Medieval Europe and the World

Other Volumes Available from Oxford University Press

The Ancient Mediterranean World: From the Stone Age
to A.D. 600
Robin W. Winks and Susan P. Mattern-Parkes

Europe in a Wider World, 1350–1650
Robin W. Winks and Lee Palmer Wandel

Europe, 1648–1815: From the Old Regime to the Age of
Revolution
Robin W. Winks and Thomas Kaiser

Europe and the Making of Modernity, 1815–1914
Robin W. Winks and Joan Neuberger

Europe, 1890–1945: Crisis and Conflict
Robin W. Winks and R. J. Q. Adams

Europe, 1945 to the Present
Robin W. Winks and John E. Talbott

Medieval Europe and the World

From Late Antiquity to Modernity, 400–1500

Robin W. Winks
Late of Yale University

Teofilo F. Ruiz
University of California, Los Angeles

New York   Oxford
OXFORD UNIVERSITY PRESS
2005

Oxford University Press

Oxford   New York
Auckland   Bangkok   Buenos Aires   Cape Town   Chennai
Dar es Salaam   Delhi   Hong Kong   Istanbul   Karachi   Kolkata
Kuala Lumpur   Madrid   Melbourne   Mexico City   Mumbai
Nairobi   São Paulo   Shanghai   Taipei   Tokyo   Toronto

Published by Oxford University Press, Inc.
198 Madison Avenue, New York, New York, 10016
www.oup.com

Oxford is a registered trademark of Oxford University Press

Library of Congress Cataloging-in-Publication Data
Winks, Robin W.
   Medieval Europe and the world : from Late Antiquity to modernity, 400-1500 / Robin W.
Winks, Teofilo F. Ruiz.
      p. cm.
   Includes bibliographical references and index.
   ISBN-13: 978-0-19-515693-5 (alk. paper)—ISBN-13: 978-0-19-515694-2 (pbk. : alk. paper)
   ISBN-10: 0-19-515693-5 (alk. paper)—ISBN-10: 0-19-515694-3 (pbk. : alk. paper)
      1. Middle Ages—History. 2. Europe—History—476-1492. I. Ruiz, Teofilo F., 1943–II.
Title.
   D117.W56 2005
   940.1—dc22   2004054721

Printing number: 9 8 7 6 5 4 3 2 1

Printed in the United States of America
on acid-free paper

Contents

Maps and Boxes

Maps

Boxes

Preface

The Value of History

History is a series of arguments to be debated, not a body of data to be recorded or a set of facts to be memorized. Thus controversy in historical interpretation—over what an event actually means, over what really happened at an occurrence called "an event," over how best to generalize about the event—is at the heart of its value. Of course history teaches us about ourselves. Of course it teaches us to understand and to entertain a proper respect for our collective past. Of course it transmits to us specific skills—how to ask questions, how to seek out answers, how to think logically, cogently, lucidly, purposefully. Of course it is, or ought to be, a pleasure. But we also discover something fundamental about a people in what they choose to argue over in their past. When a society suppresses portions of its past record, that society (or its leadership) tells us something about itself. When a society seeks to alter how the record is presented, well-proven facts notwithstanding, we learn how history can be distorted to political ends.

Who controls history, and how it is written, controls the past, and who controls the past controls the present. Those who would close off historical controversy with the argument either that we know all that we need to know about a subject, or that what we know is so irrefutably correct that anyone who attacks the conventional wisdom about the subject must have destructive purposes in mind, are in the end intent upon destroying the very value of history itself—that value being that history teaches us to argue productively with each other.

Obviously, then, history is a social necessity. It gives us our identity. It helps us to find our bearings in an ever more complex present, providing us with a navigator's chart by which we may to some degree orient ourselves. When we ask who we are, and how it is that we are so, we learn skepticism and acquire the beginnings of critical judgment. Along with a sense of narrative, history also provides us with tools for explanation and analysis. It helps us to find the particular example, to see the uniqueness in a past age or past event, while also helping us to see how the particular and the unique contribute to the general. History thus shows us humanity at work and play, in society, changing through time. By letting us experience other lifestyles, history shows us the values of both subjectivity and objectivity—those twin conditions of our individual view of the world in which we live, conditions between which we constantly, and usually almost without knowing it, move. Thus, history is both a form of truth and a matter of opinion, and the close study of history should help us to distinguish between the two. It is important to make such distinctions, for as Sir Walter Raleigh wrote, "It is not truth but opinion that can travel the world without a passport." Far too often what we read, see, and hear and believe to be the truth—in our newspapers, on our television sets, from our friends—is opinion, not fact.

History is an activity. That activity asks specific questions as a means of arriving at general questions. A textbook such as this is concerned overwhelmingly with general questions, even though at times it must ask specific questions or present specific facts as a means of stalking the general. The great philosopher Karl Jaspers once remarked, "Who I am and where I belong, I first learned to know from the mirror of history." It is this mirror that any honest book must reflect.

To speak of "civilization" (of which this book is a history) is at once to plunge into controversy, so that our very first words illustrate why some people are so fearful of the study of history. To speak of "Western civilization" is even more restrictive, too limited in the eyes of some historians. Yet if we are to understand history as a process, we must approach it through a sense of place: our continuity, our standards, our process. Still, we must recognize an inherent bias in such a term as "Western civilization," indeed two inherent biases: first, that we know what it means to be "civilized"and have attained that stature; and second, that the West as a whole is a single unitary civilization. This second bias is made plain when we recognize that most scholars and virtually all college courses refer not to "Eastern civilization" but to "the civilizations of the East"—a terminology that suggests that while the West is a unity, the East is not. These are conventional phrases, buried in Western perception of reality, just as our common geographical references show a Western bias. The Near East or the Far East are, after all, "near" or "far" only in reference to a geographical location focused on western Europe. The Japanese do not refer to London as being in the far West, or Los Angeles as being in the far East, although both references would be correct if they saw the world as though they stood at its center. Although this text will accept these conventional phrases, precisely because they are traditionally embedded in our Western languages, one of the uses of history—and of the writing of a book such as this one—is to alert us to the biases buried in our language, even when necessity requires that we continue to use its conventional forms of shorthand.

But if we are to speak of civilization, we must have, at the outset, some definition of what we mean by "being civilized." Hundreds of books have been written on this subject. The average person often means only that others, the "noncivilized," speak a different language and practice alien customs. The Chinese customarily referred to all foreigners as barbarians, and the ancient Greeks spoke of those who could not communicate in Greek as *bar-bar*—those who do not speak our tongue. Yet today the ability to communicate in more than one language is one hallmark of a "civilized" person. Thus definitions of civilization, at least as used by those who think little about the meaning of their words, obviously change.

For our purposes, however, we must have a somewhat more exacting definition of the term, since it guides and shapes any book that attempts to cover the entire sweep of Western history. Anthropologists, sociologists, historians, and others may reasonably differ as to whether, for example, there is a separate American civilization that stands apart from, say, a British or Italian civilization, or whether these civilizations are simply particular variants on one larger entity, with only that larger entity—the West—entitled to be called "a civilization." Such an argument is of no major importance here, although it is instructive that it should occur. Rather, what is needed is a definition sufficiently clear to be used throughout the narrative and analysis to follow. This working definition, therefore, will hold that "civilization" involves the presence of several (although not necessarily all) of the following conditions within a society or group of interdependent societies:

1. There will be some form of government by which people administer to their political needs and responsibilities.
2. There will be some development of urban society, that is, of city life, so that the culture is not nomadic, dispersed, and thus unable to leave significant and surviving physical remnants of its presence.
3. Human beings will have become toolmakers, able through the use of metals to transform, however modestly, their physical environment, and thus their social and economic environment as well.
4. Some degree of specialization of function will have begun, usually at the workplace, so that pride, place, and purpose work together as cohesive elements in the society.
5. Social classes will have emerged, whether antagonistic to or sustaining of one another.
6. A form of literacy will have developed, so that group may communicate with group and, more important, generation with generation in writing.
7. There will be a concept of leisure time—that life is not solely for the workplace, or for the assigned class function or specialization—so that, for example, art may develop beyond (although not excluding) mere decoration and sports beyond mere competition.
8. There will be a concept of a higher being, although not necessarily through organized religion, by which a people may take themselves outside themselves to explain events and find purpose.
9. There will be a concept of time, by which the society links itself to a past and to the presumption of a future.
10. There will have developed a faculty for criticism. This faculty need not be the rationalism of the West, or intuition, or any specific religious or political mechanism, but it must exist, so that the society may contemplate change from within, rather than awaiting attack (and possible destruction) from without.

A common Western bias is to measure "progress" through technological change and to suggest that societies that show (at least until quite recently in historical time) little dramatic technological change are not civilized. In truth, neither a written record nor dramatic technological changes are essential to being civilized, although both are no doubt present in societies we would call civilized. Perhaps, as we study history, we ought to remember all three of the elements inherent in historical action as recorded by the English critic John Ruskin: "Great nations write their autobiographies in three manuscripts, the book of their deeds, the book of their words, and the book of their art."

The issue here is not whether we "learn from the past." Most often we do not, at least at the simple-minded level; we do not, as a nation, decide upon a course of action in diplomacy, for example, simply because a somewhat similar course in the past worked. We are wise enough to know that circumstances alter cases and that new knowledge brings new duties. Of course individuals "learn from the past"; the victim of a mugging takes precautions in the future. To dignify such an experience as "a lesson of history," however, is to turn mere individual growth from child into adult into history when, at most, such growth is a personal experience in biography.

We also sometimes learn the "wrong lessons" from history. Virtually anyone who wishes to argue passionately for a specific course of future action can find a lesson from the past that will convince the gullible that history repeats itself and therefore that the past is a map to the future. No serious historian argues this, however. General patterns may, and sometimes do, repeat themselves, but specific chains of events do not. Unlike those subjects that operate at the very highest level of generalization (political science, theology, science), history simply does not believe in ironclad laws. But history is not solely a series of unrelated events. There are general patterns, clusters of causes, intermediate levels of generalization that prove true. Thus, history works at a level uncomfortable to many: above the specific, below the absolute.

If complex problems never present themselves twice in the same or even in recognizably similar form—if, to borrow a frequent image from the military world, generals always prepare for the last war instead of the next one—then does the study of history offer society any help in solving its problems? The answer surely is yes—but only in a limited way. History offers a rich collection of clinical reports on human behavior in various situations—individual and collective, political, economic, military, social, cultural—that tell us in detail how the human race has conducted its affairs and that suggest ways of handling similar problems in the present. President Harry S. Truman's secretary of state, a former chief of staff, General George Marshall, once remarked that nobody could think about the problems of the 1950s who had not reflected upon the fall of Athens in the fifth century B.C. He was referring to the extraordinary history of the war between Athens and Sparta written just after it was over by Thucydides, an Athenian who fought in the war. There were no nuclear weapons, no telecommunications, no guns or gunpowder in the fifth century B.C., and the logistics of war were altogether primitive, yet twenty-three hundred years later one of the most distinguished leaders of

American military and political affairs found Thucydides indispensable to his thinking.

History, then, can only approximate the range of human behavior, with some indication of its extremes and averages. It can, although not perfectly, show how and within what limits human behavior changes. This last point is especially important for the social scientist, the economist, the sociologist, the executive, the journalist, or the diplomat. History provides materials that even an inspiring leader—a prophet, a reformer, a politician—would do well to master before seeking to lead us into new ways. For it can tell us something about what human material can and cannot stand, just as science and technology can tell engineers what stresses metals can tolerate. History can provide an awareness of the depth of time and space that should check the optimism and the overconfidence of the reformer. For example, we may wish to protect the environment in which we live—to eliminate acid rain, to cleanse our rivers, to protect our wildlife, to preserve our majestic natural scenery. History may show us that most peoples have failed to do so and may provide us with some guidance on how to avoid the mistakes of the past. But history will also show that there are substantial differences of public and private opinion over how best to protect our environment, that there are many people who do not believe such protection is necessary, or that there are people who accept the need for protection but are equally convinced that lower levels of protection must be traded off for higher levels of productivity from our natural resources. History can provide the setting by which we may understand differing opinions, but recourse to history will not get the legislation passed, make the angry happy, or make the future clean and safe. History will not define river pollution, although it can provide us with statistics from the past for comparative measurement. The definition will arise from the politics of today and our judgments about tomorrow. History is for the long and at times for the intermediate run, but seldom for the short run.

So if we are willing to accept a "relevance" that is more difficult to see at first than the immediate applicability of science and more remote than direct action, we will have to admit that history is "relevant." It may not actually build the highway or clear the slum, but it can give enormous help to those who wish to do so. And failure to take it into account may lead to failure in the sphere of action.

But history is also fun, at least for those who enjoy giving their curiosity free reign. Whether it is historical gossip we prefer (how many lovers did Catherine the Great of Russia actually take in a given year, and how much political influence did their activity in the imperial bedroom give them?), the details of historical investigation (how does it happen that the actual treasures found in a buried Viking ship correspond to those described in an Anglo-Saxon poetic account of a ship-burial?), more complex questions of cause-and-effect (how influential have the writings of revolutionary intellectuals been upon the course of actual revolutions?), the relationships between politics and economics (how far does the rise and decline of Spanish power in modern times depend upon the supply of gold and silver from New World colonies?), or cultural problems (why did western Europe choose to revive classical Greek and Roman art and literature instead of turning to some altogether new experiment?), those who enjoy history will read almost greedily to discover what they want to know. Having discovered it, they may want to know how we know what we have learned and may want to turn to those sources closest in time to the persons and questions concerned—to the original words of the participants. To read about Socrates, Columbus, or Churchill is fun; to read their own words, to visit with them as it were, is even more so. To see them in context is important; to see how we have taken their thoughts and woven them to purposes of our own is at least equally important. Readers will find the path across the mine-studded fields of history helped just a little by extracts from these voices—voices of the past but also of the present. They can also be helped by chronologies, bibliographies, pictures, maps—devices through which historians share their sense of fun and immediacy with a reader.

In the end, to know the past is to know ourselves—not entirely, not enough, but a little better. History can help us to achieve some grace and elegance of action, some cogency and completion of thought, some harmony and tolerance in human relationships. Most of all, history can give us a sense of excitement, a personal zest for watching and perhaps participating in the events around us that will, one day, be history too.

History is a narrative, a story; history is concerned foremost with major themes, even as it recognizes the significance of many fascinating digressions. Because history is largely about how and why people behave as they do, it is also about patterns of thought and belief. Ultimately, history is about what people believe to be true. To this extent, virtually all history is intellectual history, for the perceived meaning of a specific treaty, battle, or scientific discovery lies in what those involved in it and those who came after thought was most significant about it. History makes it clear that we may die, as we may live, as a result of what someone believed to be quite true in the relatively remote past.

We cannot each be our own historian. In everyday life we may reconstruct our personal past, acting as detectives for our motivations and attitudes. But formal history is a much more rigorous study. History may give us some very small capacity to predict the future. More certainly, it should help us arrange the causes for given events into meaningful patterns. History also should help us to be tolerant of the historical views of others, even as it helps to shape our own convictions. History must help us sort out the important from the less important, the relevant from the irrelevant, so that we do not fall prey to those who propose simple-minded solutions to vastly complex human problems. We must not yield to the temptation to blame one group or individual for our problems, and yet we must not fail to defend our convictions with vigor.

To recognize, indeed to celebrate, the value of all civilizations is essential to the civilized life itself. To understand that we see all civilizations through the prism of our specific historical past—for which we feel affection, in which we may feel comfortable and secure, and by which we interpret all else that we encounter—is simply to recognize that we too are the products of history. That is why we must study history and ask our own questions in our own way. For if we ask no questions of our past, there may be no questions to ask of our future.

Robin W. Winks

Introduction

In contemporary western culture, the term "medieval" has been deployed in various and often contradictory ways. The most common usages denote backwardness and often cruelty. Movies, news reports, popular literature, even public political pronouncements often allude to "medieval practices, medieval torture, medieval attitudes." References to religious fanaticism, the Inquisition, the absence of manners among the poor, the dirt and squalor of medieval cities, unspeakable cruelties, and bizarre practices drive the point convincingly home. In this rendition, the Middle Ages appears uncivilized and barbaric, with the gargoyle as a most fitting emblem of its grotesque environment. By infiltrating our everyday speech and imagination, these pejorative views of the Middle Ages have reinforced the notion of a sharp divide between the "Dark Ages" and our "civilized" present.

At the same time a different, gentler usage of the term has held sway. In this depiction—as cultivated in many popular movies and fiction—the Middle Ages is romantic, exotic, even glamorous, inhabited by elegantly clad and comely ladies about whom brave and handsome knights hover. The latter always stand out from the crowd of uncouth, smelly peasants and the handful of heinous, evil-plotting villains, magicians, or witches. A few dragons may be thrown in for effect, and romantic castles, beautiful horses, and armor complete the decor. This medieval world of honor and courtliness has had a long ancestry. Harkening back to twelfth-century epics and romances, its revival in the fourteenth and fifteenth centuries in books of chivalry, the early nineteenth-century romantic movement, and the rebirth of Camelot in the literary imaginings and codes of conduct of certain social groups on the eve of the twentieth century, this nebulous world has filtered down to our own time in such mass popular culture phenomenon as J. R. R. Tolkien's *The Lord of the Rings*.

These usages are, of course, not only contradictory but also incorrect. Both brutal and glorious, the Middle Ages was far more complex and creative than the stereotypical reductionism of modern popular culture would lead us to believe. The terms themselves—the Middle Ages, medieval—were coined by Renaissance humanists as belittling labels for the long arc of time spanning

the collapse of classical civilization in the West and the rebirth of ancient culture in Italy from the mid-fourteenth century onward (the Italian Renaissance). Italian humanists—most notably Petrarch, Leonardo Bruni, and
Coluccio Salutati—viewed their own literary and philosophical oeuvre as the
rebirth (or renaissance) of a superior classical culture (mostly Roman); seeking to reinstate the Latin that had been written by ancient authors, they
intended to abandon the medieval Latin "polluted" by an almost millennium
of linguistic accretions. They measured their work in direct opposition to the
scholasticism of northern centers of learning, such as Paris, and found it superior to the "Gothic" (by which they meant German) culture of the time-in-
between (the *medium aevum*). With its excesses and lofty aspirations, medieval
architecture and art, in their eyes, could not compare with the simple rational
proportions of classical architectural style and thought. The invention of new
literary and poetic forms and the embrace of Ciceronian rhetoric and ethics led
to similar rejection of medieval literature and philosophy.

But the break between medieval and Renaissance was never as sharp as
late fourteenth- and fifteenth-century Italian humanists depicted it to be. In
many ways, the Renaissance and the transition to the early modern period
are inexplicable without reference to the Middle Ages, for many of the successes and pitfalls of subsequent periods (including our own) were foreshadowed in medieval developments. The Renaissance in Italy and the first
stirrings of modernity in the early sixteenth century were deeply connected
to medieval social, economic, political, and cultural transformations. What,
then, was the Middle Ages?

The Middle Ages

We must begin by emphasizing the complexity and long span of the historical period we call the Middle Ages. It begins roughly with the decline and
eventual demise of the Roman Empire in the West (the third to the early sixth
century), although a very good argument can be made for its being triggered
by the early spread of Christianity throughout the Mediterranean world in
the first and second centuries c.e. (The "common era," the period common to
both Christians and Jews). The formulation of Christian theology and
dogma—a great deal of it borrowed from classical sources—played a signal
role in the fomenting of unique medieval values. As to its chronological end,
medieval cultural forms and institutions endured long after the commonly
accepted terminus for the Middle Ages in the traditional periodization of
western European history. Nonetheless, the late fifteenth and early sixteenth
centuries witnessed a series of developments—the fall of Constantinople to
the Ottoman Turks (1453), the beginning of printing (1460s), the encounter
between the Old World and the New (1492 and beyond), Vasco da Gama's
epoch-making voyage to India (1494), and the dramatic rupture in religious
culture with the Protestant Reformation (1520s)—that clearly marked a shift
into a new and different era.

Covering a period of over a millennium, the Middle Ages as a whole can itself be divided into distinct subperiods. In the medieval West, the period of transition between the classical world and the early Middle Ages has become a separate field of inquiry, known as "Late Antiquity." These centuries, roughly from the third to the sixth centuries, have become distinct from, as well as a gateway to, the "Early Middle Ages." The latter had originally encompassed the period between the demise of the Roman Empire in the West and the year 1000. It now begins around the late sixth century, while the "Late Middle Ages" is usually understood as the period between the end of the first millennium and that of the fifteenth century. These chronological benchmarks are usually drawn for heuristic purposes, and, often, social, economic, political, and cultural developments flow from one of these artificial periods to the next without any distinguishable sharp change. Likewise, social, political, economic, and cultural developments varied dramatically according to geographical location. To view the experiences of, let's say, the French or the English in the twelfth century as paradigmatic for the entire medieval West is to obscure the peculiar historical developments of places such as Mediterranean Europe, Scandinavia, or Hungary. We cannot see this history through one single lens or experience; rather, we need to see it from a variety of perspectives to appreciate its richness and complexities. Similarly, such catchall terms as "feudalism" or "manorialism" have little meaning in ever-evolving contexts. Thus, different geographical locales and chronological periods yield myriad Middle Ages, one as distinct from the other as the Middle Ages is from other historical periods. What then do we mean by the Middle Ages?

One way to answer this question is to emphasize medieval complexity and diversity, refusing to reduce the Middle Ages to a standard narrative from the center. Essentially, this means seeing the medieval past from the so-called center as well as from the peripheries. We must admit that there are many Middle Ages, all of them linked together by the West's evolving definition of itself as a particular kind of Christian world for over a millennium. Although medieval history is, as Marc Bloch, a great French medievalist, once argued, a history of localities, all these diverse histories rest upon a common ground. And that common ground, complex as it is, provides a basic unit to the history of the Middle Ages.

The Middle Ages and Rome

We must imagine the millennium between the collapse of the ancient world in the West and the beginning of the early modern period as an elaborate tapestry. Many strands were woven into it to create something new and distinct. Of the different threads that were woven into the larger pattern of medieval life, classical civilization and Christianity played, perhaps, the most significant role. There were, however, other influential strands. Medieval men and women always lived in the shadows of Rome, particularly in the ancient core of the great empire: the Mediterranean basin. But Rome's pervasive influence reached into the peripheries of the vast Roman world: into England, parts of

Germany, North Africa, the Balkans. Rome's impact could be seen not only in the survival of legal systems, vestiges of Roman taxation, or the ruins of Roman buildings strewn upon the face of Europe but also in the patterns of land exploitation, social relations, and other social and economic legacies that pervaded, and still pervade, most of everyday life in the Western world.

Christianity

Rome's legacy became Christianized in the early fourth century. Constantine's tolerance and support for Christians after 312 and the eventual Christianization of the empire in the century afterward colored ancient Roman practices and traditions with new values. Roman civilization was not so much overthrown as it was taken over. Slowly, Christianity became the common bond for all those who lived in the former lands of the empire in the West and even beyond. But Christianity borrowed heavily from Roman structures and traditions. Christian churches imitated Roman architectural forms. Sometimes, as was the case in the early Middle Ages, parts of Roman buildings (columns, marble pieces taken from destroyed Roman temples, and so on) became parts of churches and can still be seen throughout most of southern Europe. Christianity and *Romanitas* thus became deeply intertwined, each altering and transforming the other. This is best exemplified by the selection of Rome, the paradigmatic pagan city, as the center for western Christianity.

The Germans

Roman culture and Christianity were also influenced by Germanic culture and Germanic migration into the heartlands of the western Roman Empire. The coming of German groups into Roman territory—sometimes through peaceful settlement and by invitation of Roman imperial authority, sometimes by half-hearted intrusions from German groups fleeing the wrath of the Huns, sometimes through bold invasions of mostly western lands—coincided with the decline of Roman institutions and with the slow Christianization of the empire. Most of the German invaders were already Christians, but since they were Arian Christians (a heresy—that is, a form of Christianity that did not conform to the orthodox doctrines and dogmas of the church—of the early fourth century that rejected the idea that the three persons in the Trinity were co-eternal) they were considered heterodox Christians in the eyes of westerners. The reality is that by the time many of these Germans came into the empire in the fourth, fifth, and sixth centuries, they were already half Romanized, while the Romans had become half Germanized. Dress style, beards, and even Roman armies—which by the fourth century were staffed mostly with Germans and fought in traditional German military formations—dramatically attest to the manner in which Roman civilization was transformed by the settlement of Germans in its midst. Germanic social structures, culture, and traditions became significant foundations of medieval society.

The Eastern Empire or Byzantium

Rome, however, did not really fall. In the eastern portions of the empire Rome survived, although much transformed, until the very end of the Middle Ages. These parts of the empire survived the Germanic invasions and prospered. By the late sixth century, the Roman Empire in the East reverted to the Greek language and traditions for its administrative and cultural life. Known by historians in its Greek incarnation as Byzantium, the city (Constantinople) and the empire remained a constant reminder to the West of the permanence of Roman imperial forms. Byzantium contributed a great deal to the makings of western Europe. The long hold of its architectural influence can still be seen in places like Ravenna, Venice, Monreale, and other locations. Byzantium was the other face of the Middle Ages, and throughout most of the centuries after the fall of the Roman Empire in the West (certainly until the late twelfth century) western Europe measured itself against Byzantine models.

These two civilizations did not evolve in isolation; rather, they interacted and borrowed from each other, but throughout most of the long thousand years of medieval history, the Byzantines enjoyed a marked cultural superiority. Even at its end, when Byzantium had lost most of its territory and awaited its demise at the hands of the Ottoman Turks in the 1440s and early 1450s, Byzantine scholars fled to the West, carrying with them a treasure trove of Greek learning. This included most of Plato's work, and some of these texts (skeptical, magical, scientific) served as a catalyst for the revolution in learning of the early modern period. More to the point, Byzantium served as a gateway to a wider world. For many centuries, eastern goods as well as ideas flowed through Byzantium to the West. Thus, the eastern Roman Empire served as a bridge to other cultures and other worlds.

Islam

Later we will have an opportunity to examine Islam and its meteoric rise as a religion and political entity. The Middle Ages cannot be understood without reference to Islam; its social, economic, and cultural contributions were instrumental in the making of the western Middle Ages. A great portion of this history took place in areas controlled by Islam: most of Iberia, Sicily for a century, North Africa, Egypt, Palestine, and elsewhere. These ancient components of Rome's Mediterranean world were deeply shaped by Islamic influence. The Muslims were also among the main transmitters of classical culture to the West. In the former lands of the great Hellenistic empires, the Muslims discovered most of the great classical works, commented on them, shaped them to their purposes, translated them, and brought them to the West to the intellectual benefit of medieval men and women.

When Dante writes about Aristotle, he refers to him simply as the "philosopher." When he writes about the greatest of Aristotle's commentators, Averroës, a Muslim, he refers to him simply as the "commentator." Dante understood well what most learned men knew in the early fourteenth century, that their mental world was largely shaped by Muslim science and contributions.

Through the introduction of new crops, new agricultural techniques, and new forms of husbandry, irrigation, silk production, and iron and leather works, the Muslims also shaped the material culture of the West, leaving an indelible mark on its intellectual and everyday life.

Celts, Vikings, and Magyars

Celtic lore and culture had a deep impact on the cultural transformations of the West. This ancient culture successfully resisted centuries of Roman domination, keeping some of its religious practices and lore alive. In the late eleventh and twelfth centuries, many treasures of Celtic oral culture found their way into the written word. The romances of the twelfth century, from the cycle of stories woven around Arthur and the Round Table to the narratives of the quest for the Holy Grail, owed a great deal to the enduring spirit and magic of the Celtic people.

To the Celts we can add the signal contributions of the Vikings (Normans [Northmen, Norsemen], Danes, and other Scandinavian people). Although the Vikings, as was the case with the Magyars, brought untold disruptions to many parts of western Europe in the ninth and tenth centuries, they also became important components in the mix that would lead to the emergence of a distinct western civilization. The Vikings, a dynamic and enterprising people who expanded the boundaries of Europe, played a major role in the first stages of kingdom-building in both East and West. The Magyars or Hungarians, after their conversion to Christianity around the year 1000, played a significant role in western Europe's eastern frontier. The list goes on, and many players appear in the pages that follow. The history of the Middle Ages is the history of these different cultures, strands in a complex tapestry of interaction and mingling into a new and distinctive world. But there is always the danger of thinking of medieval Europe as a world unto its own, in isolation from the rest of the known world. It was not.

Europe and the World

For many years, the history of the Middle Ages was written as a history of fall and rise. The Roman Empire collapsed in the West under the impact of Germanic invasions. The areas of what today is France, Germany, England, and the Low Countries sank into the "Dark Ages." Even Italy, gripped by contending Germanic groups and by a Byzantine invasion in the sixth century, descended into chaos. Iberia, after the fall of the Visigothic Empire in 711 and the Muslim occupation, also suffered a precipitous decline. Part of this history of decline emphasized the growing isolation of the West, as men and women turned inward to the labors and concerns of everyday life. Education declined. Culture flickered in a few monasteries throughout the land. Central power, especially after the collapse of the Carolingian dynasty, became fragmented and privatized. Only with the revival of culture in the twelfth century and the embryonic beginnings of feudal monarchies did Europe embark on its long road to modernity.

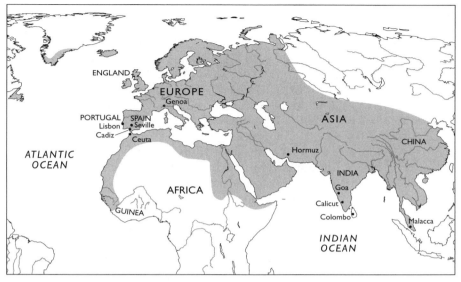

Overseas Exploration in the Fifteenth Century

Some aspects of this picture are not completely untrue, but the works of Peter Brown, most recently his *The Rise of Western Christendom,* and those of others have shown that western Europe was far less isolated than has been thought, that education could flourish, and that commercial and cultural exchanges, although diminished, remained. There were indeed isolated villages and small towns. In these places, the world did not extend beyond the limited horizons of most of the inhabitants. But even these people knew of other worlds. The outside came to them in myriad ways. The images from outside the boundaries of Europe served to western men and women as a continuous reminder that they were part of a wider world.

This is not a book about the history of the world or Europe in a global context. It is a book about the history of western Europe in the Middle Ages, but throughout these pages we must remember that European developments did not take place in isolation. They were shaped by long-distance commercial contacts and by religious and political antagonisms against those beyond the borders of Europe. Faraway places were inscribed in sacred history. Biblical stories, heard in church or preached by itinerant preachers, brought distant lands into clear relief. Merchants followed the Silk Road, the ancient thoroughfare linking China to Europe, carrying luxury items and valuable spices for the tables of the powerful. Some Christian missionaries traveled in the other direction, or, as was the case in the later Middle Ages, intrepid voyagers, such as Marco Polo, set off in search of knowledge and trade. Recent archaeological discoveries testify to maritime routes linking India, China, and the Spice Islands with Egypt. From Egypt, trade moved westward to the great commercial depots in Italy and elsewhere on the Mediterranean.

Gold, salt, and other products flowed from sub-Saharan Africa to the Maghreb. Caravans departed from fabled Timbuktu across the Sahara and into North African ports. From there goods went to Iberia and to the rest of western Europe. The Vikings, bold and gifted voyagers, sailed to Iceland, Greenland, and North America. They also directed their expeditions eastward. Following the river networks from Staraia Ladoga and from their later foundation of Novgorod on the Baltic Sea, the Vikings or Northmen traveled south into what is today the Ukraine, reaching the Black Sea, before being checked by the Pechenegs, a steppe people.

The Muslims' control of the southern shores of the Mediterranean projected them into continuous contact with Christianity. In the "garden protected by our [Muslims'] spears," Dar al-Islam (the lands of Islam), Arabs, Jews, Syrians, and local populations engaged in active trade, cultural production, and exchanges. That trade reached deep into the northern regions of Europe, testifying to the unity of the medieval world and to its contacts with the world beyond its boundaries. Muslims and Christians also captured, enslaved, and sold each other into captivity. Germans moved deep into their eastern frontier after the eleventh century. A league of cities and merchants, the Hansa connected Baltic urban centers and goods with western European markets. By the fourteenth century Europeans were in a traveling mood, although as one can attest by their frequent perambulations to pilgrimage sites, Europeans were always in the mood for travel. The Portuguese, wonderful innovators and the true pioneers of the Age of Discovery, began their extraordinary explorations down the coast of Africa, on their eventual way to India, China, and Japan. They also sailed into the Atlantic to the Azores islands, as the Castilians did to the Canaries. The sea lanes that led to the New World and, with it, to the end of the Middle Ages had long been opened by European awareness of and, in a few cases, intimacy with the world. Throughout these pages, we must always keep in mind that the history of the European Middle Ages took place always in the context of and in relation to other histories.

ONE

The End of the Ancient World: Christianity and the Western Empire

On 28 October 312, Constantine (Roman emperor in the West, 312–337, and in the whole empire, 324–337) defeated his rival Maxentius at the Milvian Bridge, near Rome. This was one of the many battles that the children of the tetrarchs (those associated with Diocletian in the running of the empire in 286) fought over Diocletian's (284–305) inheritance. But what made this battle significant in western history is that Constantine claimed that the night before the battle he had a vision of a Christian symbol, the two Greek letters of the word "Christ," that is, the Messiah (although popular belief often describes Constantine's vision as a cross against the sun, with the words: *In hoc signis vincit* [With this symbol, you will conquer]). Displaying the sign on his soldiers' shields, Constantine routed and killed Maxentius, guaranteeing his rule over the western sections of the empire. Shortly afterward, in 313, he, jointly with his co-emperor Licinus, proclaimed an edict at Milan granting Christians the right of worship throughout the empire and ending the restrictions on Christians that had so effectively checked their preaching and proselytizing under Diocletian.

In the early fourth century, Christianity was one of many other religions and cults competing for the hearts and minds of those living under Roman rule. Constantine's conversion to Christianity or support of the new religion, a much debated event among late antique historians, set the course for the subsequent development of the empire and for western culture. Although in reality Constantine was not baptized until he was close to his death in 337 (and was possibly baptized by an Arian bishop at that), he gave Christians a privileged access to imperial power and took an active role in some of the most crucial Christian controversies and gatherings.

Yet despite imperial support for Christianity, the ancient classical deities' hold on the Roman imagination was not yet finished. One last formal attempt

The colossal head of Constantine. Constantine (315–337) was the first Roman emperor to grant Christians the right to worship freely throughout the empire. He also converted to Christianity and favored Christians in his administration. The sculpture dates from the fourth century C.E. and was a fairly accurate representation of the emperor's face. (Scala/Art Resource)

was made to reconstruct the old polytheism of the empire. The emperor Julian, called the "Apostate" (361–363), a ruler with strong philosophical leanings and much influenced by the Neoplatonists, sought to merge the old classical and rational philosophical systems of the Greek and Roman worlds with the mysticism of Egypt. However, Julian's attempts to restore the traditional cults died with him, and Christianity quickly regained and extended its now-favored position. In 375, Emperor Gratian gave up the title of Pontifex Maximus (as head of the official cult of Rome), a title very dear to earlier emperors, and refused to use the public treasury to support ancient Roman festivals associated with the traditional gods of the city and the empire.

Theodosius I (379–395) made Christianity the official religion of the empire, abolished the ritual religious Roman calendar, and in 394 began to persecute those still adhering to traditional religious practices or to some of the new eastern religions. Paganism, a pejorative term deployed by Christians against their rivals and connoting lack of sophistication and rural origins, continued to thrive in the countryside, in the army, and among some of the upper classes and intellectuals for another century or so, but in the cities it was no longer an organized force.

In 313, the final victory of Christianity was still almost a century away, and we must strive to understand the social, economic, cultural, and religious setting in which Constantine's support for Christianity took place. After all, the Rome in which Constantine defeated Maxentius and eventually rearranged the social and political structures of the empire was a very different one from the Rome that almost collapsed in the crucible of the third-century crisis. The transition from antiquity to medieval took place against the framework of three distinct but interrelated historical developments: the widespread series of crises of the ancient world in the third and later centuries, leading to the social, political, economic, and cultural reconfiguration of the empire; the further development of Christianity in the fourth and fifth centuries; and the afterlife of the empire in the West after Constantine's reforms.

The Crises of the Ancient World

During the second century, Rome benefited from the enlightened rule of the "good emperors." Following Nerva's (96–98) short rule, a series of gifted emperors—Trajan (98–117), Hadrian (117–138), Antonianus Pius (138–161), and Marcus Aurelius (161–180)—restored order within the empire; strengthened the borders against the growing menace of Germans, Persians, and other foreign threats; and presided over what Edward Gibbon (1737–1794), author of the influential *The Decline and Fall of the Roman Empire,* in an Enlightenment exaggeration described as the happiest and most peaceful age of mankind. These emperors consciously selected the best man in the empire to succeed them, avoiding the dynastic problems that had plagued Rome in the late first century. But all was not well in Rome. Peace and order were bought at the price of freedom, and the empire began slowly to suffocate. The Antonines, as these group of emperors were known, ruled well and kept order, but they did so as enlightened military despots. When Marcus Aurelius designated his incompetent and insane son, Commodus, as his heir, the empire entered a crisis from which it would emerge only in the mid-280s.

The Roman Empire, as it existed in the second century, came fairly close to disintegrating during the crisis. Weather changes, the decline and inefficiency of slavery as a method of production (with fewer conquests, there were fewer sources of slaves), technological backwardness (because of the dependency on slave labor), and other factors led to a downturn in agricultural production, widespread famines, epidemics, and inflationary pressures. Rome was, in the famous depiction of Ferdinand Lot, a French historian of the late nineteenth and early twentieth century, "a giant with feet of clay," a world structurally unprepared for the social and economic chaos that ensued in the early third century.

Politically, provincial armies began to compete for control of the empire. They selected their own emperors, marching on Rome to place their candidate on the throne, extorting financial rewards from those they had selected as rulers, and violently disposing of them when they could no longer come up with the money to pay for their exorbitant salaries and excesses. On the borders of the empire, German tribes either hired themselves to the different contending armies, infiltrated Roman lands and settled in Roman territories (often, however, at the invitation of Roman authorities), or engaged in the systematic plundering of frontier areas. The vast empire became a battleground, as different Roman armies fought for power. Classical art declined or became simply imitative, although it must be noted that other innovative artistic and architectural forms began to develop at the same time. Civic life lost its vigor and was replaced by a search for redemption and mysticism. An endless succession of emperors occupied the throne throughout the third century with little apparent success. Some sought to restore a semblance of order with some success; others failed. Few of these rulers died of natural causes, instead falling victims to the whims of the army or to political assassination. In the 270s, the empire tilted perilously on the edge of a precipice, ready to collapse.

If Rome had perished then, our world would look very different indeed. None of the structures that allowed for the transmission of culture from the classical world to the Middle Ages were yet in place. In the third century, Christianity might have never succeeded in the fragmented political world that would have emerged with the demise of the empire. There would not have been a Byzantium to serve as a bridge to the medieval world and a preserver of classical texts. All these statements are, of course, sheer speculation. For the empire did not collapse. The reforms of Diocletian and Constantine, foreshadowed in some of the programs of early third-century emperors, breathed new life into Rome. The western empire endured for almost two hundred years, before it was replaced by German kingdoms and Christendom. The eastern parts of the empire, what we will later know as Byzantium, lasted into the fifteenth century.

There was a price to pay for these additional years. Rome was transformed from the illusion of a *Res publica,* a republic in which the emperor was first among equals and sovereignty was vested, theoretically, on the senate and people of Rome, to an absolute monarchy. Many of the peasants in the western parts of the empire became bound to the soil. The city of Rome was almost abandoned and neglected and a new capital, Constantinople, was built in the East. Christianity became the main religion of the empire. Thus, in those two hundred years, bought by harsh administrative and political reforms, the Middle Ages were forged.

One should not exaggerate, however, the negative aspects of the third-century crisis. Many of the most fundamental aspects of Roman civilization endured in the West. Roman urban life and civic institutions, the centerpiece of classical civilization, remained a living historical model, although much diminished, to be imitated and admired in later centuries. Roman buildings and material monuments (aqueducts, arenas, amphitheaters, and complex road networks) made a permanent imprint even in faraway peripheries of the empire. They, especially the roads, dictated the life of, and patterns of movement in, these regions for centuries to come. Roman aristocratic lifestyles and values in Gaul, Spain, Italy, and other areas, although Christianized, lived on into the seventh century, with traditions of learning and emphasis on culture and country life modified but still vital. Trade patterns, radiating from the Mediterranean to inland areas, survived, as did the basic structures of agricultural production and organization of rural labor. The crisis of the late antique world transformed many things, but it did not obliterate the legacy of the empire. In the West, men and women, the learned and the unlearned, lived in the shadow of Rome for more than a millennium.

Nonetheless, social, economic, and political crises were not the only ills that plagued the Roman world. The collapse of civic life, Rome's true religion, and the sense of pessimism that pervaded the Roman world from the second century onward created a sense of anxiety that led to the spread of mystery religions. Thinking about those enlightened rulers of the second century C.E., specifically of the twentieth-century novelist Marguerite Yourcenar's vivid fictional account of Emperor Hadrian's life, one is reminded of a quote she attributes to the nineteenth-century writer Gustave Flaubert: In the second century the gods were dead, and Christianity was not yet. Men stood alone. For many, that was a terrifying and difficult thought to bear.

Christianity: The Importance of Religion in the Later Roman World

In reality, however, late antique women and men did not stand alone. Many of them had embraced Christianity and, with it, a new and radical way of thinking about the relationship between the individual and God, control over their own bodies, holiness, and the role of redemption in human life. But Christianity developed and triumphed within a complex cultural and religious atmosphere. Its final victory and its eventual conquest of the Roman world resulted from the transformation of classical culture and from a bitter struggle with traditional Roman cults and a host of new religious and quasi-philosophical doctrines vying for the minds of the people in the late antique world.

The Failure of Reason

Throughout the Roman Empire, as political rule became concentrated in the hands of the few and as social and economic conditions turned to the worse, pessimism mounted. This was often accompanied, in some circles, by a lack of faith in humanity's ability to work out its own future. The old gods seemed powerless to intervene, and to many life appeared to be a matter of luck. Beginning as early as the third century b.c. and gathering increasing momentum, the cult of the goddess Fortune became immensely popular in the Mediterranean world. Chance governed everything: Today's prosperity might vanish tomorrow, so the best thing to do was to enjoy good fortune while the goddess smiled upon you. Closely related was the belief in Fate. What happened was inevitable because it had been fated from the beginning; when you were born, the moment of your death was already fixed. Virgil attributed both fate and fortune to the will of divine providence, but most Romans seem to have felt helpless to change their own fates or to influence events. This growing sense of despair and the rejection—by some segments of the Roman population—of the formidable philosophical approaches (Platonism, Aristotelianism, Stoicism, and other reason-based attempts to explain human behavior and the workings of the world) led to the embrace of a variety of new redemptive religions. They promised either salvation, as Christianity did, or predetermined explanations for the vagaries of life, as was the case with astrology.

Astrology

By the third and fourth centuries, many Romans came to believe that the movements of the heavenly bodies influenced their fortunes and fates and governed their decisions. If one could do nothing to change one's destiny, one could at least try to find out what that destiny might be by consulting an expert astrologer. The astrologer would study the seven planets (Saturn, Jupiter, Mars, the Sun, Venus, Mercury, and the Moon), each of which had its own will, character, gender, plants, numbers, and attendant animals, and each of which was lord of a sphere. Seven itself became a mystic number: There were seven ages of man, seven wonders of the world. Then, too, there were the twelve Houses of the Sun—constellations of stars through which the sun passed on its way around the earth. These were the signs of the zodiac, itself an imaginary belt of the heavens. From the position of the heavenly bodies and the signs of the zodiac at the moment of conception or birth, astrologers would draw up a horoscope foretelling a person's fate.

The Roman emperors, like most of their subjects, profoundly believed in astrology. Especially valuable for the art of prophecy were so-called unnatural events: the appearance of a comet, the birth of a monster. Similarly, people believed in all sorts of magic and tried by its power to force the heavenly bodies to grant their wishes. The magus, or "magician," exercised enormous power.

New Cults: Cybele, Isis, Mithras

The state religion of the Olympian gods and of the deified emperors still commanded the loyalty of many Romans, who regarded the proper observance of its rites as the equivalent of patriotism. But by the first century c.e. the old faith no longer allayed the fears of millions who believed in blind fate and inevitable fortune: People increasingly sought a religion that would hold out the hope of an afterlife better than the grim reality on earth. So, along with astrology and magic, mystery religions began to appear in Rome. These new faiths, which often required elaborate and secret rituals, taught that the human soul could be saved by its union with the soul of a savior, who in many cases had experienced death and a form of resurrection. This union was accomplished by a long initiation, marked by purification, ritual banquets, and other ceremonies designed to overcome human unworthiness. The god would enter the candidate, who would be saved after physical death. The initiate sought a mystical guarantee against death by survival in the hereafter. One could join as many of these cults as one liked and still practice the state religion.

Many of these ideas were not new, but they had been limited to small groups of followers. The Greeks had such cults in the rites of Demeter at Eleusis and in the mysteries of Dionysus. The rites of Dionysus, now called Bacchus, became popular in Rome, celebrating as they did carnal pleasures and the abandonment of all restraint. Hundreds of late Roman sarcophagi depict the Bacchic procession celebrating the joys of drink and sex. Another major competitor for the mind of the late Roman people was the cult of the great mother-goddess Cybele, which came from Asia Minor at the end of the Second Punic War. Cybele's young husband, Attis, died and was reborn annually (like Demeter's daughter Persephone). Attis was thus a symbol of renewed fertility. The rites of Cybele included fasting, frenzied processions, self-flagellation, and self-mutilation by the priests. The first temple to Cybele at Rome dated from 204 B.C., but the zenith of the cult was reached in the second century C.E.

Even more popular, mainly with women, was the cult of the Egyptian goddess Isis, whose consort, Osiris, died and was reborn each year. Either lascivious or chaste aspects of the cult were concentrated in an elaborate ritual of worship for Isis, the loving mother-goddess who promised her adherents personal immortality. Conversion to Isis worship often emphasized her chastity and morality and the prospect of salvation for her followers, in contrast to the presumed depravity and growing commercialism associated with Cybele.

From Persia, around the first century C.E., came the cult of the god Mithras, allied to the supreme powers of good and light, and so connected with the Sun. The male initiates passed in succession through seven grades of initiation, qualifying for each by severe tests. Baptism and communion were also part of the ritual. Unconquered, physically rough, and self-denying, Mithras became a model for the Roman soldier, to whom he held out the hope of salvation. Temples of Mithras have been found in every province of the empire, and prominently in Rome itself.

These cults appealed widely to the masses rather than to the educated. But several trends in mysticism were also popular among intellectuals. The philosopher Epicurus had taught that unnecessary fear lay at the root of the troubles of humanity. Whatever gods might exist, if they existed at all, took no interest in what humans might do; life after death was only untroubled sleep. A quiet life and the cultivation of friendships would bring happiness; if evil came, one could endure it. But as ordinary people could hardly banish fear or pain or desire by following Epicurean formulas, the Epicureans were few in number. So were the Stoics, who prescribed the suppression of human emotions; people should accept the universe and simply defy evil to do its worst.

Perhaps halfway between religion and philosophy was the school of the so-called Hermes Trismegistus (Thrice-Great Hermes), which prescribed abstinence, concentration, and study as a preparation for a flash of ecstasy and a spiritual rebirth. Hermeticism survived the rise of Christianity and the long Middle Ages and witnessed a vigorous rebirth, as did many other astrological and philosophical movements, during the Italian Renaissance. Stronger than Hermeticism, and far more wedded to its philosophical origins, was Neoplatonism, whose adherents claimed to be disciples of Plato. They taught that each human soul makes a pilgrimage toward an eventual union with the divine spiritual essence.

No single mystery religion or philosophical movement appealed to men and women of all classes in Rome. Mithraism, which perhaps had the most adherents, especially in the army, was not inclusive of women. Neoplatonism, with its philosophical bent and inclination toward asceticism, had no appeal for the masses. Christianity, which shared many of the redemptive notions of many of these different religions, competed with these diverse cults and philosophies for the soul of the Roman world for more than three centuries after the death of its founder.

The Development of Christianity in Late Antiquity

Born out of Judaism, Christianity had developed slowly over the three centuries between its founding in Palestine and Constantine's Edict of Milan in 313. Over these centuries, Christianity had developed a body of doctrines and dogmas, and its message, first aimed at the poor and the oppressed, now addressed and attracted some of the learned and powerful. Martyrdom, holiness, and new definitions of the body served as powerful magnets for popular devotion. Christians fought for their faith in several fronts. First, Christians engaged Judaism from its inception. While each claimed to be the true Israel, Christians and Jews engaged in bitter polemics as to whether Jesus was the Christ, that is, the Messiah; as to the proper observance of Jewish laws; and as to the propriety of preaching to the Gentiles. Second, Christians dealt, sometimes harshly, with heresies and deviations within Christianity itself. Determining what Christianity was, that is, what orthodox belief was to be and what dogmas and doctrines were acceptable, was not an easy task. Christianity was forged by continuous struggle against internal dissent and heterodoxy. Third, Christians had to combat the appeal of those mystery religions and philosophical quasi-religious movements outlined previously. Sharing many aspects with them, Christianity entered a fierce struggle with classical philosophy and eastern religion for the minds of Rome. Finally, Christians lived within the borders of the Roman Empire. Stubbornly refusing to blend within the variegated and tolerant Roman religious world, and stubbornly claiming to have sole monopoly of the truth, the Christians could not but be in conflict with Roman authorities.

Christianity and Rome

The imperial authorities did not consistently seek to stamp out the Christian religion, and persecutions were sporadic over the course of three centuries, varying in severity at different times and different places. The first persecution was under Emperor Nero in 64 C.E., who had some Christians torn to pieces by wild beasts and others set alight as torches in the dark. A generation or so later, in circa 110–111, an imperial administrator, Pliny the Younger, wrote from his post in Asia Minor to Emperor Trajan that he was puzzled about how to treat the Christians and asked for instructions. Should he make allowance for age or punish children as severely as adults? Should he pardon a former Christian who now recanted? Should he punish people simply as Christians, or must he have evidence that they had committed the crimes associated publicly with their name? Up to now Pliny had asked the accused if they were Christians, and if they three times said they were, he had them executed. Pliny had interrogated the alleged Christians partly on the basis of an anonymous document listing their names. He had acquitted all who denied that they were Christians, who offered incense before the emperor's statue, who cursed Christ, and who admitted that they had once been Christians but had recanted.

Trajan answered with moderation that Pliny had done right. He left the question of sparing children to Pliny's own judgment. He said that Christians need not be sought out, although any who were denounced and found guilty must be punished, as Pliny had done. Any who denied that they were Christians, even if they had been suspect in the past, should gain pardon by penitent prayer to the Roman gods. As for "any anonymous documents you may receive," they "must be ignored in any prosecution. This sort of thing creates the worst sort of precedent, and is out of keeping with the spirit of our times." Trajan thus established the guidelines by which the Romans dealt with the Christians under the law until the reign of Decius, in 249–251, when vigorous persecution was renewed.

Alone among the emperor's subjects, however, unrepentant Christians might be killed "for the name alone," presumably because their "atheism," as Trajan saw it, threatened to bring down the wrath of the gods on the community that tolerated it. The Jews, equally "atheist" in this sense, could be forgiven because they were continuing to practice their ancestral religion— worthy in itself in Roman eyes—and because Rome had long since officially tolerated the Jewish faith, provided that the Jews did not rebel against the Roman state, paid their taxes like everyone else, and participated in the civic life of the empire. For suspected Christians a single act of religious conformity brought acquittal. Not until the third century, when the Roman world felt threatened from within and without, did persecutions become frequent and severe. By then Christians were far more numerous than in the previous two centuries, as the faith had spread rapidly. After an anti-Christian riot in Alexandria, Decius commanded that on a given day everyone in the empire must sacrifice to the gods and obtain a certificate to prove having done so. The bishops of Rome, Antioch, and Jerusalem; nineteen Christians of Alexandria; and six at Rome are known to have been executed for refusing to comply. No bishop in North Africa died, although there were cases of torture. In Spain two bishops recanted. Many Christians who had not obeyed the edict escaped arrest afterward for failing to have the certificate; some hid until the persecution had died down, and in parts of the empire the edict was not enforced. In the Latin West others bribed officials to issue them false certificates saying that they had sacrificed; later they were received back into their churches with some protest. In the Greek East, the same bribery probably took place but apparently was not regarded as sinful.

Under Valerian in 257–259, the government for the first time tried to interfere with the assembly of Christians for worship, and the clergy were ordered to sacrifice. After Valerian had been captured by the Persians, however, his successor granted toleration. But the systematic persecution begun in 303 by Diocletian was the most intense of all, especially in the East, where it lasted a full decade, as compared to about two years in the West. Churches were to be destroyed and all sacred books and church property handed over. In Palestine nearly a hundred Christians were martyred.

Persecution as a policy was a failure; it did not eliminate Christianity. Quite the contrary, many influential persons in the empire became Christians. Moreover, persecution did not avert disasters, which continued to befall the Roman state whether it persecuted Christians or not. In 311 and 313, respectively, the persecuting emperors Galerius and Maximinus officially abandoned the policy. In 313 the Edict of Milan confirmed that Christians might worship again with some semblance of freedom, own property, and build their own churches, as long as they did nothing against public order. The state was to be neutral in matters of religion.

The Organization of the Church

The expansion of Christianity and the development of the church in the first three centuries was a complex phenomenon. Early Christianity, embattled and persecuted, prospered along a wide arc that extended from trading cities on the Silk Road (the main trade route connecting Asian markets with the eastern Mediterranean and from there to the West) in the East to the outskirts of the Roman Empire in the West. Its message was carried out by a heady combination of combative Christian saints and by exemplary and ascetic-minded holy men, who articulated a message of piety and asceticism that fit perfectly into the moral and spiritual climate of late imperial Rome. Its redemptive message—the powerful image of a god who died to save humanity—its charitable works, its support network (some of these aspects shared with other eastern religions), its insistence on monotheism, and its vigorous polemical stance against so-called pagan beliefs propelled Christianity to a unique place among the multitude of religious sects within the empire and beyond. From the religion of the poor, it soon became the religion of the learned and powerful as well. Most of all, a great deal of Christianity's success depended on its well-developed administrative and pastoral institutions.

The Christian community developed well-defined lines of authority to discipline or even oust those who misbehaved. Christians had to organize to survive in the midst of an empire originally committed in principle to the suppression of Christianity. Prophets, or teachers, appeared in the very first churches, the informal groups of Christians organized by the missionaries; soon elders, overseers, and other officials followed. More and more, an overseer (Greek *episkopos*) exercised authority over a compact administrative area, referred to as his see; this was the bishop, who became the key figure in church administration. It was claimed that each see had been founded by one of the original apostles, and its bishop thus held office through apostolic succession. Since it had been Jesus himself who had chosen the apostles, every bishop, in effect, became his direct spiritual heir. Groups of bishoprics or episcopal sees were often gathered together into larger units under an archbishop, or head overseer (*archiepiskopos*).

Claiming to be at the top of the hierarchy was the bishop of the imperial capital, Rome itself. The prestige of Rome contributed powerfully to his claim, although Rome was also closely associated with the rituals of the ancient imperial cults. Moreover, by the late third century Rome had lost a great deal of its centrality as an administrative, military, or ceremonial center, and it entered into precipitous decline after Constantine moved its capital to the East, to a new Christian "Rome." Nonetheless, in the earlier centuries of Christianity, the association of Peter and Paul with Rome played an important role in the identification of the city with the emerging Christian religion. Jesus had said to Peter, "Thou art Peter and upon this rock I will build my church"—a celebrated pun, since the Greek word for Peter is *Petros,* and that for rock is *petra.* Because Peter had been martyred in Rome, the bishops of that city could claim that Christ himself had picked Peter and his diocese, Rome, as the "rock" upon which to build, a claim that was embodied in the "Petrine theory." The so-called Petrine doctrine, that all the bishops of Rome were the direct descendants of Peter and had inherited his primacy and prerogatives, dates from a later period, and as Christianity became part of Roman life and its institutions paralleled those of Rome, it was not clear yet where the center of the new religion was to be. In many respects, there were far more Christians in the eastern parts of the empire than in the West. The preeminent cities and centers of ancient culture were there, as were those cities deeply connected to the early history of Christianity, such as Antioch, Ephesus, Jerusalem, and others. In the same vein, some of the most doctrinal and spiritually innovative developments of the early church (monasticism, theological pronouncements, and the like) occurred first in the eastern parts of the empire.

It should be not surprising that the bishops of the great cities of the eastern Mediterranean—Alexandria and Antioch—claimed to exercise a paternal rule equal in authority to that of the bishop of Rome. They called themselves *patriarch* (fatherly governor). Still later, after Constantinople had been made the imperial capital (C.E. 330), its bishop, also a patriarch, would oppose any claims to supremacy by the bishop of Rome. Nonetheless, with the removal of imperial government from Rome, the bishops of the ancient capital gradually made themselves more and more responsible for the government of the great city. As German and other invaders began to pour into the empire's territory, and Rome itself came under attack, the bishops of the old imperial city became the surviving symbol of the old Roman sense of order and certainly a rock to their congregations and even to the non-Christian population of the cities. A succession of outstanding men became bishops of Rome, notably Leo the Great, also known as Pope Leo I (440–461). A theologian, splendid administrator, and brave man, he may have helped save the city from the invading Huns. By the time of the breakup of the Roman Empire in the fifth century, few in the West would have disputed the claims to supremacy by the bishops of the city. By then, what we now know as the papacy had emerged as the firmest institution in a new and unstable world.

But how did the administrative organization of the church develop? The government of the church had taken shape gradually, in response to need. The church strengthened its organization by utilizing the existing political machinery of the Roman Empire, placing its major officials in centers that were already administrative capitals. Bishops and archbishops, meeting in council, determined which religious ideas or practices would be accepted and which rejected, which writings were truly Christian and which false. In this way the church selected the twenty-seven canonical books of the New Testament, written in Greek, and the Old Testament writings as preserved in a Greek translation from the Hebrew. In the Greek (or eastern) church today these orthodox versions are still in use; in the Roman (or western) church the Latin version, called the Vulgate and made by Jerome after 386, is used.

Bishops and Their Duties

Each bishop presided over several churches. Each church was under the care of a priest (Greek, *presbyteros*) who had been qualified by special training and by a ceremony of ordination. The area served by each church and its priest came to be known as the parish. In the early church the office of deacon had much importance. Before long, then, a distinction between those who were merely faithful worshipers (the laity) and those who conducted the worship and administered the affairs of the church (the clergy) became well defined. By the seventh century, the broad lines of church government in both the East and the West had been established. The organization was hierarchical, that is, there was a regular series of levels from subordinate to superior, from priest to bishop, from bishop to pope or patriarch. But at almost every level there were councils made up of officials who met to debate problems and to make decisions.

After the conversion of Constantine, the first Christian emperor, the election of bishops became a matter of particular concern to imperial authorities. To retain the initiative, the officials of the church worked to put the election of each new bishop into the hands of the clergy of the cathedral or of the see. Practice remained uneven, however; sometimes the clergy, and in some cases the people, simply gave assent to an accomplished fact by approving elections; at other times the people had real power, as when Roman mobs under the sway of rival political leaders controlled the choices for the bishop of Rome. Since bishops often exercised actual governing power and had their own law courts, lay rulers often insisted on approving or even selecting them. The degree to which laymen could participate in the choice of the bishops remained an important point of contention in the West down to the eleventh century.

Monasticism

Deacons, priests, bishops, and archbishops all served the laity and were called secular clergy, as their pastoral duties were in the *saeculum* (in the world). Early in the history of the church, however, another kind of devotee to Christianity appeared in Syria and Egypt: the monk, a man or sometimes, in the case of prophetesses and anchorites, a woman who felt that he or she must become an ascetic. The New Testament extolled the merits of abstaining from sexual relations if possible and from all other fleshly indulgence. Therefore, monks, hermits, and/or anchorites would leave civilization behind and go into the desert to live in solitude, meditation, and prayer, subsisting on the minimum of food and drink. By the third century there were many of these hermits, who enjoyed reputations for extreme holiness and often competed with each other in torturing themselves or in self-denial. Some lived in trees or in holes in the ground; others on the top of columns, to which they would haul up food supplied by pious followers.

Others, such as the Egyptian hermit Pachomius, formed communities of monks living by a rule. Certain monks, such as Anthony (whose life written by Athanasius became one of the foundational hagiographic texts [those that described the lives of the saints]), engaged in such extreme lives of asceticism that they served as models for others. The most famous of these rules was written by Basil (330–379) and became standard in the Greek church. Basil prescribed celibacy and poverty but required that the monks work in the fields or elsewhere to make their communities as self-supporting as possible. Because after Basil monks lived by a rule, they are known as the regular clergy (Latin *regula*, "rule"), as contrasted with the secular clergy.

In the West the perception of the church's growing materialism and of the Christians' involvement in the world and in politics after Constantine's Edict of Milan led to the rule of St. Benedict of Nursia (c. 480–c. 547), who founded an abbey at Monte Cassino in southern Italy. According to Pope Gregory the Great's (590–604) *Life of St. Benedict* (written almost half a century after Benedict's death), Benedict, a member of a prestigious Roman senatorial family, gave up his wealth and status and embraced a wandering life in the wilder-

The Written Record

THE RULE OF ST. BENEDICT

The Benedictine rule blended Roman law with the new Christian view to produce the most enduring form of monasticism in western society. Consider the concepts of authority, rule, and equality contained in the following portions of the rule of St. Benedict:

An abbot who is worthy to preside over a monastery ought always to remember what he is called, and carry out with his deeds the name of a Superior. For he is believed to be Christ's representative, since he is called by His name, the apostle saying, "Ye have received the spirit of adoption of sons, whereby we call Abba, Father." And so the abbot should not—grant that he may not—teach, or decree, or order, any thing apart from the precept of the Lord; but his order or teaching should be sprinkled with the ferment of divine justice in the minds of his disciples. Let the abbot always be mindful that, at the tremendous judgment of God, both things will be weighed in the balance: his teaching and the obedience of his disciples. And let the abbot know that whatever the father of the family finds of less utility among the sheep is laid to the fault of the shepherd. . . . [The abbot] shall make no distinction of persons in the monastery. One shall not be more cherished than another, unless it be the one whom he finds excelling in good works or in obedience. A free-born man shall not be preferred to one coming from servitude, unless there be some other reasonable cause . . . for whether we be bond or free we are one in Christ; and, under one God, we perform an equal service or subjection; for God is no respecter of persons.

The Rule of St. Benedict, in *Select Historical Documents of the Middle Ages*, trans. E.E. Henderson (London: George Bell, 1982), 176–77.

ness. Overcoming numerous temptations by the Devil and severe tests of his faith, Benedict made his way eventually to Monte Cassino (a high place near the road between Naples and Rome). There he founded a monastery and wrote a rule (also included in Gregory the Great's work). His Latin rule, like Basil's Greek rule, prescribed hard work for all and urged the monks to be tolerant of one another's interests and infirmities.

Benedict's rule and example served as the foundations for the spread of monasticism throughout the West. When Gregory the Great sent missionaries, such as Augustine of Canterbury, to England (596) and sponsored campaigns to convert people in Gaul and elsewhere to Christianity, monastic ideals and institutions (the monastery) became the backbone of Christianity's eventual penetration into rural areas and in the conversion of Germanic groups to orthodoxy (read here obedient to the pope) in western Europe. Over the next thousand years and beyond, Benedict's rule and monasteries remained at the center of life, culture, and spirituality in the medieval West.

In the West during the sixth and seventh centuries, the monks acted as pioneers in opening up the wilderness, performing missionary service, and providing much charitable and medical work among the poor and the sick. In both East and West, scholarship also became one of the recognized occupations for monks. The monastic scribe, who copied the works of the ancients and built up the library of his foundation—a development of the sixth and seventh centuries—helped preserve the literature of the past.

Tensions often arose between secular and regular clergy, each feeling that its own work was more valuable to Christianity as a whole. Constant care and strict government were needed to maintain the high ideals of the monasteries and of similar female institutions that soon appeared throughout Christendom. This continuing need prompted successive monastic reform movements that played a major role in Christian history.

The Dynamics of the Spread of Christianity

In earlier paragraphs we described some of the elements that assured the victory of Christianity throughout the Roman world. In the West, the rapid decline of Roman authority and institutions—prompted by internal factors and Germanic invasions—led to the rise of Christianity as a viable haven in the midst of political uncertainty and cultural change. If Christianity succeeded, it did so not only because of its elaborate administrative organization or because monasticism attracted some of the best minds in both East and West. Monasticism was, after all, the outcome of deeper transformations and of new dynamics in the nature of Christianity. We hinted at some of these factors earlier. The works of Peter Brown, Claudia Rapp, and others, show that holiness, the veneration of saints, or what Brown describes as "to join Heaven and Earth at the grave of a dead human being,"* had an extraordinary impact in the construction of early Christianity and its rapid spread throughout the Roman Empire.

Christianity's embracing of the poor and the downtrodden, the substantial role that women played in the development of the religion in its early centuries, its aggressive preaching, and its redemptive message provided a heady religious and social context for the rise of new spiritual values. Holiness, demonstrated in heroic fashion by the early Christian martyrs and saints, the worship of dead martyrs (both women and men), and the formalization of the cult of saints around the tombs and shrines of holy men and women, provided Christianity with a charismatic and divine appeal. Ascetic practices—above all sexual renunciation—empowered men and, most of all, women. In the ancient world women had been often restricted to interior spaces, their social and economic roles predetermined. Under Christianity the role of women changed. The human body became the site for a struggle between temptation and the nefarious appeal of the flesh and the yearning

---

*Peter Brown, *The Cult of Saints. Its Rise and Function in Latin Christendom* (Chicago: The University of Chicago Press, 1981), 1.

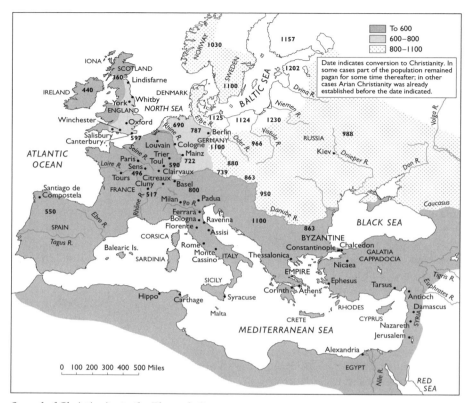

Spread of Christianity to the Eleventh Century

for purity and the divine. Sexual abstinence became associated with piety and holiness and gave women and men outlets beyond marriage and traditional lives. The cult of the saints, the worship of relics, the role that holy graves came to play in late antique Christianity marked, to a large extent, the victory of the "vulgar," to use Peter Brown's description, that is, of the popular understanding of religion over that of the elite. But it also marked the deep imprint that these new practices and models had on society as a whole. That many of the saints were also scholars and learned did not hurt. As Christianity developed its hierarchical structure and its wide popular appeal, it also produced vibrant and innovative cultural forms and complex rituals (sacraments) of salvation.

The Development of Christian Thought

The Christian clergy could hardly have attained its great power had it not been an essential intermediary between this visible world of actuality and an invisible other world that, to the devout Christian, is as real as this one. In Christianity certain important ideas about the other world are embodied in ritual acts called sacraments. These sacraments, administered by the clergy, are central to an understanding of Christian doctrine. Over the centuries and into the twelfth century, the sacraments grew in number to seven: (1) baptism, by which a person was washed of the stain of original sin and brought into mystical union with Christ; (2) confirmation, by which one was formally brought into the discipline of the church; (3) the Eucharist, the central act of Christian observance; (4) penance, whereby a confessed and repentant sinner was granted absolution (forgiven) by the priest; (5) extreme unction, a ceremony performed by the priest at the dying moments of the Christian in preparation for the life to come; (6) ordination, the ceremony by which a candidate was made a priest; and (7) matrimony, holy marriage. The central sacrament of Christianity was the Eucharist, or Holy Communion. It stems from Jesus' last supper with his disciples, where he took bread, blessed it, and, breaking it, gave it to the disciples, and said: "Take, eat; this is my body." And he took cup and said: "Drink you all of it. For this is my blood of the new testament, which is shed for many for the remission of sins." By the third century, the Eucharist, which commemorates Christ's sacrifice, had become a ceremony that made the Christian believer feel a personal link with God and experience the wonder of salvation. If the sacrament of baptism figuratively washed away the stain of original sin and made a person a Christian, then the sacrament of the Eucharist enabled one to remain in Christian communion and to sustain its faith and fellowship. Theological explanations were given for this symbolic act. Adam, who began with the chance for a perfect life on earth in the Garden of Eden, disobeyed God, was driven from Eden, and was exposed to death and suffering on earth. This was Adam's "original sin," and all his descendants shared his fate. But the Jews kept alive their faith in God; after generations of suffering, God took mercy and sent to earth his only son, Jesus. By suffering on the cross, Jesus atoned for human sins and made it possible in the future for faithful Christians to be saved, despite Adam's sin. After death the faithful would enjoy in the other world the immortal happiness they could only anticipate in this one.

Even so elementary an outline of the doctrine of salvation bristles with the kinds of difficulties Christians have been arguing about for centuries. What was the relation between God and his son? What was Adam's original sin? How did one attain salvation? Was it enough to belong to the church, or must there be some inward sign? This last question raises what has been for two thousand years perhaps the central point of debate in Christianity—the problem of faith versus good works. Those who believe that salvation is primarily an emotional matter for the individual Christian—a matter of faith—tend to minimize the importance of outward acts. Those who believe that a person must behave in strict accordance with God's directions to be saved put more emphasis upon good works. Either position, carried to its logical extreme, poses great dangers: on the one hand, the taking over of the priestly role by the individual believer; on the other, dictatorship over daily behavior by the clergy.

The Nicene Creed

The early centuries of Christianity saw a series of struggles to define the accepted doctrines of the religion (orthodoxy) and to protect them against the challenge of rival or unsound doctrinal ideas (heresy). The first heresies appeared almost as early as the first clergy. In fact, the issue between those who wished to admit gentiles and those who wished to confine the Gospel to the Jews foreshadowed the kind of issue that was to confront Christianity in the first few centuries. The points at issue sometimes seem unimportant to us today, but we must not regard these religious debates as trivial; people believed that salvation depended upon the proper definition and defense of religious belief and practice. Also, bitter political, economic, and regional issues often underlay theological disputes. Heresy, a departure from established beliefs or dogmas (the essential principles of the church), had a significant role in defining the nature of the nascent religion. Christian doctrine was shaped by the tensions and dialectical play of different ways of defining the faith. At the end, it was a question of power. Those who won imposed their views as the orthodox position; those who lost were branded as heretics, exiled, or persecuted. Right doctrine depended, to a large extent, on circumstances and on the context in which these doctrinal struggles took place.

One of the most significant issues for Christians was the question of evil. A good number of the so-called heretical movements that proliferated in early Christianity sought to address the presence of evil in the world. It has always been difficult to understand and explain how evil can exist in a world created by a good God. The Gnostics, a group that prospered in the second century and whose ideas owed much to Greek philosophy, astrology, and magic, affirmed that only the world of the spirit is real and good; the physical world is evil, or an evil illusion. Thus they could not accept the Old Testament, whose god created this world; they regarded him as a fiend or decided that this world had been created by Satan. Nor could they accept Jesus' human life, work, and martyrdom in this world—an essential part of Christian belief. They could not accept baptism, because to them water was matter, or venerate a crucifix, which to them was simply two pieces of wood. Like the Zoroastrians, with their god of good and their god of evil, the Gnostics were dualists. Clearly heretical, the Gnostics focused on Christ's miracles and on other sorts of magic.

Closely related to Gnosticism were the ideas of Mani, a third-century Mesopotamian prophet who called himself the Apostle of Jesus. He preached that the god of light and goodness and his emanations were in constant conflict with the god of darkness, evil, and matter and his emanations. These Manichaean dualistic views became immensely popular, especially in North Africa during the third and fourth centuries. The Christians combated them and throughout the Middle Ages tended to label all doctrinal opposition by the generic term Manichaean. As we shall see, Manichaeaism made a serious bid for the allegiance of many Christians in the twelfth century.

But we must not forget that within Christianity, heresy sometimes involved very practical problems. Emperor Constantine, and later in his polemical works St. Augustine of Hippo, faced the so-called Donatist movement in North Africa. The movement arose because a number of priests yielded to the demands of Roman authorities during the Roman persecutions of the Christians after 303 and handed their sacred books over to them. After the edicts of toleration of 311 and 313, they had resumed their role as priests. Donatus, bishop of Carthage, and his followers maintained that the sacraments administered by such priests were invalid. This belief was divisive, because once a believer questioned the validity of the sacraments as received from one priest, he might question it as received from any other. Amid much bitterness and violence Constantine ruled that once a priest had been properly ordained, the sacraments administered at his hands had validity, even if the priest himself had acted badly or sinfully.

Heresy also arose over essentially philosophical, but deeply emotional, issues. One such was Arianism, named after Arius (c. 280–336), a priest of Alexandria. Early in the fourth century Arius taught that if God the Father had begotten God the Son through God the Holy Ghost, then God the Son, as begotten, could not be exactly of the "same essence" (*homoousios* in Greek) as God the Father, but must be somehow inferior to, or dependent upon, or at the least later in time than his begetter, who was of a "similar essence" (*homoiousios* in Greek), but not the same. Arius's view threatened to diminish the divinity of Christ as God the Son and to separate Christ from the Trinity of Father, Son, and Holy Ghost.

Arius's bitter opponent, Athanasius (c. 293–373), patriarch of Alexandria and "the father of orthodoxy," fought him passionately. Athanasius and his followers maintained that Christians simply had to accept as a matter of faith that Father and Son are identical in essence and that the Son is equal to, independent of, and contemporaneous with the Father. Even though the Father begat the Son, it was heresy to say that there was ever a time when the Son did not exist. In the Greek East especially, this philosophical argument was fought out not only among churchmen and thinkers but also in the streets and among the laity. A visitor to Constantinople complained, "I ask how much I have to pay; they talk of the born and the unborn. I want to know the price of bread; they answer 'the father is greater than the son. I ask if my bath is ready; they say 'the son has been made out of nothing.'"

After trying to stay out of the quarrel and urging the bishops to stop discussing it, Constantine realized that for political reasons it would have to be settled. In 325 he summoned the first council of the whole church, an ecumenical council, at Nicaea (now Iznik) near Constantinople. A large majority of the bishops decided in favor of the Athanasian view, which was then embodied in a statement known as the Nicene Creed, issued with all the force of an imperial decree by Constantine himself. The emperor had presided over the council, and against his will found himself giving legal sanction to a purely doctrinal decision, and so playing the role both of a secular and a religious dignitary. Centuries later, this dual power became known as "Caesaropapism," the sharing of political and religious power and often associated with the relation between emperor and patriarch in the East.

The Written Record

THE NICENE CREED

The Council of Nicaea created a religious organization to run in parallel to civil administration, and in the Nicene Creed set out a basic statement of what Christians believe.

We believe in one God, the Father all-sovereign, maker
of all things, both visible and invisible:
And in one Lord Jesus Christ, the Son of God,
begotten of the Father, and only-begotten,
that is from the essence [*ousia*] of the Father.
God from God
Light from light,
True God from true God,
begotten not made,
being of one essence [*homoousion*] with the Father;
by whom all things were made,
both things in heaven and things on earth;
who for us men and for our salvation came down from
heaven and was made flesh, was made man
suffered and rose again on the third day,
ascended into heaven, cometh to judge quick and dead:
And in the Holy Spirit.
But those who say that there was once
when he was not and before he was
begotten he was not and he was made
of things that were not
Or maintain that the Son of God is of a different
essence or substance or is created or subject
to moral change or alteration
Them cloth the Catholic and Apostolic
Church anathematize [condemn to damnation].

The Nicene Creed, in *Documents of the Christian Church,* 2d ed., ed. Henry Bettenson (London: Oxford University Press, 1963), 35.

But the decree of Nicaea did not dispose of Arianism. Arians disobeyed; Constantine himself wavered (as noted earlier, he may have been baptized before his death by an Arian priest); his immediate successors on the imperial throne were themselves Arians. Between 325 and 381 there were thirteen more councils that discussed the problem, deciding first one way, then another. One pagan historian sardonically commented that one could no longer travel on the roads because they were so cluttered with throngs of bishops riding off to one council or another. Traces of Arianism remained in the empire for several centuries after Nicaea, and Arian missionaries, most notably the Arian bishop Ulfilas, successfully converted most of the German tribes on the borders of the empire. The German conversion to Christianity, but to a type of Christianity consider heterodox or heretical by most of the Christian population of the empire, had significant consequences for the settlement of Germanic groups in the western parts of the empire from the fifth century onward and for their relation with the local inhabitants of those regions.

The Debate over the Two Natures of Christ

Long before Arianism disappeared, a new and related controversy had shaken the eastern portion of the empire to its foundations. Exactly what was the relationship of Christ the god and Christ the man? He was both man and god, but how was this possible? And was the Virgin Mary the mother only of his human aspect, or, if not, how could a human being be the mother of god?

One extreme position separated the human nature of Christ from the divine and therefore refused to regard the human virgin as the mother of god. This view later became unfairly linked with the name of Nestorius (died c. 451), patriarch of Constantinople in the early fifth century, and its followers were called Nestorians. They took refuge in Asia. The other extreme view was that of the monophysites, who argued that Christ's human and divine natures were totally merged; they carried their thesis so far that they almost forgot Christ's human attributes and tended to make him a god only. Again the dispute flared into physical violence in the East; again the decision hung in the balance; again the emperor (now Marcian, 450–457) called a council, this time at Chalcedon, near Constantinople, in 451. The council condemned monophysitism and, like the Council of Nicaea, took a mystical rather than a rational position; the true believer must believe in the two natures of Christ, human and divine, coexisting yet not distinct from each other; thus the Virgin is properly called the mother of god. The council also recognized Constantinople as having the same religious status in the East as Rome had in the West.

Like the decision at Nicaea, the decision at Chalcedon did not definitely dispose of the opposition. Monophysites were concentrated in Egypt and Syria, and they apparently expressed in their religious beliefs the resentment of the ancient Mediterranean cities of Alexandria and Antioch against the new domination by the upstart Constantinople. Partly because it was identified with what we may be described as local or regional identity, monophysitism did not die out, and the emperors strove to deal with it by one compromise or another. Since there were few monophysites in the West, the Roman church regarded the issue as closed; each time an emperor at Constantinople tried to appease his Egyptian and Syrian monophysite subjects, he was condemned by the bishop of Rome (by the sixth century, the pope) for heresy.

Thought and Letters in the First Christian Centuries

Although a good deal of dislike and misunderstanding had always characterized the attitudes of most Greeks and Romans toward each other, Roman
admiration for Greek literature and art deeply influenced the work of Roman
writers and artists. The triumph of Christianity tended to contribute new
sources of misunderstanding and tension to the relationships between east-
erners and westerners. The political division between East and West imposed
by Diocletian's reform (the Edict of the Tetrarchy, 285) and repeated by many
of his successors expressed the geographic distinction between eastern and
western provinces that corresponded roughly to the old Greece and Rome.
As Germanic inroads began increasingly to disrupt communications in the
fourth and fifth centuries and to threaten all the established institutions in the
West, the opportunities for westerners to learn Greek and embrace the early
classical tradition decreased. In the eastern provinces few except soldiers and
professional administrators had ever spoken or read Latin, although it
remained the official language of legislation at Constantinople through the
fifth century. Despite the growing division, however, the literature of the late
Roman and early Christian world may be treated as a whole, often because
of subject matter.

The Rise of Christian Literature

In the West pagan literature declined or became derivative, while in the East
a few passionate devotees of the old gods still made their voices heard. Christian writings increasingly took center stage. In the East, writers devoted much
energy to polemical statements on doctrinal questions and disputes. In both
East and West, the best minds among Christians faced the problem of how to
treat Greek and Roman literature. At first, a few thinkers, mostly in the West,
advised against reading anything but Scripture. Later they acknowledged
that one had to read the great classical authors of the past to be able to refute
non-Christian philosophical ideas. Still, there was always the danger that in
the pleasure of reading a classical author one might forget to expose his errors
and refute his arguments. The Greek Christians worried far less about this
problem. In the fourth century Basil, author of the communal monastic rule;
his brother, Gregory of Nyssa (died c. 394); and their friend, Gregory of
Nazianzos (329–389) all had excellent classical educations and used the techniques of the so-called pagan philosophers to discuss religious ideas.

One of the most important writers in Latin was Jerome (340–420), who
studied with Gregory of Nazianzos and who produced the Latin Bible (the
Vulgate). Another was Ambrose (c. 340–397), a Roman civil servant and aristocrat who became bishop of Milan. Christianizing much that he found in the
classics, he transformed Cicero's Stoic concept of duty to the state into a
Christian concept of duty to God. Ambrose put his own preaching into practice when he publicly humiliated Emperor Theodosius I (379–395) and forced
him to do penance for savagely punishing some rioters. The act symbolized
the western church's insistence that, in matters of morals and faith, the

church would be supreme over the secular power—an attitude that ran exactly counter to the practice growing up in the East.

Augustine

Early Life.   The third, and greatest, of the western Christian thinkers was Augustine of Hippo. We know Augustine (354–430), probably the most influential mind of late antiquity, intimately through his famous autobiography, *The Confessions*. We also know the social, political, and geographical contexts in which he wrote and how his ideas developed through Peter Brown's biography. Augustine was born in a small market town in what is now Algeria, inland from Carthage, the administrative and cultural center of the African provinces. Here the population still spoke Punic (Phoenician), but the upper classes were Latin speaking, wholly Roman in their outlook, and deeply imbued with the classical traditions of Rome. Prosperous planters lived on their great estates, while peasants toiled in the fields and olive groves. Of modest means and often at odds with one another, Augustine's father and his devoutly Christian and possessive mother were determined that he should be given a good education, for this was the path to advancement. But all that his teachers did was force him to memorize classical Latin texts and to comment on them in detail. Augustine was so bored that he never did learn Greek, and so was cut off from the classical philosophers and forced to pick up their ideas secondhand. His parents' ambitions for him prevented him from getting married at seventeen, like most of his contemporaries. While at school, Augustine took a concubine, with whom he lived happily for fifteen years and by whom he had a son.

Disappointed with his reading of the Bible, which he found insufficiently polished and too confining, Augustine at nineteen joined the Manichaeans. The sect was regarded by pagans and Christians alike as subversive and had been declared illegal. Gone were Augustine's plans to become a lawyer, as his mother had wished; he determined to learn and teach the Manichaean "wisdom." When he went back to his birthplace, his mother was so angry with him for having become a Manichaean that she would not let him into the house. But the static quality of Manichaean belief, the nature of its rituals, and the disappointing intellectual level of the leaders he met began to disillusion Augustine, and he returned to Carthage to teach rhetoric. He also embraced astrology for a while in a deep personal search for an answer to the question on the origin and nature of evil. Highly placed friends invited him to move to Italy. At twenty-eight he was appointed professor of rhetoric at Milan, the seat of the imperial court. The job required him to compose and deliver the official speeches of praise for the emperor and for the consuls.

Conversion and **The Confessions.**   At Milan, Augustine abandoned the Manichaean faith and fell under the spell of Ambrose, the bishop of Milan. Better educated than Augustine, a superb preacher, and indifferent to the demands of the flesh, Ambrose stimulated Augustine to reexamine all his ideas. And Augustine's mother, who had followed him to Milan, eagerly drank in Ambrose's words "as a fountain of water." Ambrose's influence was complemented by Augustine's discovery of Neoplatonism. He was influenced by the Neoplatonist idea that material things of this world were reflections of ideas in the eternal other world, and that there were means by which one could move away from the external world of the senses. Augustine's world widened. Evil, instead of looming at the center of it, took a less prominent place; his god became more distant, more powerful, more mysterious than Mani's god. But in the end Augustine could not accept the Neoplatonist view that a person could attain to the vision of god by reason alone. He was ready for conversion to Christianity.

This was a major step, involving not only the abandonment of his worldly career but also the rite of baptism, which was then felt to be so great a spiritual ordeal that many Christians put it off until their deathbeds. On Easter Day 387, at the age of thirty-three, he was baptized by Ambrose. Soon afterward he returned to his native North Africa. In his hometown he soon found himself in intellectual combat with the Manichees, debating them publicly, writing pamphlets against them, arguing that evil was in large part simply bad habits; once a person had derived pleasure from an evil act, the memory of the pleasure prompted doing it again. Within three years Augustine had been forced into the priesthood by the demands of a local congregation, and in 395 he became bishop of the large town of Hippo (modern Bône). Here he wrote *The Confessions*, describing his spiritual journey in an effort to lead his reader to God.

Augustine's gravest practical problem was the Donatists, who regarded themselves as the only true church and who outnumbered the Catholics in Hippo. He preached against them, wrote pamphlets against them, and turned out a popular set of verses satirizing them. Convinced that there could be no salvation outside the church, Augustine also persecuted the Donatists after 399, when the Christian emperors began to take severe measures to suppress ancient religious practices. When the Goths sacked Rome in 410, refugees poured into North Africa with accounts of the fear that had gripped the inhabitants and the ruthlessness of the invaders. Although no longer the imperial capital, Rome was still the symbol of the imperial tradition and of all ancient culture. The North African governors, worried about the stability of the province, issued an edict of toleration for the Donatists. Augustine protested, contrasting the City of Man, the secular world where evil was commonplace, with the City of God, toward which history was moving humanity spiritually.

The City of God. In a new work, *The City of God*, written between 413 and 425, Augustine combated the pagan argument that it was Christianity that had been responsible for the catastrophic sack of Rome. It was easy to show why many empires had fallen in the past, and Augustine quickly moved beyond his original subject. He attacked traditional non-Christian worship and classical interpretations of Roman history, systematically demolishing non-Christian philosophy. Honest in seeking and generous in spending their wealth, the Romans had been allowed by God to acquire their great empire; but they became too eager for praise and glory. True glory belonged only to the citizens of the City of God (*civitas Dei*). The community of those who served the Devil in the earthly city would be separated in the afterlife from those who served God, the Christians. As the demons took over Rome because the Romans had not submitted to the authority of Christ, so only in that heavenly City of God could the Christian achieve true peace. Augustine thus elaborated a complete Christian philosophy of history, with the faithful as pilgrims passing through the here-and-now on their way to the heavenly Jerusalem.

Free Will and Predestination.   Later in life Augustine found himself engaged in a final philosophical controversy with Pelagius (c. 354–420), a Christian layman who had lived for many years in Rome and who believed that humans not only could, but must, perfect themselves. He denied original sin and believed in free will. Yet such an exaltation of human possibilities is in its essence non-Christian, since it diminishes God's majesty. Pelagius's ideas affected questions of Christian behavior. For example, if there were no original sin, then newborn infants could not be guilty of it, and infant baptism was unnecessary. The Pelagian message, that one must simply will oneself to obey God's commandments, meant that every Christian must lead a monk's life. In Rome many upper-class Christians regarded Pelagius's views as a summons to reform and purify themselves.

Augustine fought Pelagius's ideas, recognizing that for the first time he had met an intellectual opponent of his own caliber. He feared "the crisis of piety" that the Pelagians could create. On the practical level, he preferred to see rich, puritanical radicals give their property to the church rather than directly to the poor. On the theological level, he argued that not all sins were committed willfully or could be willfully avoided; some came through ignorance, weakness, or even against the desire of the sinner. It was for these sins that the church existed. Baptism was the only way to salvation. For Pelagius, humans were no longer infants dependent upon a heavenly Father; they were emancipated beings who must choose to be perfect. For Augustine, human behavior was still dependent upon God. Human beings were not perfect, for they had sinned. Pelagius had won a considerable following in the Holy Land. In 419 a young and brilliant successor, Julian, bishop of Eclanum, took up the contest with the aging and determined Augustine. Augustine defended the concept of original sin by citing the passage in Genesis in which Adam and Eve instantly cover their genitals after they have eaten of the forbidden fruit. That was the point, Augustine said, at which sin had arisen. All sexual feelings create guilt; only baptism and the Christian life could wipe it out. Julian answered in disgust that this imagery was blasphemous, making the Devil into the true creator of humanity, destroying free will, and sullying the innocence of the newborn. Sexual power, he said, was a natural good, a sixth sense.

Both positions were held by devout Christians. Yet to Julian, Augustine's god seemed unjust, a persecutor of infants, and not the loving god who sacrificed his only son for human salvation. Justice must underlie all society and all religion. For Augustine, God's justice was indisputable and could not be defined by mere human reason. God had said he would visit the sins of the fathers upon the children, and so Adam's sin had been visited upon all humanity. The world of the fifth century was large enough for both points of view to be heard, but it was Augustine's view that would prevail, for Julian was seen as too intellectual, too insistent on a solely rational god, while the clergy preferred a god whose mystery could not be fully grasped. In his old age Augustine came to believe that God had already chosen those people who would attain salvation and that a person's actions were predestined, or determined beforehand. In the face of new Germanic onslaughts—this time from the Vandals—on the hitherto safe shores of North Africa itself, predestination was a message with some comfort for those who had persevered in what was believed to be God's work.

When Augustine died, a year before the Vandals devastated Hippo, a disciple listing his writings said that no one could ever hope to read them all; and yet anyone who did would still have missed the greatest experience: knowing Augustine as a human being or seeing him in the pulpit and listening to him preach. Although the Catholic church turned away from the doctrine of predestination—always insisting that God's grace must be supplemented by good works before a person could be saved—it still considered Augustine the greatest western father of the church. More than a thousand years later, other non-Catholic Christians would return to his teaching of predestination.

The Christian Triumph as a Historical Problem

Why did Christianity triumph in the fourth century? It began as a despised sect in a rich, well-organized, sophisticated society, yet it took over that society. The Romans had undermined religion by their tolerant acceptance of myriad of religious beliefs as long as imperial authority was accepted and taxes paid. Jesus' teachings, as glossed and transmitted by preachers and missionaries, gave Christianity certain advantages over the mystery cults. The evangel was really "good news"—with its promise of salvation from sin and personal immortality and its admonition to behave with kindness and love toward one's fellow human beings. The expanding church provided a consoling and dramatic ritual and the opportunity to become part of the dangerous and challenging task of spreading the gospel. The would-be convert could find Christian ideas and rites closely related to those of Egyptians, Greeks, and Jews. The new beliefs were compatible with various already held beliefs, making possible that merging of bodies of ideas, what is called syncretism.

Yet Christianity's success was not universal. From its cradle in Jerusalem, where the new religion did not prosper, Christianity did not penetrate far into the lands of Zoroastrian, Hindu, and other eastern faiths, nor into Africa south of the Sahara. Instead, it spread westward along the trade routes of the Mediterranean and north into Europe, essentially within the structure of the Roman Empire, for it needed the political and cultural framework of the state to prosper. Christianity succeeded not only because it set itself against the earthly compromises of pagan cults and the sterility of later classical philosophy, but also because it contained so much of Judaism and of paganism. Even more important perhaps is the extent to which Christianity allowed the old rites and habits, the unintellectual, practical side of religion, to survive. Christmas celebrates the birth of Jesus, but it also marks the turning northward of the European winter sun, the promise of its returning warmth; Easter is an echo of thousands of years of celebration of the coming of spring.

Christianity thus offered a new and believable spiritual promise, yet preserved reassuringly familiar elements; it extolled mutual love; it had a capacity for adaptation; it was well led and taught. Moreover, Christianity eventually triumphed within the Roman world because of the organization of the church, something that Jesus had not foreseen, much less planned. The Roman principle of the union of civil and religious authority, with the first predominant, was applied in reversed order of importance in the West after the demise of Roman centralized government in the fifth century, the better to give humanity the sense of security it needed in a period of vast and rapid change. The Romans relied on religion, not science, to explain their world. The increasing pessimism of the late Roman Empire fostered the growth of astrology, religious cults promising personal salvation, and mystical philosophy. The Jews under Roman rule were hard to control and divided among various political and religious factions. Many Jews believed in the imminent coming of some sort of deliverer, or Messiah. Christianity began as a Jewish movement. Paul separated Christianity from Judaism and spread its beliefs throughout much of the empire.

Roman persecution of Christianity was intermittent. It arose because the Christians' refusal to sacrifice to the emperor threatened the unity of the empire. Despite persecution, Christianity continued to spread. Constantine ended the persecution in 313. Emperor Theodosius made Christianity the official religion of the empire in 380. In the West the bishop of Rome (later the pope) became the surviving symbol of the old Roman sense of order and authority. He was head of the church and an important political figure. In the East the emperor at Constantinople sometimes acted as the real head of both church and empire. Monasticism arose out of the desire of some Christian believers to escape the temptations of the world. The rule of St. Benedict became the basis for most monasteries in the West. The development of a complex Christian theology gave rise to many heresies in the early church, which led to both political and theological controversy.

The Aftermath of the Empire in the West

By the time Augustine was dying at Hippo, the western Roman Empire was facing increasing difficulties. Rome had been sacked. German tribes, some of them with legal authority from the emperor in Constantinople to occupy and rule in the West, began to settle in parts of the western empire (Gaul, Spain, Italy, and North Africa). Worse invaders thrust deep into the heartland of the western empire: the Huns led by their great leader, Attila. Roman imperial administration decayed and was replaced in many localities by the church. Taxes were not collected; trade declined. All was not hopeless, however. In the midst of a painful period of transition, a vital new civilization was in the making. In the East, the Roman Empire lived on, transformed but viable. Further East, less than a century and a half after the western empire became fragmented, Muhammad began preaching surrender to Allah. In the West itself, the Germans settled to the building of their own individual societies, often in close cooperation with those who kept the memories of Rome alive. It is to these three distinct civilizations that we turn now.

SUMMARY

The Romans relied on religion, not science, to explain their world. The increasing pessimism of the late Roman Empire fostered the growth of astrology, religious cults promising personal salvation, and mystical philosophy. Christianity began as a Jewish movement. Paul separated Christianity from Judaism and spread its beliefs throughout much of the empire. Roman persecution of Christianity was intermittent. It arose because the Christians' refusal to sacrifice to the emperor threatened the unity of the empire. Despite persecution, Christianity continued to spread. Constantine ended the persecution in 313 C.E. Emperor Theodosius made Christianity the official religion of the empire in 380.

In the West the bishop of Rome (the pope) became the surviving symbol of the old Roman sense of order and authority. He was head of the church and an important political figure. In the East the emperor at Constantinople usually acted as the real head of both church and state. Monasticism arose out of the desire of some Christian believers to escape the temptations of the world. In the West, monasticism, grounded upon St. Benedict's life and rule, developed as one of the vital institutions in Christendom. Benedictine monks became the vanguard of papal attempts to link all of the West into a coherent Christian world.

The counterpart to the religious and practical aspects of monasticism can be found in the formal elaboration of Christian theology between the first and the sixth centuries. Nonetheless, defining what Christianity was and how one ought to be a Christian generated numerous controversies and disputes. At the end, the issue was one of authority, but conflicts over questions of belief divided Christians into orthodox and heterodox (heretical). Augustine of Hippo, the most influential Christian theologian of the period, helped, through his writings and combative life, to shape the course of the church and Christianity for centuries to come.

Christianity had beliefs in common with its rivals, the other mystical religions and philosophic movements. Christianity succeeded because it set itself against the earthly compromises of ancient religions and the dryness of later pagan philosophy and because it retained much pagan religious practice and philosophic thought.

TWO

Byzantium and Islam,
500–1000

As Christianity slowly took over the institutions and the responsibilities for city government and charity from a fading Roman imperial administration in the West, different political structures and cultures began to emerge throughout the ruins of the Roman Empire. Over the next five hundred to six hundred years, between the fall of Rome in the West in the fifth century and the first stirrings of cultural revival in the late eleventh, three major cultural and political entities shared the geographical space once dominated by Roman institutions and power. These three distinct cultures—Germanic, Byzantine, and Muslim—were deeply intertwined. We cannot think of the early Middle Ages in the West as an exclusively Germanic affair. Rather, we must think of this period as an interspersing of these three civilizations—sometimes in the form of cultural and technological transfers, sometimes in the form of open religious and political conflict—over the centuries. Each of these large cultural or political entities was itself fragmented. The Germanic groups that settled in the West divided into specific subsets. They also engaged in intense social, political, and cultural negotiations with original inhabitants and with those on their borders. Germans did so with local populations (Romans, Iberians, Celtic people) in their midst and with Scandinavians, Poles, Avars, Muslims, and others in their periphery. Byzantium interacted with Slavs, Turkis, Khazars, Bulgars, Persians, Muslims, and others in its boundaries and with a variety of local inhabitants. Islam, stretching from India to the Atlantic, ruled over a population of extraordinary ethnic and cultural variety.

In this chapter we examine the development of unique political and cultural institutions in Byzantium and Islam. Each of these civilizations had a profound influence on the development of western medieval culture. In the case of Byzantium, its enduring example shaped western consciousness and the idea of the West as a place separate from the East. Often, the West sought to create a distinctive identity in imitation of, and in opposition to, Byzantium. In the case of Islam, "the enemy in the mirror" to use Barkai's brilliant

description, the influence was felt right at home, in the dazzling achievements of the Cordoba caliphate and in the dynamic Islamic culture of Sicily.
Both of these cultures, Islam and Byzantium, interacted intensely with each
other, with the new "barbarian" kingdoms in the West, and with other peoples in their sphere of influence. Byzantium served also as a bridge to faraway places. Byzantine cultural and religious forms spread over a vast area,
stretching from the Balkans and substantial parts of Central Europe to the
vast landmass in the East that is part of what today we call Russia. Islam, the
lands of Dar al-Islam (the world of Islam), encompassed a wide multicultural
and ethnic world: from Iberia in the West to the Spice Islands (what is today
Indonesia) in the East. The coast of North Africa and, for a while, Sicily and
the islands of Mallorca and Minorca represented its northern boundary. In
the South, Islam extended well beyond the great Sahara. Muslim caravans
traveled deep into Africa, Muslim merchants plying their trade widely across
sub-Saharan Africa.

Byzantium

At the far southeastern corner of Europe, on a little tongue of land still
defended by a long line of massive walls and towers, stands a splendid and
magical city, Istanbul. After 330, when the first Christian Roman emperor,
Constantine the Great, made it his capital, it was often called Constantinople,
but it also retained its ancient name—Byzantium. For more than eleven hundred years thereafter it remained the capital of the eastern Roman Empire.
The waters that surround it on three sides are those of the Sea of Marmora,
the Bosporus, and the city's own sheltered harbor. A few miles to the north,
up the narrow, swift-flowing Bosporus, lies the entrance to the Black Sea. To
the southwest, the Sea of Marmora narrows into the Dardanelles, a long passage into the Aegean. The Dardanelles, the Sea of Marmora, and the Bosporus
connect the Black Sea with the Mediterranean and separate Europe from
Asia. Together, these are the Straits, perhaps the most important strategic
waterway in European diplomatic and military history. The city dominates
the Straits. To the Slavs of Russia and the Balkans, this city has always been
Tsargrad—city of the emperor. It was the center of a civilization sharing some
of the cultural and political traditions of the West, yet it was startlingly different in significant ways.

The city, Constantinople (the term Byzantium was often identified with the
eastern Roman Empire as a whole, but also with the city), retained its fabled
reputation for over a millennium. As has been noted, Constantinople commanded a superb strategic location on the Straits, but its long survival
depended, to a large extent, on its unique identity as the strongest fortress in
the late antique and medieval world. Only in 1453, when the internal weakness of the empire and the adroit use of artillery and military force by the
Ottoman Turks led to the breaching of the city walls, did the long history of
the eastern empire come to an end.

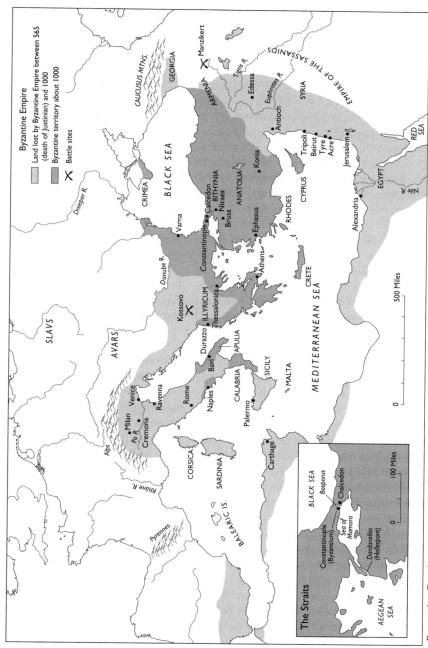

Byzantine Empire

Byzantine Empire

- Land lost by Byzantine Empire between 565 (death of Justinian) and 1000
- Byzantine territory about 1000
- ✕ Battle sites

SLAVS

AVARS

CAUCUSUS MTNS.

GEORGIA

✕ Manzikert

ARMENIA

Tigris R.

Euphrates R.

EMPIRE OF THE SASSANIDS

Edessa

SYRIA

Antioch

Dnieper R.

BLACK SEA

CRIMEA

Varna

Constantinople

Calcedon

Nicaea

BITHYNIA

Brusa

ANATOLIA

Konia

Ephesus

Athens

RHODES

CYPRUS

Tripoli
Beirut
Tyre
Acre
Jerusalem

RED SEA

Alexandria

EGYPT

Nile R.

Danube R.

Kossovo ✕

ILLYRICUM

Thessalonica

Durazzo

Bari

APULIA

CALABRIA

SICILY

MALTA

Palermo

MEDITERRANEAN SEA

CRETE

Rhône R.

Alps

Milan

Po R.

Cremona

Venice

Ravenna

Rome

Naples

CORSICA

SARDINIA

BALEARIC IS.

Pyrenees

Carthage

0   500 Miles

The Straits

BLACK SEA

Bosporus

Chalcedon

Constantinople
(Byzantium)

Sea of Marmara

Dardanelles
(Hellespont)

AEGEAN SEA

0   100 Miles

Byzantium: The "State"

It is very difficult and incorrect to speak of the "state" in the early Middle Ages, but if there was a state in early medieval Christendom in the sense in which we think of states today, Byzantium was as close to the definition as one could get. After Constantine, Byzantium called itself New Rome. Its emperors ruled, in theory, in direct succession from Augustus. Yet many non-Roman elements became increasingly important in Byzantine society. After Constantine had become a Christian, the emperor was no longer a god, but his power remained sacred. A reigning Byzantine emperor usually followed the Roman practice and chose his heir. When an emperor selected someone not his son, public opinion required that he adopt him formally. Each new emperor was raised aloft on a shield as a sign of army approval, thus becoming *Imperator* (commander-in-chief). By the mid-fifth century, he might also be formally crowned by the patriarch of Constantinople, and he would swear to defend the Christian faith. In the seventh century the emperor began to call himself *Basileus*, King of Kings, in token of his military victory over the Persians. Later still he added the term *Autocrat*, for the emperor was an absolute ruler. Empresses bore corresponding titles and played an important role in the political and ceremonial life of the empire. Three times in Byzantine history women—Irene, Euphrosyne, and Theodora—ruled alone. Often, they did so with boldness, taking far-reaching political and religious decisions.

So complex were the rules of imperial life that books were written to describe them. The emperor's subjects remained silent in his presence. The emperor spoke and gave commands through simple, brief, and established formulas. Those admitted to an audience approached with their arms held fast by officials and ceremoniously fell on their faces in homage when they reached the throne. On public occasions the emperor was acclaimed in song, to the sound of silver trumpets. The officials of the palace were the most important functionaries of the state. All officials had a title that gave them a post in the palace as well as a rank among the nobility. At Byzantium many of the greatest and most influential officials were eunuchs, the third gender or "beardless men," a feature of the Byzantine political organization that sometimes astonished westerners and made them uneasy. There was never a prime minister as such, although in practice an imperial favorite often controlled policy. While Byzantine dynasties sometimes lasted several centuries, those close to the throne or important military commanders sometimes intervened. They imprisoned and exiled emperors, murdered them, blinded or mutilated them (which made them ineligible to rule again), and then enthroned their own candidates. Revolution was viewed as the proper recourse against imperial tyranny. In the Nika revolt of 532 Justinian might have lost his throne had it not been for the coolness and bravery of his celebrated empress, Theodora, who is alleged to have said:

> Now, above all other times, is a bad time to flee, even if we get away safely. Once a man has seen the light, he must surely die; but for a man who has been an emperor to become a refugee is intolerable. . . . Now if you wish to save your-

---

The Written Record

THEOPHILUS ON JUSTICE

Emperor Theophilus (r. 829–842) appeared every week on horseback at a given church and handed down judgments so fair and equitable that they have passed into legend:

One day when the Emperor appeared, a poor woman threw herself at his feet in tears, complaining that all light and air had been shut off from her house by a huge and sumptuous new palace which a high official of the police was building next door. Moreover, this official was the brother of the Empress. But the Emperor paid no heed to this. He ordered an instant inquiry, and when he found that the woman had told the truth, he had the guilty man stripped and beaten in the open street, commanded the palace to be torn down, and gave the land on which it stood to the woman. Another time, a woman boldly seized the bridle of the horse which the Emperor was riding, and told him that the horse was hers. As soon as Theophilus got back to the palace, he had her brought in and she testified that the general of the province where she lived had taken the horse away from her husband by force and had given it to the Emperor as a present to curry favor with him. Then he had sent the rightful owner of the horse into combat with the infantry, where he had been killed. When the general was hauled before the Emperor and was confronted by the woman, he finally admitted his guilt. He was dismissed from his post, and part of his property was confiscated and given to the plaintiff.

Quoted in Charles Diehl, "La Légende de Theophile," *Seminarium Kondakovianum* (Prague: Institute Imeni N.P. Kondakova, 1931), *Recueil d'études* IV, 36.

---

self, O Emperor, that is easy. For we have much money: there is the sea, here are the boats. But think whether after you have been saved you may not come to feel that you would have preferred to die.

The Law

As the direct agent of God, the emperor was responsible for preserving the tradition of Roman law. Only the emperor could modify the laws already in effect or proclaim new ones. Thus he had on hand an immensely powerful instrument for preserving and enhancing power. Between 528 and 533 Justinian (r. 527–565) ordered his lawyers to dispose of obsolete, repetitious, and conflicting enactments. His *Code* (the *Corpus Iuris Civilis*) included all legislation since Hadrian (r. 117–138). In addition, the *Corpus* included the authoritative opinions of legal experts collected in the *Digest*. The *Institutes*, a handbook for students, served as an introduction to both compilations. All these were set down in the Latin in which they had been issued, although Justinian's own laws, the *Novels*, or newly passed enactments, appeared in Greek.

In the eighth century a new collection modified Justinian's work. Under Leo VI, the Wise (r. 886–912), a new collection rejected much that dated from an earlier period.

In the Byzantine Empire, justice could be rendered only in the emperor's name. The emperor was the supreme judge, and rendering justice was perhaps his most important function. Subordinate officials handed down decisions only by virtue of the power the emperor delegated to them, and the emperors themselves often rendered judgment in quite ordinary cases brought to them by their subjects. The emperors of the later ninth century took great care in the systematic appointment of judges and created a kind of legal aid bureau to enable the poor of the provinces to make appeals to the capital. Judges were obliged to render, write out, and sign all decisions. New courts were set up, and new officials were created. Later, even in the provinces, side by side with the martial law administered by the local commanding general, soldiers could be tried in civil courts for civil offenses.

War

As defenders of the faith against hostile invaders, the Byzantine emperors fought frequent wars, which were followed by periods of peace, for the eleven hundred years the empire lasted. Sometimes the invaders were moving north and west from Asia: Persians in the seventh century, Arabs from the seventh century on, and Turks beginning in the eleventh century. Byzantium thus absorbed the heaviest shock of eastern invasions and cushioned the West against them. The Byzantine state had also engaged in warfare a variety of enemies: the Huns of the fifth century, the Avars of the sixth and seventh, the Bulgars of the seventh and succeeding centuries, the Magyars of the ninth and later centuries, and the Pechenegs and Cumans of the eleventh, twelfth, and thirteenth centuries.

Sometimes the enemies were of Slavic origin. The Slavs had, from the sixth century onward, filtered gradually south into the eastern Roman Empire. Their steady migratory flow eventually covered the entire Balkan peninsula. In the northeastern part of the peninsula, the Slavs were conquered by the Hunnic tribe of the Bulgars but slowly absorbed their conquerors. These Bulgars fought exhausting wars against Byzantium. So did the Varangians (or inhabitants of Rus, see later), another Slavic people, whose Scandinavian upper class was gradually absorbed into a larger Slavic population. Sailing across the Black Sea, the Varangians (part of the two-pronged expansion of Scandinavian people or Northmen from the eighth century onward) attacked Byzantium by sea in 860. These Varangian or Rus attacks against Byzantium continued on and off through the next century. Beginning in the eleventh century, the enemies were western Europeans: Normans from the southern Italian state; crusaders from France, Germany, and Italy; freebooting adventurers from the new Italian cities.

For more than seven hundred years after Constantine, until the late eleventh century, the Byzantines held their own. Although hostile forces sometimes swarmed to the foot of the walls or threatened from across the Straits, Byzantium itself remained inviolable until 1204. In that year it was taken for the first time by a mixed force of Venetian traders eager for profit and French, Italian, and German crusaders, who had set out to fight the Muslims in Palestine and had been detoured to the greater profit to be had in the imperial city. Only a political entity with phenomenally good armies and navies and enlightened diplomacy could have compiled so successful a military record and withstood so many challenges over such a long period of time. From all periods of Byzantine history survive studies of the art of war, discussing new ways of fighting and new weapons. The Byzantines were adaptable, learning and applying lessons from their enemies. Often commanded by the emperor in person, carefully recruited and thoroughly trained, well armed and equipped, entertained by bands playing martial music, and served by medical and ambulance corps, by a signal corps with flashing mirrors, and by intelligence agencies far more competent than those of their rivals, the Byzantine armies, although occasionally defeated, by and large maintained their superiority.

The same is almost as true of the Byzantine navies. The appearance of a Muslim fleet in the eastern Mediterranean in the seventh century forced a naval reorganization by the Byzantines, who by the tenth century had recaptured their former control of these waters. At its height, the Byzantine fleet played a major role in imperial defense. It was equipped with one of the most deadly weapons of the Middle Ages: Greek fire, a chemical compound squirted from tubes or siphons that would set enemy vessels aflame, burn even when in contact with water, and strike terror into the hearts of enemy sailors.

Diplomacy

The Byzantines, however, preferred negotiating to fighting, and they brought diplomacy to a high level. The subtlety of the instructions given their envoys has made "Byzantine" a lasting word for complexity and intrigue. First Persia and then to some extent the Muslim caliphate were the only states whose rulers the Byzantine emperors regarded as equals. All others were "barbarians," and that included, in some manner, western rulers. Nonetheless, in their endless effort to protect their frontiers, the Byzantine emperors dealt realistically with those peoples whom they could not conquer. They negotiated treaties, obtaining military assistance and allowing the vassal peoples to enjoy the luxuries that Byzantine money could buy. A kind of "office of barbarian affairs" kept imperial officials supplied with intelligence reports on the internal conditions of each of these people. As in Roman times, when the emperor sent arms to the chieftain of a foreign tribe, it was the equivalent of adoption. The Christian Byzantine emperor could make the paternal relationship even stronger by sponsoring a non-Christian ruler at his baptism. The son of such a chief might be invited to be educated at Byzantium, and thus introduced to all the glories of Byzantine civilization. Titles in the hier-

The Written Record

DAZZLING THE "BARBARIAN"

A solemn formal reception at the imperial court usually dazzled a foreign ruler or envoy, even a sophisticated western bishop like Liudprand of Cremona (d. 972), ambassador of the king in Italy, who has left us his account from the year 948:

Before the emperor's seat stood a tree made of bronze gilded over, whose branches were filled with birds, also made of gilded bronze, which uttered different cries, each according to its varying species. The throne itself seemed so marvellously fashioned that at one moment it seemed a low structure and at another it rose high into the air. It was of immense size and was guarded by lions, made either of bronze or of wood covered over with gold, who beat the ground with their tails and gave a dreadful roar with open mouth and quivering tongue. Leaning upon the shoulders of two eunuchs I was brought into the emperor's presence. At my approach the lions began to roar and the birds to cry out, each according to its kind. . . . After I had three times made obeisance to the emperor with my face upon the ground, I lifted my head and behold! The man whom just before I had seen sitting on a moderately elevated seat had now changed his raiment and was sitting on the level of the ceiling. How it was done I cannot imagine, unless perhaps he was lifted up by some sort of device as we use for raising the timbers of a wine-press.

Liudprand, *Antapodosis*, V1, *v*, in *The Works of Liudprand of Cremona*, trans. F. A. Wright (London: Routledge & Kegan Paul Ltd., 1930), 207–8.

archy of the palace were bestowed on "barbarian" rulers. Marriage was also a most useful instrument. These enemy leaders were pleased to marry Byzantine women of noble family; when it was a question of a particularly desirable alliance, the emperor himself might marry a "barbarian" princess. And the Byzantines could think and write about diplomacy in ways unthinkable at that time in the West. Constantine Pophyrogenitus's *De administrando Imperio* is a superb example of the level of sophistication and expertise in the Byzantine administration.

The Byzantine Economy

Byzantium was a great center of trade to which vessels came from every quarter of the compass. From the countries around the Black Sea came furs and hides, grain, salt, wine, and slaves from the Caucasus. From India, Ceylon, Syria, and Arabia came spices, precious stones, and silk; from Africa, slaves and ivory; from the West, especially Italy, came merchants eager to buy the goods sold in Constantinople, including the products of the imperial industries. The Byzantine emperors were able for centuries to maintain a monopoly over the manufacture and sale of silk textiles, purple dye, and gold embroidery. Long a closely guarded secret of the Persians, silk manufacture came to Byzantium in the mid-sixth century. The power derived from control over the manufacture and sale of silk has been compared with modern control over such strategic materials as oil. But it was not only the imperial treasury that profited. The rich were able to embellish their persons and their homes; many middle-class merchants and craftsmen found a livelihood in the industry; and the flow of revenue into the imperial treasuries allowed the emperors to tax the lower classes less than would otherwise have been necessary for defense and other official expenses.

Besides controlling silk, the emperor forbade the export of gold. The *nomisma,* as the Byzantine gold coin was called, was standard all over the Mediterranean and even in the East. Until the mid-eleventh century it was rarely debased, and even then only gradually under the impact of civil strife and foreign invasion. For eight hundred years this money was stable. Throughout Byzantine history the sources of state income remained much the same. Money came in from state property. This money was distinct from that which came in the emperor's personal estates. Booty seized in war or fortunes confiscated from rich men in disgrace provided cash. And of course there was also revenue from taxation on land and persons, sales and profits, imports and exports, and inheritances.

From Diocletian (r. 284–305) the Byzantines inherited the concept that land and labor were taxable together. The territory of the empire was considered to be divided into units called *yokes,* each of which was defined as the amount of land that could feed a single laboring farmer. To be taxable as a unit of land, each yoke had to have its farmer to work it; to be taxable as a person, each farmer had to have a yoke to work. The government thus had to find a person to cultivate every yoke; otherwise there would have been no revenue. This concept led to the binding of many peasants to the soil. Large private landowners flourished under such a system, since it was easier for the state to lease them large tracts of land and leave it to them to find the supply of labor. Moreover, inferior land or abandoned or rundown farms were assigned to nearby landowners, who were then responsible for the taxes on such property as on their more productive acres. Only a landowner with rich and productive farmland could pay such taxes on the more marginal farms. So this aspect of the system also contributed to the growth of large private estates. Yet although the large estate may have predominated in the early period, the small private freeholder seems never to have disappeared.

The typical Byzantine *oikos,* or "household," included slaves. Byzantium was a patriarchal society; thus, in the upper classes' *oikos,* women were often segregated to apartments of their own. Daughters were literally kept under lock and key, for an unchaste daughter brought disgrace upon every family member. Women could not consume alcohol before others, even at family dinner. Everyone in the family took part in decisions about marriage, since one of its purposes was social advancement. The delivery of children was an important social, and thus economic, function for women. But women also played a role in the rural economy and in artisan work. Moreover, as was discussed before, women held an important position in the political sphere, either as influential figures behind the throne or as outright rulers.

Byzantine Christianity and Relations with the West

For most of its history Byzantium was not defined by its relations with the West. Although sharing the same religion and concerned by some of the same theological issues, the rulers of Byzantium interacted most intensely with its neighbors to the east, north, and south. Although there was a keen awareness of the legacy of Rome and dreams of reconquering and uniting the empire once again, those hopes were not realistic. Moreover, the West had little, certainly before the eleventh century, to offer in terms of trade or culture. Nonetheless, the histories of the West and Byzantium were bound together. Byzantine influence was particularly strong in Italy and other Mediterranean areas. Byzantine armies and administrators maintained a long presence in Ravenna and southern Italy. Byzantine culture and architecture also influenced the development of Italian art forms. The cathedral of St. Mark in Venice is only one of the most notable examples.

Not unlike the West, religion governed Byzantine life from birth to death. The church governed marriage and family relations and filled leisure time. Religion also dominated the arts and literature, economics and politics, and intellectual life. What was the true relationship of the members of the Trinity to one another? What was the true relationship of the human to the divine nature of Christ? Was it proper to worship holy images? Such problems were argued not only in monasteries and centers of secular learning but also in the streets. The questions were desperately important. The right answer meant salvation and future bliss; the wrong answer, damnation and eternal punishment. Foreign policy was also pervaded by religion. When the emperor went to war, the enemies were infidels, heretics, or schismatics. The emperor went into battle against them with a sacred picture borne before him, an icon (image) of the Virgin, perhaps one of those that legend said had been painted by St. Luke, or one not even made by human hands at all but miraculously sent from heaven itself.

Contrast with the West

Yet much of this was also true in the medieval West. The real contrast is most apparent when we compare the relationship between ecclesiastical and secular authority in the West with that in the East. In the West, the departure of the emperors from Rome permitted local bishops to create centers of authority, especially in Rome after the sixth century, and to challenge, although not always successfully, kings and emperors. In Constantinople, however, the emperor remained in residence, and no papacy developed. Constantine himself summoned the Council of Nicaea in 325; he paid the salaries of the bishops, presided over their deliberations, and as emperor gave to their decrees the force of imperial law. When he intervened in matters of Christian dogma, he was doing what no layman in the West would do. In the East the emperor regularly deposed patriarchs and punished clerics. In short, the church often functioned as an adjunct to the needs of the state, of which the emperor was the effective head. Such a system, in which a single authority plays the role of both emperor and pope, is known as *Caesaropapism,* although the term is essentially incorrect, as it fails to recognize that there were no popes in the West until later and, certainly, no popes in Byzantium.

Sometimes a patriarch of Constantinople successfully challenged an emperor. Moreover, absolute though they were, none of the emperors could afford to impose new dogma without church support or risk offending the religious beliefs of the people. The power of the emperor seldom applied to the inner, or "esoteric," form of the church, for the sacraments remained the preserve of the clergy. Thus the emperor was more an "imitator of Christ"— the deputy of God on earth—with authority in both spiritual and secular realms. As we saw in the previous chapter, Constantine had not wanted to intervene in the theological quarrel over Arianism, but he did so because the very structure of the empire was threatened. The Council of Nicaea failed to impose a settlement, and the quarrel continued for another three quarters of a century. New battles began over the relationship between the human and divine natures in Christ. Egyptian and Syrian Christians were mono-physites—believers in a single, divine nature for Christ—and they success-fully resisted attempts to force them to compromise.

In the East, more so than in the West, monasticism became an ideal of the Christian life; to become a monk was to take a direct route to salvation. Worldly men, including many emperors, became monks on their deathbeds to increase their chances of going to heaven. At Byzantium, but also in the West, monks enjoyed enormous prestige and often influenced political deci-sions. Rich and powerful laymen, from the emperor down, founded new monasteries as an act of piety. Often immune from taxation, monasteries acquired vast lands and much treasure in both the East and the West.

For the ordinary Christian, the sacraments of the church provided the way to salvation. In the East every religious act took on a sacramental quality. Every image, every relic of a saint, was felt to preserve the essence of the holy person in itself. God was felt to be actually present in the sanctuary; he could be reached only through the proper performance of the ritual. The emphasis also fell more on mystery, ritual, and a personal approach to the heavenly savior than on the ethical teachings of Christianity. Once believers accepted the proper performance of an act as the right way to reach God, they could not contemplate any change in it; for if the old way was wrong, then their parents and grandparents were all damned.

Theological Quarrels with the West until 1054

A difference in the wording of the liturgy, it is sometimes argued, caused the so-called *schism,* or split, between the eastern and western churches in 1054.

The Greek creed states that the Holy Ghost "proceeds" from the Father; the Latin adds the word *filioque,* meaning "and from the son." But this and other differences might never have led to a break had it not been for increasing divergences between the two civilizations and the two forms of Christianity. More than three hundred years earlier, in the eighth century, a religious controversy arose in the Byzantine Empire over the use of sculpted and painted sacred images (icons) and the nature and amount of reverence that a Christian might properly pay them. Twice, for long periods (726–787 and 813–842), the emperors adopted the strict Old Testament rule that all images must be banned. (This policy is termed *iconoclasm,* from the Greek words for "image breaking.") The western Christians, who believed that images were educational and might be venerated (although not worshiped), were shocked. In the end the emperors restored the images, but as early as the 730s an emperor had punished the pope by removing from papal jurisdiction southern Italy and Illyricum (the Balkan provinces) and placing them under the patriarch of Constantinople. The papacy was determined to recover its rights in these territories. Even more decisive was the papal belief that Byzantium could not, or would not, defend Italy and the papacy against Lombards and Muslims.

Competition in the 860s between papal and Byzantine missionaries to convert the Bulgars again led to a political quarrel. It was then that the Byzantines "discovered" the Roman "error" in adding *filioque* to the creed. In 867, at the Council of Constantinople, the Patriarch Photius charged the pope with heresy and challenged any papal claims to supremacy. Although this quarrel, too, was eventually settled, an underlying mistrust persisted. The Byzantines became accustomed to going their own way without reference to the bishops of Rome.

Under these circumstances the Byzantines were unprepared for a revival of the old papal efforts to recover jurisdiction over southern Italy. Norman adventurers began just after the year 1000 to conquer Byzantine territory in southern Italy and to restore its churches and revenues to the pope. The pope naturally welcomed this, but the Byzantine patriarch Michael Cerularios was unhappy over his losses. A violent and powerful man, he dug up the old *filioque* controversy and opposed papal jurisdiction in southern Italy. In answer to his complaints, the pope sent to Byzantium one of his most energetic and unbending cardinals, Hugh Silva Candida, in 1054. Patriarch and cardinal thereupon excommunicated each other.

The issues that separated eastern and western Christianity, however, went beyond a struggle for ecclesiastical jurisdiction or the *filioque* dispute. They also involved the proper use of unleavened bread for communion and the desire by both pope and patriarch for more uniformity in liturgy, doctrine, and church lines of authority, resulting respectively from the Patriarch Michael Cerularius's reforms in Byzantium and the monastic and papal reform movement in the West. Eastern and western Christians were also increasingly suspicious of and resistant to each other's cultures. To the visiting westerner, the Greeks seemed soft, effeminate, and treacherous, although this is, as all these kinds of reports are, a stereotypical representation. To the

Byzantine, the westerner seemed savage, fickle, and dangerous. Nowhere is the western animosity toward the Byzantine shown better than in the writings of Bishop Liudprand, who had been so impressed by the emperor's movable throne when he first visited Constantinople in 948. On a second official visit in 969 as ambassador from Otto I, he describes his reception by the emperor Nicephorus Phocas:

> On the fourth of June we arrived at Constantinople, and after a miserable reception . . . we were given the most miserable and disgusting quarters [that] . . . neither kept out the cold nor afforded shelter from heat. Armed soldiers were set to guard us and prevent my people from going out and any others from coming in. . . . To add to our troubles the Greek wine we found undrinkable because of the mixture in it of pitch, resin, and plaster. The house itself had no water, and we could not even buy any to quench our thirst.*

On the other side, the Byzantine ambivalence toward westerners is illustrated by the *Alexiad,* written by the princess Anna Comnena more than a century later. She says that two Normans, Robert Guiscard and his son Bohemond, might rightly be termed

> the caterpillar and the locust for whatever escaped Robert . . . Bohemond took to him and devoured. . . . For by nature the man was a rogue and ready for anything; in roguery and cunning he was far superior to all the Latins [Westerners]. But in spite of his surpassing them all in superabundant activity in mischief yet fickleness like some natural appendage attended him too. . . .

> A certain charm hung about the man but was partly marred by a sense of the terrible. There seemed to be something untamed and inexorable about his whole appearance . . . and his laugh was like the roaring of other men. . . . His mind was many sided, versatile, and provident. His speech was carefully worded and his answers guarded.**

The mutual dislike between Byzantines and westerners was to grow steadily more intense after the late eleventh century, until it climaxed in tragedy in 1204, when a coalition of western crusaders diverted an expedition against Jerusalem into an attack on and conquest of the city.

The Fortunes of Empire, 330–1081

Despite their efforts, the emperors at Constantinople could not reconquer the West fully and thus reconstitute the Roman Empire of Augustus. Indeed, theological controversy—reflecting internal political strain—combined with Persian and Muslim expansion cost the empire Syria and Egypt. The internal structure was modified to meet the new situation. From 717 to 867 the threat

---

*Liudprand, *The Works of Liudprand of Cremona,* trans. F. A. Wright (London: Routledge of Kegan Paul Ltd., 1930), 235–36.
***Alexiad* (New York: Barnes & Noble, 1901), 37–38, 226, 347. Translation partly the author's, partly from Elizabeth A. S. Dawes.

of Arab conquest was safely contained, the Bulgars were converted, the major religious and political struggle over church images was fought and decided, and the large landowners began to emerge as a threat to the financial and military system. From 867 to 1025 the Byzantine Empire was at its height. The emperors counterattacked the Muslims and regained much territory and prestige, the grim struggle with the Bulgars was fought to a bloody conclusion, the people of Kievan Rus converted to Orthodox Christianity, and the emperors made every effort to check the growth of the great landowning aristocracy. But the years 1025–1081 represented a period of decline, slow at first and accelerating as the period drew to a close.

Constantine to Leo III, 330–717

The emperors immediately following Constantine were Arians until Theodosius I (r. 379–395), who in 380 proclaimed orthodox Nicene Athanasian Christianity to be the sole permitted state religion. All those who did not accept the Nicene Creed were to be driven from the cities of the empire. The empire, East and West, was united under Theodosius, but his sons Arcadius (r. 395–408) and Honorius (r. 395–423) divided it, with Arcadius ruling at Constantinople. Until the accession of Justinian in 527, the eastern portion of the empire successfully used Goths and other Germanic groups as troops and usually managed to deflect invaders further westward. Despite the challenge from Huns and Persians, the eastern Roman Empire continued to prosper. Only the monophysite controversy warned of internal weakness.

In a series of wars, Justinian's armies, led by the capable general Belisarius (a eunuch), reconquered North Africa from the Vandals, parts of Italy from the Ostrogoths, and small portions of southern Spain from the Visigoths. It was a last desperate effort to reunite all of Rome's Mediterranean lands. But the long campaigns and a vast new system of fortifications proved extremely costly. By limiting his wars with the Persians on the eastern frontiers to defensive efforts, Justinian permitted the Persian danger to grow. The empire, however, did not have to pay the full bill for Justinian's policies until the early seventh century. During the reign of Phocas I (r. 602–610), internal bankruptcy and external attacks from the Persians seemed to threaten total destruction. But Heraclius (r. 610–641) sailed in the nick of time from Carthage to Constantinople and seized the throne. He spent the first years of his reign in military preparations, absorbing heavy losses as the Persians took Antioch, Damascus, Jerusalem, and Alexandria. The Persians threatened Constantinople from the Asian side of the Straits, while the Slavs and Avars were besieging it in Europe.

In 626 Heraclius defeated the Persians in their own territory and recaptured all the lost provinces. But only a few years later, the new movement of Islam exploded out of Arabia and overran the very provinces that Heraclius had recaptured from the Persians. In both the Persian and the Muslim victories over Byzantium, the antagonism of the monophysite Syrians and Egyptians played a major role. From Egypt the Muslims pushed westward to

Carthage in 698, putting an end to Byzantine North Africa. Muslim ships began to operate from Cyprus and Rhodes. Heraclius's work and that of Justinian were seemingly undone.

Despite the desperate crisis, the emperors completely overhauled the administrative machinery of the state. Gradually they extended the system of government previously introduced into Italy to their remaining territories in Asia Minor and the Balkans. The loss of Syria and Egypt required the transformation of Asia Minor (Anatolia) into a reservoir of military manpower and state income. Moreover, the frequent raids of Slavs, Avars, and Bulgars into the Balkan provinces made the emergency more acute and increased still more the dependence on Asia Minor. Eventually the emperors divided Asia Minor and the Balkans into army corps areas, with the local military commanders also exercising civil authority. These new military districts were called *themes,* from a word meaning permanent garrison. In each theme the troops were recruited from the native population; in return for their military services, the independent farmers were granted land, but they were not allowed to dispose of it or to evade their duties as soldiers. Their sons inherited the property along with the obligation to fight.

Although in theory responsible to the emperor, the commanding generals of the themes often revolted, and in the late seventh and early eighth centuries such rebellious generals seized the imperial throne. The imperial government strove to combat this danger by dividing the large original themes into smaller ones. From seven big themes at the end of the seventh century the number mounted to about thirty smaller ones by the year 900. This system also embodied a change in concepts of taxation. As new immigration and settlement apparently ended the labor shortage of earlier centuries, it was now possible to separate the land tax from the tax on persons. The latter was transformed into a hearth tax, which fell on every peasant household without exception. For purposes of the land tax, each peasant village was considered a single unit. Imperial tax assessors regularly visited each village, calculated its total tax, and assessed each inhabitant a portion of it. The community as a whole was held responsible for the total tax, and often the neighbor of a poor peasant or of one who had abandoned a farm would have to pay the extra amount to make up the total. This obligation was onerous, and when the tax could not be collected the state itself sometimes had to take over the property and resell or rent it. Displaced officials, overburdened landowners, and harried peasants weakened the idea of unity for a common purpose. Nonetheless, the empire experienced sustained economic growth well into the twelfth century.

Leo III to Basil I, 717–867

In 717–718 Leo III, who had come to the throne as a successful general, defeated the Muslims who were besieging Constantinople. Thereafter the Byzantine struggle against the Muslims gradually became stabilized along a fixed frontier in Asia Minor. But the Muslim capture of Crete and Sicily in the ninth century opened the way for repeated pirate raids against the shores of Byzantine Greece and southern Italy. In northern Italy the Lombards conquered the Byzantine exarchate of Ravenna in 751, and Byzantine claims in Italy were further damaged by the alliance between the Franks and the papacy. And in the Balkans the Bulgars' menace reached a new peak of severity. Under the iconoclastic emperors, iconoclasm took a violent anti-monastic aspect, since the monks of Byzantium were the great defenders of iconographic representations. During this phase of the struggle some of the monks challenged the right of emperors to legislate in matters of religion. But the worship of images was twice restored by imperial decree. As a result of the struggle, the Byzantines drew more careful distinctions between superstitious adoration paid to images and proper reverence.

Although the new system of small military holdings and the growth of a free peasantry retarded the development of large estates during the eighth and ninth centuries, landlords were nevertheless again beginning to accumulate properties. One cause may have been the ruin of the small farmers in Anatolia as a result of disorders that accompanied a great rebellion under a Byzantine general, Thomas the Slav, who with the support of the poor in Anatolia and the Arabs twice sought to conquer Constantinople until defeated and executed in 884.

Basil I Through the "Time of Troubles," 867–1081

Although intrigue and the violent overthrow of sovereigns remained a feature of Byzantine politics, the people developed a deep loyalty to the new ruling house that was established in 867 by the Armenian Basil I (r. 867–886) and called the Macedonian dynasty because of Basil's birth there. As political disintegration began to weaken the opposing Muslim world, the Byzantines counterattacked in the tenth century. They captured Crete in 961 and Antioch and much of northern Syria in 962. A new Muslim dynasty in Egypt, which also took over in Palestine, stopped the Byzantine advance short of Jerusalem. But like the later crusaders from the West, the Byzantine emperors still hoped to liberate that city from the Muslims. While pushing back the Muslims, the Byzantines allied themselves with the Armenians and gradually annexed Armenia. In the West, firmly reestablished in southern Italy after defeating the Saracens (or North African Muslims) in 915, the Byzantines dominated the neighboring Lombard duchies until after the advent of the Normans in the early eleventh century. From then on the emperors would find themselves under attack on three fronts—in Asia Minor, in southern Italy, and in the north from the Bulgars.

Under the early emperors of the Macedonian dynasty, the large landowners continued to flourish. Whole dynasties of nobles lived on their great estates, constantly acquiring more land at the expense of the poor. They bought up the holdings of the poor and made the peasantry once more dependent upon them. The growing might of the local magnates meant that the state was losing both its best taxpayers (the free peasants) and its best soldiers (the military settlers). During the tenth and eleventh centuries, a great struggle developed between the emperors and the nobles. The nobles thwarted all imperial attempts to check the growth of their power and eventually seized the throne. Laws intended to end the acquisition of land by magnates could not be enforced; in times of bad harvest especially, the small free proprietor was forced to sell out to his rich neighbor.

The great Emperor Basil II (r. 976–1025) made the most sustained efforts to reverse this process. He confiscated the estates of those who had acquired their lands since the rule of his grandfather. Other could keep their holdings on satisfactory proof of prior ownership. As a final blow to the nobles, Basil II ordained that they would have to pay all the tax arrears of the delinquent peasants. But a few years after Basil died, this law was repealed under the influence of the magnates. As the landlords turned more of the free military peasants into tenants on their estates, they became virtual commanders of private armies. After Basil, only the civil servants acted as a counterweight to the landowners. To reduce the landlords' power, the civil servants tried to cut down the expenses of the army. Strife between these two parties weakened the imperial defenses.

The Macedonian dynasty died out in 1057, and a "time of troubles" began. The Normans drove the Byzantines from the Italian peninsula by taking the great southern port of Bari in 1071. In the same year, the Seljuk Turks defeated the imperial armies at Manzikert in Armenia and captured Emperor Romanos IV. Asia Minor, the great plains of Anatolia, Byzantium's most important reservoir of manpower and taxes, now lay open to the Turks, who pushed all the way to the Straits and established their capital in Nicaea. Meanwhile other Turkic tribes raided southward into the Balkans. In 1081 one of the powerful magnates of Asia Minor, Alexius Comnenus, seized Constantinople. By then the first Crusade was a mere fifteen years away, and, with the coming of western Christians into Byzantine lands, so was a dramatic shift in the political landscape.

Byzantium and the Slavs and Turkic People

One of Byzantium's most enduring legacies was the transmission of its civilization and religion to the Slavs. Much as Rome had Christianized large groups of Germanic invaders in western Europe, so Constantinople, the new Rome, Christianized diverse groups in eastern Europe.

Conversion of the Bulgars

The first people to fall under Byzantine influence were the Bulgars. Although present-day Bulgarians are of Slavic provenance, the medieval Bulgars were of Turkic origins. From the time they crossed the Danube in the late seventh century, the Bulgars had engaged in intermittent warfare against the Byzantine Empire. At the same time, a Slavic people called the Moravians had established a kingdom of their own. Their rulers associated Christianity with their powerful neighbors, the Germans, and feared both German and papal encroachment. To avoid German or papal influence, the king of the Moravians sent to Byzantium and asked for a Greek missionary to teach the Moravian people Christianity in 862. The Byzantine emperor, Michael III, sent to Moravia two missionaries, Cyril and his brother Methodius, called the Apostles to the Slavs. They knew Slavic and invented an alphabet in which it could be written. That alphabet proved to be too complicated and another was designed later by Constantine of Preslav and named after Cyril. It is still employed by the Russians, the Bulgarians, and the Serbs, and it is still called *Cyrillic* after the early missionary. As a countermove to Byzantine influence, Boris, ruler of the Bulgars, asked for Christianity from the Germans. But these efforts by the two rulers, that of the Moravians and the Bulgars, to avoid conversion at the hands of their powerful neighbors failed.

In Moravia, the efforts of the German clergy and of Roman Christianity eventually triumphed. However, in the lands of the Bulgars (what is today Bulgaria), conversion played out differently. The power of nearby Byzantium was too strong. Boris, the Bulgar ruler, found that he could not obtain a church independent from the papacy. Only in the fold of the eastern church could Boris unify his country and consolidate his own power. From the late ninth century on, the language of the church became the native Slavonic tongue used in preaching by the followers of Cyril and Methodius.

But the ambitions of the Bulgars' kings were ultimately too great to permit friendly relations with Byzantium. Under Simeon (r. 893–927), second son of Boris, there began a bitter hundred years' war between the Bulgars and Byzantium. In 981, Samuel, the Bulgar ruler, defeated Basil II. But in 1014 Basil won an important victory over the Bulgars, and shortly afterward, Byzantine domination over the land of the Bulgars became complete. The country was ruled as a conquered province. But its inhabitants were never deprived of their own church, whose archbishop had as much ecclesiastical jurisdiction as in the days of Bulgar independence.

The great expenditures of money and manpower incurred in the long pursuit of the Bulgar war played their part in weakening Byzantium for the military disasters that were to come at Manzikert and at Bari in 1071. But the war helped to determine where the line between East and West would be drawn for future history. The Bulgarians, the people who inhabit the lands of the Bulgars, are an Orthodox people to this day, and their civilization throughout the Middle Ages directly reflected the overpowering influence of Byzantium. In much the same way, more than three hundred years later, the western neighbors of the Bulgars, the Serbs, also took their faith from the Greek East after a flirtation with the Latin West.

The Conversion of the Rus

Beginning in the eighth century, the Scandinavians expanded into the area that is today European Russia. First taking control of the Baltic shore, they moved south along the rivers to the Sea of Azov and the northern Caucasus.

Their name was *Rus,* which has survived in the modern term Russian. Gradually, the Rus overcame many of the Slavic, Lithuanian, Finnish, and Magyar peoples who were then living on the steppe. The story told in the Old Russian *Primary Chronicle,* compiled during the eleventh century, is suggestive of what may have happened among the inhabitants of Russia sometime in the 850s:

> There was no law among them, but tribe rose against tribe. Discord thus ensured among them, and they began to war one against another. They said to themselves, "Let us seek a prince who may rule over us, and judge according to the law." They accordingly went overseas to the Varangian [i.e., Scandinavian] Russes . . . [and] said to the people of Rus, "Our whole land is great and rich, but there is no order in it. Come to rule and reign over us."*

This is known as the "calling of the princes." The *Chronicle* goes on to tell how the Viking Rurik accepted the invitation in 862 and settled in the Slavic trading town of Novgorod. Scandinavian princes then moved south along the Dnieper River. They seized the settlement called Kiev and made it the center of a realm at first only loosely controlled and devoted to trade. In 860, for the first time, their warships appeared off Constantinople, where they caused panic before they were repulsed. During the next two centuries there were three further attacks as well as other wars, which the Byzantines won.

Although a brisk trade developed between the Byzantines and the Rus people, the continuing religious influence that Byzantium exercised upon the Rus people was even more important. There is evidence in a trade treaty of 945 that some of the Rus envoys were already Christians, swearing by the Holy Cross to observe the provisions of the treaty. The Rus were converted during the late 980s during the reign of Vladimir. He felt the inadequacy of the old faith, about which we know little except that the Rus worshiped forest and water spirits and a god of thunder. But the cautious Vladimir did not accept Orthodox Christianity until after he had sent a commission to visit various countries where all the faiths were practiced. Shortly after he received their report he was baptized and married a Byzantine princess. Returning to Kiev, he threw down all the idols in the city. It is said that in one day he forcibly baptized the entire population in the waters of the Dnieper.

Despite its legendary features, the story of Vladimir reflects the various cultural influences to which the Kievan realm was exposed. It had Muslim, Jewish (the Khazars), and Roman Catholic Christian neighbors, but the most powerful and influential neighbor was the Orthodox and Greek Byzantium. Doubtless the marriage alliance with the Byzantine princess played a part in Vladimir's decision. To secure the conversion of the Rus to the Byzantine form of Christianity was also important for the Byzantines, who needed to protect their possessions along the Black Sea and their capital itself against

---

*Samuel H. Cross, *The Russian Primary Chronicle,* in *Harvard Studies and Notes in Philosophy and Literature* (Cambridge, Mass.: Harvard University Press, 1930), XII, 145. Reprinted by permission.

renewed Rus attacks. The church became an important social force in Kievan society, and the Slavic clergy formed a new and influential social class. Although the Byzantine patriarchs always asserted theoretical sovereignty over the Kievan Rus church, the latter church asserted its independence in practical matters quite early. From the first, the church in Kievan Rus became an important landowner, and monasteries multiplied. The clergy came to have legal jurisdiction over all Christians in cases involving morals, family affairs, and religious matters. The concept that crimes should be punished by the ruler replaced the old concept that punishment was a matter of personal revenge. For the first time formal education was established; the Cyrillic alphabet was adopted, and literature written in Slavonic began to appear; Byzantine art forms were imported and imitated. However, pre-Christian beliefs persisted in rural areas, and the new culture was largely confined to the few cities and to the monasteries.

Kievan Rus

Scholars have disputed whether agriculture or commerce was economically more important in Kievan Rus; the answer appears to be commerce. In trade, with Byzantium in particular, the Russians sold mostly furs, honey, and wax—products not of agriculture but of hunting and beekeeping. Since the Byzantines paid in cash, Kiev had much more of a money economy than did western Europe in the ninth and tenth centuries. Thus, from the economic and social point of view, Kievan Rus in the eleventh century was, in some ways, more advanced than feudal western Europe. Moreover, before the Tatar invasions, which started in the early 1200s, the Kievan kingdom developed close diplomatic and political relations with the West. Dynastic marriages were arranged between the ruling house of Kiev and the royal families of Sweden, Norway, and France, and alliances were reached with principalities in Germany. Merchants from the West appeared in Russia, especially at Novgorod and at Kiev.

The Kievan political structure, however, suffered from many internal weaknesses. It failed to make any rules for the succession to the throne, and it followed the practice of dividing the land among a prince's sons, as was the case in Iberia and other western regions. The resulting fragmentation into often mutually hostile provinces weakened the realm. Thus when the Mongol Tatars appeared in the early thirteenth century, Kievan Rus had been softened for the blow. Never entirely centralized politically, Kievan Rus, nonetheless, strove for unity. It bequeathed the ideal of unity, together with a literary language and a single Christian faith, to the future Russian state of Muscovy (Moscow) that was to emerge after more than two centuries of Mongol domination. Moscow would also take from the Byzantines, by way of Kievan Rus, not only their religion but also their political theory of autocracy. In time, Moscow would come to see itself as the natural heir to the rulers in far-off Byzantium.

A Closer Look

THE STORY OF IOASAPH

Unique among the stories of saints' lives is an extraordinary document of the tenth century, a highly polished tale of an Indian king who shuts away his only son, Ioasaph, in a remote palace to protect him from the knowledge of the world, and especially to prevent his being converted to Christianity. But the prince cannot be protected; he sees a sick man, a blind man, and a dead man. And when he is in despair at life's cruelties, a wise monk in disguise, named Barlaam, succeeds in reaching him by pretending to have a precious jewel that he wishes to show. The jewel is the jewel of the Christian faith, and the rest of the long story is an account of the wise Barlaam's conversion of Prince Ioasaph.

During the conversion, Barlaam tells Ioasaph ten moral tales, illustrating the Christian life. One of these reappears in Elizabethan literature as the casket story in Shakespeare's *Merchant of Venice*; another is the tale of *Everyman*, which later became common in all western literatures; other Barlaam stories were used by hundreds of western authors and preachers of all nationalities.

What is most extraordinary about this piece of Byzantine literature is that the story originally comes from India. The life of Ioasaph is a Christianized version of the life of Buddha, the great Indian religious leader of the sixth century B.C. His life story passed through Persia via the Arabs to the Caucasian kingdom of Georgia before it was turned into Greek legend and transmitted to the West. And the stories that Barlaam tells to convert Ioasaph are also Indian in origin and are either Buddhist birth-stories (recitals of the Buddha's experiences in earlier incarnations used as comment upon what was going on around him) or Hindu moral-cosmic tales. Indeed the very name Ioasaph was once *Bodasaph*, and so is the same as the Indian word *bodhisattva*, which means a person destined to attain Buddhahood. Prince Ioasaph has been canonized a saint of both the Orthodox and the Roman Catholic churches, and thus through this legend Buddha himself became and has remained a Christian saint in the eyes of many commentators.

Sometimes nearly identical, and certainly quite similar, legends can be found in different cultures. These legends are taken as evidence of major migrations of peoples, of movement of key individuals between cultures, and of a common reservoir of legends and cultural material.

Byzantine Learning and Literature

Byzantine achievement was varied, distinguished, and of major importance to western culture. Byzantine literature may suffer by comparison with the great achievements of the classical age, but the appropriate society with which to compare medieval Byzantium is the Europe of the Middle Ages. Both were Christian and both the direct heirs of Rome and Greece. The Byzantines maintained learning on a level much more advanced than did the West, which, indeed, owes a substantial cultural debt to Byzantium. In the West, the knowledge of Greek had diminished considerably, and few schol-

ars enjoyed access to the works of ancient Greek philosophy, science, and literature in their original form. During all this time the Byzantines preserved
these masterpieces, copied and recopied them by hand, and studied them
constantly. Study was not confined to monasteries but was also pursued in
secular libraries and schools. The teacher occupied an important position in
Byzantine society; books circulated widely among those prominent in public
life. The imperial academy at Constantinople supplied a steady stream of
learned and cultivated men to the bureaucracy, the church, and the courts. Its
curriculum emphasized secular subjects: philosophy, astronomy, geometry,
rhetoric, music, grammar, law, medicine, and arithmetic. The School of the
Patriarch of Constantinople, also in the capital, provided instruction in theology and other sacred subjects.

The most substantial part of Byzantine prose literature consists of theological writing. Early Byzantine theologians hotly debated the controversies that
rent the empire about the true relationship between God the Father and God
the Son, or between the divine and human natures of Christ. Too difficult for
most people to read or understand, such works nonetheless enormously
influenced the lives of everyone. The leaders of the society were directly or
indirectly affected by the answers to the problems of human social and economic life in general, or of the life of the human individual in particular, and
of a person's prospects for eternal salvation or damnation. The early theologians also drew up appropriate rules for monks, balancing the need for denying the desires of the flesh with the provision of reasonable opportunities for
work. Later, in the eleventh century, Byzantine theologians developed a mystic strain in which they urged contemplation and purification as stages
toward illumination and the final mystic union with God.

Saints' lives (hagiographies), usually written for the ordinary person,
depicted adventure, anxiety, deprivation, violence, and agony of various
sorts before the final triumph of virtue and piety. The eyes of the reader were
directed upward toward a heavenly reward, since the hero of the story, if a
saint before the fourth century and the triumph of Christianity, was often
martyred. Exciting, edifying, and immensely popular in their day, these stories supply valuable bits of information about daily life, especially among the
humbler classes, and about the attitudes of the people. It should be noted
here that hagiography also became an intense endeavor in the Latin West.
The purpose and result were similar; in both, the contemplation of the saints'
lives was a function of education and doctrine. Around each saint arose a
cult, and the saint became a patron, protector, even friend and intimate with
whom the worshiper could communicate. By projecting the real into the
supernatural world, the Christian societies in the early Middle Ages found a
source of authority and security close at hand, when the secular authority of
the emperor seemed far away and unable to respond quickly.

In the late fourth century, debates over the growing role of the saints and
over the development of sanctuaries devoted to specific patrons reflected the
tendency of the wealthy to make religious practice more private and exclusive, as opposed to the common people's desire for access by all in the Chris-

Hagia Sophia. The greatest church built under the emperor Justinian in Constantinople (today Istanbul), the capital of the eastern part of the empire (Byzantium). The church served as a model for numerous architectural projects over the following centuries. The four towers or minarets were added after the Ottoman conquest of the city in 1453—when the church became a mosque—and were used to call the faithful to prayer.   (Vanni/Art Resource, NY)

tian community. The issue was not an arid one, for access to a heavenly patron depended on who was that patron's representative or intermediary on earth. When the bishops—that is, the church—emerged victorious, episcopal power became fully entrenched in the West. In the East the powerful families were generally successful in preventing the growth of a truly mass religion.

The Arts

The Church of Hagia Sophia (Holy Wisdom) in Constantinople, built in the sixth century, was designed to be "a church the like of which has never been seen since Adam nor ever will be." The dome, says a contemporary, "seems rather to hang by a golden chain from heaven than to be supported by solid masonry." Justinian, the emperor who ordered it to be built, was able to exclaim, "I have outdone thee, O Solomon!" The Turks themselves, who seized the city in 1453, have ever since paid Hagia Sophia the compliment of imitation; the great mosques that throng present-day Istanbul are all more or less the result of an architectural engagement and negotiation with the great church of the Byzantines.

Before Hagia Sophia could be built, other cities of the empire, particularly Alexandria, Antioch, and Ephesus, had produced an architectural synthesis of the Hellenistic or Roman basilica with a dome taken from the Persians.

This is just one striking example of how Greek and eastern elements were to be blended in Byzantine society. In decoration, the use of brilliantly colored marble, enamel, silk and other fabrics, gold, silver, jewels, and paintings and glowing mosaics on the walls and ceilings reflect the sumptuousness of the East. Along with the major arts of architecture, painting, and mosaics went the so-called minor arts. The silks, the ivories, the work of the goldsmiths and silversmiths, the enamel and jeweled book covers, the elaborate containers made to hold the relics of a saint, the great Hungarian sacred Crown of Saint Stephen (which was, itself, of Byzantine provenance), and the superb minia- tures of the illuminated manuscripts in many European libraries all testify to the endless variety and fertility of Byzantine inspiration.

Even in those parts of western Europe where Byzantine political authority had disappeared, the influence of this Byzantine artistic flowering is often apparent. Sometimes actual creations by Byzantine artists were produced in the West or ordered from Constantinople by a connoisseur; these are found in Sicily and southern Italy, in Venice, and in Rome. Sometimes the native artists worked in the Byzantine manner, as in Spain, in Sicily, and in the great Romanesque domed churches of southern France. Often the native product was not purely Byzantine, but rather a fusion of Byzantine with local elements.

Byzantium lived long after western conquest in 1204, but to focus on the Byzantine relationships with the West, although critical to the writing of the history of western Europe, misses the point completely. Byzantium was far more defined by its relations to Slavs, Bulgars, and other peoples than it was by its relation to the West. Most of all, from the seventh century onward, Byzantine history was intimately bound to that of the Arabs and to the expansive world of Islam.

The World of Islam, Circa 570–1096

Between 1325 and 1354 or so, Ibn Batutta, a Muslim legal scholar from Morocco, traveled widely through Dar al-Islam and beyond. His journeys, which he recorded for posterity in one of the most extraordinary travel nar- ratives ever written, were centered around the *hajj* (the Muslim obligation to go on a pilgrimage to Mecca), but his endless curiosity and taste for new things took him in restless wanderings across the Sahara desert to the fabled city of Timbuktu; to the Niger River area (the kingdom of Ghana) in sub- Saharan Africa; to the regions south of the Horn of Africa; and to Jerusalem, a Muslim city in the fourteenth century, where he visited Christian, Jewish, and Muslim holy sites. From the Middle East he traveled east to India and the Malabar coast, visiting Cochin, Calicut (the great spice trading centers), and other fabled Indian cities. He continued onward to China and what is today Indonesia. Wherever he traveled across the known world (from Muslim Granada to China), he was in or close to the world of Islam. From one corner of northern Africa to Southeast Asia, the language of worship was one and the same: Arabic. Traveling though this multiethnic world, he was always at

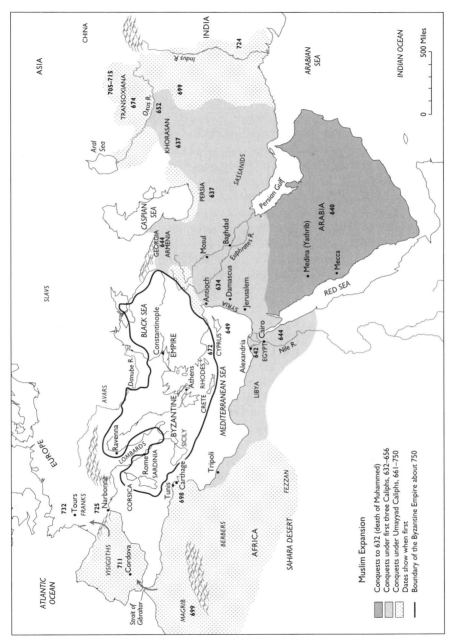

Muslim Expansion

Muslim Expansion

- Conquests to 632 (death of Muhammed)
- Conquests under first three Caliphs, 632–656
- Conquests under Umayyad Caliphs, 661–750
- Dates show when first
- Boundary of the Byzantine Empire about 750

0 500 Miles

ATLANTIC OCEAN

EUROPE

SLAVS

ASIA

CHINA

INDIA

ARABIAN SEA

INDIAN OCEAN

Strait of Gibraltar

MAGRIB 699

VISIGOTHS 711 • Cordova

FRANKS 732 • Tours 725

Narbonne

AVARS

BERBERS

AFRICA

SAHARA DESERT

FEZZAN

CORSICA

SARDINIA

Tunis
698 • Carthage

Rome

LOMBARDS

Ravenna

SICILY

Tripoli

BYZANTINE EMPIRE

Danube R.

BLACK SEA

Constantinople

Athens

CRETE RHODES 672

CYPRUS 649

MEDITERRANEAN SEA

LIBYA

Alexandria 642

EGYPT • Cairo 644

Nile R.

RED SEA

GEORGIA 644
ARMENIA

Antioch 634
• Damascus
SYRIA
• Jerusalem

Mosul •
Baghdad •
Euphrates R.

Persian Gulf

CASPIAN SEA

Aral Sea

PERSIA 637

SASSANIDS

KHORASAN 637

Oxus R. 652

TRANSOXIANA 674

705–715

699

724

Indus R.

ARABIA 640

• Medina (Yathrib)

• Mecca

home in Islam. Not unlike today, when the world of Islam reaches from the Muslim communities in northern Europe to the heart of Africa to central and southeast Asia, medieval Islam was the most widespread of all the religions of the Book (the religions based upon the Old and New Testament), and the one that most easily bound people of diverse linguistic, racial, and ethnic differences. How did Islam come about?

Islam

Islam (the Arabic word means "submission to God") is the most recent of the world's great religions. Its adherents (Muslims, "those who submit" to God) today inhabit, not very differently from Ibn Batutta's day, the entire North African coast, much of central and west Africa, parts of former Yugoslavia, and Albania, Egypt, Turkey, the entire Near and Middle East, Pakistan, parts of India, the Malay peninsula, Indonesia, and the Philippine Islands, as well as central Asia and portions of China. Relations with the Muslim world have been crucial to western civilization since Muhammad founded Islam in the early seventh century, and they have become even more significant in the last decade.

Muhammad, Circa 570–632

What we know of Muhammad is derived from Muslim authors who lived sometime after his death. The Arabia into which he was born about C.E. 570 was inhabited largely by nomadic tribes, each under its own chief. Some of these nomads lived on the meat and milk of their animals and on dates from palm trees. They raided each other's flocks of camels and sheep and often feuded among themselves. Others lived in cities and engaged in the ancient long-distance trade that carried goods from the Far East into the Mediterranean ports. The religion of the Arabs centered upon the worship of sacred stones and trees. Their chief sacral center was the city of Mecca, fifty miles inland from the coast of the Red Sea, where there was a holy building called the *Ka'ba* (the Cube), in which the Arab worshipers revered many idols, especially a small black stone "fallen from heaven," perhaps a meteorite. In the sixth century Mecca was inhabited by the Quraysh, a trading people who lived by caravan commerce with Syria. Muhammad was born into one of the clans of the Quraysh. Orphaned early, he was brought up by relatives and as a young man entered the service of a wealthy widow, Khadija, a woman older than himself and who later became Muhammad's first wife.

Muhammad, trading far from Mecca, became well acquainted with Christianity and Judaism. As an insightful observer of the political realities of his world, he also knew of the factionalism of Arabic politics and of the great struggles between Byzantium and Persia for control of the Middle East. In the early 610s, Muhammad received God's revelation through visions and direct commands from heaven. These utterances, believed by Muhammad and the faithful to be the word of God, became eventually the Qur'an, the Muslims'

Fragment from the Qu'ran (Iraq or Syria, ninth–tenth centuries). This fragment from an early Qu'ran reveals the elaborate design and beautiful calligraphy used by Muslim artists and scribes of the period. Since Islam did not allow representations of the human form, the Muslim world reached high levels of creativity and aesthetic achievement in their lacework design. (Bildarchiv Preussischer Kulturbesitz/Art Resource, NY)

sacred text, containing god's direct revelation to his messenger, Muhammad. Through a series of "recitations," the exact rendering of God's words, Muhammad lay the foundation of a new, dynamic, and revolutionary religion. While Muhammad imbedded Islam within Judaic and Christian traditions and teachings (not unlike what Christianity had done with Judaism), Islam, as the new religion was known, emphasized that Allah was the only God (linking thus with the monotheism of the Judeo-Christian tradition) and that Muhammad, the messenger of God, was the last prophet in a long chain of great prophetic figures that included Moses and Jesus. Thus no further revelation could occur. "There is no God but Allah and Muhammad is his Prophet."

The whole body of revelation was not assembled in the Qur'an until after Muhammad's death. The chapters were not arranged in order by subject matter, but by length, with the longest first. Moreover, the Qur'an is full of allusions to things and persons, reflecting the circumstances and politics of early seventh-century Arabia. Nonetheless, God's revelation—the sacred Qur'an—established the rules by which Muslims (those who accept Islam and thus surrender to Allah) had to live. These obligations were clearly spelled out, and this accounts, in part, for the great success of Islam in converting large populations. Muhammad declared that it was idolatry to worship more than one god (although he never argued that his fellow Arabs did not also have a knowledge of God). If Judaism emphasizes God's justice and Christianity his mercy, Islam may be said to emphasize his omnipotence. Acknowledgment of belief in God and in Muhammad as the ultimate prophet of God and acceptance of a final day of judgment are the basic requirements of the faith. A major innovation for the Arabs was Muhammad's idea of an afterlife, which was to be experienced in the flesh.

The formal demands of Islam were not severe. Five times a day in prayer, facing toward Mecca, the Muslim, having first washed face, hands, and feet, would bear witness that there is no God but Allah and that Muhammad is his prophet. During the sacred month of Ramadan, Muslims may not eat, drink, or have sexual relations between sunrise and sunset. They must give alms to the poor, and, if they can, they should at least once in their lifetime make a pilgrimage (the *hajj*) to the sacred city of Mecca. Polygamy was sanctioned, but four wives were the most a man could have.

Historians note many similarities between Islam, Judaism, and Christianity. All are monotheistic. Muslims worship together but do not require an organized church to attend: Individual prayer is at the heart of expressing faith. Jews, too, worship together and also require no formal church. Muslims and Christians both believe in the Last Judgment. To Muslims, Jews and Christians were "people of the Book," that is, people who worshiped through a holy scripture. Both (but also Zoroastrians) were the *dhimmis* (protected religious minorities). The *dhimmis*'s religious practices were tolerated and a small tax levied on them. Allah's message also appeared in a text, the Qur'an, but it did not represent a series of commandments as much as a guide to living in such a way as to achieve salvation. The Qur'an describes the tortures of the damned at the Last Judgment, as did Christian texts and illustrations, but the vision of the rewards of the saved differed: To the Muslim, heaven was a place of running water and green parks and gardens, and the saved would retain their riches, dressing handsomely and eating well in the company of physical beauty.

But the Qur'an was a great deal more than just another sacred text. The book served as a legal code; as a guide to right Muslim behavior, the *shari'a*; and as the basic text for the learning of Arabic. The teachings of Muhammad and the Qur'an also transcended the divisions between tribal antagonism and the hostility and differences between desert and urban Arabs. The *Umma* (the community of believers) brought together all these disparate groups into one people. While tribal customs operated for the individual members of the tribe, Muhammad's preaching and the Qur'an superseded all long traditions and allegiances.

Muhammad's Preaching

At first Muhammad preached this faith only to members of his family; then he preached to the people of Mecca, who rejected his teachings. In 622 some pilgrims from a city called Yathrib, two hundred miles north of Mecca, invited Muhammad to come to their city to settle a local war. He accepted the invitation. This move from Mecca is the *Hijra* (flight), from which the Islamic calendar has ever since been dated. Thus the Christian year 622 is the Muslim year 1. Yathrib had its name changed to al-Medina, the city. Medina became the center of the new faith, which grew and prospered. When the Jews of Medina did not convert, Muhammad came to depend more upon the Arabs of the desert and became less universal in his appeal. Allah told him to fight against those who had not been converted. The *jihad* (the struggle against the enemies of Islam or the infidels) would become an important aspect of Islamic expansion, and it may have influenced the development of the concept of the Christian Crusade later on. Those who die in battle against the infidel believe that they die in a holy cause.

In 630, Muhammad, after a series of successful raids and disruption of Mecca's trade, returned in triumph to Mecca. He cleansed the *Ka'ba* of all idols, retaining only the black stone, and he made it a shrine of his new religion. Two years later, in 632, Muhammad died, but the foundations for a dynamic new power were already laid. Abu Bakr, who had been appointed by Muhammad as community worship leader, was selected as the first caliph.

Expansion of Islam, 633–725

Within a few years of the death of the Prophet, Arab Muslim armies were on the move under the banner of Islam. Syria, Palestine, and Persia were conquered almost simultaneously by two armies between 633 and 641. The Syrian province fell easily. By 639 Jerusalem had been captured, a sacred city for the Muslims both as the cradle of their religious tradition and as the place from which on the site of the Dome of the Rock Muhammad leapt into heaven. In 651 the native Persian dynasty was ended. During 639–642 the Arabs added Egypt, with Alexandria as the major Byzantine naval base and as one of the great repositories of ancient learning. Launching ships, they seized Cyprus and Rhodes and began attacking southern Italy and Sicily. Moving west across North Africa, they took Carthage in 698 and conquered the native Berber tribes. In 711, with a mixed force of Berbers and Arabs under the command of Tariq, a freed slave, they invaded Spain across the Straits of Gibraltar. (The name Gibraltar is a corruption of Arabic words meaning "Rock of Tariq.") By 725 the first Muslims had crossed the Pyrenees. Seven years later, a Muslim army was defeated by Charles Martel near Poitiers and withdrew south of the Pyrenees. Meanwhile, they had been spreading east from Persia throughout what is today Soviet Turkestan, and in 724 they had reached the Indus River and the western frontiers of China. They also moved south from Egypt and North Africa into the desert regions of central Africa. In the early ninth century, Muslim forces based in North Africa conquered Sicily and established Muslim rule in the island for the next century. These conquests of the first centuries of Islam were virtually final. Only the Mediterranean islands and Spain were permanently reconquered by Christians—Sicily in the early tenth century, Spain not fully until the end of the fifteenth century.

Disunity in Islam, 634–1055

The Arabs had overrun a vast collection of diverse peoples with diverse customs. Moreover, internal dissensions among the Arabs themselves prevented the establishment of a permanent unified state to govern the whole of the conquered territory. After Muhammad's death, there was disagreement over the succession. Finally, Muhammad's eldest companion, Abu Bakr (r. 632–634), was chosen *khalifia* (caliph, the representative of Muhammad). Abu Bakr died in 634, and the next two caliphs, Omar (r. 634–644) and Othman (r. 644–656), were also chosen from outside Muhammad's family. Many Arabs resented the caliphs' assertion of authority over them and longed for their old freedom as nomads. In 656 Othman was murdered. By then those who favored choosing only a member of Muhammad's own family had grouped themselves around Ali, an early convert and cousin of the Prophet. This party also opposed all reliance on commentaries, or supplemental works, explaining the Qur'an. Fundamentalists with regard to the holy teachings, they became known as Shi'ites (Shia Ali, the followers or partisans of Ali). Together with their opponents, the Sunni, these two religious and political interpretations remain a significant divide in the Muslim world today. Opposed to Shi'ite interpretation of doctrinal truth was a prominent family, the Umayyads, who backed one of their members, Muawiyah, as caliph.

In 656 Ali was chosen caliph, and civil war broke out. Ali was murdered in 661. His opponent, Muawiyah, had already proclaimed himself caliph in Damascus in 660. Thus began the dynastic Umayyad caliphate (661–750). On the whole, it saw ninety years of prosperity, good government, brisk trade, and cultural achievement rivaling those of Byzantium. The civil service was run by Greeks, and Greek artists worked for the caliph; the Christian and Jewish populations, except for the payment of a head tax, were on the whole unmolested and better off than they had been before. Shi'ite opposition to the Umayyads, however, remained strong. The enemies of the Shi'ites, as noted earlier, called themselves Sunnis (traditionalists). There was, in reality, little difference between the two groups with regard to religious observances and law, but the Shi'ites felt it their duty to curse the first three caliphs who had ruled before Ali, while the Sunnis deeply revered these three caliphs. The Shi'ites were less tolerant of the unbeliever, opposed the government, and celebrated the martyrdom of Ali's son Hussein, who was killed in battle in 680 as the result of treachery.

In 750 the Shi'ites were responsible for the overthrow and murder of the last of the Umayyad caliphs at Damascus, together with ninety members of his family. The leader of the conspirators was Abu'l Abbas—not a Shi'ite himself, but the great-grandson of a cousin of Muhammad. The caliphate was shortly afterward moved east to Baghdad, capital of present-day Iraq and close to the former capital of the Persian Empire, and was thereafter known as the Abbasid caliphate. The days when Islam was primarily an Arab movement under Byzantine influence were over.

Other groups appeared in Islam with varying views of how to interpret the Qur'an. Some were Sufis who attempted to lose themselves in divine love and whose name was given them from *suf,* wool, for the undyed wool garment they wore. Politically the rest of the Muslim world fell away from its dependence upon the Abbasids. One of the few Umayyads to escape death in 750, Abd al-Rahman, made his way to Spain and built himself a state centered in the city of Cordoba. Rich and strong, his descendants declared themselves caliphs in 929. Separate Muslim states appeared in Morocco, Tunis, and Egypt, where still another dynasty, this time Shi'ite, built Cairo in the tenth century and began to call themselves caliphs, although they were soon displaced by Sunnis. Rival dynasties also appeared in Persia, in Syria, and in the other eastern provinces. At Baghdad, although the state took much of its character and culture from its Persian past, power fell gradually into the hands of Turkish troops. Although the caliphate at Baghdad lasted until 1258, during its last two centuries the caliphs were puppets in Turkish hands.

Islam in the West

Muslim domination of western Mediterranean waters and control of North Africa and of ancient trade routes linking western Europe to sub-Saharan and eastern Asian markets from the late seventh century onward meant that the historical development of the medieval West was intimately linked to the fortunes of Islam. But Muslim political practices and power had a direct and long-term presence in the political landscape of western Europe. This was most evident in Spain and in Sicily.

Spain

From 711, when a small North African expeditionary force smashed the Visigothic Empire in Iberia, until the demise of the Cordoba caliphate in 1035, Islam was the dominant power in the peninsula. Muslim armies had the upper hand in the fields of battle, imposing their will on the fledgling Christian kingdoms (Asturias-Leon, Castile, Aragon, and the County of Barcelona) in the northern regions of Spain. As late as the end of the tenth century, Cordovan armies could strike deep into Christian territory. A Muslim army led by al-Mansur (Almanzor in Spanish), the prime minister and power behind the throne in Cordoba, sacked Santiago de Compostela, the great pilgrimage site in far northwest Spain, and Christian captives carried the cathedral of Compostela's bells on their backs to Cordoba as a sign of Muslim hegemony. From 800 onward the city of Cordoba reached dazzling heights. It was a great center of learning, a city of more than 100,000 inhabitants, a place of beauty. No other western European city matched its size and achievements in this period. Sitting on the banks of the Guadiana river, the city of Cordoba dominated a vast hinterland. There, the tending of olive trees, vineyards, and irrigated fields (producing cereal grains and fruits) provided for great wealth. The city and al-Andalus, as the region under Islamic rule came to be known, greatly benefited from the agricultural revolution and technical innovations that the Muslims introduced into Iberia. With its royal palace and fortress

The interior of the Great Mosque of Cordoba (late eighth or early ninth centuries). Begun in the late eighth century, the Great Mosque of Cordoba's interior encloses a veritable forest of graceful horseshoe-shaped arches in distinctive patterns of red and white. When the city was conquered by the Christians in 1236, a Gothic cathedral was built within the space of the mosque, destroying the overall architectural unity of one of the most extraordinary buildings in western Europe.   (Werner Forman/Art Resource, NY)

(the Alcazar), extensive walls, and large and magnificent mosque, the city served as a center for one of Islam's flourishing political entities.

Islamic rule in the Iberian peninsula was not limited to military superiority and cultural achievements. Before 1000, Islamic agriculture, technology, political institutions, the Arabic language, culinary tastes, and social relations deeply influenced the development of Christian society. The history of Christian Spain in the central Middle Ages and until 1212—when the Christians won a signal battle at Las Navas de Tolosa and became the dominant power in the peninsula—was often defined (in the early period) by Christian relations with their Muslim masters and superior culture. Jews in Muslim Spain also benefited from the tolerant policies of the Cordoba caliphs and reached their "golden age" in terms of intellectual achievements and political and economic prominence under Muslim protection. Christians and Jews wrote in Arabic and adopted Muslim dress and customs even when retaining their own religion. Christian princes from northern Spain came to Cordoba to be treated by Muslim and Jewish physicians at the caliph's court. They also often married Muslim princesses—as Christian princesses married Muslim noblemen—as a sign of their dependence on al-Andalus.

We know now that there were numerous conversions to Islam by the Christian population of southern Spain in the aftermath of 711. We also know that Andalusi society proved to be extraordinarily resilient. Even after the Christians gained the upper hand after the demise of the caliphate in 1031 and the fragmentation of Muslim power into numerous small kingdoms (the kingdoms of *taifas*) in 1035, and even after the Christians made great territorial gains in the early thirteenth century, most Muslims remained faithful to their religion, culture, and language into the early seventeenth century. Although Christian-Muslim-Jewish relations could be antagonistic in this early period, on the whole, before the Christians gained the upper hand, the three religions lived in a fairly peaceful manner. Economic, social, and cultural exchanges created a pluralistic society that was unique in western history. Through Muslim civilization in Iberia and, to a lesser extent, in Sicily, western Europe remained open to a wider world that stretched into the Far East and into southern Africa.

Sicily

Sicily was the other melting pot in the West. From ancient times the island had been a meeting point for different civilizations: Phoenician, Greek, Roman, Byzantine, Lombard, and others. Each of these civilizations has left its imprint on the island, and their enduring presence can be seen in the ruins and monuments that dot the Sicilian landscape. From the mid-eighth century onward Muslim naval forces, operating out of North Africa, placed tremendous pressure on Mediterranean lands. The Saracens, as these raiders were known, occupied areas of southern France and southern Italy and, by the early tenth century, had conquered all of Sicily. With a sizable population of Jews and Christians, the island became, as was the case with Spain, an encounter point for the three religions. For almost a century and a half, the Muslims ruled over Sicily until Roger (the Great Count), one of the Norman nobles who had come into southern Italy in search of fortune, wrested the island from Islam in a series of campaigns between 1061 and 1091. Although the Islamic presence in Sicily did not match that of Muslims in Spain, the Muslims left a signal cultural, political, and architectural legacy in the island.

Islamic Civilization

The Arabs brought their new religion and their language to the peoples they conquered. The religion often stimulated new artistic and literary development, and, by requiring a pilgrimage to Mecca, it fostered mobility among the Muslims and encouraged the exchange of ideas with fellow Muslims from other parts of the Muslim world. Since Arabic had to be learned by everyone who wished to read the Qu'ran, it became the standard written language of the whole Islamic world.

Spreading their religion and clinging to their family and social traditions, the Arabs in the early stages of their expansion founded new cities in the conquered territories that were purely Arabic in population. But as conversions increased, the Arabs absorbed non-Arabs. And in their way of life, they borrowed much from the older urban societies they were absorbing. So, aside from religion and language, the chief contribution to Muslim culture came from the civilizations of Persia and of the Greco-Roman world. Islamic government learned much from the Persian tradition, Islamic philosophy learned much from the classic world, and Islamic literature learned much from both.

Christians and Muslims felt themselves to be members of religions that were on the same level of intellectual advancement. Together with the Jews, these two religions developed along parallel courses in many respects—in their attitudes toward creation, human history, the last judgment, and the instability of everything mortal. When at peace with the Muslims, the Byzantines thought of them as the successors of the Persians and as such the only civilized nation worth dealing with as equals. The caliph's ambassadors were given the highest places at the imperial table. This was appropriate, for if there was a city that rivaled Constantinople, it was Baghdad. In the late eight and early ninth centuries, under the rule of the fabled Harun-al-Rashid, Baghdad was a city without compare. A magnificent city with great gardens and a site for literary, scientific, and artistic achievements, Baghdad also sat at the center of a vast commercial network that generated the income to sustain such dazzling cultural production. The Muslims excelled in a wide range of scholarly and artistic areas, and here we can only provide a rather succinct account of these accomplishments.

Science

The reign of Mamun the Great (r. 813–833) is often said to mark the high point in the development of Arabic science and letters. In Baghdad he built an observatory, founded a university, and ordered the great works of Greek and Indian scientists and philosophers translated into Arabic. The works of Aristotle and other philosophers and scientists of the ancient world were also available to the Arabs, whether in the original Greek or in Syrian or Persian translations. Under Harun al-Rashid (r. 785–809), the fifth Abbasid caliph, schools of translators were set up, and manuscripts were ordered from Constantinople and elsewhere.

One of the chief fields of interest was medicine, which the Muslims developed far beyond the standard works of the Greek masters. Muslim scientists wrote textbooks, for instance, on diseases of the eye, on smallpox, and on measles, which remained the best authorities on those until the eighteenth century. Al-Razi, a Persian, wrote a twenty-volume compendium of all medical knowledge, and the philosopher Avicenna (980–1037) was even more famous for his systematization of all medical science. Al-Kindi (d. 870) wrote

---

The Written Record

THE CALAMITIES OF LOVE

A poetic treatise on the calamities of love describes the kinds of "avoidance" in which lovers may engage.

The first kind is the avoidance required by circumstances because of a watcher being present, and this is sweeter than union itself. Then there is the avoidance that springs from coquetry, and this is more delicious than many kinds of union. Because of this it happens only when the lovers have complete confidence in each other. Then comes avoidance brought about by some guilty act of the lover. In this there is some severity, but the joy of forgiveness balances it. In the approval of the beloved after anger there is a delight of heart which no other delight can equal. Then comes the avoidance caused by boredom. To get tired of somebody is one of the inborn characteristics of mankind. He who is not guilty of it does not deserve that his friends should be true to him. Then comes the avoidance brought about when a lover sees his beloved treat him harshly and show affection for somebody else, so that he sees death and swallows bitter draughts of grief, and breaks off while his heart is cut to pieces. Then comes the avoidance due to hatred; and here all writing becomes confused, and all cunning is exhausted, and trouble becomes great. This makes people lose their heads.

Adapted from *Medieval Islam* by G. E. von Grunebaum. 1946. Reprinted by permission of The University of Chicago Press.

---

more than 250 works on musical sounds, optics, and the tides. Muslim scientists adopted Indian numerals (the ones we use today and call "Arabic"). The new numerals included the zero, without which higher mathematical research could not be carried out. The Muslims began analytical geometry and founded plane and spherical trigonometry, and they progressed much further than their predecessors in algebra.

Philosophy, Literature, and the Arts

In philosophy, the Muslims eagerly studied Plato, Aristotle, and the Neoplatonists. Like the Byzantines and the western Europeans, they used what they learned to enable them to solve theological problems. These focused on the nature and the power of God and his relationship to the universe or on the distinctions to be drawn between the apparent (outer) meaning and the true (inner) meaning of the Qu'ran. Al-Ghazali (d. 1111), having written a *Refutation of Philosophy,* became a Sufi mystic for a decade before returning to his desk to write an autobiography and more theological works, all Sunni. The great Spanish Muslim scholar Averröes (1126–1198) strove to reconcile philosophy and the Qur'an. Averröes's commentaries on Aristotle, translated from Arabic into Latin, were available to the Christian West by the 1240s. Thus the Muslims came to surpass the Byzantines in the role of preserver and modifier of the classical works of philosophy and science. In the twelfth century and later, when the West was eager for ancient learning, it was the Muslims as well as the Greeks who could set it before them.

Indeed, the process had begun even earlier in Cordoba. In 854 a Spanish Christian complained that his fellow Christians were irresistibly attracted to Muslim culture:

> My fellow Christians delight in the poems and romances of the Arabs: they study the works of Muslim theologians and philosophers, not in order to refute them, but to acquire a correct and elegant Arabic style. Where today can a layman be found, who reads the Latin Commentaries on the Holy Scripture? Who is there that studies the Gospels, the Prophets, the Apostles? Alas! The young Christians who are most conspicuous for their talents have no knowledge of any literature or language save the Arabic; they read and study Arabian books with avidity, they amass whole libraries of them at immense cost, and they everywhere sing the praises of Arabian lore.*

The Arabic poems of which the Spaniard spoke portrayed life in the desert, with its warfare and hunting, its feasts and drinking bouts. Love was a favorite subject. Composition was governed by a strict code of convention; it was customary, for example, for the poet to praise himself, but not possible for him freely to portray human character. Still, much understanding of fundamental human experience shines through.

Arabic love poetry, especially as developed in Spain, deeply influenced the poets (called troubadours) across the Pyrenees in Provence, in the south of France. Earthly love became an important element of medieval literature. The troubadours' songs spread to Germany, where the *minnesinger* adopted the convention. The troubadour, as shall be seen later, created an interest in the theme of courtly love, or highly mannered and elegantly elaborate formal relations between men and women, and in the twelfth and thirteenth centuries troubadour literature helped preserve and, for the aristocracy, elevate chivalric attitudes. Some of the greatest masterpieces of Western love poetry thus find their ancestry in the songs of the Muslims of Spain. Love, however, was not the only theme of Arabic verse. The famous blind Syrian poet al-Ma'arri (979–1057) lamented human helplessness in the face of the vicissitudes of life, sometimes in verses of a haunting beauty:

> My friend, our own tombs fill so much space around us,
> imagine the space occupied by tombs of long ago.
> Walk slowly over the dust of this earth;
> its crust is nothing but the bones of men.**

---

*From G. E. von Grunebaum, *Medieval Islam* (Chicago: University of Chicago Press, 1946), 57–58.

**From Wilson b. Bishai, *Humanities in the Arabic-Islamic World* (Dubuque, IA: Wm. C. Brown Company, 1973), 94. Slightly modified.

Besides poetry there is much interesting autobiography and excellent history in Arabic. Fiction is of a limited sort only—sad misfortunes of a pair of lovers; exciting incidents of urban life in the capital, with the caliph and his chief minister, the vizier, participating; the adventures of a rogue. These stories were collected in the celebrated *Arabian Nights* between 900 and 1500. Stories of Persian, Indian, and Jewish origin are included, as well as some that derive from Greek and Hellenistic works. Thus Sinbad the Sailor's famous roc (a gigantic mythical bird) with its enormous egg came from the Greek romance of Alexander, and the *Odyssey* supplied the adventure with the blinded giant.

Deeply appreciative of secular music and dancing, the Arabs in the early Islamic period seem to have preferred the role of spectators to that of performers, most of whom were slaves or former slaves. Stringed instruments like lutes, as well as whistles, flutes, and drums, were popular in the Islamic world. Many musical words we take for granted derive from Arabic: lute, tambourine, guitar, and fanfare, for example. From the Muslims of Spain across the Pyrenees into France and thence to the entire western European world came not only the poetry of courtly love but also the instruments the singer played as he sang of his beloved. Similarly, recent research has emphasized the role that Qu'ranic recitation had in the evolution of chant in the Mediterranean world and beyond. The more we know about Islam, the deeper we find the connections between Muslim culture and that of the Christian West to be.

Conclusion

Through Sicily and Spain Greco-Roman and Muslim science, philosophy, and art came into the West. When considering the contributions of the Byzantines and the Muslims to the culture of Western society, historians are altogether justified in saying that much light came from the East. The Christian Middle Ages did indeed receive its light from the East, but that, to return to the point made at the beginning of this chapter, implies a separateness that is not historically accurate. Byzantium and Islam were not just powers in the East. Muslim society, as noted earlier, extended from the Iberian peninsula all the way to India. It still has an enduring Mediterranean presence today. And, in this new Islamic *mare nostrum* of the eighth and ninth centuries, Muslim and Jewish merchants plied their trade between the great al-Andalus ports of Valencia, Almería, Málaga, and other Mediterranean ports and the busy commercial entrepots of Alexandria, Jaffa, and other Levantine cities. More than that, Islamic culture was an integral part of the European experience. Around 800, Cordoba was probably the largest city in western Europe. It had schools, a police system, street lights, and a superb postal service—this at a time when Paris and London were little more than overextended villages, with little to show as either political or cultural centers, and when Rome was barely populated, a city of ruined monuments and decaying houses. Not until the breakdown of the caliphate in 1031 and its final demise in 1035 would Christianity begin to gain the upper hand in the long conflict for control of the peninsula. Even then, as shall be seen in a later chapter, in the twelfth century Christian scholars flocked to Toledo and other centers of Muslim culture in search of the unique offerings of Greek culture, preserved and augmented by Muslim scholars.

Muslim power also waxed strong in Sicily. Throughout the late ninth and most of the tenth century Sicily was in the hands of Islam, and Muslim culture left a deep imprint on the island—one that is visible to this day—despite the Norman occupation in the eleventh century and more than a millennium of Christian life there. From their outpost in the Baleric Islands and strongholds on the North African coast (in what is today Tunis, Morocco, and Algeria), Muslim merchants and pirates dominated the western Mediterranean into the early modern period. Many a Christian ended as a slave in North Africa, a testimony to the military hegemony of Islam.

SUMMARY

The Byzantine Empire survived in the East with its capital at Constantinople until 1453. The emperors were absolute rulers chosen in theory by God and were responsible for preserving the traditions of Roman justice. Byzantium was the buffer that cushioned western Europe against frequent invasions from the north and east. The Byzantine armies and navies were well organized and well led. The Byzantines also developed great diplomatic skill. Byzantine strength was based on a rich economy. Trade and a monopoly of silk and luxury goods were important, but agriculture was the mainstay of both the economy and society. The Byzantines faced constant problems caused by the absorption of small farms into large estates.

Religion dominated Byzantine life. The emperor was also the effective head of the church, a system known by some historians as Caesaropapism. Religious controversies such as the iconoclast heresy were also political issues. Differences between Latin western Christianity and Greek eastern Christianity multiplied after the fall of the Roman Empire in the West. In 1054 these differences came to a head in a schism between the two churches that has never been repaired. One of the greatest Byzantine cultural achievements was the transmission of their civilization to Russia and the eastern Slavs, who were converted to Byzantine (Orthodox) Christianity in the ninth and tenth centuries. Because of its Byzantine heritage, Kievan Rus developed very differently from western Europe. Byzantium preserved and transmitted the works of ancient Greece. Byzantine literature and art were of a high standard and were influential in the West.

Islam, a monotheistic religion, was founded in Arabia by Muhammad in the seventh century. Muhammad's teachings are collected in the Qur'an, the Islamic holy book. His followers are called Muslims. Their holy city is Mecca. Muhammad converted and united most of Arabia. After his death in 632 the Muslims conquered all of the Near East, Egypt, North Africa, much of Spain, Persia, and northern India. This rapid conquest was the result of the Muslims' religious zeal, the weakness of the Byzantine and Persian empires, and the Arabs' need to expand to reduce the overpopulation of the Arabian peninsula.

In the eighth century the Arab empire split into several rival states, the chief of which was the caliphate of Baghdad. Islamic civilization was based on religion and on the Arabic language. In government, literature, and philosophy, the Arabs borrowed extensively from, and improved on, the Greeks and Persians. In science, philosophy, and literature, the achievements of Arab civilization were impressive indeed.

THREE

Medieval Society in the West: From Late Antiquity to the Central Middle Ages

The Breakdown of Roman Civilization

As noted earlier, during the period from the collapse of the Roman Empire in the West to about C.E. 1000, a great deal of Roman civilization was transformed and, in the worst of cases, lost, but much was retained and developed, and many new ways of life were adopted. New types of social relationships arose, combining Roman and Germanic practices. New inventions, such as deeper plowing and better drainage, the horse collar (a great improvement on the old yoke), and the seaworthy Norse ships (which could face the hazards of Atlantic navigation in a way the old Mediterranean vessels never could) marked technological advances over the ancient ways of farming and sailing.

The more than half a millennium between the collapse of Roman authority in the West and the flowering of late medieval society was marked by a complex process of integration of Roman and barbarian (meaning those who did not speak Latin in this case, but a name inappropriately given to the Germans and other groups who migrated, settled, or, sometimes, even conquered portions of the western empire) civilizations, through accommodation, cultural and political negotiations, and strife. These processes of bringing new societies into being have been the subject of many insightful recent studies. We now know that the ethnogenesis (the emergence of a distinct people or ethnic group—as a political, cultural, and linguistic entity—out of motley Germanic and other groups) was the outcome, to a large extent, of the imposition of classical ethnographic categories, harkening back to Herodotus, on those outside the boundaries of the Greco-Roman world.

As Patrick Geary, Roger Collins, and others have shown, the mechanisms by which Germans and Romans came to form, in time, "nations" were indeed quite different from the ones proposed by historians until a recent date. We can no longer accept the idea, as presented in maps and other artistic representations, that this Germanic group settled in this particular region, while another group settled elsewhere, and that each of them had a unique history and constituted a "unique" people, leading to the origins of modern nations. As Collins and Geary have argued, the Germanic groups entering the Roman West were, each of them, composed by many different groups, some of them not even Germanic. Their ethnic and linguistic heterogeneity belies the claims of later historians and politicians as to foundational myths of national origins. Thus, the construction of local and regional identities, language, politics, and culture, between roughly the late fourth and early ninth centuries, was not a lineal process and evolved according to changing local and regional circumstances. Moreover, the differences between Roman and "barbarian" were, more often than not, minimal. In some cases, they dressed alike, spoke the same languages, had the same habits, married each other, and lived in one cultural context. What follows therefore is a simplified version of a far more complicated story, and it cannot begin to convey the complexities of these processes and the emergence of "barbarian" kingdoms out of the wreckage of Roman society in the West.

The Germans

The Germans, people without a common political, geographical, or cultural identity but sharing a common language, held most of the lands outside the borders of the Roman Empire in the third century. From the shores of the Baltic to the Ukraine, the Germans interacted with Rome on the outer boundaries of the empire. Very early in ancient times some migrated southward. When the Romans first began to write about them, they were already divided into tribes, although with no overall political unity. One group of Germanic tribes—the Visigoths, also called Goths, themselves the result of the amalgamation of different groups—had settled in what we now call Romania and in the adjacent plains. In the fourth century, a fierce Asian people known as the Huns, led by their remarkable leader Attila, invaded the territory of the Goths. The Hunnic tribes were themselves conglomerations of diverse peoples, drawn to Attila's leadership by conquest, force, or perceived opportunities for profit. Living on horseback for days, traveling swiftly, and reveling in warfare, the Huns started a panic among the Goths and other Germanic tribes. The shock waves, beginning in the last half of the fourth century, continued throughout the fifth and into the sixth. They shattered Roman control of the West and left its fragments in Germanic hands.

Besides barbarian military raids and conquests, there were slower and more peaceful infiltrations. German laborers settled and worked on the large Roman estates, especially in Gaul. Individual Germans joined the Roman armies, often rising to high positions and defending the old empire against their fellow tribesmen. Roman legions openly recruited Germans into their ranks, and after the mid-fourth century, entire units of the Roman army were manned by Germans. Often, the integration of Germans and Romans was peaceful. In fact, most German groups came into the western portions of the empire at the request of Roman officials, and some Roman writers, for example Orosius, a Hispano-Roman writing in the early fifth century, praised the coming of the Visigoths into Spain. In the same manner, the absorption of the Roman peoples was also peaceful, with the Germanic groups establishing permanent settlements into which the Romans were then assimilated. Although there was much bloodshed and numerous genuine invasions of the land of one people by another, in general the process might more properly be thought of as a steady migration of peoples that was achieved sometimes peacefully, sometimes by force.

Thanks to chronicles and histories, almost all written in Latin by monks (although some German accounts survive in Latin form), we know a great deal about the routes of the encroaching bands, about their chiefs, and about the politics of the separate realms they set up. These accounts are inferior to the best Greek and Roman historical writings not only in style and in wealth of detail but also in psychological insight and accuracy. Moreover, they almost certainly exaggerate the cruelty and destructiveness of the invasions. In reality, we do not fully know how numerous the invaders were in proportion to the invaded population; we do not know to what degree the invaders replaced peoples who were there before them; we do not know whether the total population of western Europe was greater or less under Germanic rule than under the late Roman Empire.

How complete was the breakdown of Roman civilization in the West? This question has been debated for a long time. Although originally it was argued that Roman civilization in the West collapsed, we know today that Roman social structures endured and that cultural patterns and literary tropes—inherited from the classical world—showed, in specific areas and at specific times, remarkable vigor. Transformations did occur. They can be seen most clearly at the level of large-scale political and economic organization. In the early Middle Ages, substantial political entities did exist. Among them, one must note the Visigoths in Spain in the sixth and seventh centuries, Merovingian (from the supposed founder of the Salian Franks royal family, Merovech) Frankland in the same period, and the important and fruitful interlude of the Carolingians' revived empire in the eighth and ninth centuries. But these Germanic kingdoms, although still attempting Roman fiscal organization and integrating the remnants of Rome's legal system into their own codes, as the Visigoths did with their *Lex Visigothorum* or law of the Visigoths, began slowly to lose the sense of "public" authority and to often fall back to the primacy of private personal and familial relationships of power, which were essential parts of the Germanic inheritance. As a result, one finds a failure to organize and administer any large territory as an effective political entity. Only the church consistently asserted its authority beyond the relatively narrow limits of the medieval duchy, county, or other small unit and maintained an effective organization to which millions of persons adhered.

Roads, postal systems, and communications deteriorated from the Roman efficiency that had allowed both persons and goods to travel in freedom and ease. Thousands of little districts came to depend upon themselves for almost everything they used, and thus became relatively autarkic (self-sufficient). Some invading Germanic tribes did exercise loose control over sizable areas, but these areas were much smaller than the old empire had been. The network of habits of command and obedience that held a great, complex community together had waned. Most common people in the early Middle Ages reverted to their local dialects or languages in the countryside. Spoken and most certainly written Latin were the almost exclusive monopoly of the clergy and of a few powerful men. The slow process by which, over the centuries, Latin gave birth to the Romance languages—Italian, French, Romanian, Galaic-Portuguese, Castilian, Catalan, and Provençal—began in the late empire. Even where Latin survived as a learned tongue, written as well as spoken, it was debased and simplified. The general level of cultivated literature and philosophy fell, and traditional skills in the arts underwent a profound change. This is, of course, also a simplistic view, and one may advance a very different perspective on these developments. Under the impact of cultural transformations and the influx of new people, Latin became a dynamic, evolving language. Medieval Latin, with a vitality that is common to all living languages, gave rise to new words, new grammatical forms, which transformed its syntax and pronunciation. It was very different from classical Latin, the much-adored language of Italian humanists, but it was alive.

But much of ancient civilization did survive the early Middle Ages. People could weave, farm, use horses, and make the necessary implements of peace and war as well in the year 1000 as in the year 100; in some ways and in some places, they could do these things better. Among churchmen there survived an admiration for and some familiarity with the classics. The Germanic chiefs so admired the Rome they were replacing that they retained a reverence for its laws and institutions, even if they understood them only in part. Moreover, in the last three decades, our knowledge of the early Middle Ages has been profoundly transformed and expanded. The works of Peter Brown, Patrick Geary, and others have shown these centuries to be far more dynamic and formative than previously thought. Archaeological research and new critical ways of looking at the extant sources have revealed a world far removed from its former pejorative description as the "Dark Ages" or the "barbarian West." It was a new world a-borning. In the next pages we shall try to identify some of the different Germanic groups that settled in the western lands of the Roman Empire, emphasizing, once again, their heterogeneity and the manner in which most of these different groups intermingled with Roman and other local populations.

Visigoths, Vandals, Celts, 410–455

The people we know now as the Visigoths had entered the lands of the eastern Roman Empire by imperial leave. Conflict soon arose, however, as to the terms of their presence in Roman territory and to their relationship to Roman authority. In the year 378 at Adrianople, a motley coalition of Germans, Huns, and others defeated the Roman legions of the eastern Emperor Valens, who was killed in battle. This variegated group of people became a collective entity known as the Visigoths. After the battle at Adrianople, more and more Goths now freely entered the empire. Unable to take Constantinople or other fortified towns, they proceeded south through the Balkans, under their chieftain Alaric, ravaging Greece and then marching around the Adriatic into Italy. In 410 they sacked Rome itself. Alaric died soon afterward, and his successors led the Visigoths across Gaul and into Spain.

Here, in the westernmost reaches of the Continental Roman Empire, the Visigoths founded a kingdom that lasted until the Muslim invasions of the eighth century. In southern Gaul a large area (Aquitaine) was given to them by the western Roman Emperor Honorius (r. 395–423), into whose family their king married. Since the Visigoths were Arians, they had some difficulty in ruling the orthodox Christians among their subjects. After the Visigothic king Recared converted to Catholic Christianity in 589 and abandoned his Arian beliefs, Visigothic Spain reached its high point. Toledo became the capital of a renewed and energetic empire, sustaining such scholars as Isidore of Seville, the author of the famous *Etymologies*. Church councils held at Toledo and elsewhere within Visigothic Spain reached new landmarks in promoting a vital ecclesiastical culture throughout most of the seventh century. Nonetheless, the Visigoths, as was the case with other Germanic kingdoms, never fully resolved the question of royal succession. On the one hand, they embraced a Germanic elective principle of regal power and the idea that power came from below; on the other hand, Germanic rulers were enticed by the idea—promoted by the church—that power descended from God and that royal power was therefore unassailable (see later in this chapter). The tendency of Germanic rulers to divide their kingdoms among their children, together with a principle of partible inheritance based on a conception of the kingdom as the private property of the king, lessened the possibility of a stable and enduring public political culture. These crises of succession and authority explain, to a large extent, Islam's successful conquest of the peninsula in 711.

Preceding by a few years the Visigothic migration, another Germanic people, the Vandals, crossed the Rhine westward into Gaul and moved southward into southern Spain, where they settled in 411. The Vandals entered North Africa from Spain, moved eastward across modern Morocco and Algeria, and established their capital at Carthage in 439. Here they built a fleet and raided Sicily and Italy, finally sacking Rome (455) in a raid that has made the word *vandalism* synonymous with wanton destruction of property. They held on in North Africa until 533, when Emperor Justinian conquered their kingdom.

Under pressure on the Continent, the Romans early in the fifth century began to withdraw their legions from the British Isles. As they left, Germanic tribes from across the North Sea in what are now northern Germany and Denmark began to filter into what is today England, parts of Scotland, and Wales. These Angles, Saxons, and Jutes gradually established their authority

A celtic cross from County Leith, Ireland (probably late ninth or early tenth century). Highly decorated crosses or book illuminations, such as the Book of Kells, *reflected the unique contributions and artistic sensibilities of Irish (Celtic) monasticism in the early and central Middle Ages.*   (The Irish Picture Library)

over the Celtic Britons, many of whom survived as a subject class. The invaders soon founded seven Anglo-Saxon kingdoms, of which Northumbria, Mercia, and Wessex successively became the most important. Scotland and Wales remained Celtic, as did Ireland, which was in large measure converted to Christianity in the fifth century by Catholic missionaries coming from Gaul. The missionaries were led by a Briton, Patrick, whose preaching and activities can be dated with some uncertainty to the late fourth and or first half of the fifth century.

Ireland escaped the first great wave of barbarian invasions, and its Celtic church promoted learning, poetry, and the illustration of manuscripts by paintings. By the end of the sixth century, Catholic Christianity was moving into England from both Celtic Ireland and Rome. Thus, Irish monasticism played an important role in the conversion of western Europe. At its height in terms of scholarship, hagiographical writings, and proselytization, during the period from the sixth to the early ninth centuries the Irish church sent Irish scholars out from Ireland as missionaries to convert non-Christian populations. Inspired by charismatic missionaries and saints—Columba, Columban of Leinster, and others—the Irish brand of Catholicism spread throughout England, Scotland, and the Continent.

Intellectually, one must note the activities at the monastery of Clonard, which reputedly housed thousands of scholars, and the ecclesiastical school at Aranmore. Ireland has a rich history, one that differs in some respects from other western European countries. It may not have saved civilization as a recent book has claimed, but in the early Middle Ages, having escaped the brunt of the Germanic invasions and the disintegration of Roman institutions, Ireland combined its Celtic heritage with classical learning—most evident in the *Book of Kells*—making Irish cultural centers important repositories of ancient knowledge and new artistic forms.

Huns and Ostrogoths, 451–526

Not only the Germanic peoples but also the Huns, originating further east, participated in the onslaught on Roman territories. Early in the fifth century the Huns conquered much of central and eastern Europe. Under their domination lived a large collection of German tribes. The Hunnic rulers also extracted tribute money from the eastern Roman emperors at Constantinople. Under their ruler, Attila, the Huns pressed westward, crossed the Rhine, and were defeated in 451 at Châlons in northeastern France by an army led by the Roman general Aëtius, with the help of Theodoric I, the Visigothic king, who died in the battle. After retreating to his strongholds in central Europe, Attila marched marched into Italy the next year—his armies already ill and reeling from the battle of Châlons. As they threatened Rome, Pope Leo the Great apparently persuaded Attila (probably through bribes and payments) to withdraw without attacking Rome. Illnesses in the region around Rome may have also played a role in Attila's withdrawal.

Like many nomad empires, that of the Huns in central Europe fell apart after the death of its founder in 453. A plague decimated their ranks, and many withdrew into Asia. But other central Asian peoples entered Europe before the age of the barbarian invasions was over: Avars in the sixth century, Bulgars in the sixth and seventh, and Magyars in the ninth. The Magyars eventually set up a state in the Danubian plain, and their descendants still inhabit modern Hungary. As the first distant eastern invaders, the Huns had not only precipitated the invasions of the Germanic tribes but also directly helped to smash Roman influence in central Europe.

Among the German tribes liberated after the collapse of the Hunnic Empire, the first to make a major impact were the Ostrogoths (East Goths). They moved into the general disorder left in Italy after the last of the western emperors, Romulus Augustulus (the little Augustus), was dethroned by his German protector Odovacar in 476. Roman imperial power, however, continued uninterrupted in the East. Like many other Christianized German tribes, the Ostrogoths were Arians. To the bishops of Rome (the popes) and the Roman Christian population, they were therefore heretics as well as German foreigners. Although their leader, Theodoric the Great (r. 493–526), hoped to benefit from the civilization of the Roman Empire for the improvement of his Germanic subjects, he did not have enough time to bring about any real assimilation. Moreover, toward the end of his reign, Theodoric became suspicious of the empire and planned to go to war against Constantinople.

Many other Germanic peoples participated in the breakup of Roman territory and power in the West during the fifth and sixth centuries but failed to found any lasting political entity. They remain tribal names: Scirae, Suevi, Alamanni, Gepides. There were two other German tribes, however, whose achievements we do remember—the Burgundians, who moved into the valleys of the Rhine and Saône rivers in Gaul in the 440s and gave their name to a succession of "Burgundies"; and the Franks, from whom France derives its name. But most of all, we must remember that these names, as preserved for us by late antique historians, represented heterogeneous groups of people, not all of them belonging to the same ethnic or linguistic group. As Roger Collins has pointed out, the old migration theory showing the net movement of people across Europe is now untenable. While most Vandals, to cite just one example, ended up in North Africa after passing through Spain, substantial numbers of Vandals could be found fighting in the Balkans during the same period in which they were supposed to be wreaking havoc in Roman North Africa.

The Franks: The Building of an Empire

The Franks engaged in no long migrations, expanding gradually west and south from their habitat along the lower Rhine. They were eventually to create an empire that would include most of western Europe except for the Iberian peninsula and the British isles. Clovis (r. 481–511), a descendant of the house of Merevig or Merovech (called Merovingian), was the primary founder of Frankish power. Moving into Gaul, he successively defeated the last Roman governor (486), the Alamanni (496), and the Visigoths of Aquitaine (507). Large areas of modern France, northwest Germany, and the Low Countries were then under Frankish rule. One should note that the Franks, unlike other Germanic groups, had not embraced Christianity, either the Arian version, which predominated among the Germans, or the orthodox one. Thus, the Franks were a target for Catholic missionary activity. The most important factor in Clovis's success, aside from his skill as a general, was therefore his conversion circa 496 to Christianity as an orthodox Catholic. This gave him the instant support of the clergy of Gaul, especially of the powerful bishops of Aquitaine, who welcomed the Franks as a relief from the Arian Visigoths.

The advantages of clerical support were somewhat denied by the Frankish custom of dividing up their lands among the king's sons in every generation. In time, Clovis's sons and grandsons gained control of Burgundy and much of present-day Germany, but this meant not only a periodic parceling out of territory into petty kingdoms and lordships but also constant secret intrigues and bloody rivalries among brothers and cousins and other relatives who strove to reunite the lands. According to the sixth-century historian Gregory, bishop of Tours, King Childeric, Clovis's grandson, married Fredegund, who stopped at nothing to achieve her ambitions. She sent her husband's son by an earlier marriage into a plague-infested region in the hope of killing him off, and when that failed she stabbed him. Next, she sent an assassin to kill her sister-in-law, Brunnhild, and when the assassin returned unsuccessful, Fredegund had his hands and feet cut off. Brunnhild, nearly eighty, was dragged to her death by wild horses. Gregory's vivid account provides an example of the Franks' frequent feuds and familial disputes, a pattern common also among the Visigoths and other Germanic groups.

By the end of the seventh century, the divisive Merovingian kings became so weak that they became known as *rois fainénts* (do-nothing kings). They delegated real power to their chief officials, the "mayors of the palace." By the eighth century one particular family, the house of Pepin of Heristal, had made this office hereditary from father to son. In 732, one of the majors of the palace, Charles Martel (r. 714–741), defeated a Muslim incursion from Spain near Poitiers. Shortly afterward he organized some of his nobles into a dependable cavalry. Because this was the farthest north the Muslims ever came, later historians saw the battle as a landmark in European history. In reality, this was a small Muslim probe into lands that held little or no attraction for them. The significance of the battle, which was fought in the traditional Germanic fashion, with all the free men fighting on foot, resides in the social and military transformations that the introduction of the stirrup, shortly afterward, brought about, and in the rise of the mounted soldier, the knight, as supreme in European battlefields until the end of the fifteenth century. Based upon the prestige of his victory and of far-flung economic and military reforms carried out by his father, Charles Martel's son, Pepin III, the Short (r. 751–768), assumed the title of king of the Franks (with papal approval and cooperation) and consolidated the kingdom once again. Pepin's rule as king and the subsequent destiny of the Carolingians, as the new dynasty came to be known (from *Carolus,* the Latin form of Charles), became intimately tied to Italian affairs.

Italy from Theodoric to Pepin, 527–768

Soon after the death of Theodoric, the great eastern Roman emperor, Justinian (r. 527–565), launched from Constantinople an ambitious effort to reconquer the major areas of the West that had been lost to the Germanic invaders and their allies. The imperial forces tackled the Vandals in North Africa in 533, and then invaded Italy from Carthage via Sicily. For almost twenty years, savage and destructive warfare ravaged the peninsula, and Rome changed hands several times. The towns and countryside were devastated and the survivors reduced to misery. Three years after Justinian's death, a new Germanic tribe, the Lombards, entered Italy from the north. They easily conquered the north Italian plain that still bears their name (Lombardy) and established a kingdom with its capital at Pavia. Farther to the south they set up the duchies of Benevento and Spoleto. Ravenna, Rome, and Naples remained free of Lombard rule. Italy lay once again in fragments, even though the emperor at Constantinople appointed an exarch, or governor, who had his headquarters at Ravenna and was responsible for the defense of Italy. Constantinople was far away; danger threatened the emperors from the east, and they often could not afford to pay much attention to Italy's needs or send money and troops to help the exarchs fight the Lombards. In this chaotic situation, the church emerged more and more as the protector of the Catholic population; the bishops often received privileges from the non-Catholic Lombard conquerors that conferred upon them virtual governing rights in the towns if they would keep them peaceful. Among the bishops, the pope took the lead; and among the popes, the most remarkable was Gregory I, the Great (r. 590–604).

Born into a rich and aristocratic Roman family, Gregory abandoned worldly things and became a monk. His administrative talents were extraordinary; he served as papal ambassador to the Roman imperial court at Constantinople before becoming pope in 590. Besides his religious duties, he had to take virtually full responsibility for maintaining the fortifications of Rome, for feeding its population, for managing the great financial resources of the church and its lands in Italy, for conducting diplomatic negotiations with the exarchate and Lombards, and even for directing military operations. Gregory had an exalted conception of papal power, and he stoutly defended its supremacy over the eastern church.

During the seventh and early eighth centuries, the differences between the empire in the East and the papacy was greatly increased by religious disagreements and related political and economic disputes (see Chapter 2). Simultaneously, the Lombards were gradually consolidating and expanding their power, taking Ravenna and putting an end to the exarchate. Menaced by the Lombards and unable to count on help from Constantinople, Pope Stephen II paid a visit to Pepin III of the Franks in 753. Pepin was unsure of his position, being only a descendant of a line of mayors of the palace. In exchange for papal approval of his new title of king, he attacked the Lombards and forced them to abandon Ravenna and other recent conquests. Pepin, although these lands did not truly belong to him, gave a portion of them to the pope, in what became later the celebrated Donation of Pepin. Together with Rome and the lands immediately around it, the Donation of Pepin formed the territory over which the pope ruled as temporal sovereign until 1870. These were the Papal States, and Vatican City is their present-day remnant. Pepin's son, Charles the Great (Charlemagne, 742–814), completed the destruction of the Lombard kingdom in 774.

Carolingian Empire

The new alliance with the Franks marked the end of papal dependence upon the empire at Constantinople and the beginning of the papacy as a distinct territorial power. The Franks did not try to dictate to the popes. Sometime between 750 and 760 the clerks of the papal chancery forged "proof" that Pepin had been confirming a gift of lands to the church made long ago by the emperor Constantine. For about seven hundred years, until the Italian Renaissance scholar Lorenzo Valla proved it a forgery in 1440, people believed the document on which the "donation" of Pepin was based to be genuine.

Charlemagne and the Revival of Empire, 768–814

Charlemagne (r. 768–814) was a vigorous, lusty, intelligent man who loved hunting, women, and war. All his life he wore Frankish costume and thought of himself as a Frankish chieftain. A man interested in the culture of the past—he had Boethius's *Consolation of Philosophy* read to him—and a great conqueror, Charlemagne crossed the Rhine and in campaigns lasting more than thirty years conquered the Saxons, who lived south of Denmark, and converted them at sword's point to Christianity. Charlemagne also added to his domain the western areas of modern Bohemia, much of Austria, and portions of Hungary and Croatia. The eastern boundaries of his realm reached the Elbe and the Danube. Along these wild eastern frontiers and in the southern borders with Islam he established provinces (*marks* or *marches*). His advance into eastern Europe also brought him victories over the Avars, successors to the Huns along the lower Danube. Far to the west, Charlemagne challenged Muslim power in Spain and set up a Spanish march in what is today Catalonia. A defeat of his rear guard at the hands of the Basques or Gascons at the pass of Roncesvalles in the Pyrenees Mountains in 778 formed the theme of the heroic epic *Le Chanson de Roland* (*The Song of Roland*), although in the *Chanson* the enemy is depicted as Muslim.

By the end of the eighth century, Charlemagne had reunited under Frankish rule all of the western Roman provinces except for Britain, most of Spain, southern Italy, Sicily, and North Africa, but had added to his domains areas in central and eastern Europe that the Romans had never possessed. On Christmas Day 800, Pope Leo III crowned Charlemagne emperor in Rome. So mighty was the tradition of the Roman Empire and so great its hold on people's minds that the chief bishop of the Christian church crowned him "Roman Emperor Carolus Augustus." A great deal of scholarly debate surrounds whether the pope's action caught Charlemagne by surprise or not, and he may not have been pleased by the coronation and the role played by the pope and the implication that the pope had the right to choose and crown emperors. He seldom used the title, but it is clear that the crowning had an impact on Charlemagne's own sense of his rule. Since Irene was a ruler in Byzantium, and a contested ruler at that, this may have prompted the pope to seek support elsewhere and to select a male ruler over a female one.

A king by the "grace of God," Charlemagne claimed spiritual rights and duties as well as temporal ones as emperor. His lofty concept of his office and his personal power enabled him to influence the church. He named his son, Louis the Pious, his successor in 814, and the pope played no part in the ceremonies. Charlemagne's government was quite innovative, and a series of reforms streamlined the administration of the Carolingian territories, allowing the emperor or king greater access to their subjects, their military service, and their fiscal contributions. Members of his personal household staff were also the government officials: the chamberlain, the count of the stable (constable), and so on. On major decisions the emperor conferred with great nobles of state and church, asking them for advice and permission. The decisions of these great gatherings of warriors, bishops, and powerful men, called capitularies, were sent out to the outlaying areas of the empire, providing a sense of unity to Charlemagne's vast possessions. Since the Franks, like other Germans, believed that law preexisted and could not be made by humans, even Charlemagne could not, in theory, legislate. But he did issue instructions to his subjects, which usually dealt with special administrative problems.

Charlemagne's territories included about three hundred counties, each governed by a count. The count had to maintain order, render justice, and recruit and command soldiers. Alongside the count, the bishop of the diocese and the various local magnates might have considerable powers of their own when on their own lands. Only a powerful king could keep the local authorities from taking too much power for themselves. Charlemagne required his counts to appoint teams of judges, whose appointment he would then ratify and who would actually take over much of the counts' role in rendering justice. He also sent out from his own central administrative staff pairs of royal emissaries, usually a layman and a cleric, to investigate local conditions and to correct abuses. As representatives of the emperor, they could overrule the count.

The Carolingian Empire depended heavily upon Charlemagne's personality—on his energy, on the brilliance that all observers attributed to him, on his administrative talents, and on the happy fact that, having only one surviving son, Charlemagne did not divide the empire among heirs. But he had assembled more territory than could be effectively governed, in view of the deterioration of administrative machinery and communications since Roman days. Under his less talented successors, the Frankish practice of dividing lands and authority among the heirs to the throne continued. Quarrels over the allotment of territory raged among brothers and cousins. Although the title of emperor now descended to a single heir in each generation, it had become an empty honor by the middle of the ninth century.

Thus Charlemagne's achievement was short-lived, if brilliant. Historians have taken differing views of it. Some have emphasized its brevity and denied its lasting influence. Others have stressed its achievements and declared that the mere resurrection of the Roman imperial title in the West helped determine the future direction of European political action; the next time a new revival began, statesmen instinctively launched it by reviving the Roman Empire once again. Some insist that Charlemagne's revival of the imperial title at least kept alive the ideal of a unified Christian western society, as opposed to a collection of parochial states devoted to cutthroat competition. Others maintain that, thanks to Charlemagne's act, an ambitious secular power could oppose the temporal claims of a spiritual power, the papacy. Of course, a spiritual power well anchored in Italy could oppose a weak temporal power. A great deal of the evolution of western politics hinges on the uneasy balance between temporal and spiritual power in medieval Christendom.

In the struggle among Charlemagne's successors, one episode deserves special notice: the Strasbourg Oaths of 842. Two of his grandsons, Charles the Bald, who held the western regions, and Louis the German, who held the eastern regions, swore an alliance against their brother, the emperor Lothar, whose lands lay between theirs. Each swore the oath in the language of the other's troops—Louis in a Romance Latinlike language on its way to becoming early medieval French, and Charles in Germanic. The symbolism was a striking sign of things to come. We should not, however, read too much into this. Patrick Geary has recently debunked the notion that the origins of modern European states can be traced back directly to Carolingian and post-Carolingian developments. The process of nation-building was far more complex than that, and it is erroneous to link specific events in the eighth and ninth centuries to the earlier and very embryonic medieval origins of the state in thirteenth-century France, England, or Castile. Nonetheless, Carolingian achievements resonated throughout western history in other ways. As shall be seen later, the revival of culture in Charlemagne's and his successors' courts, above all in the areas of grammar, orthography, and educational reform, lay the foundations for subsequent and far more enduring cultural production in the twelfth century. In the ninth century there were as yet no national states in western Europe. Indeed, instead of coalescing into larger units, the Frankish dominions were even then breaking up into much smaller ones, despite the formal settlement reached at the Treaty of Verdun in 843. As the power of the fairly complex Frankish kingdom was frittered away in family squabbles, smaller entities—duchies or counties—emerged as virtually autonomous units of localized power.

After Charlemagne: The Northmen or Vikings

Charlemagne's rule was also open to the world. It borrowed some of its symbols and political language from Byzantium. It benefited from the great treasure-taking from the Avars. It maintained constant, and not always hostile, contacts with the Muslims in Spain and with the great Caliph Harun al-Rashid, the ruler of Baghdad. The Frankish Empire at its height was heterogeneous enough to provide a sense of the complexities of the world beyond its borders, but by the early ninth century new people, the Vikings, the Magyars ("Hungarians"), and the Saracens, were already converging on the core areas of western Europe. Their coming would deeply affect Frankish territories and the rest of the West.

Charlemagne's conquests in Germany had for the first time brought the home ground of many of the barbarians into Christendom. Still outside lay Scandinavia, from whose shores there began in the ninth century a new wave of invasions that hit Britain and the western parts of the Frankish lands with savage force. The Northmen or Vikings conducted their raids from small ships that could easily sail up the Thames, the Seine, or the Loire. Their appetite for pillaging grew with their successes, and soon they organized fleets of several hundred ships, ventured farther abroad, and often wintered along a conquered coast. They ranged as far east as Yaroslavl in what is today northern Russia and as far south as Spain, penetrated into the Mediterranean through the Straits of Gibraltar, and raided Italy. To the west they proceeded far beyond Ireland to reach Iceland and Greenland. About 986 some of them almost certainly sighted Newfoundland (Vinland), Labrador, and perhaps New England.

Desire for profit does not by itself account for Viking expansion. Polygamy was common among the upper classes of the pagan Scandinavians, and the

The Oseberg Viking Ship, circa mid-ninth century. In seaworthy ships, such as the one depicted here, the Viking or Northmen struck deep into England and western France; reached the Mediterranean, Iceland, Greenland, and the New World; and sailed through the extensive river networks in eastern Europe, the Ukraine, and the Black Sea.   (Werner Forman/Art Resource, NY)

younger sons of these chiefs probably had to leave home to seek more wives. Like most migrations, however, the chief motivation most likely was to find new lands to settle in the face of growing overpopulation. Cultivable land became scarce, throwing families onto marginal lands to face the fear of famine in a bad year. The Northmen's first captured base was along the lower Seine River, which is still called Normandy after them. In 915 the Frankish king was forced to grant the Norse leader Rolf, or Rollo (r. 860–c. 931), a permanent right of settlement. The Normans became an efficient and powerful ruling class—in fact, the best administrators in the new feudal age. From Normandy soon after the year 1000, younger sons would go off to found a new Norman kingdom(s) in the southern Italian and Sicilian territories that belonged to the eastern Roman Empire and to the Arabs. And from Normandy in 1066, as we shall see, Duke William and his followers would conquer England. Kinsmen of these Northmen who had settled in Normandy also did great deeds. In the 860s the first wave of Viking invaders crossed the Baltic Sea to what are now the Baltic States and penetrated deep inland to the south along the river valleys. They conquered the indigenous Slavic tribes and, at Kiev on the middle Dnieper, consolidated a political entity known as Rus.

The Anglo-Saxon Kingdoms and the Danes, 871–1035

In England, violent and frequent Danish attacks on the northern and eastern shores were soon followed by settlement. The chief barrier to the Danes was the Anglo-Saxon kingdom of Wessex under Alfred the Great (r. 871–899). Although Alfred defeated the Danes, he acquiesced in the Danish control of the whole northeast of England, a region thereafter called the Danelaw. By the mid-tenth century, Alfred's successors had reunited the Danelaw to Wessex, whose royal family ruled over all England. Soon after the turn of the eleventh century, new waves of Danes scored important successes under the command of Canute, or Knut (b. 994 and king of Denmark in 1018). In 1016 Canute was chosen king of England by the Anglo-Saxon *witenagemot*, a "council of wise men." Able ruler of a kind of northern empire (he was also king of Norway), Canute allied himself with the Roman church and helped in the process of Christianizing Scandinavia. His early death (1035) led to the breakup of his holdings, and England reverted to a king of the house of Alfred, Edward the Confessor, who reigned from 1042 until 1066.

Anglo-Saxon royal revenue came in part from an ancient practice, the *feorm*—originally a tax of food levied for the support of the monarch and his household as they moved about England, although by the time of Edward the Confessor it was sometimes paid in money. There was also the *Danegeld*, a war tax on land first levied in 991 to bribe the Danes, which continued to be collected long after its original purpose was unnecessary. The king also had income from his own estates and from fines levied in court cases. His subjects were required to work on the building and repair of bridges and defense works and had to render military service in the *fyrd*, the ancient Germanic army. The Anglo-Saxon king was the guarantor of law, and serious crimes were considered to be offenses against him as well as against the victims; he was also a lawgiver. His council of wise men, made up of important landholders, churchmen, and officials, advised him on major questions of policy and sometimes acted as a court to try important cases. The council also played a major role in the election and deposition of kings. The king's personal household staff moved with him and did his business from day to day, a practice found among Continental chieftains as well.

The Saxon Empire, 911–996

By the end of the ninth century, Carolingian power in the German territories had almost disappeared in the face of challenges by ambitious local magnates and threats from Northmen, Slavs, and Magyars (the latter a confederation of Finno-Ugric groups, with some added Turkic elements). When the last nominal Carolingian ruler, Louis the Child, died in 911, the German magnates

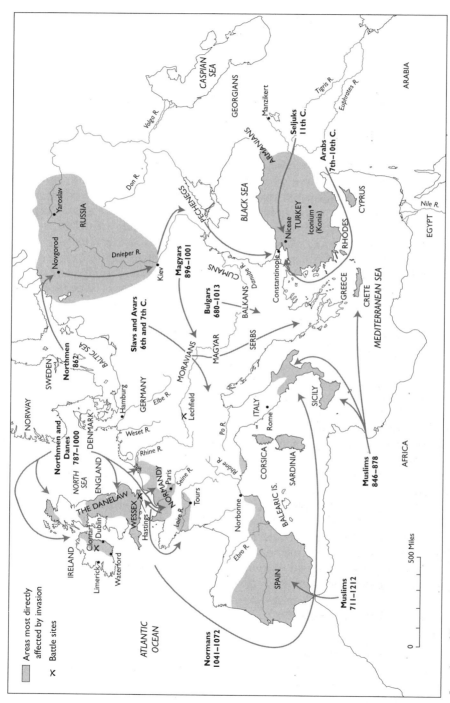

Invasions of Europe, Seventh through Eleventh Centuries

elected the duke of Franconia as King Conrad I (r. 911–918). The most important units in Germany were now duchies—Franconia, Saxony, Swabia, and Bavaria—each under an autonomous ruler. Conrad I failed to control either the other dukes or the "Hungarians" (as Nora Berend names them in her recent book), and eventually his strongest enemy, Henry the Fowler, duke of Saxony, succeeded him. Henry's son, Otto I (r. 936–973), the Great, checked the rival dukes and defeated the Magyars or "Hungarians" at the battle of Lechfeld in 955, ending their threat to western Europe.

Master of his German territories, Otto next sought to revive Charlemagne's title of Roman emperor, which had passed from one Carolingian prince to another. After the reign of the great pope Nicholas I (r. 858–867), the papacy had fallen into the hands of rival Roman noble families. Without strong central administration and under attack from Muslims in the south and Magyars or "Hungarians" in the north, Italy had fallen into anarchy. Yet Rome was an irresistible magnet that attracted all who sought supreme power. Like Charlemagne had done 162 years earlier, Otto went to Italy and had himself crowned emperor by Pope John XII in 962. Otto then deposed John and installed his own candidate on the papal throne. He forced the Roman aristocracy to promise that imperial consent would hereafter be necessary for papal elections, and he renewed the Donation of Pepin and the subsequent grants of the Carolingians to the papacy. Although the papacy for the next hundred years was hardly more than an instrument manipulated by his successors, Otto's action eventually ensured the continuity of the papacy as an independent institution; it also tightly linked the political fortunes of Germany and Italy for centuries to come.

In the western Carolingian lands, which we now call France, partitioning, strife, and feebleness led to the fragmentation of both territory and power among several ambitious landowners. As early as 887 one faction of these magnates chose a non-Carolingian, Odo, count of Paris, as king, and civil war between him and the Carolingian claimant added to the chaos. For the next century the families of the two rivals alternated in power. Finally, in 987 the magnates elected as king Hugh Capet (r. to 996), a descendant of the early count of Paris. Although several of the nobles who chose Hugh were actually more powerful than he was, he founded the Capetian dynasty that lasted until 1328.

Society and Culture in the Early Medieval West

The different Germanic tribes and their allies settling within the borders of the western Roman Empire from the late fourth century onward brought with them their own institutions, forms of social organization, and political associations. The intertwining of Germanic customs and practices with Roman civilization led to a new society. Both the German and Roman populations in the West were transformed into a new people, and western Europe into a new society.

The Written Record

SLAVERY IN THE EARLY MIDDLE AGES

A Christian prelate, Theodore, archbishop of Canterbury, drafted a set of rules pertaining to male and female slaves in seventh-century England. The following is from the second penitential book—that is, a book on penances arising from the failure to adhere to discipline—of Theodore at Canterbury, section XIII:

1. If he is compelled by necessity, a father has the power to sell his son of seven years of age into slavery; after that, he had not the right to sell him without his consent.
2. A person of fourteen [years] can make himself a slave.
3. A man may not take away from his slave money which he has acquired by his labor.
4. If the master of a male and a female slave joins them in marriage and the male slave or the female slave is afterward set free, and if the one who is in slavery cannot be redeemed, the one who has been set free may marry a free-born person. If any freeman takes a female slave in marriage, he has not the right to put her away if they were formerly united with the consent of both. If anyone acquires [as a slave] a free woman who is pregnant, the child that is born of her is free. If anyone sets free a pregnant slave woman, the child which she brings forth shall be [in a state] of slavery.

Early Welsh law also speaks of slavery. For example, the so-called Welsh Canons, dating from circa 550–650, include entries such as these:

1. If anyone commits homicide by intention, he shall pay three female slaves and three male slaves and shall receive security. . . .
4. If a slave kills a freeman, and this was through the freeman's fault, and if he was slain with a cudgel or an axe or a hoe or with a knife, that murderer shall be given over to the parents, and they shall have the power to do [with him] what they will.
5. If any master permits his slave to bear arms and he slays a freeman, the master shall be prepared to hand over the slave and another with him. . . .
22. If any freeborn man or slave commits a theft by night and in the act of committing it is struck with a spear and killed, he who slays him shall have no need to make restitution. . . .
38. If any slave kills another's slave, he shall remain alive as the joint property of the masters.

Published by Octagon Books, a division of Hippocrene Books, Inc.

Free and Unfree

From the third century onward, slavery in the West declined. At the same time, the formerly free *colonus*, the farm worker laboring in the Roman village (the village) or estates, came to be legally tied to the soil by Constantine's Edict of the Colonate (332). Slavery did not disappear, however, and remained a feature of European history into the modern period. However, its preeminence in the society and economy of the ancient world was no more. All Germanic law codes prescribed enslavement as a penalty for many violations of laws or rights. We have evidence that slavery was relatively commonplace, especially in Spain, Italy, and the eastern Mediterranean. Although the church recognized that slaves had souls and would intervene to some extent to protect slaves, the church was often a major slaveholder itself and thus resisted movements for general emancipation. However, slaves could be freed, thus adding to the ranks of freemen. We have no reliable figures on the numbers of slaves or the extent of slavery, although it is believed that slavery declined after the collapse of the Roman Empire and was at its low point in the ninth century.

A new group of people, a hereditary servile population bound to the soil yet not slaves or chattel, as well as a host of other diverse social arrangements that bound men and women to the soil or to other men, could be found in growing numbers in such dissimilar places as the Asturian-Leonese kingdoms, Lombardy, Frankland, and elsewhere. These emerging social categories appear in Germanic legal codes and in daily practice. They would eventually become common to most part of western Europe with the full emergence of serfdom (see Chapter 4).

Family and People: From Public to Private

Freedom began to be associated with membership in overlapping social groups—family, village, tribe—and with the right, and obligation, to fight in the frequent wars between local lords and regional groups. Thus the family and the far more encompassing idea of a people or *gens* came to replace the Roman state as the central defining social category. Blood ties, whether real or constructed, also played a significant role in the social negotiations between different groups. Blood also held a central place in the literary and cultural imagining of early medieval people. This shift from civic associations and citizenship to blood-based ties was paralleled by a decline in government's public nature and in the wielding of power as a public act. Rome did survive in myriad ways. Roman law, the heart of Roman civilization, was preserved in fragments within Germanic codes. The *Lex Visigothorum* (the law of the Visigoths), as noted earlier, is a very good example of this. Aspects of Roman fiscal structures also survived, although now transformed by Germanic practices and by expediency, but one must admit to the slow and inexorable decline of the Roman public sense of the state.

In the Germanic kingdoms emerging in the West after the collapse of imperial authority, kings and the great men played a significant role. German rulers saw the source of their authority in a complex mix of Germanic strains. One Germanic tradition emphasized the elective principle. Brave and capable warriors could be raised upon a shield by the soldiers and "elected" as king. This elective principle, or ascending theory of power, played a significant role in the evolution of political thought throughout the Middle Ages. It remained as a valid principle of rulership in Visigothic Spain, Germany, and

Frankland. Power ascended from below, from the "people," although the people usually meant the great magnates, warriors, and high ecclesiastics. An elective kingship undermined the hereditary principle or any serious claims to sacral kingship. Another strain, however, traced the origins of some of the Germanic royal houses to ancient gods or even mythical animals. The Merovingians are an example of this, and these associations with an ancient past and lineage provided a great deal of political capital and prestige, buttressing royal houses against the ambitions of great men.

Germanic kingship also borrowed from Christian tradition and Roman legal forms. In Christianity, power comes from God. It descends from God to humans. Thus, the king is a ruler by the grace of God and holds power from God. It is easy to see why the church's support and Christianity were so attractive politically to Germanic kings. Nonetheless, these two principles competed into the late Middle Ages. Although most kings sought to claim God as the ultimate source of their power, the elective principle remained an enduring feature of early medieval political life. Moreover, God's power was mediated by the church and thus diminished. What is obvious is that from the sixth century onward until the late Middle Ages, the public nature of government and power—the salient feature of Roman political life—had been replaced by private arrangements that bound one man to another, or the ruler to his subject. Even the rule of Charlemagne was distinguished by these constant personal and private negotiations between the king and the barons, dukes, and counts of the realm. Although some of the ancient structures of governance and power remained in place, the very sense of the corporate and public nature of state was lost in the West. And only the church retained a sense of the former way of ruling.

In this sense the widespread use of the *wergild* (the value set in Germanic and Anglo-Saxon codes for the life of an individual or for any serious crime, and to be paid in compensation to the victim's family or lord by the offender) signaled the privatization of justice, although it also served as an important deterrent to blood feuds or family vendettas. Since the amount paid in *wergild* corresponded very closely to social and economic status, gender, age, and whether one was free or not, the privatization of crime and punishment also served as an important marker of the medieval society's hierarchical character. Slaves were worth far less than free women and men. Men's *wergild* was superior to that of women of the same social standing. Women still capable of bearing children counted for more than those beyond the age of procreation, and so forth.

The careful detailing of *wergild* payments according to these categories also gives us a very good sense of the role of women in early medieval society. Christianity in its first three centuries had empowered women by providing them with direct access to the sacred, through their roles as prophetesses and virgins. As Peter Brown has shown and as noted in an earlier chapter, chastity and sanctity gave women a control over their bodies that was quite different from that of Roman matrons. By the early Middle Ages, the church had become less flexible in its acceptance of women, and the sacrament of the mass had become a male monopoly, but notable female saints served as reminders to society as a whole of the role of women in religion. Moreover, as was the case before and as would be the case later, women played a significant role in the agricultural life of Europe. We know that they tended the fields and worked side by side with the male members of their families in squeezing the fruits from the earth. Yet misogyny and patriarchy, themes that will be explored in some detail later and that had a long history and roots in both the classical and Judeo-Christian tradition, remained powerful presences in the daily relations between women and men. Germanic codes and customs established the right of the male over the female members of the family, and women's rights to property and inheritance were severely limited or nonexistent. In places such as Spain and Italy, where elements of Roman law were incorporated into Germanic codes, women enjoyed greater rights over property and inheritance.

Culture

In the past, the early Middle Ages was seen as a cultural wasteland. A few monasteries here and there kept, as barely as a flickering light, a few fragments of the great glories of the ancient past. Today we know a great deal better. Perhaps, when judged by comparison with the achievements of Greek, Hellenistic, or Roman civilizations, or by those of the Byzantine and Muslim East, those of western Europe in these centuries may sometimes seem feeble or primitive. But this is what one would expect in a world where life was often too turbulent to allow much leisure for the exercise of creative skills. The efficient Roman communication system had deteriorated. Cities were often mere shells of the vibrant centers of communication they had once been. Technical skills were lost, as was command over Latin, the western European language of intellectuals and writers. Many Germans loved and admired the Roman world that their fellow barbarians were destroying. They painstakingly kept alive the Roman literary and artistic tradition. Moreover, the widely traveled invading tribes brought with them art forms of their own—poetry, sculpture, and painting—that have only recently been widely appreciated by scholars. But even the achievements of the classical age seemed to have survived far more widely and extensively than previously thought.

Everywhere in the West, then, the story in general is the same, although it varies greatly in detail. The people of these centuries were gradually moving away from their Roman past, while still cherishing Roman models. They were also creating new and original writings and works of art. While the Christian faith gave them a more permanent and firmer link with Rome and its traditions than they would otherwise have had, they neither entirely absorbed the Roman heritage nor wholly abandoned their own traditions.

Latin Literature

Two distinct periods can be identified in the cultural production of the early Middle Ages. The first, which corresponds to the period in late antiquity, witnessed the transmission of classical themes and learning to the Middle Ages.

The second was far more autonomous and, while borrowing from classical (Roman) models, led to many novel hagiographical, philosophical, and literary works, as well as to architectural and artistic works. The latter could not have happened without the first, and it may be useful to revisit the manner in which culture was transmitted in the dying days of the western empire.

It was in Italy that the fight against the loss of the classical heritage was waged most vigorously and most successfully. Under the Ostrogothic King Theodoric (r. 493–526), two distinguished intellectuals combated the general decline: Boethius and Cassiodorus. Unlike most of his contemporaries, Boethius (c. 480–524) knew both Greek and Latin. Learned and versatile, he advised Theodoric on many points. A recognized authority on music, he selected the best available harpist to play at the court of Clovis, king of the Franks. He thwarted an effort of Theodoric's military paymaster to cheat the troops by showing that the paymaster had "sweated" the silver from the coins. He held the posts of consul and of Master of the Offices, something very much like a prime minister.

Boethius planned a Latin translation of the works of Plato and Aristotle, and in the small portion that he completed he took care to make his translation as literal as possible. Boethius was keenly interested in education. Borrowing from Martianus Capella's fourth-century description of the seven liberal arts, he wrote most of the textbooks that served as introductions to the arts through the next five centuries. Boethius also made the first efforts to apply to Christian theological writings the logical methods of Aristotle. These were to inspire scholars and thinkers who lived six hundred and more years after his death. Had Boethius survived to carry out his plans for rendering the greatest Greek philosophers into Latin, western Europe perhaps would not have been denied these materials for another five hundred years. But only two years after making him Master of the Offices, Theodoric imprisoned Boethius on a charge of treason. After a year in jail, Boethius was executed, perhaps because he was sharply opposed to the Arian Christianity practiced by Theodoric and the Ostrogoths.

In jail he wrote his most famous work, *On the Consolation of Philosophy* (or *Consolation of Philosophy*), a dialogue between himself and the female personification of Philosophy. Written in excellent Latin, the *Consolation* is a moving and noble book in which the prisoner seeks answers not only to why he is suffering injustice but also to the larger questions of human life and death and the relationship between humans and God. The book dwells on the prevalence of suffering, the fickleness of fortune, and the transitoriness of worldly triumphs. Everything we gain here on earth, even fame, will vanish. *On the Consolation of Philosophy* became one of the most popular books of the Middle Ages, and was read to Charlemagne and by Chaucer. Remarkably, the book never mentions Christ; it serves as a reaffirmation of the values of classical civilization in its twilight.

Cassiodorus (c. 490–575) managed to stay in Theodoric's good graces and, like Boethius, became consul and Master of the Offices. He collected Theodoric's official correspondence, providing a model to Germanic kings on how to write official letters. He wrote a history of the Goths that intertwined the histories of the Roman and German people and, by granting the Goths equal antiquity with the Romans, lay the foundations for a common world. But his great ambition was to found a new Christian seminary in Rome, where a revival of learning and scholarship might take place. The terrible disorders that accompanied Justinian's reconquest of Italy from the Goths between 535 and 554 made this impossible. Instead, Cassiodorus founded a monastery in southern Italy where he tried to keep learning alive in its Christian form. Writing a guide to the appropriate readings for each of the seven liberal arts, Cassiodorus created, in a sense, the curriculum of the western Middle Ages, one that would remain in place into the early modern period. The monks at Cassiodorus's monastery, Vivarium, copied by hand not only the Bible but also the best pagan Latin authors. Cassiodorus himself wrote books on spelling, on the Psalms, and on the soul. Some of his monks translated Greek works into Latin, helping turn the monasteries into centers of rote learning.

In Gaul, a highly Romanized province, there remained even during the invasions a cultivated group of Gallo-Roman aristocratic landowners and churchmen who still found it natural to communicate with each other in Latin. Perhaps the most distinguished writer of all was chiefly a prose stylist, Sidonius Apollinaris (fl. 455–c. 475). Born of a family long prominent in imperial affairs and educated at the school of Lyon, Sidonius became bishop of Auvergne in southcentral France during the invasions of Visigoths and Burgundians. Yet in 147 letters, written with an eye to preservation and future publication, Sidonius writes almost as if nothing very alarming were happening in the outside world. With gentlemanly distaste, he refers to the Germanic invaders as underbred and coarse. He had no apprehension that they were bringing with them the doom of Sidonius and all his friends.

Far more typical of the period and already fully ushering a new cultural world were the views of Pope Gregory the Great (590–604). Practical in every way, Gregory was ready to abandon the classical past if he could bring more order into the barbarian and Christian present. "The same lips," he wrote one of his bishops, "cannot sound the praises of Jupiter and the praises of Christ," and he enjoined him to stop holding conferences where ancient literature was read. In Gregory's own writings, the same practical tendency appears; his *Dialogues* deal in four volumes with the lives and miracles of the Italian church fathers, providing edifying anecdotes to attract Christian readers away from pagan authors. But perhaps the most important of Gregory's writings is his surviving correspondence, more than a thousand letters. Sent to all corners of the Christian world and dealing with every sort of problem in the management of the church and its relations with secular rulers, these letters reflect Gregory's humanity, commanding nature, and, at times, unexpected humor.

By the time of the Frankish triumph, the Gallo-Roman culture that Sidonius so proudly represented had virtually died. Whatever literary activity there was, it was different in its themes and style, and closer to the cultural world of Gregory the Great than to that of Sidonius. We have some moving sixth-century Latin hymns and descriptive poems by a writer known as Fortunatus, who deeply influenced Radegund of Poitiers, a Thuringian princess brought to Frankland to become queen and whose asceticism and piety led her to a monastery and to a life of holiness and power. While embracing Christianity fully, she still delighted in Fortunatus's poetry. We have the history in which Gregory, bishop of Tours, chronicles the unedifying behavior of the Merovingian rulers. Gregory's Latin prose may have shocked Sidonius, but there is a vigorous quality about him, a mixture of credulity, native goodness, and calm acceptance of atrocities that gives the reader deep insight into the Merovingian age. In Spain, too, there was a good deal of writing in Latin, at least into the seventh century, which saw the *Etymologies* of St. Isidore (c. 570–636), archbishop of Seville, a sort of encyclopedia. Isidore became perhaps the most influential and certainly the most representative literary figure of his time. His work was known in Ireland by the middle of the seventh century, and his listing of the cleric's duties became so well established that it was accorded semiofficial status by the middle of the twelfth century. The Iberian peninsula before the Muslim invasion in 711 was a site for important intellectual exchanges and artistic production. The great Visigothic church councils generated a continuous stream of edicts and religious ordinances. In the court, Visgothic customs, intertwined with Roman legal formulas, led to the writing of important law codes.

Besides the many works that can be attributed with reasonable accuracy to a specific writer, there were many accounts of the lives of the saints, known as *hagiographies*. Many people read or learned about the saints through these anonymous works. Homely tales about the virtues of the saints as well as rousing exhortations to bravery in the manner of the early Christians created what may be the most influential literary sources of the period. For a different spirit one turns to Britain and to Ireland. Christianity came to Britain in three waves: one with the Roman troops, which virtually died out; one from Ireland, where it was of Gallic origin; and the third from Rome, at the end of the sixth century and the beginning of the seventh. In England Christianity produced the first original writing in Latin. The combined influence of the Celtic and the Roman traditions brought such fruitful results that by the end of the eighth century missionaries from Britain stimulated a revival on the Continent.

Of several cultivated writers, the greatest was Bede (c. 673–735), called the Venerable for his learning. Abbot of his monastery, he could read Hebrew and Greek, knew the Latin writings of the church fathers intimately, and wrote the famous *Ecclesiastical History of the English People,* the story of the spread of Christianity in England from the arrival in 597 of the missions sent by Gregory down to 731, almost to the moment of Bede's death. Written in Latin of astonishing vigor and purity, it tells almost everything we know of the progress of the new religion among the pagan Anglo-Saxons, about the church's relationship with the Anglo-Saxon kings, and about the foundation of the many monastic houses, where monks found a shelter for themselves and their books.

Churchmen from Britain, Spain, Italy, and other parts of Europe helped make possible the great flowering of Latin letters that took place under Charlemagne. Alcuin of York (735–c. 804) went to Charlemagne's court in 781 and helped to transform the palace school there into a serious and practical educational institution where men studied the seven liberal arts. Alcuin wrote much prose and verse and took the lead in reviving biblical scholarship and in teaching such practical subjects as legible handwriting to the scribes, who now began to copy, once again in the model of Cassiodorus' Vivarium, manuscripts in monasteries. We owe the survival of much of Latin literature to the efforts of these Carolingian scribes, as we owe them the invention of lowercase letters and the importation of musical notations into the West. Theodulfus, a scholar and philosopher from Spain, was at the center of a philosophical revival, as Einhard was the leader in historical writing. His biography of Charlemagne remains one of the most important sources for our understanding of the period.

The foundations laid by scholars such as Alcuin and others permitted their successors in the next two generations, after Charlemagne's empire had disintegrated, to write history, poetry, hagiographies, works on theology and ethics, and vast numbers of personal letters in Latin. In new monastic centers, with libraries far more extensive than originally thought, the literary work made possible by the "Carolingian Renaissance" went on, and the continuity of knowledge in western civilization was assured.

Vernacular Literature: *Beowulf*

Britain's distance from Rome and its failure to become completely Latinized during antiquity allowed it to profit greatly from the double wave of Latin Christian missionaries—Celtic and papal—and so provide the needed stimulus for the Carolingian Latin literary revival. But the thinness of the Latin veneer probably encouraged the Angles, Saxons, and Jutes to produce a literature in their own language (called Anglo-Saxon or Old English). Sometimes they were translators; Boethius's *Consolation of Philosophy* was rendered into Old English, and King Alfred the Great himself translated Bede's *Ecclesiastical History*. Sometimes they were original writers, setting down a group of proverbs or the life of a saint or a chronicle. By far the most remarkable Old English literary survival is *Beowulf,* a poem of almost 3,200 lines written down about the year 1000. It is clear that the poem was composed well before the date of the surviving manuscript, perhaps as early as about 680, perhaps as late as 800 or even later. Until 1939 some scholars thought it had been composed in Northumbria, some in Mercia; but in that year a spectacular archaeological discovery at Sutton Hoo in Essex (East Anglia) turned up the ship tomb of a king of the East Angles dating from the late seventh or early eighth century and containing a harp, jewels, and armor like those described in *Beowulf,* which also includes a description of a ship-funeral. Some scholars now think the poem may be of East Anglian origin. The poem has been described as "a museum for the antiquarian, a source-book for the historian,

The Written Record

BEOWULF

Beowulf begins in Denmark, where it tells of the founding of the Danish royal line and the building of a great hall by King Hrothgar. The hall is repeatedly raided by a savage monster, Grendel, who seizes and eats the Danish warriors as they lie asleep after dinner, until from over the sea in southern Sweden comes a hero, Beowulf. He lies in wait for the monster and in single combat so severely grips his hand that Grendel has to flee, leaving his entire arm, ripped out at the socket, in Beowulf's hands. The wound is fatal, but Grendel's mother tries to avenge him and Beowulf has to slay her at the bottom of a wild and lonely lake. Here Hrothgar's queen, Wealhtheow, thanks Beowulf for killing Grendel:

To him she carried the cup, and asked in gracious words
if he would care to drink; and to him she presented
twisted gold with courtly ceremonial
two armlets; a corselet and many rings,
and the most handsome collar in the world.
I have never heard that any hero had a jewel
to equal that.

Applause echoed in the hall.
Wealhtheow spoke these words before the company:
"May you, Beowulf, beloved youth, enjoy
with all good fortune this necklace and corselet,
treasures of the people; may you always prosper;
win renown through courage, and be kind in your counsel
to these boys [her sons]; for that, I will reward you further.
You have ensured that men will always sing
your praises, even to the ends of the world,
as far as oceans still surround cliffs,
home of the winds. May you thrive, O prince,
all your life. I hope you will amass
a shining hoard of treasure. O happy Beowulf,
be gracious in dealing with my sons.
Here, each warrior is true to the others,
gentle of mind, loyal to his lord;
the thanes are as one, the people all alert,
the warriors have drunk well. They will do as I ask.

Then Wealhtheow retired to her seat
beside her lord. That was the best of banquets.

Beowulf, ll. 1190–96, 1215–34, trans. Kevin Crossley-Holland. Reprinted by permission of Farrar, Straus & Giroux, Inc., and Macmillan & Co. Ltd. Translation 1968 by Kevin Crossley-Holland; introductory matter 1968 by Bruce Mitchell.

a treatise for the student of Christian thought, and a gymnasium for the philologist." It is, however, also unmistakably a poem meant for oral recitation.

The Arts

Like literature, the arts also gradually moved away from the standardized Roman forms toward newer achievements that were introduced as the Germans merged their arts with those of the lands they settled. The early great churches of such important imperial cities as Milan or Trier were still large rectangular structures taken over from the secular architecture of the Romans, but innovations were tried for certain smaller Christian structures, especially baptisteries, which were detached from the main church. Some were square, others many-sided; rich mosaic decoration became common. As soon as a barbarian tribe was firmly established in its new territory, its kings, as a matter of prestige, built churches—often small, and generally imitative of the Roman models. While most of these structures have disappeared, we know from contemporary written accounts and archaeological research that they often had domes and tin or gilded bronze roof tiles that shone in the sun.

To find clear-cut examples of the kind of art the Germans brought with them into the western empire, it is easiest to turn to goldsmithing and jewelry. Fleeing before the Huns, the Germans who had settled along the shores of the Black Sea brought with them objects made by local craftsmen characterized by brilliant color and the use of gems or colored glass for ornamentation. The Vikings also produced magnificent jewelry often embellished with gold, silver, and niello, in which silver, copper, lead, and sulfur were combined. The influence of the East, especially evident in Ravenna's great churches and mosaic work, led to the gradual abandonment of realistic representation of humans and beasts in art. Imported Byzantine silver, ivories, and textiles, as well as Byzantine monuments like those mentioned already in Ravenna, helped speed the change in styles. The Carolingian period brought a new flowering of the arts. Surviving monuments in Italy gave the artists some of their inspiration, and Charlemagne's ability to attract the best craftsmen from everywhere in Europe enabled them to put their ideas into practice. Charlemagne's palace in Aix-la-Chapelle or Aachen directly borrowed from Byzantine and classical architectural languages, but it also reflected the theological and philosophical speculations of intellectuals at his court.

It was largely through book illustration—the illumination of manuscripts—that inspirations from one region or one school could intermingle in other regions with influences from other schools. Northern Italian books that embodied all these classical and Byzantine influences traveled across the Alps into Gaul and into Britain with Gregory the Great's missionaries. In due course the same influences penetrated into Germany. Charlemagne enjoyed receiving foreign travelers, many of them, especially officials, bringing rich gifts, relics, books, textiles, jewels. In 796 arrived a treasure trove captured from the Avars, who had been pillaging for two centuries. It filled sixteen

A depiction of the four horsemen of the Apocalypse found in Beatus of Liébana's doctrinal polemical work, Commentary on the Apocalypse. *It shows the highly stylized rendition of religious subjects by local artists in tenth-century northern Iberia.*   (The Pierpont Morgan Library/Art Resource, NY)

oxcarts. The most sensational present—a white elephant—was sent in 802 by the caliph at Baghdad, Harun al-Rashid. Harun also sent Charlemagne a clock of gilded bronze with twelve mounted mechanical knights who, on the stroke of noon, emerged from twelve doors that shut behind them. Perfumes, silken tents, and oriental robes abounded. The exotic atmosphere of the court remained a vivid memory for many centuries after the glory had departed.

The Spread of Christianity

One significant cultural aspect of the early Middle Ages was the slow but bold spread of Christianity to northern lands. In the crucial centuries between the collapse of Rome in the West and the high point of church reform in the eleventh century, Christianity made significant inroads. Peter Brown's book *The Rise of Western Christendom* dramatically shows the manner in which missionaries from Rome, England, Frankland, and other areas carried the banner of a militant, warriorlike Christianity to Scandinavia and Iceland. Micro-Christendoms, to use Brown's term, emerged in northern areas of the British Isles. Further east, Christianity came to what we now know as Hungary. German expansion in the East brought western Christianity into competition with Orthodox Christianity in Bohemia and Moravia in the late ninth century. Poland was converted by Bohemian Catholic missionaries in the late tenth century, sealing the history of vast areas of central and eastern Europe into western Catholicism. The Viking rulers of Kiev chose, as we saw in an earlier chapter, orthodox Christianity after examining the advantages and disadvantages of other religions. With Christianity came books, the Bible most of all, but also a whole host of interpretative works, hagiographic literature, and other patristic literature. All of them breathed the accumulated learning of the past.

Reflecting upon the Carolingian artistic explosion as well as upon a galaxy of writers that ranges from Boethius and Pope Gregory the Great to Isidore of Seville, the Venerable Bede, and the author of *Beowulf,* no scholar would now seriously maintain that the early Middle Ages in the West were "dark." Troubled? Yes. Often agonizingly wretched? Yes; but certainly not dark.

SUMMARY

In the fifth century the structure of Roman government in the West collapsed under the pressure of invasion and migration by Germanic tribes. Much of the Roman heritage, however, was preserved by the church and the barbarians' own reverence for Roman civilization. The Franks founded the most lasting political entity to arise from the ruins of Roman power. In alliance with the papacy, the Frankish king Charles the Great (Charlemagne) sought to revive the Roman Empire in the West.

In the tenth century, Viking invasions severely disrupted Britain, Ireland, and northern France. By the year 1000 those invasions had died down, and medieval Europe had begun to take shape. Early medieval culture was a blend of Germanic and Roman influences. Most serious writing was in Latin, especially in Italy and Gaul. Latin also enjoyed a revival in eighth-century England. Literary use of the vernacular languages was rare except in England, where the remarkable epic poem *Beowulf* was written in Old English. The arts of this period combined Roman, German, and Byzantine elements. A significant artistic revival occurred under Charlemagne. The rise of Christianity also represented an important cultural watershed, leading to the spread of specific cultural forms throughout the world of Christendom.

FOUR

Medieval Society: Warriors, Peasants, and Merchants

In the last three chapters we followed the development of the West in a fairly chronological fashion. In this and subsequent chapters, while still following loosely a chronological format, we shift our narrative to a more thematic approach. This and the following chapter examine the social, economic, and religious structures of medieval Europe after the year 1000. Following chapters focus on culture and politics.

Introduction

It may be useful to summarize the story up to this point. After the collapse of the Roman Empire in the West, diverse German kingdoms struggled for supremacy in the region that we know today as western Europe. As we saw in previous chapters, Byzantium made its bid for supremacy in the West in the sixth century, and, for a brief period of time under Justinian, it sought to reunite most of the former Roman territories under imperial authority. That failed. Islam mounted its challenge in the eighth and ninth centuries, establishing its almost millennial presence in Iberia, as well as a century-long occupation of Sicily. Against this background, and often in open confrontation against Islam and Byzantium, new political entities came into being from the fifth century onward. As was discussed in the last two chapters, we must abandon the idea that these three different civilizations were monolithic. Islam split sharply along religious and political lines. Byzantium was also torn by religious controversy. Similarly, the different Germanic groups that settled within the borders of the Roman Empire developed along distinct social, political, religious, and cultural lines.

In the West, new institutions and new methods of wielding power, of production, and of social relations emerged out of the wreckage of the Carolingian Empire. What was western Europe like around the year 1000?

Europe and the World Around 1000

Around the year 1000, England was organized politically along patterns closely related to those of the original Germanic-Northmen kinship-based monarchy. Neither Ireland nor Wales had yet been conquered by the English, nor had England been conquered by the Normans. France was nominally ruled by an elected king who was feebler than his great supporters. The new king of the Franks ruled the Ile-de-France, the small region around Paris. His powers did not extend much beyond that. Germany was divided into duchies, one of which, Saxony, had asserted its supremacy and claimed the old imperial title; and Italy still remained anarchic, although the papacy had begun to revive. In the northern regions of the Iberian peninsula, a number of small Christian kingdoms—Leon-Asturias, Castile, Aragon, Navarre, and the County of Barcelona—were beginning to mount a serious challenge to Muslim power in the South. These Iberian kingdoms were—because of the exigencies of continuous warfare and the growing importance of pillaging and tribute—far more centralized than their northern counterparts. As a "society organized for war," medieval Spain also was a land in which even peasants were sometimes liable for military service and, thus, enjoyed greater freedoms. In Cordoba, the caliphate still commanded the fear of its fledgling Christian neighbors, but its downfall was just thirty years away. Portugal was not yet an independent country.

Thus, out of the debris of the Roman Empire, buffeted by two successive waves of invasions and held together only by a common Christian faith, the major political Germanic units had begun to take on certain features that we can recognize today. Elsewhere, the Scandinavian kings had imposed some semblance of order on their turbulent peoples. The great German thrust into the eastern borders of Europe was ready to get underway. In the East, the Byzantine Empire stood firm at Constantinople, despite many shocks. It had started Christianizing the Slavic peoples nearest to it—the Bulgarians, the Russians, the Serbs. But Byzantium was entering a period of uncertainty. The Macedonian dynasty was coming to a close and a new and formidable threat, that of the Seljuk Turks, would become, in a few years, a menace to the lifeline of the empire in Anatolia. In 1055, Tughril Beg, a leader of the Seljuk Turks, conquered Baghdad and established his rule throughout the Middle East and the Fertile Crescent. But these conquests did not yet affect the flow of trade along the Silk Road and the connections with India, China, and the Spice Islands; nor did they radically transform the world of Islam.

In central Europe, Hungary, a complex political entity in which Muslims, Jews, and Christians would share, as Nora Berend shows, an uneasy life, joined Catholic Europe under Stephen I's (997–1038) rule. Kievan Rus, the Viking state centered in Kiev, had embraced Christian Orthodoxy under Vladimir the Saint and became a fairly vigorous political entity and cultural center under the rule of Iaroslav (1019–1054). Poland under Boleslav the Brave advanced briefly into Bohemia and Moravia and conquered Krakow, soon to be one of the devotional centers of the Polish people. The western Slavs—Czechs, Poles, Croats, and others—and the Magyars, lying between the Germans and the influences radiating from Constantinople, had received Roman missionaries. By the year 1000, there was already visible a fateful line of demarcation between the western Catholic world and the eastern Orthodox world. This religious boundary would have an important impact for the political future of Europe. But the question must be posed again, after this lengthy interlude: What were the social and economic structures of the West?

Feudal Europe: The Structures of Everyday Life

It is all very well to speak of relative anarchy before and after Charlemagne, but what was anarchy like? What was the nature of human relations? What were the structures of everyday life and of social relations? Did everyone just slaughter everyone else indiscriminately? What were the rules that enabled life to go on, however harshly? In fact, of course, mutual arrangements allowed people to work and fight, to survive if they could, to seek out some way of assuring at least temporary security. In these arrangements we find elements surviving from Roman times, innovations introduced during the Germanic invasions, and changes linked to the conversion to Christianity. The settled inhabitants of western Europe and the invaders underwent a long and slow mutual adjustment, as new and old ways of regulating human affairs competed and often combined with each other.

Feudal society, by which is meant the complex set of customs, rights, and obligations that bound warriors (lords and vassals) to each other, and the dominant social groups (warriors and clergy) to dependant peasants, was essentially one of the ways to organize society in this period. This was, to a large extent, a response to the political fragmentation of western Europe, resulting from the demise of the Carolingian Empire and the wave of invasions. But it was also a way to extract surpluses from the land and from those below for the benefit of the ruling groups. When we speak of "feudalism," a term we try to avoid because of its elusive meaning, we mean the entire structure of society and the ties that bound lords, peasants, and clergymen into webs of mutual obligations and rights. This interconnectedness brought all men and women—except for those utterly on the margins—within Christian society. For the sake of clarity, however, we examine here each group individually.

Feudal society was long in the making, as it borrowed from the past and made practical and on-the-spot adjustments to construct a world in which some semblance of order and recognizable hierarchies of authority were present. Order was often ruthlessly enforced. But feudal society differed markedly from one geographical area to another. Traditional feudal structures prospered in the areas around Paris (the Ile-de-France), Normandy, western Germany, areas of southern France, England after the Norman invasion in 1066, what today we know as Belgium, Burgundy, and Catalonia. Feudal relationships were weakest or almost nonexistent in the northwestern

Iberian kingdoms (Leon-Asturias, Castile), Italy, Scandinavian countries, and other regions in the so-called periphery of western Europe.

We must think of feudal society as an organic whole. By the late twelfth and early thirteenth centuries, as feudal relations became undermined by the rise of a monetary and commercial economy and by the rise of feudal monarchies (which stood against the private and arbitrary arrangements of feudal western Europe), contemporary thinkers and clergymen defined the tripartite division of society. According to this ideological imagining, medieval society was divided into three distinct orders: those who pray, those who fight, and those who work. In the next chapter we look in detail at the church, but in the early sections of this chapter we focus on the other two orders. This tripartite division of society was thought to be divinely sanctioned. There were no individual rights or privileges; rather, each man or woman in the Middle Ages derived his or her rights and obligations from membership in one of the social orders. One depended on the other. There could not have been lords without peasants. After all, peasants generated the income and food to feed and keep the lords living in style. There were no peasants without a lord.

The very nature of society rested, or so it was argued, on the peasants' reliance on lordly protection. Briefly, this system of social organization was centered around some brutal facts. A few men, the knights, enjoyed a monopoly of weapons or, in the case of the clergy, a monopoly of the sacred and exercised their power or religious authority, often in violent fashion, to extract surpluses from the land. Peasants comprising as much as 95 percent of the population worked, often under exceedingly harsh and oppressive conditions, to support knights and clergymen. The knights' (the mounted soldiers) function was, in theory, to defend their own particular peasants and their respective lords. The clergymen's duty was to pray for the well-being of all Christians. In reality, the few (knights and ecclesiastics) enjoyed positions of privilege at the expense and oppression of the many (the peasants). Conditions, of course, changed from place to place. Even in areas where full feudal structures never developed or where serfdom was rare or nonexistent, peasants were bound to their lords by a series of traditional dues, work obligations, and taxes.

We must note something else. The bonds that tied one lord to another, or between lord and peasants, were private. As we indicated in the previous chapter, most of the sense of the public nature of government had disappeared in the wreckage of the Carolingian Empire. Powers of government and, more importantly, powers of justice were exercised at the local level by individual lords. The ties between lord and vassal (the warriors) were regulated by private oaths and ceremonials. The relations between a lord and his peasants were regulated by the customs of the village and by the inability of lords, because of tradition and their own limited coercive powers, to exercise their control over peasants fully or excessively. Nonetheless, because of their private nature, these relationships were arbitrary and often unpredictable. Tradition, custom, and the attempts of the church to formalize and sacralize the ties between free men, or between free men and lesser or servile men and women, provided some lessening of the harshness and brutality of the system. In theory, everyone was to do their divinely ordered duty: peasants to work, knights to fight, ecclesiastics to pray.

If everyone did what they were expected to do, then society would function harmoniously. The king, where there were kings, was the glue that bound the three orders together. This imagining of medieval society by ecclesiastical writers of the twelfth and thirteenth centuries was not always so neat. Merchants and townsmen—growing in numbers and power from 1000 onward—religious minorities, and other marginal groups presented, as shall be seen later, a serious challenge to the well-constructed and protected feudal structures. The system therefore has to be seen as a whole.

Lord and Vassal

One of the most significant precedents for the lord-vassal relationship was the war-band of the early Germans (or the *comitatus,* as Tacitus called it in Latin). In the war-band the leader commanded the loyalty of his followers, who had put themselves under his direction for fighting and for winning booty. Chief and followers consulted together before a raid or before making peace; those who disagreed might go and serve another chief. Profits and goods from war and pillage were divided among all the fighters. In the Roman provinces, too, local landowners often built their own private armies, while in Rome itself the magnates had long maintained their groups of clients, to whom they acted as patron and gave legal protection. When a humble man wanted to enter the client relationship, he asked for the *patrocinium* of the great man and secured it by performing the act of *commendation,* recommending or entrusting himself to the patron. He remained free, obtaining food and clothing in exchange for his services, whatever they might be. If the man was of the upper classes, he was called *fidelis,* a faithful man. By the Carolingian period, the term *vassus,* originally denoting a man of menial status, had come to mean a man who rendered military service to his patron, or lord. To be a *vassus,* or vassal, meant no disgrace; it was the new name for status gained by the act of commendation.

A Roman patron sometimes retained title to a piece of property but granted a client temporary use of it, together with the profits to be derived from it, as long as he held it, often for life. The Romans used the term *precarium* for this kind of tenure, and the Carolingian rulers commonly adopted the old practice, sometimes using the old Roman term, sometimes the newer term *beneficium* (benefice) to describe land temporarily held by a vassal in exchange for service. By the year 1000 the act of becoming a vassal usually meant that a man got a benefice; he might even refuse faithful service or loyalty unless he was satisfied with the land he received. In the later Carolingian period, the benefice came more often to be called a *feudum,* the term that has given us the words feudal and feudalism. When the benefice became hereditary, it also became a *fief.* Although title to the fief remained with the lord who granted it,

Pe lan deſſus dit
monſeigneur mō
le de rumeſnỹ et
monſeigr raſſe de gauires che
ualiers tous deur ſeigneurs
Se chicrue donnerent liberte⸗
et franchyſes a la ville de chia⸗
ue et aur bourgois pareille

A highly ornate book illumination (fifteenth century) shows a vassal pledging fidelity to his lord. Although the clothing would have been different in an earlier period, the gestures and rituals of enfeoffment remained the same throughout the Middle Ages. (Giraudon/Art Resource, NY)

the fief itself passed, on the death of a vassal, to the vassal's heir, who inherited with it the obligations to serve the lord and his heirs.

The benefice or fief was often granted in the form of land, but land was worthless without labor to work it. The lords or, in this case, the vassals who were given fiefs also received with them peasants who lived and worked on the lands that made up the feudal grant. This practice, too, had its precedents. In late Roman times the emperors had often granted an immunity to those residing on their own estates—an understanding that imperial tax collectors or other law-enforcing officials would stay away from the inhabitants. Because, in theory, the immunity exempted the farmers from onerous duties, it was hoped that they would enjoy their privileged status and therefore stay put and supply the emperor with predictable quantities of badly needed produce. By 332, when these expectations failed, the peasants were legally tied to the land by an imperial edict. Much later, the Frankish kings adopted some of these practices, sometimes extending it to the lands of the church and even to those of private proprietors. By the tenth century an immunity meant that the king undertook to keep his officials off the privileged lands and that the holder of the lands would himself perform such governmental functions as collecting taxes, establishing police arrangements, and setting up a court of justice.

From late Roman times, too, came the local offices of duke and count. Originally military commanders, they took over civil authority as the power of the central government diminished or collapsed. In Frankish times they were sometimes very powerful rulers, kings in all but name. In the disorders of the Carolingian decline, these offices gradually became hereditary; at the same time the dukes and counts were the vassals of the Carolingians. So the title and office, the duties of the vassal, and the fief (or territory that went with the office) all became hereditary.

As was noted earlier, feudal practices varied from place to place and developed and altered with the passage of time. In the western Iberian kingdoms, most of all in Castile, royal grants of land were given outright to vassals as reward for help in the wars against the Muslims. The word vassal itself was used indiscriminately to refer to either noblemen or peasants. With more centralized authority, the nobility had far less autonomy and independent rights of justice than in the heartlands of feudal Europe. In England, when full feudal relations were introduced after the Norman Conquest of 1066, lords held their fiefs from the king in ways that were unusual for central France. Nonetheless, certain general conceptions were accepted almost everywhere. One of the most significant was that of a feudal contract. The lord owed something to the vassal, just as the vassal owed something to the lord. When they entered into their relationship, the vassal rendered formal homage to his lord; that is, he became the lord's "man." He also promised him aid and counsel.

Aid meant that he would appear fully armed when summoned and fight as a knight in the lord's wars. This obligation was subject to limits on the number of days of service owed in any one year. As part of the aid, he might also be required, at his own expense, to entertain his lord for a visit of specific length and to give him money payments on special occasions—the marriage of the lord's eldest daughter, the knighting of his eldest son, to ransom the lord when he had been captured, and, after the late eleventh century, on the lord's departure on a crusade. Counsel meant that he would join with his fellow vassals—his peers, or social equals—to form the lord's court of justice, which alone could pass judgment on any one of them. The vassal also swore fealty (fidelity) to his lord. In his turn, the lord was understood to owe protection and maintenance to his vassal.

In theory, if the vassal broke this contract, the lord would have to get the approval of a court made up of the vassal's peers before he could proceed to a punishment, such as depriving the vassal of his fief (forfeiture). If the lord broke the contract, the vassal was expected to withdraw his homage and fealty in a public act of defiance before proceeding to open rebellion. Sometimes the contract was written; sometimes it was oral; sometimes the ceremony included a formal investiture by the lord in which he would give his kneeling vassal a symbol of the fief that was being transferred to him—a twig or a bit of earth. When lord or vassal died, the contract had to be renewed with the successor. The son of a vassal, upon succeeding to his father's fief, often had to pay relief, a special and often heavy cash payment similar to a modern inheritance tax. If the vassal died without heirs, the fief would escheat, or revert to the lord, who could bestow it on another vassal or not, as he saw fit. If the vassal's heir was still a minor, the lord exercised the right of wardship, or guardianship, until the minor came of age; this meant that the lord received the revenues from the fief, and if he was unscrupulous he could milk it dry. Widows could be forced to marry someone chosen by the lord or pay a substantial amount to avoid an unpleasant husband. In theory, the lords sought to extract as much income from the vassalitic relationship as possible. In reality, local circumstances and the natural give-and-take of daily practices determined the type and amount of payments.

The lord and vassal relation depended, in fact, on the unequal power of the participants. We should be very wary of the traditional depiction of feudal society as a pyramid. Kings around the year 1000 were either scarce or, with some of the noted exceptions, fairly powerless. Sub-infeudation (where a vassal had a vassal or many vassals of his own); allegiances to many different lords; and vassals who, as was the case of the dukes of Normandy (also the kings of England after 1066, although as kings they were not vassals for England), were far more powerful than their lord and who gave, in fact, no military service or counsel to him, made the system very complicated and confusing. If one had the means, one could challenge one's lord and get away with it. An oppressive lord could lay heavy demands on his vassals; he could also be resisted quite successfully.

At the end, the system, despite its precarious nature, prevented anarchy. One could not expect to break fealty to others continuously (to be a felon) without others breaking their oaths and obligations to oneself. Moreover, around the year 1000 the ceremonies surrounding vassalage had become highly formalized and ritualized. Free men bound themselves to each other in a language highly charged with religious symbolism and emotional content. Loyalty to one's lord was celebrated in epic poems and debated in later romances. The gestures of lordship were inscribed in manuscript illumination and other iconographic sources. These gestures and words meant a great deal. They sacralized and institutionalized the bonds that linked society together.

There were ways also to make these arrangements work. A person might receive fiefs from more than one lord, and so owe homage and fealty to both. What was he to do if one of his lords quarreled with the other and went to war? Which of his lords would have a prior right to count on his military help? This happened very often; one Bavarian count had twenty different fiefs held of twenty different lords. Gradually, therefore, there arose a new concept, that of a *liege* lord, the one to whom a vassal owed service ahead of any other. Military service could be avoided by a money payment (scutage). Lords liked that, for it gave them access to income and the possibility to hire a more reliable fighting force. At the end, the difficulties often persisted. Even though feudal law became more subtle and more complex, as was indicated earlier, arms and might ultimately counted far more than legality. At the end, it was about power, the power of one lord over another, the power of the lords over the peasantry.

Lord and Peasant

The complex and highly ritualized arrangements of power directly between lord and vassal involved only the governing class who fought on horseback (the knights) and whose fiefs consisted of landed property known as manors, estates, or villages. Even if we include their dependents, the total would hardly reach 10 percent of the population of western Europe. Most of the other 90 percent of the people worked the land. In late Roman times, the large estate, owned by a magnate and worked by tenant farmers, had been called a *latifundium*. The tenant farmers, or *coloni*, were often descendants of small landowners who had turned over their holdings to the magnate in exchange for a guarantee of protection and a percentage of the crop. While the *coloni* were not slaves, Constantine's Edict of the Colonate (332) forbade them to leave the ground they cultivated, nor could their children leave either, legally binding them to the land. Although this may seem the most obvious origin of medieval peasant servitude, the medieval peasantry was forged from a variety of circumstances. We are not far wrong if we think of the late Roman latifundium becoming the medieval village or manor and the late Roman *coloni* becoming the medieval serfs, but the social revolution created by the rise of a mounted military class and of new kind of warfare also transformed the social structure of Germanic kingdoms. Some of the warriors rose to the ranks of lords and vassals. Some ended up as peasants.

Medieval peasants occupied a range of social categories. For the sake of brevity, we may classify them as free or unfree (serfs). Freedom, of course, meant something very different than what it means for us. The distinction was whether the peasant was tied to the land or not, whether his status was hereditary (inherited through the mother) or not. Were we to be transported back in time to a medieval village or manor in the eleventh century, we would have great difficulties in determining who was free and who was not. In reality, some serfs were better off than free peasants, with more access to land, better working conditions, and more wealth. But the differences depended on a large number of variables: size of family, how many surviving children one had, location, individual lords' demands, and the like. Both free and unfree toiled under heavy obligations. They both worked for the lord or lords (many villages were divided among different lords and the peasants may have owed work and dues to several lords). Most of all, the peasants owed

This fourteenth-century book illumination shows a plowman working the land. The illustration shows the typical wheeled plow, pulled by horses, employed in northern Europe from the tenth century onward. (Giraudon/Art Resource, NY)

work to their lords (remember that these lords could be vassals to another lord). The number of days of work owed varied according to custom, season, and amount of land held. Free and servile peasants paid a census, a rent for the use of the land. They paid a tenth of their production, theoretically to the church, but in this period mostly to the lords. Peasants were also liable for occasional work, for cleaning roads, for rebuilding structures (*corvée*), for providing lodging for their lords, and for aids that paralleled those given by the vassal to his lord (on the occasion of their lord's daughter's marriage, his son's knighting, ransoming, and crusades).

As if this was not enough, both free and servile peasants paid to their secular and ecclesiastical lords a fee for the right to inherit their meager possessions. They also paid for the right to grind their grain or press their wine in villages where lords exercised their bans (monopoly) over these facilities. Woods and game in the forest also belonged to the lords. Serfs had additional financial obligations. They paid for the right to marry outside the village. Most symbolic of their status, at the time of his marriage, a male serf paid a head tax as a recognition of his bondage, and a fee in lieu of the lord's right to the first night with the bride. The latter was a right found only in places of oppressive lordship, and there is no evidence that it was ever enforced. The lords, who could and often did behave as sexual predators, preferred a financial compensation instead.

We should attempt to capture, even if briefly, the sense of rural life. Peasants worked together or died separately. No peasant ever lived in isolation, and their lives were bound tightly around the village. Most medieval villages or hamlets—from small concentrations of population of ten to fifteen families to very large villages with as many as a thousand inhabitants—were a collection of ill-made huts with dirt floors. The cycle of planting, haymaking, harvesting, and vintage paralleled the liturgical calendar. Winter crops were planted in late fall. The vintage took place no later than St. Michael's Day (29 September). Taxes and village dues were paid by St. Michael's Day or by St. Martin's Day (11 November). On the latter day, the stubble that remained on the arable land was burned to provide some nutrients to the soil. Animals that could not be kept through the winter were slaughtered and turned into salted meat or sausages. By 2 February, the feast of Candlemas, as the harshness of winter began to wane, the cycle began again with the preparation of the fields and the planting of the spring crops. St. John's Feast (23 June) was the beginning of harvesting and haymaking, which continued through August. Vintage began once again in September.

This cycle varied in Mediterranean Europe or in the northmost parts of Europe. Social conditions differed in other parts of Europe. In Castile, to give an example, peasants were not tied to the soil. The repopulation of the frontier had given them greater freedoms, but this did not necessarily mean release from financial and work obligations. In Old Catalonia (the northern parts of the county), servile obligations were strengthened in the thirteenth century, at a time when servitude was waning in the rest of western Europe. It is difficult to calculate how heavy was the burden imposed on the peasantry. Depending on location, one may assume that as much as 50 percent of a peasant's income went to his lords or to ecclesiastical masters (in church lands). In some places, the obligations were more onerous. Famines were quite common and localized. The rate of infant mortality was appallingly high. In time of need, infanticide, especially female infanticide, was not rare. One cannot convey fully the harshness of peasants' lives. Theirs was a world of fear, and life was lived on the edge of doom. A turn in the weather, a war, or an epidemic meant instant catastrophe.

Peasants were caught in an inexorable biological cycle. When young women began to menstruate (as late as fifteen years old or even later), they were expected to assume their God-given role as mothers (while still working the fields). One pregnancy followed another since there were no reliable forms of contraception, and the church preached continuously the sanctity of reproduction. Children died at an appalling rate, as did mothers. In some parts of Europe, the children were often buried at the door's threshold, a throwback to systems of belief predating Christianity. Life was short and brutish, to quote an English philosopher of a later age. Nearby forests were the refuge of truculent brigands, coal-makers, and other undesirable types.

Nonetheless, village customs and traditions provided a modicum of protection for the peasants. Serfdom itself could be seen as a status laden with religious significance. Many gave themselves into servitude to monasteries in highly symbolic ceremonies. But remember, a serf was not a slave. There were still slaves in Europe, mostly in the Mediterranean world, but serfs had rights, limited as they were. There was also not as clear a distinction between gender roles. Men and women worked the fields side by side. Women, in many cases, worked holdings of their own and paid rents to lords. In some areas, as late as the thirteenth century, the frequent use of matronymics tell us of the enduring role of women in village society. Children also worked side by side with their parents from a very tender age. Adulthood, if one was lucky (or unlucky) enough to survive the first year, came swiftly. Death also came swiftly as well. Modern young people cannot imagine what it is to lose teeth very early in life, to look as if one was sixty years old when barely thirty. In a world without antibiotics, infections could be fatal. In a world without analgesics, pain was a constant fact of life. Yet, there was some solace.

Most of all, the village was a community, one in which a rough equality existed among its inhabitants. If one held land and had a household, if one was a "citizen of the village," then one had access to common pasture lands, rights to the use of the woods—an important place for keeping pigs, for picking up brush and fallen limbs to stoke one's hearth, and for some small hunting to complement the peasant's meager diet. The peasants' fare was monotonous and seldom sufficient. Their usual diet consisted of bread, some bacon from time to time (eaten in a stew), some cheese, some greens, and badly watered-down wine or beer in the north. The universal crops were wheat (to be given to lords, who loved wheat bread), barley, rye, and oats. Lords and monks ate white bread; peasants ate black bread. There was some justice after all, since the bread the peasants ate was, unbeknownst to them, more nutritious than that of the lords. Grapes were cultivated wherever possible for the importance of wine in the liturgy of the mass and for its significance in the rituals of hospitality. Where viticulture was impossible, beer or mead (a wicked concoction made of fermented honey) was made to provide some solace from the harshness of life. Most importantly the peasants, whether free or unfree, had rights to their lands. They could not be evicted. The land belonged to the lords, but peasants were so bound to the land that, in a sense, it was theirs. In time, far beyond the Middle Ages, this de facto occupation and claims did become legal rights of ownership.

In the period around 1000, a medieval village usually produced only what was needed to feed its own population. The oldest method of cultivation was the two-field system, typical of the Mediterranean world and the classical period, alternating crops and fallow so that the fertility of the soil could be recovered. Later, especially in grain-producing areas in the north, a three-field system was devised—one field for spring planting, one for autumn planting, and the third lying fallow. Elsewhere—in the mountains, in wine-growing areas, in the "Celtic fringes" of Brittany and Wales, and in the new areas of pioneer settlement in eastern lands—there were many variant agricultural techniques and social arrangements. In the South, where the soils were thin and poor, the three-field system never made any serious inroads. Here, as so often was the case, there was no "typical" medieval way.

In the village, oxen had originally pulled the plow (although in poor villages cows and even humans also did the work), but the invention of the
horse collar and the use of horseshoes helped make it possible to substitute
horses for oxen (mostly in the North), although this was not as common as
once believed. So did the increasing use of tandem harnessing, enabling the
horses to work in single file instead of side by side. A heavy-wheeled plow
also made its appearance in northern regions, where the heavy soils allowed
for that type of device. Once again, the pattern of agricultural settlement varied from region to region. Insofar as a "typical" village existed, each of its
peasant families had holdings, usually scattered long strips of land in the
large open fields. In theory, this gave each family a bit of the good arable land,
a bit of the less good land, a bit of woodland, and so on. The strips might be
separated from each other by narrow, unplowed *balks*, but there were no
fences, walls, or hedges in northern Europe, although in the South, fences
and short, crisscrossed cultivation of the land were the norm. The village lord
or lords had their own strips, or *demesne* (perhaps a quarter to a third of the
land), reserved for the production of the food that their households needed.
It was understood that the peasants had to work this demesne land for the
lords, often three days a week throughout the year, except perhaps in harvest
time, when the lords could command their services until the crops were
safely in the barns.

Undoubtedly the bulk of the hours of labor on the village went directly into
farming, mostly grain farming. But some of the manor's inhabitants were
also craftsmen, such as blacksmiths or tanners, and they, too, cultivated their
own plots of land. Sometimes a village had at least one church of its own,
with a priest. If the lord was a great lord, he might have several priests,
including his own chaplain for the household and a village priest for the local
church, but only after the reform of the church in the eleventh century did
Christianity come to all villages. Peasant beliefs were a complex mixture of
some vague notions of Christianity and their own long-held pre-Christian
traditions. We now know that practices harkening back to the earliest agricultural cults survived in western Europe into the modern age.

The organization of the countryside by villages or manors represented a
survival from late Roman times, and it developed earliest, in its new
medieval forms, in eastern France and in parts of Italy and Germany. Within
the Roman heartland in the West, the old Roman landlord's economic power
over his tenants had fused with the traditional Germanic village chief's political power and with the governing rights that the lord received with his fief.
Custom prevailed in the lord's court of justice, where he or his steward sat in
judgment on the serf-tenants and free peasants, enforcing the traditional
rules of the village community. No village was totally isolated. All peasants
had access to the outside world. The iron for agricultural implements had to
be bought, as was salt, and often such luxuries as furs or occasional spices
had to be bought also. The village, then, had surpluses and deficiencies that
gave it the motivation and the means for trade with outsiders. Above all, the
village generated income for the lords. Peasant dues were paid mostly in

kind, and the amount of coinage or commercial exchanges was quite limited around the year 1000. After 1000, dues continued to be paid mostly in kind, but over the next three centuries payment in species (coins, money) became widespread throughout most the medieval West.

The Feudal Revolution and the Expansion of the Arable

We must emphasize, once again, that our description of feudal society in the previous paragraphs is essentially a model. Around the year 1000, this static view of feudal society was being dramatically altered. Although not all historians agree, Georges Duby, Pierre Bonnassie, Thomas Bisson, and others have argued for or against whether the transformations of European society around the year 1000 were a "mutation" (a slow transformation) or whether they amounted to what has been described in a famous article by Bisson as a "feudal revolution." In the latter formulation, lesser lords, vassals in fact, began to build their power and control over the countryside. Castles lay at the center of this revolution, as these lords, the castellans or keepers of the castle, used these strong places to terrorize and extort nearby peasants. These lords developed a new discourse of power and lordship, as they imposed harsh duties and obligations on their dependant peasantry, or worse, as they enserfed previously free peasant populations. Peasants' complaints to a distant king, or the church's attempts to deal with the new levels of violence through the preaching of the Truce of God (which banned lords from warfare in certain days of the week) or the Leagues of Peace (armed bands of knights, burghers, and even peasants attempting to restore peace to the countryside and punish predatory lords), are just a few examples of the new conditions that transformed feudal society. Part of the controversy surrounding whether there was a mutation or a revolution focuses on the extent of lordly power against the peasantry. As Bisson has shown in a recent book about the complaints of Catalan peasants against their lords, violence was real and ever present.

At the same time, the year 1000 witnessed the culmination of an expansion of the arable and the victory of new agricultural technologies, some of them dating to the eighth century. New lands came into cultivation; new villages were founded. Some of the new technological innovations mentioned earlier—the horse collar, the heavy plow, the three-field system, the cultivation of legumes—and milder weather increased food production dramatically. New villages were founded, and the population increased. Peasants' lives, despite the new types of harsh lordship emerging in some areas of western Europe, improved in some regions. Lords found it more profitable to enter into different economic agreements with their peasants—crop-sharing, rental of lands—than to be caught up in fixed customary rents at a time of a slow inflation. New economic conditions were translated into greater freedoms for the peasantry. Beyond the rural world, towns began to emerge. We will soon examine what this meant for European society, economy, and culture, but for now, new forms of lordship, an increase in food production and peasants' rights, and the rise of towns and the bourgeoisie were harbingers of change.

Urban Societies

We must remember that great cities existed in this period in the Islamic and Byzantine world. Cordoba was a very large metropolis, as were Alexandria, Constantinople, and the fabled Baghdad. Larger cities existed in the East and in Central America and the Yucatan peninsula. This was not the case in tenth-century northern Europe. But after the year 1000, towns began to emerge into being for a variety of reasons. Castles, which began to spread throughout the western European countryside in the eleventh century, became, because of the protection they offered against random violence, a magnet for population. Peasants, still tending their fields within eyesight of the castle's walls, built their huts in the vicinity. The castle also provided employment: servants to tend to the soldiers, inns, blacksmiths, and other trades necessary for warfare. A bishop's see, that is, the town where a bishop had his church (a cathedral) and the site for the cathedral chapter (usually as many as forty canons with their respective families and attendants), and the bishop's ecclesiastical court also generated enough business and jobs to attract settlers. Pilgrimage sites, such as Vezelay, Conques (in France), Compostela (in Spain), and others, or towns along a popular pilgrimage route became new centers of population. This was certainly the case of the roads that led to the tomb of the apostle St. James in Compostela. The many pilgrims crowding the feeder roads that, through France, Aragon, and Castile, led to the shrine of St. James prompted the emergence of new towns or to the revival of old foundations. In them, pilgrims often settled and took trades. Businesses to tend to the pilgrims' needs came into being. Country people migrated to the new economic opportunities available in urban centers and bolstered the population of the new towns.

The Bourgeoisie

Most of all, the true origins of towns in western Europe and of their dynamic role in medieval society came from merchants and artisans. Itinerant merchants had kept the ties of trade alive in western Europe. This had been, at best, a modest enterprise, as they brought the most indispensable of goods— salt, iron, a few spices—into the most remote of locations. By the eleventh century, merchants began to settle in the outskirts of nascent towns. Settling in the burgh (a German term), these *bourgeois*—merchants and craftsmen— injected a new element into feudal society. These were people who lived from the exchange of goods, who were not tied to the soil, and who made profits out of selling their wares. Those contemporaries writing on the social orders as late as the fourteenth century still insisted that urban dwellers were just another component of the tripartite organization of society, to be classified among those who work. But the reality was very different. Towns became islands of freedom in a sea of feudal obligations. The German saying "Stadtlufte Macht Frei" ("The air of the city makes you free") captures precisely what urban centers represented. A serf who fled to a city and lived in it for a year and a day became a free man or a free woman.

The development of urban society is a complex topic, and here we offer a simplified account of its development from its origins in western Europe to the thirteenth century. First and foremost, few towns truly developed as commercial or manufacturing centers. Most towns remained overgrown villages, and most of the inhabitants still depended on agricultural work for their survival, but, and this is a big caveat, they did so while enjoying the freedoms of the city and often were exempted from feudal obligations. Only a few regions witnessed an intense urban life with manufacturing and trade underpinning urban developments. Towns in Flanders, Hainault, and Brabant (areas that are today in northern France or southern Belgium), such as Lille, Arras, Ghent, Bruges, and others, became great producers of textiles, importing wool from England and, after the 1350s, from Castile. Italy always had cities, for the Roman urban tradition always waxed strongly there. Florence, Naples (always a large city), Milan, Venice, Genoa, and Rome, which experienced a revival after the newly found power of the papacy in the late eleventh century, were large cities, functioning as either administrative and liturgical centers, as was the case with Rome, or as industrial (Florence) or commercial hubs (Venice and Genoa). These towns could reach very large populations. Florence may have had as many as 100,000 inhabitants in the late thirteenth century, as did Paris. Most towns, however, did not exceed 5,000 to 10,000. Burgos, an important mercantile center in northern Castile, probably had between 6,000 and 8,000 inhabitants in the late thirteenth century. London never reached more than 30,000 in the late Middle Ages.

Urban Society, Economy, and Culture

Although the cities began as places of freedom, they soon ceased to be so. Throughout most medieval towns, three types of struggle went on simultaneously. The first involved the growing social differences that developed within towns as patrician elites were formed. In theory, all the town's inhabitants were equal. They were collectively under the jurisdiction of the town's lord (the king, a powerful nobleman, a bishop, or a monastery). In reality, from the eleventh century onward, social and economic distinctions began to emerge. Those with a house within the city walls and with enough income to pay taxes became "citizens" of the town, with franchise and rights. They were able to elect town officials and to serve in the governance of the town. Those without enough income and without a house of their own in the city became disfranchised. From among the franchised citizens, the well-to-do merchants and artisans became an elite at the top. By the late twelfth century throughout most towns in western Europe, this small group came to monopolize urban political and economic life. A few families, organized as extensive clans or familial networks, gained a monopoly on power within the city. Their clothes and manners (aping those of the nobility), their membership in social and pious confraternities, and their lavish display of their superiority through festivals and processions (in which they rode on horseback) were part of a complex discourse of power and difference that marked their social

This late fifteenth-century view of Florence, one of the largest western European medieval cities, shows the landscape of a sizable urban center. Note the urban sprawl extending on both sides of the Arno river, the prominence of Florence's medieval walls, and the Ponte Vecchio. (New York Public Library Picture Collection)

and political hegemony within the city. This did not happen everywhere at the same time or in the same manner, but with very few exceptions, urban government became oligarchical, as a small group of people, the bourgeoisie or patrician elites, accumulated power.

The second struggle paralleled the first. Throughout most of western Europe, towns rose in rebellion against their lords in the eleventh and twelfth centuries. In towns like Laon, Compostela, Sahagún, and others, the bourgeois stormed the bishop's palace, established communes, and asked for their liberties. In most cases they succeeded. Cities stood against and outside the feudal world, undermining, through their money economy and new mentality, the traditional society of orders. Medieval writers, as mentioned earlier, went on with the fiction that their society was neatly arranged into three orders, and sought to lump merchants and artisans with peasants. It did not work. The third struggle followed from the first. If feudal society was the enemy of urban enterprise and freedom, then the rising monarchs of the twelfth century and afterward were the natural allies of the bourgeoisie and vice versa. Since kings sought to weaken the power of the feudal nobility, they found a ready-made ally in the towns. In exchange for charters and tax privileges for the town and for the patrician elites, the Crown gained access to the towns' financial resources and to their military support. Urban militias acquitted themselves very well against noble armies. This is a little known aspect of medieval life. In Reconquest Iberia, urban contingents carried the burden of the struggle against the Muslims and stood as defenders of the Crown against the violence and rapacity of the high nobility. They did so as well in Italy and the Low Countries, although there, urban contingents fought for their own particular cities' well-being rather than for the Crown. In Italy, the Italian urban armies routed the imperial forces, gaining a de facto independence from imperial control in the twelfth century. In other parts of Europe, the king guaranteed the peace of the roads, the movement of commerce, and, most importantly, the status and privileges of the urban ruling elites.

All these political and social developments were made possible by the dynamics of money and profit. Great fairs—those of Champagne are the most famous—lured merchants from all over Europe. The fairs led to the development of banking and to large regional economies of scale. In these developments the Italians were at the vanguard. Italian merchants linked eastern Mediterranean markets with the West. Similarly, Muslim and Jewish merchants, trading out of Alexandria and other Muslim commercial centers, carried on an energetic trade with Muslim Spain and, through Spain, with Africa and the rest of Europe. Merchants on the Silk Road continued to bring eastern luxury goods and rich spices into the West until trade was disrupted by the Mongol invasion in the thirteenth century. By the late twelfth century, merchants carried wine from Gascony (Bordeaux) to England. Castilian sailors took hides, honey, and tallow to England and Flanders. By that century, the Genoese had formidable mercantile and banking outpost in Muslim Seville, and the Venetians were important intermediaries in East-West commercial exchanges. The rise of Venice as a great commercial power would lead in 1204 to the capture of Constantinople by the armies—prompted by Venetian insistence—of the Fourth Crusade.

Within the cities a number of trades were practiced. Master craftsmen organized themselves into guilds. Guilds are not at all the equivalent of unions today. They were conservative associations, formed to prevent unfair competition and to regulate the quality and production of goods. Beyond their economic aspects, guilds played an important role in the social and religious lives of townsmen. In pre-Medici Florence, the guilds, the *artes,* controlled the government of the city. Women worked in many of the trades. Most of the public baking of bread and the brewing of beer for sale was done by women. We find women working as dyers, weavers, and in many other occupations, although women's guild membership was rare indeed. In fact, women were some of the earliest victims of the towns' political, social, and economic stratification, as they were progressively pushed to the economic and social margins of medieval society.

The presence of urban capital also had important economic and cultural consequences. The bourgeois began to invest heavily in the land market. Most of the leading city dwellers had houses in the nearby countryside, in the vast hinterland or *contado* (the Italian word) ruled by the city. In the villages under the town's jurisdiction, the bourgeois began to build sizable estates. They provided food for the owner's table in the cities, as well as the prestige associated with land-owning. The consequences for the village community were nefarious. By the early fourteenth century, social stratifications began to be noticeable within villages as well. For the bourgeois, or at least for some of them, rural estates also signaled their first step in their ascent to a noble status, either through marriage, purchase, or royal grant.

A monetary economy, profit, and urban life itself had important cultural consequences. Many cities became sites of culture. Universities, emerging in the twelfth century as shall be seen later, were intensely urban places. The children of the bourgeoisie flocked to these new centers of learning. They joined the church and bent it to their purposes, developing new forms of spirituality. The rise of the Mendicant Orders in the early thirteenth century (see later) is a manifestation of this new bourgeois search for salvation and for new ways of relating to the sacred. Jacques Le Goff, one of the greatest French medievalists of the last fifty years, has already shown us how merchants developed a new sense of time: merchants' time, standing in opposition to the idea of church time or God's time. If a merchant could charge extra for the time it took to carry goods from one location to another, then time was measurable in novel and disturbing ways. Time is money. Workers in the nascent industrial centers of medieval Europe worked according to different schedules from peasants in the fields. Time was no longer measured by the singing of canonical hours through the day, a sacred measuring of time. Clock towers, emerging throughout medieval towns by the late thirteenth and fourteenth centuries, served as a vivid reminder of the new secular meaning of time.

There was more. Since merchants and craftsmen were in business to make money, and wealth, so the Gospel said, was a sure way to hell, then new ways of securing salvation were needed. Out of the intense bourgeois preoccupation for the salvation of their individual souls, purgatory was born in the twelfth century. The idea of an intermediate place between heaven and hell already existed, but purgatory did not acquire its spatial character until, as Le Goff has shown, the twelfth century. With new notions of purgatory came new ways of deploying bourgeois wealth through wills. These legacies sought to secure either remission for one's sins or a shorter stay in purgatory. The lower nobility and the bourgeoisie entered into an intense negotiation for their souls, making pious donations, asking for masses, and distributing their wealth through their wills to a large number of ecclesiastical institutions.

Urban dwellers were the first to think of property in new ways and to deal with the rising number of the poor, now often degraded and denied the spiritual blessings of poverty, in new and harsher ways. Urban cultural and political life was in many ways revolutionary, marking the beginning of a long process that concluded with the ultimate victory of the bourgeoisie during the French Revolution.

On the Margins of Society

It may not be proper to think of certain social groups as outside society. In western medieval Europe, religious minorities (Jews and Muslims), heretics, the ill, and criminals were pushed with increasing virulence to the margins of society. Jews could be found throughout most of Christian society, but Jews and Muslims were found, most of all, in the Iberian peninsula and, to a lesser extent, Sicily. Their social and economic roles were often restricted by law. In most countries in western Europe, Jews engaged in money lending, practiced medicine, or worked in commercial and artisanal activities usually circumscribed to business with their coreligionists. In Castile and the Crown of Aragon, however, Jews were found in diverse economic pursuits: as farmers, merchants, artisans, doctors, royal agents, and money lenders. Jews were victims of sporadic violence, and anti-Jewish sentiment and outright persecution began to rise at the waning of the twelfth century. In paradoxical ways, the kings, great lords, and high dignitaries of the church sought to protect the Jews. They belonged to the king, to the lords, or to the bishops and were an important source of income. Moreover, in theory, the church did not admit forced conversions of Jews. Nonetheless, the decrees of the Fourth Lateran Council (1215) forced Jews to wear an identifying mark on their clothing. Jews were expelled from England in 1290, and it has been calculated that around sixteen thousand Jews left England. They were expelled from some parts of France in 1306, from southern Italy between 1288 and 1294, and from Spain in 1492. Ghettoes, however, did not officially appear in western Europe until the sixteenth century.

Muslims could be found in great numbers in western Europe only in Iberia. The fairly fluid relationship between Christians and religious minorities in what we call Spain today also experienced a change for the worse after the early thirteenth century. As the Christians gained the upper hand in the peninsula, restrictive and punitive legislation began to set rigid, and dangerous, boundaries between the dominant group (the Christians) and those below them. As for heretics, the ill, and the poor, they all were, in some manner or another, part of Christian society. As such, they all played a role in the moral economy of salvation. Even heretics needed to be reintegrated into Christian society or punished and excluded. Again, as was the case with Jews and Muslims, heretics, the ill (mostly lepers), and the poor increasingly became targets for persecution or segregation within Christian society. The end of the twelfth century and the early thirteenth century marked a radical change in the manner in which those who were different were either severely punished (death by fire for relapsed heretics) or excluded from the community of Christians.

The Changing Status of Women

Women are a difficult group to discuss, and they should not be placed as separate from men when discussing social and economic structures. Nonetheless, here we make a few observations as to the manner in which some women gained important footholds in medieval society, while others saw their status diminished. Women cannot be included rightly among those on the margins of society. Unlike heretics, lepers, Jews, or Muslims, women occupied a variety of positions dependent on their place in the social order, wealth, locale, age, and many other factors. Although patriarchy and misogyny waxed strong throughout the Middle Ages, the status of an aristocratic woman or a female member of the royal family was incommensurably higher and better than that of a male peasant or artisan. The intersection of gender, class, ethnicity, and religion yielded many different types.

We already know that women played a significant role in the rural economy and that they also held similar positions in urban crafts and shopkeeping. We find women, even Muslim and Jewish women, running small shops in Iberian towns and working as healers and even as small money lenders. We also have numerous examples of women who, either as regents or as queens, ran the affairs of government and did so very well. In Castile women could and did inherent the throne. Urraca was queen of Castile-Leon at the end of the eleventh and beginning of the twelfth centuries with mixed results. Isabella who ruled in the late fifteenth century was probably the best ruler Castile ever had. She was certainly no pushover and kept her consort, Ferdinand of Aragon, from interfering in Castilian affairs without her consent. Blanche, queen and regent of France for her son, Louis IX, in the first half of the thirteenth century, was a formidable ruler and mother. Her sister, Berenguela, played the same role in early thirteenth-century Castile. Both cousins, Louis IX of France and Ferdinand III of Castile, ended up as saints and as exemplary kings. A great deal of their successes were the result of their respective mothers' iron hands. Eleanor of Aquitaine's career is very well known, and she had the power of her great possessions in Aquitaine to support her imperious ways.

Women, then, could and did hold power, and these examples are only the most distinguished from a long list of women who held power or exercised it behind the scenes. Some of them, as shall be seen, also excelled in learning and piety, but these examples do not change the fundamental manner in which women were subordinate to males, in which for many of them the cloister or marriage were the only options. In most places, with the exception of Iberia and some Italian regions, the law limited their right to property and inheritance. Custom and religious ordinances excluded them from attending universities or other places of learning until the modern age. They were also excluded from the celebration of the mass and, aside from some very powerful abbesses and saints, were subordinate to men in the ecclesiastical hierarchy. It was, in Charles Radding's formulation, a world made by men and, one could add, for the benefit of men. How did all this work out at the end?

Courtly love emphasized feminine nobility and erotic play, while the cult of the Virgin Mary glorified virginity (see later). But the role of women was changing, and those changes were, as indicated earlier, related to social status. The peasant's wife worked as a partner to her husband in the fields, while the lady of the castle did not. The wife of the peasant was recognized as rendering service, and daughters could inherit land in some parts of western Europe. In the early Middle Ages women of childbearing age were in short supply, and this enhanced their value in marriage, so that they could demand a larger dowry from prospective husbands. Noble families, wealthy town dwellers, and the more prosperous peasants had more children than the poor did. As infant mortality was high, large families were essential.

If the chivalric ideal enhanced the position of women, changes in the church offset any advances. Gregorian reforms in the late eleventh century, with their emphasis on clerical celibacy—long an official although unenforced church policy—meant that members of the clergy no longer took wives. Women lost their status in parish activities. As bishops became more powerful, no female position of similar authority developed. Earlier, when monasteries were so central to the church, women had been prioresses and abbesses of important nunneries; now church leadership became increasingly male. To escape from this dominance, convents were established throughout the thirteenth century, but they were made subordinate to the male religious orders. Some women fled to heretical groups, notably the Waldensians and Cathars, in order to preach and administer the sacraments.

Perhaps the best-known figure associated with this trend is Hildegard of Bingen (1098–1179). Born near Mainz, she experienced a mystical vision before she was five years old, and her parents placed her in a nunnery when she was eight. She became head of her convent and a mystic of extraordinary visions, which, when she recorded them, so impressed Pope Eugenius I (1145–1153) that she was encouraged to preach, found new convents, and perform exorcisms. She composed a cycle of seventy-seven sacred songs in plainchant, wrote at length on medicine and natural history, and attained the informal status of a saint. She also acknowledged human sexuality to a degree unusual for her time, refuted the popular idea that women felt lust more than men did, and admitted women to church services while they were menstruating, which most male religious leaders did not. Far more important, Hildegard emphasized the role of Eve and Mary in the economy of salvation. Jesus had been born of a woman, and Mary's intercession erased Eve's fault by begetting a redeemer. Thus Hildegard granted a centrality to the Virgin Mary and, by extension, to women that was crucial in the development of the representation of Jesus as Mother, to paraphrase the title of one of Caroline Bynum's books, and the role of women's spirituality in the church.

By the fourteenth century the male-female balance in population had been reversed. There were more women than men in Italy by the thirteenth century. Women of that period also controlled more wealth, and they therefore needed to know how to read and to calculate, so their education was extended beyond handicrafts, especially among the rich merchant class. Upper-class women were usually willing to play the roles assigned to them, however, since this would assure both salvation and inheritance. Since Christianity associated nakedness with shame and sexual licentiousness, society developed strong dress signals to distinguish between the sexes at a glance. In the thirteenth century this need to obscure the body was combined with an aesthetic impulse to initiate through tailoring a concept of "fashion," which in turn became related to luxury. Although the role of women was ambivalent and changing, two developments brought the idea of womanhood into prominence. First, as has been seen, was the rise of the veneration of the Virgin Mary, which began in the ninth century and reached extraordinary

The Written Record

WOMEN OF THE GENTLE CLASS

Robert of Blois, a thirteenth-century poet, wrote of the correct behavior for women "of the gentle class."

En route to church or elsewhere, a lady must walk straight and not trot or run, or idle either. She must salute even the poor. She must let no one touch her on the breast except her husband. For that reason, she must not let anyone put a pin or a brooch on her bosom.

No one should kiss her on the mouth except her husband. If she disobeys this injunction, neither loyalty, faith nor noble birth will avert the consequences.

Women are criticized for the way they look at people, like a sparrowhawk ready to pounce on a swallow. Take care: glances are messengers of love; men are prompt to deceive themselves by them. . . .

A lady does not accept gifts. For gifts which are given you in secret cost dear; one buys them with one's honor. There are, however, honest gifts which it is proper to thank people for.

Above all, a lady does not scold. Anger and high words are enough to distinguish a low woman from a lady. The man who injures you shames himself and not you; if it is a woman who scolds you, you will break her heart by refusing to answer her.

Women must not swear, drink too much or eat too much. . . .

Ladies with pale complexions should dine early. Good wine colors the face. If your breath is bad, hold it in church when you receive the blessing. . . .

Cut your fingernails frequently, down to the quick, for cleanliness' sake. Cleanliness is better than beauty.

From *Life in a Medieval City* by Joseph and Frances Gies. Copyright © 1969 by Joseph and Frances Gies. Reprinted by permission of Harper-Collins Publishers.

heights by the twelfth century, when the Virgin was more likely to be the subject of an artist than was Jesus or the apostles. Second was the celebration of courtly love and its accompanying forms of "manly combat" by the troubadours in France and Germany.

Because women participated in many significant ways in the spiritual movements of the twelfth century, their role became more significant within the medieval Christian tradition. It is also clear that, as noted earlier, in certain places women of the aristocracy were vigorously conducting affairs of state and church as early as the tenth century. But it is also clear that as medieval society entered a series of long systemic crises in the early fourteenth century, many of the gains made by some women deteriorated. The unabashed misogyny of the revived courtly literature (see later) of the fourteenth and fifteenth centuries was a harbinger of even worse things to come.

The Middle Ages concluded with the *Malleus Maleficarum Hammer of Witches*, 1486), the opening salvo in the persecution of witches (mostly women) and in the misogynist nightmare into which European society descended in the early modern period. But that was still in the future.

SUMMARY

Feudal society was the system of social and political arrangements that replaced the centralized Roman administration. Basically, it was a means of coping with the absence of strong central government and of extracting income from a servile or semi-servile peasantry. Local lords ruled over the peasants on their estates. In turn, these lords were the vassals of other lords, meaning that they owed them allegiance and services. Still other lords might be above these. This complex system varied from one part of Europe to another.

Most of Europe was organized into units called villages or manors, owned and ruled by a noble (or several nobles) or by the church. Many of the peasants on these manors were serfs, hereditary laborers who could not leave the land they worked. In return for protection given by the lord of the manor, the serfs were required to fulfill various obligations and hand over part of their crops. In time, many lords came to prefer cash payments, so that they could purchase goods that the manor could not produce.

The European economy and population began to expand in the eleventh century. New technology such as the windmill, the three-field system, and the heavy plow led to increased food production. Towns grew with increased trade and the growth of a money economy. The role of women improved, as more women came to be educated and to control property. But this improvement in the position of women was countered by rising restrictions and misogyny.

FIVE

Those Who Pray: Priests, Monks, and Crusaders

Those Who Pray

The medieval church was deeply imbedded within the feudal structures. Monasteries and churches often depended on servile labor. Ecclesiastics were vassals and lords, holding lands and jurisdictions from other lords. Beyond the obvious spiritual gains to be made from a close association with the sacred, lords benefited from their close economic and social ties with the church. If lordly families controlled the church, as they often did before the final victory of the reform movement in the late eleventh century, they could provide ecclesiastical benefices and dignities for their relatives and retainers. They could also tap into the financial resources of the church. Moreover, in the violent world of the central Middle Ages, the rituals of Christianity and the sacralization of feudal ceremonies provided legitimacy for lordly violence and oppression. But the bonds that linked churchmen and secular lords worked to the advantage of the church as well. In perilous times, great lords provided protection from the violence of everyday life, and through their donations and wills, lords gave to the church vast landholdings and steady income.

We must emphasize, once again, the extent to which the church was imbricated in the feudal world and vice versa. Nonetheless, from the tenth century onward, the Peace of God (which forbade feudal lords from fighting on Christian holidays, on Sundays, or on the eve of such days), the Leagues of Peace (leagues of urban dweller, knights, and even peasants formed under the sponsorship of the church to attack exceptionally violent or arbitrary lords), the reforms pioneered by Cluny and other monastic centers, and the growing importance of the sacraments (and those who administered them, the priests) drove a wedge between laity and clergy. This represented a veritable revolution in the manner in which men and women experienced religion throughout the West.

This linking of the spiritual with the materiality and violence of the feudal world did not serve the church well, and the growing split became focused on a few issues that were perceived as diminishing church's efficacy and its ability to minister to Christians. The first problem was simony—the buying and selling of ecclesiastical offices. When the positions of bishop or abbot were up for sale, this guaranteed two things. First, those purchasing the office were not the most spiritually minded or those who would lead exemplary lives. And second, this led ecclesiastics to become part of the violence and private nature of feudal society.

What had been common until the eleventh century, that ecclesiastics received the symbols of spiritual power from laymen (lay investiture), became intolerable. This new source of conflict worked at two levels: at the important symbolic level determining the relationship of power between lay and secular and at the practical level of landholding, collection of tithes, and other material concerns. Another substantial issue troubling the laity in the tenth and eleventh centuries was the corruption of churchmen. Priests, and even monks and nuns, did not observe their vows of chastity as well as they should have. Although in the tenth century it was not uncanonical for priests to be unchaste, and the eastern church priests could marry, the widespread violation of vows shattered general confidence in the church and opened the possibility of a hereditary church, as ecclesiastics sought to make their children heirs to their positions. Moreover, most churchmen and monks were barely educated, incapable of singing the liturgy in the correct form. Finally, the papacy in Rome had fallen victim to local politics. In the ninth century, the position of bishop of Rome became the focus for violent factional warfare. Many of those elected to the throne of St. Peter were notorious for their criminal and impious behavior. How did the church emerge and confront these problems?

The Church Universal

The medieval church had many of the attributes of the modern state. Once baptized, everyone, in theory, was subject to its laws, paid its taxes, and lived at its mercy. Yet while the rulers of the church often strove to create the machinery that would make allegiance to orthodoxy universal, they never fully succeeded. The story of their efforts, the degree of their success, the measure of their failure, and the nature of the opposition to them is in some degree the political history of the Middle Ages in the West. Having no armies of their own in this period, the popes depended upon kings and princes to raise armies for the purposes of the church. Even a mighty secular ruler often bowed to the commands of a pope. The pope had powerful spiritual weapons at his disposal: excommunication and interdict. Excommunication deprived the believer of the sacraments and threatened that person with hellfire if he or she died while excommunicated. Interdict stopped all church services in a given area except baptism and the rites for the dying; none of the population could be married, take communion, confess and be absolved, or be buried with the assurance of salvation. A population under interdict sometimes became desperate, and its ruler often yielded.

The medieval church gradually saw its authority diminished by the growth of increasingly more secular kingdoms. Yet even rulers of those realms who challenged the popes took it for granted that they, and all their subjects and the subjects of other kings and princes, were automatically Christians. Holy relics were inserted into hollows built in the throne of Charlemagne, who often disagreed with the pope. The proudest possession of Otto the Great was the holy lance, which, legend said, had been thrust into the side of Christ and had belonged to Constantine the Great. Such relics symbolized the total dependence of even the most powerful ruler upon the will of God and served as a sign that he had God's favor.

Coronation and anointing ceremonies in France, the Holy Roman Empire, and England emphasized the sacred origins of monarchical power and were an important component in the public acceptance of royal authority. But, as shall be seen later, sacred kingship was not necessarily the norm throughout the medieval West. In Castile and Portugal, kings, with some notable exceptions, were neither anointed nor crowned from the mid-twelfth century onward. In Italian cities, the sources of authority were also popular and laic. But the economic expansion of the eleventh century tended to diminish the sacred character of some European monarchies. As society grew more complex, more sophisticated methods of government needed to be devised. Clergymen played a significant role in the running of bureaucracies in western Europe, but their strict monopoly of spirituality was about to be challenged.

Theories of Papal Monarchy

The eleventh and twelfth centuries witnessed a sustained effort to build what has often been called a papal monarchy, to develop a system of ecclesiastical (canon) law, and to think through an overarching theological system. They also saw the expansion and proliferation of monasteries as new orders of monks came into being, often with reform as their aim. Those who use the term papal monarchy believe that the papacy strove steadily to dominate the temporal as well as the spiritual government. Others argue that Christian theorists had always understood that human affairs must be governed jointly by a lay and a religious authority and that the popes would never have wished to see lay rulers altogether powerless. A third group maintains that, at least in the heat of battle with secular authorities, the popes did in fact voice extreme claims to complete supremacy. In the controversies that marked the period between the eleventh and fourteenth centuries, both the papacy and lay rulers expressed many extreme views. They were deeply felt and went to the heart of a heated controversy as to where power came from and who held this power.

Christ himself had cautioned the faithful to distinguish between the things that are Caesar's (meaning belonging to the world and to lay rulers) and the things that are God's (Luke 20:25). Paul cautioned all Christians that "the powers that be are ordained of God" (Romans 13:1), so for Paul the secular powers were there to be obeyed. But at the time that Christ and Paul spoke, Christians were a tiny minority in the Roman world; the precepts became difficult to interpret later when the Christian church was supreme. As early as the fourth century, St. Ambrose, as bishop of Milan, excommunicated an emperor (Theodosius I) and forced him to do penance. Augustine had conceded the necessity of a civil state with laws and police to enforce them, while cautioning true Christians to lift their eyes above the affairs of the mere earthly city. It was Pope Gelasius (r. 492–496) who wrote to the emperor at Constantinople that there were "two by which the world is ruled"—the "sacred" authority (*auctoritas*) of priests and the royal power (*potestas*)—and that the priests had the higher responsibility.

Scholars have argued whether *auctoritas* meant "moral authority" or "the natural right to rule"; whether *potestas* meant "sovereign power" or only "a power delegated by a superior instructing church"; or even whether both words really meant essentially the same thing. Gelasius was surely thinking of the still more cryptic words of Luke 22:28, in which the apostles said to Christ, "Lord, behold, here are two swords," and Christ answered, "It is enough." This passage was constantly used in the Middle Ages to refer to the roles of the church and the state in human society.

Having broken with Byzantium and having been strengthened by the Frankish alliance and the protection of Pepin, Charlemagne, and their successors, the papacy in the tenth century sank into impotence, as the individual popes became instruments in the hands of rival Roman aristocratic families contesting for power in the city. Drunkenness, incest, arson, and murder were among the charges against the pope whom Otto deposed in 962. In such an atmosphere, the buying and selling of church offices (the sin of simony) was not uncommon, and immorality of other kinds—including the marriage or irregular union of priests or monks—was not curbed. As early as the year 910, at Cluny, in eastern France, a Benedictine monastery was founded whose powerful abbots refused to tolerate, among their own flock or elsewhere, concubinage, the sale of church offices, and other abuses; they created a series of "daughter" monasteries all inspired with the same reforming principles. More than three hundred new monastic foundations were inspired by Cluny. Living in strict accordance with the ascetic rule of Benedict, the Cluniac monks acted as an organized pressure group to spread reform everywhere in the church. Cluny was not the only reformed monastery. In other parts of Europe, monasteries, Gorzy most notably among them, also joined in the attempts to reform the church.

Cluny's example, and the examples of similar reformed monastic establishments, transformed medieval sensibilities and spirituality in two distinct ways. First, laymen saw the benefits of a reformed church (an assurance of their own salvation and more dependable ecclesiastic administrators) and began to appoint observant and pious ecclesiastics to vacant clerical dignities. Second, Cluniac monks became the vanguard of the reformed church. As advisers to kings, emperors, and popes, as bishops and even popes, they placed the reform ideals—ecclesiastical celibacy, clerical education, an end to simony, and the exclusion of the laity from spiritual jurisdiction—at the center of the church's new and revitalized vision of itself and of its role in Christendom. At the end, however, Rome remained the core of the church. There, papal business continued to be conducted, even when the popes were viewed as unworthy. Ultimately, the battle for reform had to be fought there, but it was not until the mid-eleventh century that full-fledged reform came to the papacy itself. The reform of the church and of the papacy, however, was deeply intertwined with the political interests of the German emperors and other western European kings, with their piety and sense that Christendom must be reformed.

The Investiture Controversy

The open conflict between lay and spiritual as to who had the upper hand in Christendom was played out in a variety of ways throughout western Europe. These conflicts were not limited to the late eleventh and early twelfth centuries, nor were they restricted to the single issue of lay investiture or to the struggle between the empire and the papacy. Henry II (r. 1154–1189) of England's confrontation with Thomas à Becket (d. 1170), the archbishop of Canterbury, over who had jurisdiction over clerics in the 1160s was one aspect of the broader struggle for domination. Similarly, Alfonso VI (1072–1109) of Castile's imposition of the Roman rite in his realm in 1080 and his insistence in naming bishops without papal consent and tapping into ecclesiastical resources with impunity are yet other examples of the wide-spread conflict for control of the church and its resources. Finally, the French kings, most notably Philip Augustus (1180–1223) and Philip IV (1285–1314), wrestled continuously with the papacy, and Frederick II (1211–1250), the Hohenstaufen ruler of Sicily, who confronted the church and the papacy most successfully, are among the most visible manifestations of the growing divide between lay and ecclesiastical views of how Christendom was to be organized in the late Middle Ages. To describe all the different variations of this conflict would require a book in itself. Here, we focus on the most obvious and dramatic events of the struggle over lay investiture between the German emperors and the popes.

As the Carolingian Empire gradually disintegrated in the late ninth and early tenth centuries, four duchies—Franconia, Saxony (of which Thuringia was a part), Swabia, and Bavaria—arose in the eastern Frankish lands of Germany. They were military units organized by the local Carolingians, who took the title of duke (army commander). When the Carolingian dynasty became extinct, they chose one of their own number—Conrad, duke of Franconia—as their king in 911 to protect their lands against Magyar invaders. But Conrad was a failure, so the dukes asserted themselves as rivals to the Crown. They built their duchies into petty kingdoms, made themselves hereditary rulers, and took control over the church in their own duchies.

Saxon Administration and the German Church, 911–955

Conrad's successor, the duke of Saxony, became King Henry I (r. 919–936). He and his descendants—notably Otto the Great (r. 936–973) and Otto III (983–1002)—successfully combated the ducal tendency to dominate the counts and to control the church. In 939 the Crown obtained the duchy of Franconia; thenceforth, the German kings, no matter what duchy they came from, would also have Franconia as the royal domain. The Saxon dynasty established by Henry I relied on the church to perform much of the work of governing Germany. The church welcomed the alliance because a strong central government was its best guarantee of stability; the papacy itself recognized the right of the German kings to appoint their own bishops. The Saxon monarchs gave church and abbey lands their special protection, exempting them from the authority of the counts and bringing them directly under the Crown. Like the former counts, the bishops obtained the right to administer justice within their own domain.

The church also supplied the German king with much of his revenue, and tenants of church lands furnished three quarters of his army. The church participated in the German expansion to the east, in the defeat of the Magyars at Lechfeld (955), in the push into Slavic lands along the Elbe and Saale rivers, and in the advance into Silesia. New German bishoprics were set up, with Magdeburg as center, and subject sees were established east of the Elbe. The kingdoms that the western emperor was likely to control were Germany, Burgundy, and Italy. Burgundy had grown up under ambitious rulers in the region between the eastern and western Frankish lands. Italy, on the other hand, was weak, divided, and open to invasion. Thus the king of Germany had much to gain if he could secure the title of emperor. And, if he did not make himself emperor, he faced a real danger that somebody else might.

In a later chapter we will have the opportunity to examine the development of the German Empire in the late Middle Ages, but now we must consider political and religious developments in Germany and how they relate to the attempts of the papacy to chart an independent course from secular power.

The Investiture Controversy, 1046–1122: The Triumph of Papal Reform

The struggle had its origins in the emperor's desire to reform the papacy and to name a pious and reforming pope. In many respects, what occurred after the mid-eleventh century was the conflict and contradictions between three overlapping type of reforms. First, monastic reform swept through monasteries throughout Europe eager to imitate the example of Cluny, Gorzy, and other reforming ecclesiastical establishments. Second, lay reform was the laity's embracing of the reform ideals. Pious lords and rulers throughout Christendom took special care to appoint reforming ecclesiastics to church dignities. Finally, under the sponsorship of lay rulers, mostly the German emperors, the papacy itself was reformed. But lay rulers had little understanding of the storm they were unleashing by their actions.

In 1046, Emperor Henry III found three rival popes simultaneously in office while mobs of their supporters rioted in the streets of Rome. He deposed all three. After two successive German appointees had died— perhaps by poison, but most likely because of the endemic malaria in and around Rome—Henry named a third German, Bishop Bruno of Toul, who became pope as Leo IX (r. 1049–1054). Leo was committed to the Cluniac program of monastic reform; the whole church hierarchy, he insisted, must be purged of secular influences, and over it all the pope must reign supreme. Henry III had thus put into power reformers whose chief target would be his own imperial system of government in Germany. Leo began to appoint cardinals, who now served as key advisers and administrators instead of merely ornamental dignitaries. By 1059 the papacy had given these cardinals the power to elect new popes, depriving the German emperors of that role. And the Normans of southern Italy promised to give the cardinals military backing, so that they could do their job without fear of German intervention.

In 1073 the monk Hildebrand, one of the fiery reformers who had come to Rome with Leo IX, became pope as Gregory VII (r. to 1085). He was determined to push ecclesiastical reform by ensuring the canonical (legal) election of all bishops and abbots. This would mean sweeping away the system of royal selection and appointment and its subsequent ceremony of lay investiture—that is, the conferring of the prelate's insignia of office by a layman, the emperor. Yet the German royal administration largely depended on this royal appointment of prelates, which involved not only lay investiture but also the granting of royal estates to bishops. Gregory declared that the pope was subject to no human judgment; that the Roman church had never erred and never could err; that the pope alone could make new laws, create new bishoprics, depose bishops, and change his own mind; that all temporal princes should kiss his feet; that the imperial insignia were his alone to use; and that he could absolve the subjects of a temporal prince from their allegiance and could depose emperors. Although Gregory VII's pronouncements, collected in a papal document known as the *Dictate of the Pope,* were not part of the church's official policy, they resonated with Gregory's sense that the pope, by Christ's mandate, had full authority and power within Christendom.

In 1075 Gregory forbade lay investiture. Henry IV's bishops responded in 1076 by declaring Gregory deposed. Gregory then excommunicated Henry as a usurper, declared him deposed, absolved his subjects of loyalty to him, and deprived the bishops of their offices. The Saxon nobles, opponents of Henry, thereupon joined forces with the pope and made Henry promise to clear himself of the excommunication within four months, on pain of the loss of his crown; they also invited the pope to Germany. To prevent this unwelcome visit, Henry secretly went to Italy in January 1077 and appeared before the castle of Canossa, where Gregory was temporarily staying. Henry declared himself a penitent; Gregory kept him waiting outside the castle for three days, barefoot and in sackcloth. When he was finally admitted, Henry did penance and Gregory absolved him. The drama and symbolism of this famous episode have often led historians to marvel at the power of the pope. But it struck contemporaries the other way. By allowing himself to be publicly humiliated, Henry had forced Gregory's hand; the pope had been compelled to absolve him, and while in a state of being forgiven he could not be deposed.

Before Henry returned home, his German opponents had elected a new ruler, an "anti-king," Rudolf of Swabia. By refraining for three years from making a decision between the rival kings, Gregory VII did what he could to prolong the resulting civil war. When he did decide, it was against Henry, whom he deposed and excommunicated once more. But the pope's efforts failed; Rudolf was killed in battle, and a new anti-king commanded even less support. The German clergy again declared the pope deposed, and Henry marched to Italy, took Rome in 1084 after three years of bitter siege, and installed an "anti-pope," who proceeded to crown him emperor. Gregory's Norman vassals and allies did not arrive until after Henry had returned to Germany. They looted Rome and took Gregory with them to southern Italy, where he died.

No settlement of the investiture controversy would be reached until 1122. In the Concordat of Worms, Henry V (1106–1125) renounced the practice of investing bishops with the clerical symbols of ring and staff. The pope permitted the emperor to continue investing bishops with the regalia (symbols of the worldly goods pertaining to the bishop's office). The investiture could take place before the bishop was consecrated, assuring the emperor of a previous oath of fealty from the bishop. Moreover, clerical elections in Germany were to be carried out in the presence of the emperor or his representatives, giving him an opportunity to exercise a strong influence over the decisions. In Italy and Burgundy the emperor retained less power; consecration was to take place before the regalia were conferred, and the emperor could not attend clerical elections.

But by 1122 Germany had become politically fragmented. During the years between 1076 and 1106 the princes and other nobles acted on the pretext that there was no king, since the pope had deposed him. They extended their powers and administered their lands without reference to the monarchy. Castles multiplied and became centers of administrative districts, laying the foundations for territorial principalities; free peasants fell into serfdom; and the weakness of central authority drove lesser nobles to become dependent on greater nobles. In Italy the investiture controversy had seen the further rise of the Norman kingdom of the South. The struggle had also been responsible for the growth of communes in the cities of the North. These communes had begun as sworn associations of lesser nobles who banded together to resist the power of the local bishops. In Lombardy, where they were favored by Gregory VII, the communes took advantage of his support to usurp the powers of municipal government. In Tuscany, where the ruling house was pro-papal, the communes allied themselves with the emperor, who granted them their liberties by charter. Thus, in Germany the Crown faced a newly entrenched aristocracy; in Italy it faced a new society of powerful urban communes.

The Investiture Controversy in Retrospect

The conflict between spiritual (the church) and temporal power for primacy within Christendom yielded some very important results. First, between the early tenth century (the foundation of Cluny in 910) and the Concordat of Worms in 1122, the church underwent a radical reform. Clerical celibacy was enforced. Simony became unacceptable. Ecclesiastical corruption diminished. The sacraments began to play a more central role in ordering and regulating Christian life. Gregory VII's radical stance led to the autonomy of the church in doctrinal and spiritual matters, with some notable exceptions throughout the next centuries, from the intrusion of secular rulers. We cannot speak fully of "church and state" yet because states did not fully exist in the sense in which we understand state power, but a cleavage was created within Christendom. The clergy now claimed to be the church and reiterated its monopoly of the role of intermediary between the sacred and the world.

Second, the new power and prestige of the papacy led to the consolidation of a formidable papal bureaucracy and chancery. From Rome, papal bulls and guidance went out to all of Christendom. To Rome came people to present their cases at the papal curia. The pope became the absolute ruler of the church, a divine institution that claimed exemption from civil law and from secular rulers for its members. This would prove to be a source of continuous dispute between secular rulers and the church; the dispute between Henry II of England and Thomas Becket, the archbishop of Canterbury, over ecclesiastical jurisdiction (culminating in Becket's murder and the king's public penance for his role in the assassination) was, as mentioned earlier, only the most notable example of these tensions.

Third, the investiture controversy generated a heated scholarly and political debate on the nature of power. Both sides presented their views in compelling and passionate ways. Some, like "Anonymous of York" (an anonymous cleric writing in late eleventh-century northern England), appealed to the Scriptures and argued for the supremacy of temporal kings over the pope. Others supported the papal absolute power as coming from God. Others sought to take a middle position, one that eventually became the basis for the Concordat of Worms. The importance of these intellectual activities was to lay the groundwork for the eventual autonomy of secular rule and to provide the embryonic genesis of the language of sovereignty. There were other serious consequences to the intellectual debate of papal power. In the late eleventh century, it led, as has been seen, to the emergence of an elaborate papal bureaucracy. It also led to the assertion of papal power. The Crusades, to which we turn now, became the most obvious outcome of the triumph of the church and of the reform movement.

The Crusades

Christians had struggled against Islam in western Europe and in the East since the great Muslim conquest in the seventh and eighth centuries. In Iberia, fledgling Christian kingdoms in the north of the peninsula had engaged in an alternate pattern of confrontation and adaptation. Charlemagne, as was already discussed, led a large raid against the Muslim rulers in Zaragoza. In the East, Byzantium engaged the Muslims in frequent sea and

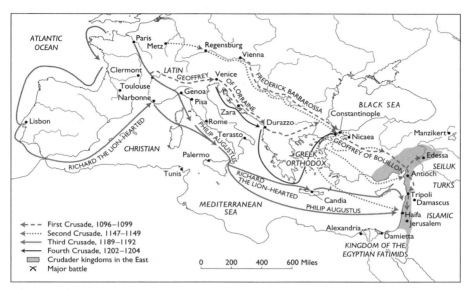

The Crusades

land battles, but it also maintained diplomatic relations with the caliphs in Baghdad. All of these conflicts were widely perceived as part of regular warfare between contending political entities, but this perception was about to change radically.

Just after the year 1000 the Cordoban caliphate weakened, and the Spanish Christian princes of the North won the support of the powerful French abbey at Cluny. Under prodding from Cluny, French nobles joined the Spaniards in waging war against the Muslims in Iberia. Soon the pope offered an indulgence to all who would fight for the Cross in Spain. In 1085 the Castilian army led by Alfonso VI with the support of a large number of Christian knights from north of the Pyrenees captured the city of Toledo. For almost a century and a half, the Muslims were able to withstand and even made gains on the Castilian and Aragonese advance on al-Andalus, but by the early thirteenth century the king of Castile, Alfonso VIII, led a large international Christian army to a signal victory at Las Navas de Tolosa in 1212. Over the next thirty years, the Iberian Christian kingdoms recovered large areas of central and southern Spain. This process, known as the Reconquest, was itself a Crusade—a holy war against the infidel supported by the papacy—and remained a battle cry in Iberia until the surrender of the last outpost of Islam in Granada on 1 January 1492.

Origins of the Crusades

From the third century on, Christians had regularly visited the sites where Jesus had lived, preached, and died. Before the Muslim conquest in the seventh century, pilgrims came from Byzantium and the West, often seeking sacred relics for their churches at home. For awhile after the Muslim conquest, pilgrimages were very dangerous and could be undertaken only by the hardiest pilgrims. During the reign of Charlemagne, conditions had improved for western pilgrims, largely because of the excellent relations between Charlemagne and Caliph Harun al-Rashid. By the tenth century the belief had grown that pilgrimage would procure God's pardon for sins. Santiago of Compostela in Spain, and of course Rome itself, had become favorite places of pilgrimage, but no place could compare in importance with the shrines of Palestine.

Obviously, stable conditions in both Muslim and Byzantine dominions were essential for the easy and safe continuance of pilgrimages. But in the early eleventh century the able though eccentric Egyptian ruler of Palestine, al-Hakim (r. 996–1021), began to persecute Christians and Jews and to make travel to the Holy Places unsafe. Although his persecution of Christians represented an exceptional development and was not in line with traditional Muslim toleration of Christians, political changes in the Middle East, most notably the rise of the Seljuk Turks in Asia, transformed the relations between Christians and Muslims.

By 1050 the Seljuks had created a state centering on Persia. In 1055 they entered Baghdad on the invitation of the Abbasid caliph and became the champions of Sunnit Islam against the Shi'ite rulers of Egypt. In the 1050s Seljuk forces raided deep into Anatolia, almost to the Aegean. Their advance culminated in the catastrophic Byzantine defeat at Manzikert in 1071, followed by the occupation of most of Asia Minor and the establishment of a new sultanate with its capital at Nicaea. Jerusalem fell in the year of Manzikert and became part of a new Seljuk state of Syria.

In 1081 Alexius I Comnenus, a general and a great landowner, came to the Byzantine throne (r. to 1118). He held off the Norman attack on the Dalmatian coast through an alliance with Venice, and he played one local Turkish potentate off against another, slowly reestablishing a Byzantine foothold in Asia Minor. Civil wars among the Turks and the multiplication of brigands on the highways in Anatolia and Syria made pilgrimages in the two decades after Manzikert ever more dangerous.

The differences between eastern and western churches provided the papacy with an additional incentive for intervention in the East. In 1073 Pope Gregory VII sent an ambassador to Constantinople, who reported that the emperor was anxious for a reconciliation. Gregory VII planned to reunite the churches by extending the holy war from Spain to Asia. He would send the Byzantines an army of western knights, which he would lead himself. It was only the quarrel over investiture with the German emperor that prevented the pope from carrying out this plan.

The First Crusade, 1095

Pope Urban II (r. 1088–1099) carried on the tradition of Gregory VII. To his Council of Piacenza in 1095 came envoys from Alexius, who asked for mili-

A late eleventh- or early twelfth-century crusader kneels before his departure for the Crusades. Note the elaborate coat of chain mail and the helmet.   (HIP/Scala/Art Resource, NY)

tary help against the Turks. The Byzantine envoys also seem to have stressed the sufferings of the Christians in the East. Eight months later, at the Council of Clermont, Urban preached to a throng of the faithful. He painted in dark colors the hardships that now faced pilgrims to Jerusalem. He summoned his listeners to form themselves, rich and poor alike, into an army, which God would assist. If a man were killed doing this work of God, he would automatically be absolved of his sins and assured of salvation. The audience greeted this moving oration with cries of "God wills it." Throngs of volunteers took a solemn oath and sewed crosses of cloth onto their garments. The First Crusade had been launched. One should note here the importance of the idea of pilgrims as soldiers, as well as the emphasis on the Crusades as a form of penance and redemption, as is obvious in Urban II's speech in the accompanying box.

The Written Record

POPE URBAN AT CLERMONT

Pope Urban proclaimed the First Crusade with these words:

The Turks, a race of Persians, who have penetrated within the boundaries of Romania even to the Mediterranean to that point which they call the Arm of Saint George, in occupying more and more of the lands of the Christians, have overcome them, have overthrown churches, and have laid waste God's kingdom. If you permit this supinely for very long, God's faithful ones will be still further subjected. . . .

I speak to those present, I send word to those not here; moreover, Christ commands it. Remission of sins will be granted for those going thither, if they end a shackled life either on land or in crossing the sea, or in struggling against the heathen. I, being vested with that gift from God, grant this to those who go.

O what a shame, if a people, so despised, degenerate, and enslaved by demons would thus overcome a people endowed with the trust of almighty God, and shining in the name of Christ! O how many evils *will* be imputed to you by the Lord Himself, if you do not help those who, like you, profess Christianity!

Let those who are accustomed to wage private wars wastefully even against Believers, go forth against the Infidels in a battle worthy to be undertaken now and to befinished in victory. Now, let those, who until recently existed as plunderers, be soldiers in Christ; now, let those, who formerly contended against brothers and relations, rightly fight barbarians; now, let those, who recently were hired for a few pieces of silver, win their eternal reward.

"The Chronicles of Fulcher of Chartres," trans. Martha E. McGinty, in *The First Crusade: The Chronicle of Fulcher of Chartres and Other Source Material*, ed. Edward Peters (Philadelphia: University of Philadelphia Press), 30–33.

Peter the Hermit, an unkempt, barefoot old man who lived on fish and wine and was a moving orator, proved the most effective preacher of the Crusades. Through France and Germany he recruited an undisciplined mob, many of them peasants living wretched lives and suffering near starvation as a result of crop failure. Often they believed that Peter was leading them straight to heaven, the New Jerusalem, which they confused with the Jerusalem on earth. In two installments, this motley group known as the Popular Crusade (to distinguish it from the actual First Crusade) marched across the Rhineland, massacring Jews, looting, and burning. Across Hungary they continued, where thousands of Hungarians were killed, and into Byzantine territory at Belgrade. The Byzantines, who had hoped for the loan of a few hundred well-trained knights, were appalled at the enormous armies about to descend on them. They proceeded to take all precautions against trouble.

Despite their best efforts, the undisciplined crusaders burned houses and engaged in looting. Once in Constantinople, Alexius Comnenus shipped them across the Straits as quickly as possible. In Asia Minor they quarreled among themselves, murdered the Christian inhabitants, scored no success against the Turks, and were eventually massacred.

Meanwhile, a considerable number of great lords had been recruited, including a brother of the king of France, the duke of Normandy, and the count of Flanders. The most celebrated, however, were Godfrey of Bouillon (duke of Lower Lorraine) and his brother Baldwin, Count Raymond of Toulouse, Count Stephen of Blois, and Bohemond, a Norman prince from southern Italy who had already attacked Constantinople a few years earlier. Better-equipped and better-disciplined, their armies began to converge on Constantinople.

The emperor Alexius was in a very difficult position. He was ready to have the western commanders carve out principalities for themselves from Turkish-occupied territory. But he wanted to assure himself that Byzantine lands would be returned to his control and that whatever new states might be created would be under his suzerainty or jurisdiction. Alexius knew of the western custom of vassalage and the importance attached to an oath taken to an overlord. Thus, he requested that each of the great western lords take an oath of liege homage to him on arrival. To obtain these oaths, Alexius had to resort to bribery with splendid gifts and to all sorts of pressure, including in some cases the withholding of food from the unruly crusading armies.

The armies were all ferried across the Straits. With the exception of the papal legate, there was no supreme command, but the armies acted as a unit, following the orders of the leaders assembled in council. In June 1097 at Nicaea, the Seljuk capital, the Turks surrendered at the last minute to Byzantine forces rather than suffer an assault from the crusader armies. This the crusaders bitterly resented, since they had been looking forward to plundering the town. Crossing Asia Minor, they defeated the Turks in a battle at Dorylaeum, captured the Seljuk sultan's treasure, and opened the road to further advance. Godfrey's brother Baldwin, leaving the main army, marched to Edessa. Here, after negotiations with the local Armenian rulers, he became count of Edessa and lord of the first crusader state to be established (1098).

The Crusader Realms, 1098–1109

Meanwhile, the main body of the army was besieging the great fortress city of Antioch, which finally was conquered by treachery after more than seven months. Antioch became the center of the second crusader state under the Norman Bohemond. The other crusaders then took Jerusalem by assault in July 1099, slaughtering large numbers of Muslims and Jews on the Temple Mount. Godfrey of Bouillon was chosen "defender of the Holy Sepulcher." The third crusader state had been founded. Venetian, Genoese, and Pisan fleets now assisted in the gradual conquest of the coastal cities. In 1109 the son of Raymond of Toulouse founded the fourth and last of the crusader states, centering around the seaport of Tripoli. The king of Jerusalem was the theoretical overlord of the other three states but was often unable to enforce his authority. To complicate matters further, the Byzantine emperors never relinquished the feudal rights that had been secured to them by the oath that the crusaders had made to Alexius.

The holdings of the westerners lay within a long narrow coastal strip extending from the Euphrates River to the borders of Egypt, more than five hundred miles long and seldom as much as fifty miles wide. Danger constantly threatened. The westerners failed to take obvious measures for the common defense. The great lords built superb castles at strategic places but often fought with one another, sometimes in alliance with neighboring Muslims. The Assizes of Jerusalem record the governmental practices of the crusader states. Essentially, the First Crusade imported feudal structures into Palestine. The great officers of the realm were the officers of the king's household: seneschal, constable, marshal, and the like. The high court of barons not only settled disputes but also acted as council of state for the king's business. The lords had rights of justice on their own fiefs. Police and civil cases were under the direction of viscounts, royal officers in the towns, and there were special commercial and maritime courts. Revenues were raised by customs dues, by monopolies on tanning and similar industries, by a poll tax on Muslims and Jews, and by a land tax on the native population.

Ecclesiastical organization was complex: The two Latin patriarchs of Jerusalem and Antioch each had a hierarchy of Roman Catholic archbishops and bishops subject to them, but Greek, Syrian, and Armenian churches continued to exist, each with its own clergy, in addition to the Muslim and Jewish faiths. Most significantly, as the crusaders settled in the Middle East, their practices, eating habits, and dress borrowed heavily from the cultural context in which they lived. Within a few years, many of the crusaders had gained new understanding of their enemies and sought some ambivalent accommodation, as shown by their frequent alliance with local Muslim powers, with the political complexities of their new world. Cultural exchanges led to new knowledge to be disseminated to the West.

For Muslims and Jews, the early impact of the First Crusade was catastrophic. The siege and capture of Jerusalem, as described by Fulcher of Chartres, a Christian chronicler, witnessed crusaders wading in the blood of the slaughtered up to their ankles. Arab accounts written after the First Crusade commented on the barbarity of the newcomers, on their ignorance of medicine or law, and on their naive view of Islam.

The Military Orders, 1119–1798

Early in their occupation of the eastern Mediterranean, the westerners founded the military orders of knighthood. The first of these were the Templars, started about 1119 by a Burgundian knight who sympathized with the hardships of the Christian pilgrims. These knights took vows of poverty, chastity, and obedience and were given headquarters near the ruins of the Temple of Solomon—hence the name Templars. St. Bernard himself inspired their rule, based on the rules for his own Cistercians. A second order was attached to the ancient Hospital of St. John of Jerusalem, and was therefore called the Hospitalers. Made up of knights, chaplains, and serving brothers under the command of a grand master, the two orders were the most effective fighting forces in the Holy Land. Each had a special uniform; the Templars wore red crosses on white, the Hospitalers white crosses on black. Later a third, purely German group became the order of the Teutonic Knights with headquarters at Acre; they wore black crosses on white. The orders had fortresses and churches of their own in the Holy Land and villages from which they obtained produce and income. Moreover, western monarchs endowed them richly with lands in Europe. They often allied themselves with Muslims and forgot their original vows of poverty so completely that they engaged in banking and large-scale financial operations. In the early fourteenth century the Templars were destroyed by Philip IV of France for fiscal and political reasons. The Hospitalers moved first to Cyprus and then to Rhodes in the early fourteenth century; they were driven to Malta by the Turks in 1522 and continued there until Napoleon's capture of the island in 1798. The Teutonic Knights eventually focused their energies on the German eastern frontier and expansion into Slavic lands.

The Muslim Reconquest and the Later Crusades, 1144–1291

It is a wonder that the crusader states lasted so long. It was not the castles or the military orders that preserved them as much as the lack of unity among their Muslim enemies. When the Muslims did achieve unity under a single powerful leader, the Christians suffered grave losses. Beginning in the late 1120s, Zangi, governor of Mosul on the Tigris, succeeded in unifying the local Muslim rulers of the region. In 1144 he took Edessa, first of the crusader cities to fall. As an answer to the loss of Edessa, St. Bernard himself preached the so-called Second Crusade in Europe. He aroused enormous enthusiasm, and for the first time western monarchs—King Louis VII of France and King Conrad III of Germany—came to the East. But the Second Crusade proved a shattering failure. As the German and French armies passed through Constantinople, relations with the Byzantines were worse than ever. The western armies were almost wiped out in Asia Minor. When the remnants reached the Holy Land, they found themselves in hopeless conflict with the local lords, who feared that the newcomers would take over the kingdom. The crusaders' failure to take Damascus in 1149 brought its own punishment. In 1154 Zangi's son, Nureddin, took it, and Muslim Syria was united against the Latins.

The next act of the Muslim reconquest was carried out in Egypt by a general of Nureddin's who was sent to assist one of the quarreling factions in Cairo. This general became vizier of Egypt and died in 1169, leaving his office to his nephew Saladin, who became the greatest Muslim leader of the Crusade period. A vigorous and successful general, Saladin brought the Muslim cities of Syria and Mesopotamia under his control and distributed them to faithful members of his own family. By 1183 his brother ruled Egypt, his sons ruled Damascus and Aleppo, and close relatives ruled all the other important centers. Internal decay in the kingdom of Jerusalem and a squabble over the throne gave Saladin his chance, and a violation of a truce by an unruly crusader lord gave him his excuse. In 1187 Jerusalem fell, and soon there was nothing of the kingdom left to the Christians except the port of Tyre and a few castles. These events elicited the Third Crusade (1189–1192). The Holy Roman emperor, Frederick Barbarossa, led a German force through Byzantium, only to be drowned in Asia Minor (1190). Some of his troops, however, continued to Palestine. There they were joined by Philip Augustus of France and Richard I, the Lionhearted, of England, each at least as interested in thwarting the other as he was in furthering any common cause. The main operation of the Third Crusade was a long siege of the seaport of Acre, which was finally captured in 1191. Jerusalem itself could not be taken, but Saladin signed a treaty with Richard allowing Christians to visit the city freely.

When Saladin died in 1193, the Christians obtained a respite. Reinforcements from the West, however, had dwindled away to a small trickle. Between the First Crusade and the fateful lunching of the Fourth, economic and political developments had transformed the crusading landscape. Venetian and Genoese merchants had set significant trade enclaves in the eastern Mediterranean and promoted intensive commercial exchanges between East and West. Their aims and policies, strongly backed by the respective city governments, differed significantly from the original crusading ideals of an earlier period. This was most evident when Innocent III came to the papal throne in 1198 and called for a new Crusade, the Fourth. Several powerful lords responded. The Venetians agreed to furnish transportation and food and also to contribute fifty armed warships on condition that they would share equally in all future conquests. The doge (duke) of Venice, Enrico Dandolo (c. 1108–1205), agreed to forgive the debt temporarily if the crusaders would help him reconquer Zara, a town on the eastern side of the Adriatic that had revolted against Venetian domination. So the Fourth Crusade began with the sack and destruction of a Roman Catholic town in 1202. Angrily, the pope excommunicated the crusaders, who settled down to pass the winter in Zara before pressing on. Their primary worry was financial; the leaders had badly overestimated the number who would join the Fourth Crusade and had committed themselves to a larger contract to which the Venetians intended to hold them.

During the winter the crusaders turned their attention to a new goal: Constantinople. The German king, Philip of Swabia, proposed that the massed army escort Alexius, a young prince with a strong claim to the Byzantine throne, to Constantinople and enthrone him in the place of a usurper. If successful, Alexius would finance the subsequent expedition. In the spring of 1204 a greatly augmented crusader fleet, with enthusiastic Venetian support, attacked Constantinople. In the initial onslaught the attackers won a resounding naval victory, although the city held. A second attack on land and sea broke through the defenses, and Alexius III fled the city. The young Alexius was then crowned as Alexius IV. While he was away pursuing Alexius III, the city was badly damaged by the worst fire in its history, probably begun when a group of Franks set fire to a mosque in the Saracen quarter. Angry, Alexius IV declined to make the promised payment. Certain that he could neither bring peace with the increasingly impatient crusaders nor defeat them in battle, a group of senators, clergy, and the populace deposed Alexius IV. In March 1204 the crusaders and Venetians agreed to seize the city a second time, to elect a Latin emperor who would receive a quarter of the empire and its booty, and to divide the other three quarters equally between Venetians and non-Venetians. The second siege ended in a second capture and a systematic three-day sack of Constantinople.

The pope himself criticized the outrages committed by the crusaders. What was destroyed in the libraries of the capital is untold. Despite general destruction, the Venetians took much of great value and beauty, shipping it all back to their city. Their booty included the four great bronze horses that had been a symbol of the city since Constantine, a host of sacred relics the Greek emperors had been collecting, and hundreds of works of Byzantine art. The crusaders now paid their debt in full to the Venetians. Any pretense of religious fervor as the driving force for the recovery of the Holy Land was thoroughly tainted by the Fourth Crusade. Perhaps most of all, the Fourth Crusade was diluted by the struggle between the papacy and its European opponents, first by the preaching of a crusade against the Albigensian heretics of southern France in the early thirteenth century and then for calling for a crusade against the emperor Frederick II between 1220 and 1250. In these affairs the popes were offering those who would fight against a European and nominally Christian enemy the same indulgence they offered those who fought Muslims. All these developments brought disillusionment when combined with the spectacle of repeated military failure.

Perhaps the culmination of tragic futility was the so-called Children's Crusade in 1212, when throngs of French and German children went down to the Mediterranean expecting that its waters would divide before them and open a path to the Holy Land along which they could march to a bloodless victory. When this failed to happen, several thousand of the pilgrims pushed on to Marsailles and other ports. There many were sold into slavery.

The Impact of the Crusades on the West

The crusading ideal remains a part of the European world even today. It fueled, as shown by Norman Housley in a recent book, most religious warfare in Europe from the late Middle Ages into the modern period. Crusading ideology was deployed against other Christians and against heretics. It became a category laden with religious significance that could be deployed for political purposes. In their short-term impact the Crusades contributed to the introduction of new products and helped create the conditions that led to modern methods of finance. The number of crusaders and pilgrims who went to the East and returned home was large. From Marseilles alone the ships of the Hospitalers and the Templars carried six thousand pilgrims a year. Ideas flowed back and forth with the people. Arabic words in Western languages testify to the concepts and products borrowed by westerners in commerce—*bazaar, tariff,* the French *douane,* and the Italian *dogana* (a customs house, from the Arabic *diwan,* the sofa on which the officials sat)—in foods—*sugar, saffron, rice, lemon, apricot, shallot, scallion, melon,* and *pistachio*—in manufactured goods—*cotton, muslin, damask* (from Damascus), and in many other areas.

The new products stimulated the growing commercial life of the West. Venice and Genoa, the ports from which much of the produce of the East was funneled into Europe, prospered exceedingly. So did the cities of Flanders, whose own manufacture of woolen goods was stimulated by the availability of eastern luxuries for trade. Letters of credit and bills of exchange became a necessity in an ever more complex commercial and financial system. Italian banking houses sprang up with offices in the Holy Land.

The Church in Society

Even with the original papal success in the struggle against the emperors on the issue of lay investiture and in its leadership of the early Crusades, the church, and Christendom in general, was severely tested by the demands of social and economic change. Corruption was often swiftly followed by new waves of reforms and by the church's inability to respond to the new spiritual needs of Christians throughout western Europe. Exceptional rulers such as Frederick II, who was long engaged in a struggle against the church, rightly believed that reforms were needed. For example, Innocent IV, in fighting Frederick, approved the appointment to a bishopric in German territory of an illiterate and dissolute young man of nineteen simply because he was a member of a powerful anti-Hohenstaufen noble family (Frederick was from the Hohenstaufen family); this bishop was forced to resign after twenty-five years, but only because his public boasting about his fourteen bastard children had become a scandal. The need for reform was constantly felt in the church itself, and successive waves of reforming zeal manifested themselves, especially in monastic movements.

Cluny continued in its determination to rid the church of abuses; its centrally organized rule over daughter houses was both its strength and its weakness. The effectiveness of centralized control depended on the personality of the abbot of the ruling house; a weak or selfish or cynical abbot would endanger the whole enterprise. Those who started out determined to leave the world and live in poverty and humility found themselves admired by the rich and often took gifts that in turn transformed them into materialistic men of business. By the late eleventh century the Cluniac houses had become wealthy and their rule had relaxed.

Cistercians and Augustinians

Founded as a reaction to the waning of the reform movement and as a rejection of the growing wealth of the church, the Cistercians sought salvation by abandoning the world in imitation of the anchorites and monks in the early centuries of Christianity. Their original house, Citeaux (Cistercium) in Burgundy, lay in a dismal wasteland far from the distractions of the world. There they pioneered land reclamation and launched a period of agricultural expansion. By the twelfth century the Cistercians were looked to for their knowledge of how to make previously uncultivated lands, often swamps, productive. In reaction to Cluny's growing worldliness, the Cistercians considered themselves the only true Benedictines, yet the self-denial, poverty, and wholly spiritual life that the Cistercians adopted was often seen by their contemporaries as arrogant, worldly, and even greedy. Perhaps the best-known Cistercian leader was Bernard of Clairvaux (c. 1091–1153), who in 1115 led a band of Cistercians to a new and remote site from which he influenced worldly affairs to a remarkable degree, preaching for a Second Crusade and attacking the scholastic method of teaching. He was one of the great mystics of the twelfth century, a period that witnessed a flowering of mystical writings and experiences. As he wrote, "There are many who seek knowledge for the sake of knowledge: that is curiosity. There are others who desire to know in order that they themselves be known: that is vanity. Others seek knowledge in order to sell it: that is dishonorable. But there are also some who seek knowledge in order to edify others. That is love." He launched significant reforms in teaching, the observance of church rules, and attitudes toward worship. The Cistercians, led by Bernard, were also influential in the dramatic development of the cult of the Virgin Mary and promoted the spread of the Gothic architectural style throughout the West (see the next chapter).

In the end, the Cistercians, too, changed. Display conquered austerity, and aristocratic traditions quenched humility. By the thirteenth century great Cistercian monasteries were wealthy centers of production. The expensive arts of architecture and sculpture were lavished on their buildings. These Cistercian monasteries had become great corporations, thoroughly tied to the increasingly complex web of medieval economic life.

One newly founded order broke with the rule of Benedict, finding its inspiration in a letter of Augustine (the great late fourth-and early fifth-century saint and philosopher) that prescribed simply that monks share all their property, pray together at regular intervals, dress alike, and obey a superior. Some of the "Augustinians," as they called themselves, interpreted these general rules severely, living in silence, performing manual labor, eating and drinking sparingly, and singing psalms; others ate meat, conversed among themselves, and did not insist on manual labor. Often beginning as small informal foundations, the Augustinians attracted donations from relatively modest donors. Unlike Cluny, with its vast collections of buildings crowned by a great and splendid church, the Augustinian foundations were simple and humble. The Augustinians preached, baptized, heard confessions, and helped the poor unobtrusively. They multiplied rapidly, playing a significant role in late medieval schools, as well as in cathedral chapters. By 1244, when the order was officially approved by the church, thousands of Augustinian houses were spread throughout England and the Continent.

Friars: Dominicans and Franciscans

In the early thirteenth century the reforming movement within the church took on new aspects. As town populations grew, the bourgeoise's new spiritual needs were no longer met by old Benedictine foundations with their distinctive rural locations and outlook. New concerns with wealth, salvation, preaching, and the afterlife found outlets in the new heterodox movements sweeping parts of Europe in the twelfth century. Most significant among these heretical movements were the Waldensians and the Cathars. Both of these movements addressed the question of the relation of the individual Christian to the material world. The mendicant orders, or begging orders, arose as an answer to the spiritual needs of the middling sorts and, not just coincidentally, as powerful responses to the heretical challenges to medieval Christianity. The two most important of these new orders of friars were the Dominicans and Franciscans.

Dominic (1170–1221) was a Spanish Augustinian canon who revived the idea of apostolic simplicity that had given birth to the Augustinians. He founded the "Order of Preachers" within the Augustinian rule, and until his death directed them in their work of preaching and living the life of simple, primitive Christians. Francis (1182–1226), the son of a wealthy Italian merchant, gave his possessions to the poor in 1206, and with a few followers, who had also given up their property, obtained Pope Innocent III's approval of his new order of the Friars Minor (little brothers) in 1209. Much against his will, Francis was soon the head of a large, loosely structured organization.

Dominic subordinated all other duties to the obligation to preach, while Francis of Assisi led a movement of protest against wealth and show. They were rivals in a sense, and both orders were soon borrowing from each other's principles. The Franciscans adopted the more efficient organizing principles of the Dominicans; the Dominicans took over the Franciscan emphasis on poverty. From the first the Dominicans had emphasized the need of study as a fundamental duty. Among the Franciscans, who began by repudiating book learning, soon some (even during Francis's life) imitated the Dominicans, moved into the universities, and became distinguished scholars. Their messages, that of the mendicant orders as a whole, however, went far beyond the brief description presented here. Dominicans and, above all, Franciscans articulated the deep spiritual needs of the urban population. Their public preaching brought a church that had grown distant and forbidding into the lives of many and provided access to the sacred to the middling sorts. Their embracing of an apostolic life and the preaching of the life of Christ had an important impact on western spirituality. Francis's preaching to the animals, his emphasis on the Christ-child, and his veneration of Nature as God's manifestation transformed popular culture and Christian teaching. He provided hope and answers where there were few.

In this and the previous chapter we discussed the transformations that social, economic, and religious structures underwent after the year 1000. Europe was poised for other transformations as well. None was more dra-

Portrait of St. Francis of Assisi (1182–1226), painted by Cimabue, a Florentine painter (1240–1302), over half a century after Francis's death. It reflects Francis's asceticism and holiness. (Alinari/Art Resource, NY)

matic than the revival of culture sweeping parts of western Europe from the late eleventh century onward. It is to this revival that we turn next.

SUMMARY

The church was the most important institution, political as well as religious, in medieval society. Successive waves of church reforms, from the early tenth century into the thirteenth century, strengthened the papacy in its relations with secular powers and reiterated the ecclesiastical leadership of Christendom. Some historians believe that the medieval papacy sought to achieve a papal monarchy that would dominate the temporal as well as the spiritual government. Regardless, the church's claim to supremacy led to a great struggle between the German emperors and the papacy over the investiture of bishops and the emperors' attempts to dominate Italy. The church emerged victorious from this struggle, and its prestige and power for the next two centuries were evident in the rise of the papal monarchy, the church's bureaucracy, and the church's sponsorship of the first three Crusades. Nonetheless, the need to reform was constantly felt in the medieval church. New religious orders—Augustinians, Cistercians, Dominicans, and Franciscans—were founded to fill this need.

SIX

Culture and Learning in Late Medieval Europe

Culture in the Medieval West, 1000–1400

Any discussion of the history of learning in the Middle Ages begins with two specific topics. The first is the manner in which classical culture was transmitted into the early Middle Ages; the second addresses the role of Christianity, or, to be more precise, of different forms of Christianity in the shaping of culture in the Middle Ages.

The Transmission of Classical Culture

In an earlier chapter we had the opportunity to examine briefly cultural developments in the early Middle Ages. It may be useful to revisit these themes as context for the literary and artistic developments of the later Middle Ages, for one cannot be explained without the other. In the nearly two hundred years of additional life for classical culture bought by Diocletian's and Constantine's drastic reforms in the late third and early fourth centuries, late Roman and Christian scholars developed the educational tools and cultural structures that allowed for the survival of specific aspects of classical civilization. This was a complex and difficult enterprise. It was often fraught with peril and, as is the case with all great cultural projects, with deep disappointments. A great deal of classical learning, works of art, and literary masterpieces were lost. We see that past only as fragments, but these fragments were important and served as central components for the making of a distinct western culture. The transmission of learning was, in many respects, a painful and heroic deed. It emerged from the recognition by a handful of scholars that something valuable, a whole way of knowing and of aesthetic sensibilities, was endangered, and that it had to be preserved and nourished. Far more important, it rested on the understanding that this knowledge had to be made accessible to new people—the Germans—who did not have the benefit of almost a millennium of Greco-Roman culture and tradition.

As was discussed earlier, the work of saving and transmitting culture was carried on at many different levels. Specific institutions, monasticism most of all, served as repositories of classical works. Monks began the tedious process of copying manuscripts—now written in parchment as the sources of papyri became too remote or inaccessible. They copied mostly liturgical books and Christian works, but monastic libraries stored and copied a diversity of Latin classics, including such openly lascivious works as Petronius's. *The Feast of Trimalchius* or Ovid's *Art of Love* and *Remedies of Love.*

The church was the great conduit for classical philosophical knowledge. Christian theologians incorporated Platonic, Aristotelian, Ciceronian, and other philosophical ideas into their own polemical and theological treatises. This was a process already underway from the first Christian century onward, but it crystalized most vividly in the fourth and fifth centuries. As we saw in Chapter 1, great Christian thinkers—Ambrose, Jerome, and Augustine of Hippo among them—took many pagan philosophical ideas and integrated them into, to use Augustine's famous title, a Christian doctrine. When faced with the question of what to do with pagan philosophy, Augustine, the greatest mind of the late antique world, answered clearly that it was there to be used and assimilated into new Christian cultural projects.

By the fifth century, the knowledge of Greek had waned in most of the West. The great philosophical works of Plato, Aristotle, and others were in peril of being lost. Boethius (d. 524) engaged in an ambitious project of translating all of Aristotle's and Plato's works from Greek into Latin. He only completed about half of the Aristotelian corpus, but the *Logic* served as the fundamental philosophical text throughout the Middle Ages until the translation of the rest of Aristotle's works in the twelfth century. Plato was lost. Only the *Timaeus,* a most puzzling Platonic work, was known to a few western medieval scholars, but Platonic and Neoplatonic ideas survived in the works of church fathers.

As was discussed earlier, Boethius was emblematic of those cultural heroes who carried out the labor of transmitting the knowledge of the past to that nascent and, in many respects, exciting new world. As we have also already learned, he was a Roman, an aristocrat, and a high official in the court of Theodoric, the Ostrogoth king of most of Italy. He was condemned to death and executed in 524 for his alleged connections with conspirators. His own Christianity was in conflict with the Arian Christianity of his German masters. He translated Aristotle, as was just noted. He wrote the last great work of the classical period, *On the Consolation of Philosophy,* a book cherished by medieval men and women from Charlemagne to Chaucer. He wrote and translated textbooks. In this Boethius followed the lead of Martianus Capella, a third-century pagan rhetorician.

In a memorable and influential work, *The Marriage of Mercury and Philology,* Martianus introduced into western culture the idea of the seven liberal arts. He had essentially reduced a great deal of classical learning to a core curriculum, recommending readings in the different disciplines or arts. Boethius took the concept and refined it. He divided the seven liberal arts into two branches: the *trivium* (from three), comprising grammar, rhetoric, and logic; and the *quadrivium* (from four), which included arithmetic, geometry, astronomy, and music. Boethius wrote or translated most of the textbooks used for learning these seven liberal arts. For the next seven hundred years, these were the texts from which medieval men and women learned about the world they had lost.

The Middle Ages and Christianity

Our second point is a simple one, to be reiterated in the following pages. Most of the Germans came into the western part of the Roman Empire as Christians. But they were, in the eyes of the Roman population, heterodox Christians, followers of the Arian heresy. The conflict over orthodox or heterodox observance of Christianity, a conflict that ended with the victory of orthodoxy by the sixth century, delayed the integration of Germans and Romans into one people. The most successful German settlers were, undoubtedly, the Franks. As was seen earlier, they came into the empire still faithful to their ancestral religion. When they converted at the end of the fifth century, they did so to the Roman version of Christianity. Their orthodox conversion guaranteed the Franks the wholehearted support of the church, with its formidable charismatic and persuasive power, providing a body of trained and literate advisers to the Frankish kings. It legitimized Frankish rule as their power became deeply intertwined with that of the church.

Christianity was also the thread running through the Germanic kingdoms. It bound Romans and Christians into a common culture. It provided an easy, and at hand, identity against the "infidel" Muslims and the suspected heretical Byzantines. Christianity buttressed the state and the social and economic systems slowly emerging in the West and underpinned German rule. It provided these mighty warriors with a sense of a wider and more sophisticated world, a memory to strive for, to imitate, to judge one's accomplishments against. By the tenth and eleventh centuries, the West was poised for a cultural revival, but the roots of many of these achievements rested with the toil of scholars in the difficult centuries between the fall of Rome and the year 1000.

The Revival of Culture

In the period between the investiture controversy (late eleventh and early twelfth centuries) and the end of the fourteenth century, Europe developed a lively and complex literary, philosophical, and scientific culture. Learning and art flourished along different paths. With educational centers, the universities above all (see later), and European courts as locomotives for this revival, late medieval literature, art, and philosophical and scientific inquiries had a signal impact on the later cultural traditions of the West. The tail end of this intellectual rebirth paralleled the first stirrings of the Renaissance in Italy, a very different type of cultural development, but one grounded in medieval precedents. Thus, it must be emphasized here that medieval Europe had already developed a robust and creative culture before the Renaissance and that cultural production in Italy in the fourteenth and fifteenth centuries has to be seen as part of a broad intellectual movement across most of the West. In Christian Europe, the long twelfth century witnessed a revival of classical knowledge and the emergence of new forms of thought. In Muslim Spain, and by implication in Christian Spain, Arabic knowledge, by which we mean the manner in which the Arabs had appropriated and commented on Greek philosophy and science, provided an alternative to the literary culture of the medieval Christian West. The borrowing from that culture by Christian scholars traveling to Spain, Sicily, and the Middle East in the twelfth century and afterward was largely responsible for the revolutions in learning of later centuries.

The Renaissance of the Twelfth Century and Beyond

From the late eleventh century onward most of western Europe underwent a dramatic cultural revival. This was limited, of course, to a small literate elite at the top, composed mostly of clerics but also including, in increasing numbers, noblemen and noblewomen and, in some cases, members of the bourgeoisie. The revival of letters, science, and education, which the great American medievalist Charles Homer Haskins described as a "renaissance," rested upon a series of significant social, political, and economic factors. The rise of towns provided a place for the exchange of ideas. Cathedral schools and universities, which came to replace monasteries as the centers of learning, were intensely urban institutions. The economic transformations of the eleventh and twelfth centuries provided capital for building projects and aesthetic endeavors. One example are cathedrals. Built in large numbers in the new Gothic style during this period, they would have been unthinkable without the wealth generated by commerce and artisan crafts. Moreover, a great deal of the architecture of the period reflected new spiritual concerns closely related to the developing values embraced by the bourgeoisie. But this feverish building program also revealed a sense of the confidence and booming economy of the period.

Cultural revival was not just influenced by urbanization and the rise of the bourgeoisie. The nobility settled down in the twelfth century and embraced a new lifestyle. Gone or diminished were the savage private wars of an earlier age. With order also came time for leisure, and courts (noble and royal) became the centers for vernacular literature and creative endeavors. In the countryside, because of the expansion of the arable and the availability of more and better food, the population increased. By the twelfth century there were more young people around. As befits a youthful culture, the elites in the twelfth century dressed in revealing dresses, with their hair uncovered, and acted in ways that were very different indeed from those of their predecessors. More significantly, Europe had not yet settled into a society sharply divided by national boundaries and identities. Knowledge and art flowed from one locality to another unimpeded by national or linguistic frontiers.

Although we may exaggerate here a bit, western medieval Europe was an open world, and a few people at the top, secular and ecclesiastics alike, experimented with new art forms and relished the pleasures of the beautiful. This cultural revival integrated many different art forms and genres. Learning had not yet developed along distinct disciplinary lines. Someone like Abelard, the greatest Christian philosopher of the twelfth century, also wrote love songs to his lover, Heloise. The latter, one of the wonders of her age, knew Latin poetry as well as the most educated of men and could write impassioned and erudite letters. Wandering clerical students wrote satirical and lascivious poetry. Alfonso X, the Wise, the king of Castile (r. 1252–1284), could compose beautiful songs for the Virgin in the vernacular (Galician language), the *Cantigas de Santa Maria,* and could write, at the same time, about law, Arabic science, and magic in Castilian. The fact that culture was fluid ought to be emphasized; nonetheless, for the sake of clarity, we explore different cultural manifestations as separate units. We follow therefore the high points of each learned tradition, tracing some of the major development in diverse areas of knowledge for over almost two hundred years of western European medieval history.

Literature

In literature, as in science and in social and economic life, Latin continued to be the language of the church and of learned communication almost everywhere in western Europe. All churchmen—John of Salisbury, Abelard, Bernard, Aquinas, and the rest—wrote Latin even when corresponding informally with their friends. Children began their schooling by learning it. It was also the language of the law and of politics; all documents were written in Latin, although property transactions were increasingly rendered in the vernacular. In Castile, however, all royal documents began to be written in the vernacular by the 1240s, and the affairs of government were conducted exclusively in Castilian (what today we call Spanish). Similar trends began to surface in Italy and other places throughout the West. Nonetheless, sermons were often delivered in Latin, and church hymns and popular songs were written and sung in it. But if Latin was widely used for all learned purposes, the period after the eleventh century marks the gradual triumph of the vernacular languages all over Europe for the literature of entertainment, of belles-lettres. Whereas *Beowulf* was the only important literary vernacular poem during the early Middle Ages, now such poems began to appear in ever greater numbers.

We may distinguish between several literary forms beginning in the twelfth century and continuing throughout most of the late Middle Ages. The first one, written in Latin, was Christian poetry. This type of literature consisted mostly of long poems that focused on Christian themes and, departing from the classical meter, conveyed deep emotions through rhyme and new poetical forms. A well-practiced genre, the most celebrated of these poems was Bernard de Morlaix's *Contempt of the World,* a very extensive poem that

---

The Written Record

GOLIARDIC POETRY

Written in Latin by clerics (wandering students in the lower ecclesiastical orders), Goliardic poems celebrated wine, love, and song. At times, as was the case with "The Gospel According to the Silver Mark," they also provided a critical outlook on church corruption or, as in the short poem "Let's Away with Studies," a reflective view of the passing of life. The poem here, "The Archpoet. His Confession," is considered the paradigmatic Goliardic poem. It was written by the "Archpoet," a pseudonym for either a German or a French cleric of knightly background, ten of whose poems (some of them political in nature) are extant. The "Confession" mocks pious Christian confessions in its embrace of gaming, drinking, love, and life.

> By the market and the crowd
> > Racketing uproarius
> Sit in quiet spots and think
> > Shun the tavern's portal,
> Write, and never having lived,
> > Die to be immortal.

From "The Archpoet," in *Mediaeval Latin Lyrics,* trans. H. Waddell (London: Constable, 1933).

---

told of the coming of the final judgment and beseeched Christians to look upward to the blessed Jerusalem (paradise).

As counterparts to these lofty works were the satirical, lascivious, and subversive poems of wandering scholars and clerics. Known as Goliards and their work as Goliardic poetry, the poems, written also in a lively Latin, emphasized the usual themes of student life: wine, the pleasures of love, and songs. We know many of these Goliardic poets by name and by the ideas advanced in that particular genre. In the Archpoet's "Confession" (1164), he vividly tells us what these young clerics were all about. The Archpoet promised his fellow Goliards and other readers that when the hour of his death would come near, he would be found in a tavern with a tankard in his hand.

Epic and Troubadour Poetry

The twelfth century also witnessed the writing down of older oral epic traditions. The epic, tracing its origins to Homer's *Iliad,* tells the heroic deeds of great warriors. In medieval epic poems, the exemplary lives of great warriors were often woven into narratives that specified the warrior's loyalty to his lord, the loyalty to one's homeland, and, in some specific cases, the Christian qualities of the warrior's sacrifice. Epic poems appear at the beginnings of all national literature. In Castile, the *Poem of the Cid,* composed around 1206 but based upon a historical figure and historical accounts dating back to the mid-twelfth century, told the story of Ruy Díaz de Vivar, el Cid—of his noble conduct to foes and friends; of his natural lord, Alfonso VI; of the king of Castile's unwillingness to acknowledge what a great vassal el Cid was; and, above all, of el Cid's unwavering loyalty to his king. In Germany, the older *Nibelungenlied* (*The Lay of the Nibelungs*) told of the tragic end of the Nibelungs (the Burgundians) at the hands of the Avars. In Russia, the late twelfth-century *Lay or Song of Igor's Campaign* recounted the failed expedition of Prince Igor against either the Polovtsy or Cumans (steppe peoples), while, in the Scandinavian lands, cycles of sagas vividly depicted the adventures of the Northmen in their journeys and adventures in the open sea.

In France, numerous epic poems recounted the deeds of French warriors. A particularly celebrated one in Old French is *The Song of Roland,* whose earliest surviving manuscript probably dates from a little after the year 1100. The poem deals with a historic episode far in the past, the defeat of Charlemagne's rear guard by the Basques (although the poem replaces the Basques with the Muslims) in 778 in the mountain pass of Roncesvalles in the Pyrenees. In *The Song of Roland* the landscape has brightened; a more intense Christian piety softens some of the worst violence. The highest virtue in the poem is loyalty to one's lord—a quality that was the first necessity in a feudal society where fealty to one's lord underpinned the entire social structure. In Roland's deep loyalty to his lord, Charlemagne, there is something new— a note of love of country.

Troubadour Poetry and Courtly Love

Very different from the epic tradition, although also written in the vernacular, troubadour poetry flourished throughout most of southern Europe in the late eleventh and early twelfth centuries, spreading its influence to other parts of Europe in later years and animating, in its particular derivation of courtly romances, some of the most significant literary works of the Middle Ages. Troubadour poetry focused on unrequited love, on the harshness of the lady, or the lord (since women wrote to their beloved as well), who refused to acknowledge the lover's devotion. At times, troubadour poetry took on lighter themes and turned the serious emotions of love into play. At other times, the lyrical forms of troubadour poetry were aimed at enemies and deployed as satirical attacks against an unwilling lady or a male competitor. The language of this poetry was mostly Provençal, the language of southern France, or Galician, the language of northwestern Spain. Troubadour lyrics and sentiments had roots in Spanish-Arabic and Spanish-Hebrew love poetry, but they also borrowed some of their forms and content from the classical tradition, above all, from Ovid. We know the name of over two hundred troubadours, including at least twenty-six women who wrote passionate and plaintive love songs to their lords. Most of those practicing these poetic forms acknowledge that the presiding genius of troubadour culture and, by implication, of courtly love, was Eleanor of Aquitaine.

The Written Record

THE SONG OF ROLAND

Roland has died on the field of battle, and Charlemagne believes that he was betrayed by Ganelon, who with his men deserted the field at a crucial moment. Ganelon is found guilty by trial, but before he can be executed one of his followers, Pinabel, challenges one of the emperor's most devoted liege men to battle. The following passage describes that battle.

In a broad meadow below Aix la Chapelle,
The barons meet; their battle has begun.
Both are courageous, both of them valiant lords,
And their war-horses are spirited and swift.
They spur them hard, and loosening the reins,
They charge each other and strike with all their might.
Both shields are shattered—they're broken into bits.
The hauberks break, the girths are split apart,
The saddles fall, and with them both the knights.
A hundred thousand are weeping at the sight.

Both chevaliers have fallen to the ground.
Losing no time, they're on their feet again.
Agile and swift is Pinabel, and strong;
They face each other—they have no horses now
And raise their swords whose hilts are made of gold
To strike and hew each other's shining helms;
Those heavy blows can cut right through the steel.
The French lament, thinking their man must fail.
"God," says Charles, "now let the right prevail!"

Says Pinabel,"Thierry, admit you've lost!
I'll be your vassal in loyalty and love,
All I possess shall be at your command
But reconcile the king and Ganelon."
Then Thierry answers, "That's easy to decide!
I'll take no offer unworthy of a knight!
Let God determine which one of us is right!"

Says Pinabel, "Almighty God forbid!
I stand here now for all my family—
I won't surrender to any man on earth!
Better to die than live to merit blame."
So once again they slash with their great swords,
Striking the helmets brilliant with gold and jewels
Great fiery sparks fly out against the sky.
Now neither champion will to the other yield
Until a dead man is lying on the field.

The Song of Roland, trans. Patricia Terry (Indianapolis: Bobby-Merrill, 1977), 141–45.

Funerary monument of Eleanor of Aquitaine at the abbey of Fontevrault (France). Divorced wife of Louis VII, King of France, wife of Henry II, King of England (whose tomb is next to hers), and mother of Richard the Lionhearted and John I (both also kings of England), she was the presiding patroness and inspirer of troubadour culture and courtly love.   (Erich Lessing/Art Resource, NY)

The richest heir in the West, with extensive lands throughout southwest France, Eleanor married the young king of France, Louis VII, in 1137. Whether in Aquitaine or in Paris, she drew around her a court of troubadours, ladies, and knights to adhere to new highly symbolic and eroticized codes of conduct. When her marriage ended in divorce—Louis resented Eleanor's alleged infidelities during the Second Crusade and her inability to bear a male heir—Eleanor returned to her lands. On her way home to her beloved South, she was seduced/kidnapped by the young Henry of Anjou, the future king of England as Henry II; she married him in 1152. As England's queen and the consort to Henry Plantagenet, the powerful ruler of the

Angevin Empire, and as mother to several formidable sons, including Richard the Lionhearted, and to gifted daughters who presided over courts of their own throughout western Europe (in Champagne, Castile, and other places), Eleanor was the inspiring genius of a new type of literary enterprise and for new bold cultural projects. Troubadour sang her praises throughout Europe.

> *God save Lady Eleanor*
> *Queen who art the arbiter*
> *of honor, wit and beauty*
> *of largesse and loyalty.*
> —Philippe de Thaun

> *Were all lands mine*
> *From Elbe to Rhine*
> *I'd count them little worth*
> *if England's Queen*
> *Would lie my arms between.*
> —Anonymous, German

Bernard of Ventadour, the greatest of the troubadours, came to Eleanor's itinerant court around 1155. He wrote that "a man without love is little worth," stating what would become the driving motif of courtly love.

Courtly Love, *fins amor*

What is courtly love, and what was its impact on European civilization? Marina Warner, a noted literary critic, stated recently that courtly love may have been one of the greatest achievements of western civilization. At a very simple level, courtly love was part of literary artifice. A young man of the knightly class loved a lady, almost always his social superior. More often than not, the lady was married to the young man's lord. Our courtly lover would compose highly lyrical and erotic poems in honor of his lady. He would undertake deeds of arms and of valor on her behalf. He would wear her colors, and his behavior and manners would testify to his love and fidelity to his lady. Courtly love flourished through lyric poetry. The code of *courtoisie* (from which would develop modern concepts of courtesy) required that the lady almost always prove unattainable. The wife of another, made inaccessible by the obligations of feudal vassalage, the lady was to be worshiped from afar. The troubadour celebrated in ecstasy even the slightest kindness she might offer him. Her merest word was a command, and her devoted knight undertook without question even the most arduous mission she might propose to him, without hope of a reward. But a lady who failed to reward him, at least to some degree, was not playing by the rules of this elaborate and artificial game. So much, however, for literary artifice, even though this description provides clues as to the complexities of courtly love. The new theories of courtly love operated at several levels simultaneously.

An illustration from Alfonso X's Cantigas de Santa Maria. *The* Cantigas *were a vast collection of Marian miracles and devotional songs to the Virgin written in Galician by Alfonso X, king of Castile in the late 1250s. This particular illumination shows troubadours and musicians performing at the king's court.*

First, this new code of behavior borrowed heavily from feudal discourse, replacing the lord-vassal relationship by the lady-devoted knight love ties. In a sense, the courtly romances challenged the culture of honor and loyalty, so vividly deployed in epic poetry, and replaced it with a new culture of love. This debate between honor and loyalty to one's lord on the one hand and love and loyalty to one's beloved on the other is one of the central motifs in works such as Gottfried von Strassburg's *Tristan* or Chrétien de Troyes's *The Knight of the Cart* (*Lancelot*). In both works, a model knight, Tristan in the eponymous work and Lancelot in *The Knight of the Cart*, are caught in the terrible dilemma of choosing between a lord they admire and respect, King Mark and King Arthur respectively, and their love for their beloved, Isolde and Queen Guinevere. At the end, love always conquers and feudal loyalty is defeated. The love was not always unattainable, but it could be highly physical.

Second, courtly romances also appropriated religious discourse. The heightened and emotional language used now to address the lady replicated the emotionally charged language present in mystical visions and used to address God. In some respects, courtly language and highly eroticized descriptions of romantic sentiments were also imitated and borrowed by mystics to express their union with God. As such, courtly love was essentially subversive and undermined both the feudal order and the grip that the church had on Christians throughout the West.

In *Tristan*, the cave of crystal—to which the lovers flee and where they lie naked with a sword separating them—is a counterpoint to the cathedral. It was a cathedral of human love. In one of the passages in the book, the author engages in a satirical attack against the ordeal, thus mocking the idea that God intervenes in the decisions of men. Because courtly love also borrowed heavily from Celtic lore, it introduced into the European imaginary a whole world of fairies, dragons, and magic that was, in itself, unchristian. Not surprisingly, the church condemned the doctrines of courtly love in the early thirteenth century.

Third, courtly love has to be seen as an important aspect of women's history. The western tradition, from both its classical and Judeo-Christian roots, was particularly patriarchal and misogynist. Courtly love did not give women of the upper classes equality with men, but it certainly changed their position. The worship of the lady, paralleled by a similar increase in Marian devotion, changed the role of certain women at the top and gave them a standing that they did not enjoy either within the church or within society as a whole. Courts of love, presided over by high-born ladies, dictated the conduct of men and bound them to the artificial, although nonetheless powerful, laws of chivalry. Something fundamental changed in the twelfth century. It was short lived, however, and by the fourteenth century, literary works such as Thomas Mallory's *Le Morte d'Arthur*, presented pejorative representations of women. But for a brief period of time and applying only to a few ladies at the top of the social pyramid, salvation was to be found in the lady's hands.

Finally, the rules of courtly love required new forms of behavior. Etiquette and manners became important. This "civilizing process," to use Norbert Elias's famous formulation, had a very significant impact on the European imagination. The concept of nobility itself is born from the idea that a certain type of behavior—a courteous behavior—combined with education and the ability to both play music and speak languages, while remaining a courageous knight, were the true ingredients of knighthood.

As the knight was always defined as a mounted man, the unwritten code that came to govern his behavior was called *chivalry*, from the French word *cheval*, a horse. As was noted earlier, the literature of chivalry and courtly love developed with particular complexity at the court of Eleanor of Aquitaine, who left Henry II of England in 1170 to live with her daughter Marie, countess of Champagne, at the court of Poitiers in western France. There the two became patrons of writers and poets. The hopes of aristocratic women were revealed through the tales of courtly love.

The most distinguished court literature can be found in the work of Chré-tien de Troyes, Andreas the Chaplain (or Capellanus), and Marie de France. Chrétien de Troyes's *Chevalier de la Charette* (*The Knight of the Cart*)—the plot seems to have been given to him by Marie of Champagne—expressed the doctrines of courtly love in their most developed form; Chrétien's work has been called "the perfect romance" for its presentation of a Lancelot who would cast aside all conventions for the love of Queen Guinevere. Marie wrote simpler tales about the physical attraction exerted by youth and beauty, while Andreas the Chaplain wrote, in *De Amore*(*On Courtly Love*), a most extensive treatise on courtly, carnal, and profane love and the attitudes of the church toward the subject. These stories, like *The Song of Roland,* were told, sung, and written in cycles, added to by troubadours (wandering min-strels) as they spread the tales to other lands.

Perhaps the best-known were the stories that evolved around King Arthur of Britain. The exploits of Arthur's knights (of whom Lancelot was one) became part of the vernacular literature in most of western Europe. Taken up in France, these stories were passed in the thirteenth century into Germany, where Wolfram von Eschenbach wrote a long poem about Arthur's knight, Sir Percival. This work marks the high point of the quest literature, centered around the search for the Holy Grail. Writers throughout most of western Europe drew upon the Arthurian cycle for romances and books of chivalry into the early sixteenth century.

In Italy, the original home of Latin, a vernacular language was somewhat slower to develop. But here, too, at the sophisticated and cosmopolitan court of the emperor Frederick II in Palermo, some of Frederick's chief advisers began to write love poetry, and soon the fashion spread northward. It was not until somewhat later, with Dante Alighieri (1265–1321) of Florence, that the vernacular Italian tongue scored its definitive triumph.

Dante and *The Divine Comedy*

For his greatest work, *The Divine Comedy,* Dante chose Italian. Among writers in the Western tradition, Dante belongs with Homer, Virgil, Shakespeare, Cervantes, and Goethe as a supreme master. As a towering intellectual figure, he heralds the new age of rebirth. But *The Divine Comedy* was a medieval poem, in some ways the most typical of all medieval literary expressions. *The Divine Comedy* is far more than a work about courtly love. It is a political and cultural summation of medieval civilization. It ends in a mystical vision of the Godhead, but a Godhead that is peculiarly Aristotelian.

Lost in a dark wood in his thirty-fifth year, "halfway along the road of our human life," Dante encounters the Roman poet Virgil, who consents to act as his guide through two of the three great regions of the afterlife: hell and pur-gatory. Descending through the nine successive circles of hell, where the eter-nally damned must remain forever, the two meet and converse with souls in

One of the earliest representations (fourteenth-century) accompanying a text of The Divine Comedy. *It shows the author, Dante (1265–1321), meeting his beloved Beatrice in the terrestrial paradise after his journey from hell.*   (Erich Lessing/Art Resource, NY)

torment, some of them historic persons, others recently deceased Florentines of Dante's own acquaintance with whose sins he was familiar. In purgatory less sinful human beings are being punished before they can be saved. The souls of the great pagan figures, born too early to have become Christians, are neither in hell nor in purgatory, but in limbo—a place of rest on the edge of hell where Virgil himself must spend eternity.

When the poet comes to the gates of paradise, Virgil cannot continue to escort him, so the guide to the final region of the afterlife is Beatrice, a Florentine woman with whom Dante had fallen desperately in love when both were in their youth, and whom he had worshiped only at a distance. Here Dante was consciously transforming one of the central experiences of his own life—his first encounter with Beatrice at the age of nine—into literature in accordance with the traditions of the code of courtly love. In paradise he finds the Christian worthies and the saints, and at the climax of the poem he sees a vision of God himself. This voyage through the afterlife is designed to show a traditional Christian concept: People's actions in this life determine their fate in the next. From the lost souls in hell, who have brought themselves to their hopeless position, through those who despite their sufferings in purgatory confidently expect to be saved, to those whose pure life on earth has won them eternal bliss, Dante shows the entire range of human behavior and its eternal consequences.

Almost a contemporary of Dante, Juan Ruiz, the archpriest of Hita, wrote the *Libro de buen amor* (the *Book of Good Love*, c. 1337), which told of a very different journey, one marked by libidinous encounters and seduction, but all of them placed within a didactic Christian framework. Similarly, Boccaccio's *Decameron* in the mid-fourteenth century provided a brilliant collection of obscene tales, written as a response to, and in the context of, the onslaught of the plague. Another important late medieval author was Geoffrey Chaucer (1340–1400).

Chaucer and *The Canterbury Tales*

By Chaucer's day the vernacular had a long history in England, and the Old English of the pre-Conquest period had evolved into a new form of the language usually called Middle English. An experienced man of affairs who served his king at home and abroad, Chaucer left behind many literary works, including a long and moving poetic narrative love story, *Troilus and Criseyde*, which derives its characters from the Trojan War stories then fashionable in western Europe. His most celebrated work, however, is *The Canterbury Tales*—tales told by a group of pilgrims on their way to the tomb of Thomas à Becket, the sainted archbishop of Canterbury murdered under Henry II. The pilgrims come from all walks of English life except the high nobility and the very poor and include a knight, a squire, a prioress, a clerk, a monk, a friar, a sailor, a miller, and others. On the way from London each tells at least one story. The knight tells a romantic story of chivalric love in which two cousins fall in love with a maiden whom they have barely glimpsed from the window of their prison cell. Deadly rivals thereafter, they cherish their mutual strife, in prison and out, without the lady being aware of them. In the end, one kills the other and wins the lady as his own. The miller tells a raw story of a young wife's deception of her elderly husband with a young lover. The prioress tells a saint's legend, the squire an unfinished story full of semi-scientific marvels, and so on. Chaucer does not hesitate to satirize his churchmen. The fourteenth century was a period of much discontent with the English church, and the poet was striking a note that was sure to be popular.

Education

With a few exceptions, the church alone directed and conducted education in medieval Europe into the early modern period. Unless destined for the

An illustration from Geoffrey Chaucer's (1348–1400) Canterbury Tales. *The illustration shows pilgrims from all social orders on their way to the tomb of Thomas à Becket in Canterbury. London is in the foreground.*   (*Art Resource, NY*)

priesthood, young men of the upper classes had little formal schooling, although the family chaplain often taught them to read and write. Young women usually had less education. The monastic schools educated future monks and priests, and the Cluniac reform stimulated study and the copying of manuscripts. In towns, especially in Italy and Flanders, merchants and members of the ruling local elites were often literate, and a growing reading public expanded the circulation of culture.

Medieval scholars, following Boethius, divided knowledge into the seven liberal arts: the *trivium* (grammar, rhetoric, dialectic) and the *quadrivium* (arithmetic, geometry, astronomy, music). The first three included much of what we might call humanities today; the last four corresponded to the sciences. In the eleventh century only a few monastic schools taught all seven, but by the fourteenth century the seven liberal arts had become a mere gateway to university education. In general monks sought to preserve rather than to advance knowledge. The cathedral schools, on the other hand, fostered a more inquiring spirit. In France during the eleventh century, at the cathedral schools of Paris, Chartres, Rheims, and other towns, distinguished teachers were often succeeded by men whom they themselves had trained, and distinguished pupils went on to join or found other schools. In Italy, a medical school had existed at Salerno since the early Middle Ages. At Bologna law became the speciality. Students were attracted to Bologna from other regions of Italy and even from northern Europe. In the early twelfth century, as education became fashionable for young men ambitious for advancement in the church or in the royal service, the number of students grew rapidly.

The student body at Bologna organized itself into two associations—students from Italy and students from beyond the Alps—and in the twelfth century the two incorporated as a whole body, the *universitas,* or university. As a corporate body they could protect themselves against being overcharged for food and lodging by threatening to leave town. They depended on their own work, or on their parents, to meet their living expenses. Since knowledge came from God, universities were essentially free and endowments and ecclesiastical benefits were set to support students and teachers.

If the students did not like a professor, they simply stayed away from his lectures. Soon the students fixed the price of room and board in town and fined professors for absence or for lecturing too long. The professors organized, too, and admitted to their number only those who had passed an examination and so won a license to teach. The university of Paris represents the best example of a university ruled by the teachers. In Paris and elsewhere in the North the cathedral schools were the forerunners of the universities. The teachers organized as a guild made up of those who taught the seven liberal arts and who got their licenses from the cathedral authorities. By the thirteenth century pious citizens had founded in Paris the first residence halls for poor students, who might eat and sleep free in these "colleges." The practice crossed the Channel to Oxford and Cambridge, where the schools' authorities stoutly resisted control by the secular powers.

Universities spread throughout Europe at a fast pace. By the fourteenth century universities existed throughout most of western Europe, but there were also communities of scholars outside the universities, advancing learning and new forms of knowledge. In the twelfth century, as cathedral schools and the first universities were on the rise, northern European scholars came to realize the trove of classical knowledge available in Spain, Sicily, and the Middle East. Many of them traveled south, mostly to Toledo, to meet Arab, Jewish, and native Christian scholars. There they learned about Greek medicine and philosophy and came in contact with the works of Arabic and Jewish commentators. For the most part, the revival of science and the new directions taken by twelfth-century philosophy can be accredited to translations of works by Galen and Hippocrates and to the recovery of the whole body of Aristotle, its translation into Latin, and its reception in cathedral schools and universities throughout the medieval Christian West.

In Italy, where the Roman past remained so vividly alive, communities of writers, artists, and thinkers pursued their interests outside the confines of the universities or the church. The Italian cities provided a rich environment in which a new kind of learning could thrive. The court of Frederick II, the Hohenstaufen ruler of Germany and Sicily, in southern Italy was an important center for philosophical and artistic inquiries. By the late thirteenth century, Italian scholars and thinkers embraced a wide range of cultural pursuits. Someone like Dante, to give just one example, could display a masterful command of Aristotle and his Arab commentator, Averroës; could deploy lyrical poetry; and could make knowledgeable references to Chrétien de Troyes's works without the benefit of a full scholastic (university) education. But despite these examples, there was, however, an important world of scholars in which ideas were hotly debated. These debates began in monastic and cathedral schools in the late eleventh century and dominated the intellectual world of Europe until the early thirteenth century and the reception of Aristotle in the West. Two main issues were debated: (1) the relationship between faith and reason and (2) the question of universals.

Medieval Philosophy: The Question of Universals

Much of the study at that time consisted of mere memorizing by rote, since in the days before printing ready reference works were scarce. Although the rules of scholarly debate and inquiry were fixed by the medieval reliance on Aristotelian logic and rhetorical training, lively discussion existed nonetheless. Discussion and teaching were particularly preoccupied with defining systems by which people could live faithfully within the expectations of Christendom. At the turn of the eleventh century, Gerbert of Aurilac, who became Pope Sylvester II (r. 999–1003), stood out as the most learned man of his day in the West. His probing mind delved into the portions of Aristotle that Boethius had translated and discovered in logic a systematic means of approaching the writings of the church fathers. By the end of the century, churchmen could debate whether it was proper to use human reason to consider a particular theological question and to explain away inconsistencies in the Bible and in the writings of the church fathers.

Once the new method became available, late eleventh- and early twelfth-century thinkers employed it in a celebrated controversy over the philosophical problem of universals. A universal encompasses a whole category of things; when we say "dog" or "table" or "person," we mean not any specific dog or table or person, but the idea of all dogs, tables, or people. The question that concerned medieval thinkers was whether universal categories exist: Is there such a thing as dogdom, tabledom, or humanity apart from the aggregate of individuals? If you said no, you were a nominalist; that is, you thought dogdom, tabledom, and humanity were merely *nomina* (names) that people give to a general category from their experience of individual members of it, but without independent reality or existence. You experience dogs, tables, and persons, and so you infer the existence of dogdom, tabledom, and humanity because the individual members of the category have certain points of resemblance; but the category, the universal, has no existence in itself. If you said yes, you were a realist; that is, you thought that general categories did exist. Many realists took this view a large step further and said that the individual dog, table, or person was far less real than the generalizing category or universal. Some said that the individual dog, table, or person was a mere reflection of one aspect of the category and existed only by virtue of belonging to the category: A person exists only by partaking of the nature of humanity, a dog because it partakes of the nature of dogdom. Medieval realism reflected, in fact, the survival and transmission of Platonic idealism through the works of church fathers. It was embraced wholeheartedly by most medieval scholars until challenged by Abelard's innovative work and by the triumph of Aristotelian philosophy in the thirteenth century.

If we transfer the question of universals to politics and think of the kingdom and the individual, we can see at once how great its practical importance may be. A pure nominalist would say that the kingdom or any type of political organization is just a name and exists only because the individuals who make it up are real. It could therefore be argued that governments and political entities must then serve their subjects, since after all they are only the sum of their individualities. A pure realist would say that the realm, or later on the state, is the only real thing, that its individual subjects exist only insofar as they partake of its general character, and that the state, by virtue of its existence, properly dominates the individual. In religion, an extreme nominalist, arguing that what we can perceive through our senses is alone real, might even have trouble believing in the existence of God, although there were yet no philosophical categories or discourse available to contemporaries to allow for atheists. An extreme realist would tend to ignore, or even to deny, the existence of the physical world and its problems.

Anselm of Canterbury. Moderate realists have to start with faith—to believe so that they may know, as Anselm (1033–1109) put it. A philosopher and theologian, Anselm was born in Aosta, Italy. He traveled to Bec in Normandy to study under Lanfranc and ended his life as archbishop of Canterbury. His life is representative of the peripatetic life of medieval scholars, who ranged throughout most of western Europe in search of teachers. Anselm's approach to knowledge is known as Scholasticism, a system of thought that, in part, dated back to Boethius. He used this approach most obviously in his so-called ontological proof of the existence of God. According to Anselm's proof, that which exists in reality as well as in the mind must be greater than that which exists in the mind alone, and since the mind can conceive the idea of a being greater than all else, it logically follows that this being must exist in reality as well as in the mind, or it is not in fact greater than anything else.

Peter Abelard. Peter Abelard (1079–1142), a popular lecturer at the cathedral school of Paris and perhaps the greatest Christian philosopher of the twelfth century, argued that universals were not merely names, as the nominalists held, nor did they have a real existence, as the realists held. They were, he said, concepts in people's minds, and as such had a real existence of a special kind. Abelard insisted on the importance of understanding for true faith. He put reason first; thus a person must understand in order to believe, instead of the other way around. His famous work *Sic et Non* (*Yes and No*) lists more than 150 theological statements and cites authorities both defending and attacking the truth of each. When Scripture and the fathers were inconsistent, he seems to argue, how could a person decide what to believe without logical thought? A rationalist and lover of argument, Abelard was nonetheless a deeply pious believer. However, Bernard of Clairvaux, the great Cistercian reformer, who was a mystic and suspicious of reason, believed Abelard heretical and had some of his views condemned and denounced repeatedly.

Abelard is also important for other reasons. His passionate love affair with Heloise, the niece of a canon of Notre Dame of Paris, led to his castration at the hands of ruffians hired by Heloise's uncle. Later, Abelard wrote an autobiography, one of the first autobiographies written in the West since St. Augustine's *Confessions* (a previous autobiographical work had been written by Guibert of Nogent a few years earlier). When Heloise read Abelard's *History of His Own Calamities,* she initiated a feverish correspondence. Although some scholars have question the authenticity of the correspondence, their letters provide a moving portrait of medieval individuality, erudition, and passion.

Thomas Aquinas.   By the time of Abelard's death, the Greek scientific and philosophical writings of antiquity were starting to be recovered, often through those translations from Arabic into Latin mentioned earlier. In the second half of the century came the recovery of Aristotle's lost treatises on logic, which dealt with such subjects as how to build a syllogism (an expression of deductive reasoning), how to prove a point, and how to refute false conclusions. Yet the recovery of Aristotle posed certain new problems. For example, the Muslim philosopher Averroës, whose comments accompanied the text of Aristotle's *Metaphysics,* stressed Aristotle's own view that the physical world was eternal; since the soul—a nonphysical thing—was essentially common to all humanity, no individual human soul could be saved by itself. Obviously, this ran counter to fundamental Christian teaching. Some scholars argued in the late thirteenth century that both views could be true—Aristotle's in philosophy and Christian in theology. But this led directly to heresy. Others simply tried to forbid the reading of Aristotle, but without success. It was the Dominican Albertus Magnus (1193–c. 1280), a Swabian, and his pupil Thomas Aquinas (1225–1274), an Italian, who succeeded in reconciling the apparent differences between Aristotle's teachings and those of the Christian tradition.

Aquinas's best-known writings were the *Summa Theologica* and the *Summa contra Gentiles.* He discussed God, humans, and the universe, arranging his material in systematic topical order in the form of an inquiry into discussion of each open question. First he cited the evidence on each side, then he gave his own answer, and finally he demonstrated the falsity of the other position. For him, reason was a most valuable instrument, but only when it reasonably recognized its own limitations. When unaided reason could not comprehend an apparent contradiction with faith, it must yield to faith, since reason by itself could not understand the entire universe. Thus the "Angelic Doctor," as Aquinas was called, worked out a systematic theology on rational principles, declaring that, since truth was indivisible, there was no contradiction between faith and reason, theology and philosophy. Nonetheless, by embracing the material views of Aristotle and by emphasizing with Aristotle the naturalness of the state, Aquinas opened the door to a more secular perception of political relations and of the place of humans in the world.

Political Thought

In dealing with problems of human relations, medieval thinkers came fairly close to a social contract theory of politics. Except for extreme realism, medieval political thought was emphatically not autocratic. To the medieval thinker the perfection of the kingdom of heaven could not possibly exist on earth, where compromise and imperfection were inescapable. Nor could full equality exist on earth. Medieval political thought accepted as its starting point an order of rank in human society. The twelfth-century *Policraticus* (*Statesman's Book*) of the English philosopher John of Salisbury (c. 1115–1180) provided a complete statement of this social theory. The prince (or king) is the head of the body of the commonwealth; the senate (legislature) is the heart; the judges and governors of provinces are the eyes, ears, and tongue; the officials and soldiers are the hands; the financial officers are the stomach and intestines; and the peasants "correspond to the feet, which always cleave to the soil." The peasant, the blacksmith, the merchant, the lawyer, the wife, the priest, and the king had all been assigned a part of God's work on earth. This "organic" theory of society was a great favorite with those who opposed change.

While medieval thought thus distinguished among vocations, it also insisted on the dignity and worth of all vocations. It accepted the Christian doctrine of the equality of all souls before God. Even the humblest person on this earth could hope to enjoy bliss as full and eternal as any king's in the next world. Furthermore, medieval political theory by no means opposed all change on earth. Medieval thinkers were certainly not democratic in the sense of believing that the people had a right to, or could, "make" their own institutions. But they did not hold that, since God had arranged authority as it was in this world, humanity should preserve existing conditions, come what may. Later Marsiglio of Padua (c. 1290–1343), the author of *Defensor Pacis* (*The Defender of Peace*), found the only true source of authority in a commonwealth to be the *universitas civium*, the whole body of the citizens. Marsiglio probably did not mean to be as modern as this may seem. But like many other medieval thinkers, Marsiglio believed that no one's place in the order of rank is such that those of lower rank must always and unquestioningly accept what is commanded of them. Moreover, Marsiglio sharply separated the two spheres or sources—ecclesiastical and secular—of power. He insisted that the pope, the "disturber of peace," should limit his authority to questions of morals and religion and should remove himself altogether from the political realm. Bartolus, writing in the mid-fourteenth century, stated in a famous formula that what touched all should be decided by all. This legal pronouncement paralleled actual practice. Kings in the Middle Ages ruled with the consent (on matters of taxation and governance) of the ruled.

If worse came to worst, medieval political thinkers were willing to approve tyrannicide. To the medieval mind, law for common everyday purposes was custom. But beyond custom lay the *law of nature,* or natural law—something like God's word translated into terms that made it usable by ordinary persons on earth. And beyond that was the imposing power of Roman law. By the mid-thirteenth century, Roman-based law codes began to be written throughout most of Mediterranean Europe. The best example of this new type of legislation is Alfonso X of Castile's *Siete Partidas.*

Science in the Medieval West

By the late twelfth century a growing interest in scientific inquiry was evident throughout the West. The Middle Ages saw considerable achievement in natural science. Modern scholars have revised downward the reputation of the Oxford Franciscan Roger Bacon (c. 1214–1294) as a lone, heroic devotee of "true" experimental methods, but they have revised upward such reputations as those of Adelard of Bath (twelfth century), who was a pioneer in the study of Arab science; William of Conches (twelfth century), whose greatly improved cosmology was cited for its particularly elegant clarity; and Robert Grosseteste (c. 1175–1253) at Oxford, who clearly did employ experimental methods. In many ways modern western science goes back at least to the thirteenth century. But science in the Middle Ages still did not question the authority of the ancients. It borrowed freely from Arabic scientific traditions and practical know-how. Thus, real progress took place in the technologies that underlie modern science—in agriculture, in mining and metallurgy, and in the industrial arts generally. Accurate clockwork, optical instruments, and the compass all emerged from the later Middle Ages. Even such sports as falconry and such subjects as astrology and alchemy (which would reach their heyday during the Renaissance) helped lay the foundations of modern science. The breeding and training of falcons taught close observation of the birds' behavior, astrology involved the same kind of observation of the heavens and complicated calculations, and alchemy relied upon the identification and rough classification of elements and compounds. Mathematics was pursued throughout the period. Through the Arabs, medieval Europeans learned Arabic (really Hindu) numerals and the symbol for zero—a small thing, but one without which the modern world could hardly get along.

Finally, and most important, the discipline of Scholasticism, as has already been noted, formed a trained scholarly community that was accustomed to a rigorous intellectual discipline. Natural science uses deduction as well as induction, and early modern science inherited from the deductive Scholasticism of the Middle Ages the meticulous care, patience, and logical rigor without which the inductive accumulation of facts would be of little use to scientists.

Mysticism

Mysticism, the idea that one may have a direct union with God, flourished in the twelfth century after a long period (from the early fifth to the late eleventh century) for which we do not have evidence for such experiences. Many mystics were known in the late Middle Ages. Hildegard of Bingen was an influential woman because her contemporaries believed that she had, in her mystical trances, become one with God. Bernard, mystic and activist, denounced Abelard, thinker and rationalist teacher. St. Francis also distrusted formal intellectual activity. For him, Christ was no philosopher; Christ's way was the way of submission, of subduing the mind as well as the flesh. The quality of Francis's piety comes out in this fragment of the *Canticle of the Brother Sun:*

Praised be thou, my Lord, with all thy creatures, especially
My Lord Brother Sun that dawns and lightens us.

Be praised, my Lord, for Sister Moon and the stars that thou
hast made bright and precious and beautiful.

Be praised, my Lord, for Brother Wind, and for the air and
cloud and the clear sky and for all weathers through which
thou givest sustenance to thy creatures.

Be praised, my Lord, for Sister Water, that is very useful
and humble and precious and chaste.

Be praised, my Lord, for Brother Fire, through whom thou
dost illumine the night, and comely is he and glad and bold
and strong.

Be praised my Lord, for Sister, Our Mother Earth, that doth
cherish and keep us and produces various fruits with
coloured flowers and the grass.*

As was seen in the previous chapter, St. Francis's preaching of poverty and of the beauty and goodness of nature had a signal impact on the western mind. His message captured perfectly the new mentality and values of the

---

*Quoted in H. O. Taylor, *The Mediaeval Mind* (Cambridge, Mass.: Harvard University Press, 1949), vol. 1, 445–46.

rising mercantile and urban groups. As the church lost a great deal of its support, the Mendicants (those who begged for their sustenance, Franciscans and Dominicans) reignited a new spirituality. Nonetheless, Francis's privileging of voluntary poverty created a sharp contrast between those who voluntarily renounced their wealth and the world and those who had always been poor. Thus, the early thirteenth century also marked the beginning of new and harsher treatment and representations of the involuntarily poor. Bonaventura (John of Fidanza, 1221–1274), a follower of St. Francis and head of the Franciscan order, preached to his students in Paris that the human mind could understand only things of the physical world. Only by divine illumination could humans hope to gain cognition of the divine or supernatural. Prayer, not study, and love and longing for God, not reason, were the answer for Bonaventura, and was also true of the mystics.

The Arts

The Romanesque style dominated church building in the eleventh and most of the twelfth centuries. Based on the principles of Roman architecture, with round arches, thick walls (to support the weight of the ceiling), and narrow windows, Romanesque architecture emphasized the interiority of belief and sought to guide the believer into inner spiritual spaces. The Gothic style, following it and developing from it, began in the late twelfth century and prevailed to the fifteenth. The great Gothic churches made the spirit of those within the building soar into the lofty nave spaces and impressed the believer, through the colors and lights filtered through the windows, with God's greatness.

Among the great Romanesque churches were those built at Mainz, Worms, and Speyer in western Germany. Another great Romanesque monastery church, with its surrounding buildings, was the complex at Cluny, and yet another was the pilgrimage church of St. James (Santiago) at Compostela in northwestern Spain. In the twelfth century thousands of pilgrims made their way to this site every year, using what may be the first "tourist guide" ever written, the *Pilgrim Guide* of circa 1130. The beautiful sculptures on the façade of the cathedral at Compostela (known as the Porch of Glory) and the striking cloisters at Moissac, Silos, and elsewhere in the West are vivid testimonies to the possibilities of Romanesque architecture and its powerful aesthetic and religious messages.

Changes in the Romanesque style were slowly in the making. The Durham Cathedral, in the north of England, shows typical Norman Romanesque rib vaulting, which permits the eye a greater sense of spaciousness as one looks up the nave toward the east window. Romanesque had become an international style, for the same type of interior could also be found in Italy, in the cathedral of Pisa and elsewhere. Variations on the typical Romanesque church can be found today throughout southwestern France. Domed roofs are representative of the style, sometimes with the domes in a row above the nave or, if built between 1120 and 1160, in a Greek (equal-armed) cross pattern, as seen at St. Front of Perigueux.

Interior of the Romanesque church of the Madeleine, Vezelay (France). The church, while retaining the round Roman arch characteristic of Romanesque architecture, borrowed new technical aspects from the Gothic. This innovation allowed for larger windows and more light. A shrine dedicated to Mary Magdalen, the church at Vezeley was an important pilgrimage stop on the road to Compostela. (Scala/Art Resource, NY)

Beginning in the late eleventh century Romanesque structures began to change substantially. The arches now gradually rose from round to pointed at the peak. Similarly, the roofs also rose more and more steeply as the smooth flow of the arch was sharply broken and two loftier curves met instead at a point. Pointed arches and great windows to let in light, the chief features of the newer medieval architecture known as Gothic, enabled the builder to carry his buildings to soaring heights. Pillars were used to take the place of a whole section of solid Romanesque wall, and the spaces between the pillars could be used for windows. Outside, too, increased lightness and soaring height were achieved by arched supports, called "flying buttresses."

Into the new window spaces the craftsmen of the thirteenth century fitted a new form of art: windows in multicolored (stained) glass, glittering with

Built in a generation in the twelfth century, the cathedral of Chartres, an important mercan-
tile, artisan, and cultural center south of Paris, is the high point of the early Gothic style. Its
spires and sculptured facades show what many art historians consider to be the most beauti-
ful manifestation of the Gothic.   (Vanni/Art Resource, NY)

gemlike colors in ruby, sapphire, and emerald and showing biblical episodes or episodes from the life of the saint whose church they illuminated. But the Gothic style was a great deal more than just technical innovations. Its rise was representative of the mental and cultural transformation that the medieval world underwent in the twelfth century and of the new relationship between men and women and their God. It invited the believer to soar upward to the vision of God and to marvel in the play of light and colors.

Gothic architecture flourished for at least two centuries everywhere in Europe. Its first and perhaps greatest moments came in northern France, at the abbey church of St. Denis, and between the 1190s and about 1269, with the building of the cathedrals of Chartres, Rheims, Amiens, Notre Dame of Paris, and other celebrated churches. Open and vast, solidly built, soaring upward,

Sculptures on the exterior of the cathedral of Chartres depict Old Testament prophets and kings and the new humanism developing in twelfth-century western Europe. (*Foto Marburg/Art Resource, NY*)

the Gothic cathedral terminated in aerial towers. Although its great windows let in the light, the stained glass covering these windows kept the interior dim and awe inspiring. In the fourteenth and fifteenth centuries ornamentation grew richer, decoration became more intricate, and Gothic architecture on the Continent moved toward its decline. In England, however, the later, richer Gothic produced such marvels as King's College Chapel in Cambridge and the Henry VII Chapel at Westminster Abbey in London. The Gothic, however, did not conquer everywhere. Italy, with its long tradition of classical architecture and with the permanent examples of Roman buildings and art within eyesight, resisted the popularity of the new style.

Shortly before 1100 a revival of European sculpture began. The tradition had never been lost, as demonstrated by early medieval Irish and English crosses and by Continental sculptures and artwork in France, Spain, and else-where. But the finest surviving examples of the art of sculpture before the Romanesque revival were in ivory and metalwork. Now the stone of the churches began to blossom out with rosettes, palm leaf ornaments, and grapevines; hiding behind the foliage would be mythical beasts. Scenes from the Bible also appeared on the capitals above the columns. Gradually sculp-ture in the round became more common. Lifelike representations of drapery and the firm balance of the figures on their feet were the principal character-istics of these statues, occurring chiefly in northern France. Similar traits were seen elsewhere in metalwork and in manuscript illumination, rather than in monumental sculpture. The influences from outside that helped make the development possible came through Byzantine art, then undergoing a kind of classical renaissance, which became available to western eyes through renewed and intensified contacts between East and West by pilgrims, travel-ers, and warriors during the period of the Crusades.

The career of the Florentine architect, sculptor, and painter Giotto di Bon-done (c. 1266–1337) is particularly illustrative of how one stage of artistic development is father to the next. A friend of Dante, Giotto often followed the Byzantine models so popular in his day, but he also sought to make his paint-ings more lifelike and emotional. He learned from Italian sculptors who had studied the sculptures on the portals of Gothic cathedrals, especially at Chartres. Giotto executed similar forms in frescoes, creating the illusion of three dimensions by the use of foreshortening and perspective. Between 1304 and 1306 Giotto painted thirty-eight frescoes depicting the lives of the Virgin and Christ. His scenes of the Kiss of Judas and of the Entombment became highly influential in the development of Renaissance art.

Even before the Renaissance, Giotto exemplified the Renaissance artist's approach to his work—individualistic, intent upon fame and success, expect-ing lucrative commissions, and engaging in business activities (in this case as a debt-collector and a landlord to weavers) for further profit. Money and art were wed through patronage, as when the great banking families of the Bardi and Peruzzi of Florence employed Giotto to apply his art to the Church of Santa Croce.

Dante, Chaucer, Giotto, and the soaring Gothic spire all attested to the pri-macy of the Christian God. Each sought to show life as a pilgrimage, a search for salvation in an ever more complex world; each sought to draw the eye upward, literally to follow the Gothic tower toward heaven. Each was lively, energetic, fond of exquisite detail. The complexity of one of Chaucer's pil-grim's tales, the intricacy of an inner circle of purgatory in Dante's vision of a netherworld, and the carefully rendered individuality of one of Giotto's fig-ures all spoke to the desire to see the individual in relation to God.

For most of the medieval West the dominant authority remained the church. Few leaders in the area that was to become Germany thought that there could be a secular state, for all theory relating to governance derived from the church, which was an intermediary with God. Even architecture reflected this view. However, in France, Castile, England, and the rising city republics of Italy, the contest between secular and ecclesiastical authorities was clearer. In these countries philosophers and statesmen felt they could discern clear boundaries between temporal and spiritual matters. And in these countries and towns science and literature were developing themes that, while Christian, nonetheless anticipated the rise of the secular domain.

SUMMARY

From the late eleventh century onward most of the medieval West underwent a dramatic cultural revival. This rebirth of education, literature, and other cultural forms had its origins in the social and economic transformations after the year 1000 and in increased contact with Muslim civilization, the great repository of classical knowledge.

Literature, in both Latin and the vernacular, dealt with heroic themes and love. Courtly love played a signal role in the civilizing of the European upper classes. Medieval thinkers sought to construct systems of thought that would have universal applicability. Nominalists opposed realists on the issue of whether universal categories could exist. The dominant approach to philosophy—Scholasticism—was primarily concerned with proving the existence of God. The leading Scholastic thinkers were Anselm, Albertus Magnus, and Thomas Aquinas. John of Salisbury's organic social theory adapted Scholastic thought to politics. Mystics distrusted human reason and relied on divine inspiration to achieve union with the divine.

Progress took place in the technologies that underlie modern science, and the discipline of Scholasticism formed a trained scholarly community that was accustomed to a rigorous intellectual discipline. Although Latin was still widely used, the vernacular languages were increasingly employed for the literature of entertainment, as in French tales of chivalry, *The Song of Roland,* Dante's *The Divine Comedy,* and Chaucer's *The Canterbury Tales.*

The Romanesque style gave way to the Gothic in the twelfth century, and Gothic dominated to the fifteenth century. Among its greatest achievements are the cathedrals of Chartres, Notre Dame in Paris, Rheims, and Amiens. The Florentine architect, sculptor, and painter Giotto best bridged the styles of the late Middle Ages and the Renaissance that was to follow.

SEVEN

Politics and Society: The Origins of Kingdoms and Communities, 1000–1300

Out of the social and economic transformations of the late Middle Ages and the cultural revival that began in the twelfth century (Chapter 6), new political institutions and ways of organizing the land emerged throughout the West. The classical world had invented important political associations— empires, city-states, and theocracies—but nations did not exist in antiquity. Between 1000 and the early fourteenth century the first steps toward the eventual emergence of the nation-state were taken. It is to the Middle Ages then that we trace the origins of our modern nations. This process of state formation in western Europe took place in two stages. The first—the subject of this chapter—was signaled by the emergence of a fairly centralized kingship; by the early stages of bureaucratic development; by the Crown's deployment of symbols and rituals of authority aimed at forging loyalty to the king and, eventually, to the kingdom; and by the emergence of a wider sense of identity among the people of a region. In the second stage—sketched briefly in a later chapter (Chapter 9)—nascent political entities weathered the late medieval crisis and emerged, at the end of the fifteenth century, as the forerunners of the nation-state. These kingdoms and, in some cases in Italy and parts of Germany, cities or loosely organized empires were very different indeed from the kind of political associations one finds around the year 1000.

We ought not to be deceived by this simple outline. The making of the nation-state, a difficult and much-debated idea, with the implications of centralization of power, elaborate bureaucracies, defined borders, and large regional identities, is not an easy or ready-made undertaking. State-building was, and is, an ongoing process. Its high point in western Europe came only in the nineteenth century, but in many parts of the world, including Europe, it remains an unfinished work. The recent wars in the Balkans and the separatist agitation in the Basque country (Spain) and elsewhere throughout the

West are grim reminders of the perils involved in the construction of national identities and of the long time that it takes for the secular or "rational" state to emerge. In truth, the late medieval and early modern proto-state was so intertwined with religion that secular states are, in fact, a very recent phenomenon.

Historians have recently questioned whether it is proper to speak of nations or states at this early stage. Indeed, we would be in error if we were to describe some of the new feudal monarchies as nations or even states. They were not. Nor can we speak yet of nationalism, although regional and national identities and concomitant ideas about love for one's country (*patria*) or "fatherland" can be found in the late thirteenth century. Nonetheless, even though one must be cautious to deploy such culturally laden words as "nation," "state," and "nationalism" in a medieval context, it is nonetheless true that by 1300 a good number of the institutions emerging around 1000 had been radically transformed. The ability of kings or city rulers to tax their citizens, to organize and keep on the fields armies not fully dependent on feudal obligations, and to assert their authority in new and intrusive ways represented a sea change from the fragmented and private ways of organizing territories and people in an earlier period.

Another caveat is that in the Middle Ages there were many different roads to political organization. The Castilian, French, or English models, to mention just a few, proved eventually to be the most successful models of political organization, but they were not necessarily the most efficient or successful in the twelfth and thirteenth centuries. Only in hindsight can we say that one type—the territorially based kingdom—proved to be more successful than the other. Nor should we accept without question the idea that the nation-state, as developed in the medieval West, was the only or best way to organize polities. The benefits, as shall be seen, were many, but much discomfort and pain were also caused by the coercive powers and expansionist policies of the rising state. There were diverse roads to political organization. The German and Italian models are significant and clear reminders that not one pattern was the norm in western Europe. These regions, which did not become nation-states until the mid-nineteenth century, are very good examples of how the absence of a unified nation did not prevent an exceedingly high level of cultural production or fail to provide a setting for good and productive lives. Other places, the Crown of Aragon for example, could form, as shall be seen later, federated political aggregations that functioned quite efficiently into the modern era. In fact, the Crown of Aragon's political organization is almost replicated by the European Union today.

Moreover, what we describe here applies mainly to certain parts of the West only. In Scandinavia, in the Baltic region, in what eventually became Russia, and in the Near East, other forms of organizing kingdom and people were as effective as those in France and England, areas that have often been thought of as paradigmatic of political development. In the East, Byzantium endured, although with many travails, as a highly centralized monarchy until the mid-fifteenth century. The great Muslim powers in Baghdad, Alexandria, North

Europe, Circa 1320

Africa, and eventually among the ruins of the Byzantine Empire had long enjoyed the kind of centralized power and elaborate bureaucracies only in the making in the West in this period. Farther East, the great emperors of China and Japan and the princely rulers in India exercised authority and held powers that were inconceivably sophisticated when compared to western standards. In the New World, Mayan lords ruled over societies far better organized than those of western Europe. The West did not have a monopoly on political centralization and statecraft. It was, in fact, far behind in its development when compared to other parts of the world.

The Early Construction of the State in the West

Several models of medieval kingship developed from the eleventh to the early fourteenth centuries in western Europe. Within each specific model were also different stages of development. Here we attempt to provide an outline of these developments and to highlight some of the salient points that went into the making of late medieval kingdoms and regions. Later we provide specific examples from the core areas of western Europe and contrast these developments in Chapter 8 with areas in the so-called peripheries of Europe. One of our guides to the theoretical assessment of the origins of centralized polities is the classic book by Ernst Kantorowicz, *The King's Two Bodies* (1957). In it Kantorowicz provides a broad view of how some kings (mostly in England and France) legitimized their rule and were able, over a long period of time, to admit no superior within the borders of their respective realms. With numerous exceptions and caveats, this process can be summarized as follows.

Christ-Centered Kingship

As was noted in an earlier chapter, one of the characteristics of early medieval kingship was the partial or, in some cases, total loss of the public nature of government. The kingdom was the private property of the king. It was often partitioned among heirs or given as benefices or as outright property to faithful vassals. What then were the sources of royal authority? The formulation was a simple one. The king ruled by the grace of God. He was the steward of his people, fostering and protecting the work of the church and the well-being of his subjects. Upon the election and/or coronation of a king, the bishop, or ecclesiastic performing the ceremony, turned to the people (the magnates and great men of the kingdom) and told them: "People, this is your king; obey him." Then turning to the king, he told him: "King, these are your people; rule them justly." The implication, within the strong Germanic tradition of contractual kingship, is that the king, as the secular representative of Christ and as wielder of the secular sword (given to him by the church), had powers that were limited and subordinated to the church, Christ's chosen bride. The king's responsibility was to his people and not to the land. He ruled as king of the Franks or the Angles without a sense of territoriality.

The Investiture Controversy: Law and Polity

The investiture controversy, although focused mainly on the conflict between the pope and the emperor (see Chapter 5), had significant reverberations in other areas of Europe. The papal claim to absolute power (*plenitude potestatis*) was based on the pope's role as vicar of Christ and on a particular interpretation of the New Testament and of patristic texts that privileged the power of the church over lay rulers. This claim, repeated through the centuries by ecclesiastical writers and church leaders, forced secular ruler to look elsewhere for their own sources of authority. This they did without abandoning their own Christological claims (i.e., that their power also came from Christ). With the revival of Roman law in the twelfth century, kings throughout the West began to claim that they were the makers of the law as well as their enforcers. The old Roman formula, *Whatever the prince desires has the force of law*, was tailor-made for new royal ambitions. Throughout the West kings became lawgivers. This was the case with the numerous charters given by Castilian, English, and French rulers, a testimony to their understanding of this newly gained power. Rising bureaucracies, a most important component in the embryonic origins of the state, pushed the limits of royal authority as far as they could. The *Domesday Book*, an eleventh-century Norman

England survey of all sources of income in the realm, is a very good example of royal authority and of its bureaucracy's newly intrusive and encompassing powers.

Territoriality

With the king as representative of the law also came a new identification of the king with the land. By the eleventh century in Castile and Aragon and by the late twelfth and early thirteenth centuries in France and England, a new sense of territoriality emerged. Kings in France and England changed their titles from kings of the French and the English to kings of England and France. This development, earlier in Mediterranean lands than in the North, was significant and had been long in the making. The final pages of the *Song of Roland* serve as a reminder of the manner in which the anonymous author represented France, "sweet France," as Roland, in the moment of death, looks upon a land which, in 1100, was not yet France. This new sense of the link between land and people was born from a rising sense of property as tangible and measurable. By the late twelfth century medieval men and women began to think of their lands not just as jurisdiction and feudal rents, but as something that could be measured and itemized. With these shifts in values, a nascent sense of the kingdom as a territorial entity came also into being. This meant the emergence of somewhat recognizable borders (although the process of formalizing national boundaries would take a long time) and, by the late thirteenth century, customs houses. The latter made very clear the liminal space between one's lands and that of others.

The Beginning of Communal Identities

This is a perilous subject. The construction of national identities, the feeling that one is French and not English, or Castilian and not Aragonese, was a long time in the making. Regional identities and allegiances to one's lord, to God, and to one's lady provided different centers for the emergence of an identity. Kings and their agents worked very hard to create an identification between the king and the land and to foster what we may call today a sense of patriotism and loyalty to the king and the land. By the late thirteenth century, political writers were already deploying sentiments such as *pro patria mori* (to die for the fatherland/motherland). Together with this new heightened sense of the land as one's mother or father and the king as synonymous with the land came the sense of the undisputed authority of the king within the newly constituted borders of his realm. By the early thirteenth century kings or their lawyers throughout the medieval West were deploying legal formulas that argued that the king is emperor in his own lands. This is a very early formulation of the idea of sovereignty (not to be fully elaborated until the mid-fourteenth century). It meant, as was noted earlier, that the king recognized no superior within his own borders. He was the equivalent of the emperor in his own land. This addressed two potential enemies: the emperor with his claims to universal hegemony and the papacy with its claims to spiritual, and political, supremacy.

A sense of community depended also on such culturally shaped categories as ethnicity, religion, language, and culture. Identity was deeply grounded in the use of a common language and in the understanding that certain people shared customs and ethnicity and that one could trace one's ancestry to a specific group. These myths—Patrick Geary discussing an earlier period calls them the "myths of nations"—are very powerful. Castilians traced their lineage back to the Visigoths; the French to the Franks; the English to either the Saxons or the Normans. The reality was very different, but these shared common histories, as mythical as they may have been, provided a powerful rallying point in the emergence of new regional and, eventually, national identities. Castilians and Aragonese described themselves as Christians as a marker of difference against Muslims and Jews in their midst. Communities of language played a significant role in this process, as they do to this day. The English upper classes spoke French or something like French into the late Middle Ages when it became obvious that their new identity required them to speak as most of the people in the land did. Dante's use of the Tuscan dialect in his *Divine Comedy* fixed Italian as the language of culture in the early fourteenth century. Similarly, the writing of all official documents in Castilian by the 1240s gave Castile a formal linguistic unity that few kingdoms enjoyed in the thirteenth century. Luther's translation of the Bible into German served as a rallying point in the emergence of a German sense of cultural and linguistic unity (although Germans spoke different types of dialect) despite political fragmentation.

The Symbols of Authority

How could kings represent and project their power in a world without television, radio, or the Internet? And how could a monarch exercise his authority in a world without sufficient means of coercion (no standing armies, no police)? The answer is that through the use of rituals, festivals, and symbols kings were able to foster a religion of monarchy, and, eventually, to command the loyalty of their people. These symbols are still used to day to foster patriotism throughout the world. It is an old and well-tried formula.

The methods to invest the king, or in the case of Italian cities the commune, with such a mystical sense of authority differed from place to place. In France and, to a lesser extent, England, coronation and anointment came to play an important role. In the case of the French, the anointment was no simple matter. French kings were anointed at Reims with sacred oil that was claimed to have come down from heaven for the baptism of Clovis in the late fifth century. Such was the power of this image that the heirs to the throne could not become kings until anointed and that French kings were still following this ritual as late as 1830. The French and English kings also claimed, from the twelfth century onward but tracing these powers to a much earlier age, that they could cure scrofula (a skin disease) with the touch of their hands. They were *thaumaturgical* kings.

In other parts of Europe, the ceremonies of coronation and anointment did not play such a significant role; in some cases they played no role at all. Frederick II, the great Hohenstaufen emperor, crowned himself, not allowing the church to play any meaningful role in the ceremonies. Without any recourse to sacrality, although he certainly thought of himself as almost sacred, Frederick II ruled over perhaps the most centralized realm (his Italian possessions in Sicily and southern Italy) in early thirteenth-century Europe. The kings of the Crown of Aragon also crowned themselves, as did the kings of Portugal. The kings of Castile abandoned crowning and anointing by the mid-twelfth century and claimed that their authority rested on the fact that they were the leaders of the Reconquest and had been acclaimed (elected) by the "people" (the magnates) and on a series of other secular ceremonies. They rejected any mediation by the church while extorting large quantities of money from ecclesiastics for the purpose of mounting crusades against the Muslims in the south. Nonetheless, even though the Castilian rulers were neither crowned nor anointed and ridiculed the French and English royal claims of thaumaturgical powers, they were quite successful in creating a territorial kingdom and in exercising their authority throughout the land. In Italy tyrants, guilds, and patrician elites legitimized their rule through the patronage of the arts and through great civic displays. Throughout western Europe, royal entries and royal coronations or ascents to power brought about great displays and festivals. They served as didactic performances, reinforcing a sense of loyalty to the king and the country. These festive displays taught also about hierarchies of power and about the obedience that was due to those on top.

The King Never Dies: Primogeniture and Inalienability of the Land

Together with these developments, primogeniture allowed for an uncontested line of descent and allowed certain royal houses (those successful like the French in having an uninterrupted male line for centuries) in strengthening their hold over their realms. By the thirteenth century the king came to be a symbolic representation of the kingdom. As an individual he could own his own property, his personal domain, but as king he held lands that belonged now to the realm and had to be passed undivided to his heir. The lands that belonged to the Crown, the national territory if we wish to call it that, could not be alienated (although in fourteenth-century England, France, and Castile it would be given away to members of the royal family). In addition, the king, as a mortal man, could and did die, but the King, as an emblem of the nation, never died. The chant "le roi est mort; vive le roi" ("The king is dead; long live the king") meant that at the moment of one king's death another king came to power, thus renewing the unbroken chain of rulership.

Capitals and Sacral Centers

Some feudal monarchies, the French and the English most of all, also bene-. fited from establishing permanent administrative centers in one location. Although medieval kings were essentially peripatetic, traveling through and from their lands and collecting their dues from scattered possessions and

The royal castle at Segovia (eleventh through fifteenth centuries) reflects the new power of kings. The castle, perched on an easy-to-defend location, dominated the city of Segovia and the surrounding countryside. It became one of the favorite royal residences in mid-fifteenth-century Castile. (SEF/Art Resource, NY)

recalcitrant vassals, the emergence of Paris and London as fixed centers for the French and English monarchies played an important role in the construction of the nation-state. Similarly, the association of royal houses with sacral sites—the English with Westminster, Canterbury, and York; the Castilians with Toledo and St. James of Compostela; the French with St. Denis and Reims; the Aragonese with Zaragoza; the Norman kings of Sicily with Palermo—contributed to the formation of a collective identity. At the same time, the establishment of royal pantheons—the creation of a family mythology through burial and remembrance—at Westminster, St. Denis, Las Huelgas of Burgos, Palermo, and elsewhere helped solidified the rising religion of monarchy.

Feudal Monarchies

Having outlined all these elements that went into the origins of the nation-state and of the rising power of kings, one must remember that royal successes depended, to a large extent, on the kings' cunning exploitation of feudal bonds. Historians have argued that by making sure that dues were exacted and by demanding military service, or payment in lieu of it, monarchs were able to centralize power and to make themselves superior to their great and powerful vassals. The process was not that simple. As shall be seen briefly in Chapter 9, civil wars in the fifteenth century in France, England, and Iberia almost wrecked the early construction of the nation-state. Nonetheless, by unceasingly claiming their feudal rights and by insisting on their suzerainty, kings came, in time, to hold the upper hand. How did this work in reality?

The Emergence of Centralized Kingdoms in the West

As it is improper to speak of nations or states, it is also incorrect to speak of centralization. In reality, the feudal monarchies emerging in the West after 1000 were not centralized in the manner in which modern states are centralized today. Nonetheless, significant changes took place in the manner in which kings ruled. There was a growing awareness of the public function of governments, a greater need—fueled by the requirements of new forms of warfare—to gain access to the financial resources of peoples and cities through taxation and for more sophisticated bureaucracies and standing armies. A great deal had changed, even though the old feudal structures and the absence of a truly centralized process often undermined the rulers' efforts.

The Iberian Peninsula

Around the year 1000 the Iberian peninsula witnessed dramatic political changes. Until then, the caliphate of Cordoba had held a firm grip on most of southern Iberia, the area known as al-Andalus. In the North, close to the Pyrenees and to the peaks of Europe's mountains, fledgling Christian kingdoms had come into being from the late eighth century onward. The oldest and most important was the kingdom of Asturias-Leon, claimant to the Visigothic legacy, firmly established in the Leonese plains but not yet able to withstand the caliphate armies. Shortly after 1000, everything began to change. By 1031, the caliphate collapsed and splintered into a series of independent Muslim kingdoms, the so-called kingdoms of *taifas.* Even though some of these new entities were quite prosperous (Granada, Seville, Zaragoza, and others), they no longer had the ability to retain their hegemony over their Christian opponents. In the north, a new power was on the rise. Under the rule of Sancho III, the Great (1000–1035), the small mountain kingdom of Navarre conquered all the other northern Iberian kingdoms. At his death, Sancho III, as was the traditional custom in Christian Iberia, divided his kingdoms among his heirs. This led to fratricidal wars between the heirs, as each of them sought to reunite the realm under one single ruler.

By 1035, one could identify a diversity of political units. In the south, Muslim kingdoms rose and fell under the pressures of invaders from North Africa. After the 1260s and spectacular Christian conquests in al-Andalus, only the Nasrid kingdom of Granada survived, but it did so as a dependent state until its final conquest in 1492. In the northeastern portions of the peninsula the heirs or relatives of Sancho III came to rule the three distinct realms (or counties) of Navarre, Aragon, and Barcelona (Catalonia). In the central and the northwestern regions of the peninsula, three different kingdoms vied for supremacy: Galicia, Asturias-Leon, and Castile. Portugal did not come into being as a separate kingdom until the early twelfth century. Of all these different political entities, Castile and the conglomerate of kingdoms known as the Crown of Aragon came in time to contest for primacy in Iberia.

The Rise of Castile, 1035–1312.   In the period between the early ninth century and 1035, Castile was a county or administrative dependence of the ancient Asturian-Leonese realm. Sitting, as it did, on the frontier with Islam, the region proved particularly dynamic in carving a political space in central Iberia against both Islamic raids and the hegemonic pretensions of the Astur-Leonese kings. Before 1035, its counts attracted inhabitants to the frontier with liberal charters or laws. Castles (from which the region took its name) rose to defend the hard-earned territory. A new vernacular language, Castilian, was already rapidly evolving. In 1035, Ferdinand I (1035–1065) ruled over the united kingdoms of Castile, Leon, and Galicia. Benefiting from the fragmentation of the caliphate, Ferdinand I was able to carry out successful raids against Muslim territories and to collect heavy tributes from the kingdoms of *taifas*. This tribute, also known as *parias,* provided substantial income to the nascent Castilian monarchy. New cities rose or were repopulated on the frontiers with Islam, Avila, Segovia, Salamanca, and others. The Cluniac order was encouraged to settle in Ferdinand's realms, and important Cluniac monasteries rose along the road that led to the pilgrimage shrine at Compostela. Unlike in northern Europe, the nobility derived most of its privileges and income from royal largesse and from shares in the booty and tributes gained in the South. On the one hand, a warring nobility continuously engaged in battles and raids on the southern frontier. Because of their military role, the high nobility always represented a source of danger for the Crown, especially in times of royal minorities or disputed successions. On the other hand, no great noble house could ever accumulate holdings that would make it, as was the case in France, an effective rival to royal power. In this respect, the tribute money collected from the Islamic kingdoms created conditions that were radically different from those in the emerging realms north of the Pyrenees. It created a financial and political dynamic that allowed for more extensive royal power. In addition, because Castile and other Iberian kingdoms were "societies organized for war," this yielded different types of social structures: greater peasant freedoms, greater mobility of the population as it was drawn to the South in the wake of the reconquest of lands from the Muslims, different types of economic structures (less mercantile active, with an emphasis on livestock and movable goods).

Ferdinand I divided his kingdoms among his three sons. This is not surprising. After all, the Iberian kingdoms had distinct histories and had remained as separate entities for a long time, and, although the most prestigious (not necessarily the most powerful) went always to the oldest son or, in the absence of a male heir, oldest daughter (in Spain women could inherit the throne), it was traditional to partition the realms. After the usual struggle between the brothers, Alfonso VI emerged as the sole ruler of the three realms. Alfonso VI (1065–1109) was an energetic and competent ruler. He continued the policy of protecting and fostering Cluniac and French influences in northern Spain. Under his reign, Castile accepted the Roman or Cluniac liturgy and abandoned its traditional Mozarabic ritual, thus firmly linking his realm with the rest of Europe. He was very successful in advancing the work of the Reconquest, and the crowning success of his campaigns and policies was the capture of Toledo in 1085, the ancient capital of the Visigothic Empire and liturgical center of the peninsula. With Toledo also came rulership over large populations of Jews and Muslims. Respectful of their religions (as long as they paid tribute to the king), Alfonso VI represented himself as the "emperor of the three religions," ruling fairly peacefully and justly over his heterogeneous subjects. Toledo also became a center for Arabic learning and a magnet for northern scholars eager to have access to Arabic science and classical texts long lost in the West. Alfonso VI's court took on administrative responsibilities not unlike those described later for twelfth-century English kings. He was able to collect territorial taxes throughout the land (in March and November), since all the lands, in theory, belonged to the king. He also advanced claims to supremacy over all the other kings within Iberia. In 1086, however, his progress into the rich lands of the South was thwarted by an Almoravid invasion from North Africa. Even though the Almoravids prevented any further Christian expansion for a while, Alfonso VI was able to keep Toledo under his rule and established Castilian hegemony over the center of the peninsula once and for all.

Urraca (1109–1126), Alfonso VI's daughter, inherited the throne in the absence of male heirs. Her first marriage to Raymond of Burgundy had produced a son, the future Alfonso VII, but Raymond's premature death led to Urraca's wedding to the king of Aragon, Alfonso the Battler. This was a formidable couple and, since Alfonso died without children, their marriage could have led to an early union of the crowns of Castile and Aragon. But Urraca and Alfonso could not get along at all. Their marriage was punctuated by continuous personal and political conflict. At home, Urraca had also to face the wrath of the bourgeoisie. Throughout the towns along the road to Compostela, urban dwellers rose up in arms demanding freedom from their ecclesiastical lords and new privileges. At Compostela, the queen was dragged into the streets and humiliated. Despite these setbacks, Urraca was able to neutralize the ambitions of her troubling husband and eventually abandon him. She was also able to pass the kingdom of Castile undivided and undiminished to her son, Alfonso VII.

The reign of Alfonso VII (1126–1157) marks a watershed in peninsular history. During his rule, the administration of the realm continued to develop. Royal and municipal officials went out throughout the land, marking the royal presence in everyday affairs. The king's peace protected pilgrims trekking on their way to Compostela or merchants plying their trade with al-Andalus and with northern Europe. Taxes were collected. The Reconquest picked up steam once again, as the Almoravid power waned. Alfonso VII called himself "emperor of all the Spains," and although other peninsular kings did not take this very seriously, it marked Castile's claims to hegemony in Iberia.

All of his accomplishments, however, were somewhat detoured by the death of his son Sancho III one year after assuming the throne of Castile in 1158. Leon had gone to Alfonso VII's second son, Ferdinand II. The minority of Sancho III's son, Alfonso VIII (1158–1214), was a wicked period. Great noble families, the Laras and the Castros, fiercely competed for the regency. Civil wars raged across the countryside. Aragon and Leon took over Castilian lands in their respective frontiers. When Alfonso VIII came to age, he proved to be perhaps the most gifted of all medieval Castilian rulers before Isabella the Catholic. A pious and honest man, married to one of Eleanor of Aquitaine and Henry II's daughters, Alfonso VIII restored peace in the realm, provided justice for his subjects, and began an arduous campaign to recover the lands taken by his peninsular rivals. In 1212, he organized and led a large international army against a new wave of North African invaders, the Almohads. The crucial Christian victory at Las Navas de Tolosa in that same year signaled the turning point in the relationship between Islam and Christianity in Spain. From henceforth, the days of a Muslim independent political entity existing in Spain were numbered. Christians were now firmly on top.

One must note that in 1188, the king of Leon, Alfonso IX (r. 1188–1230), called a meeting of the Cortes. Although there had been earlier gatherings of magnates and high clergymen to discuss the affairs of the realm in 1020 and afterward, the 1188 meeting was the first one to include representatives from the towns. As such, this constitutes the first parliament (a gathering of the three different orders of society: clergy, nobility, and urban representatives) in medieval Europe and one in a long line of representative assemblies called by the Leonese and Castilian kings from the late twelfth century onward. Almost a century before the first English parliament, Leon-Castile had Cortes, where urban representatives came to decide on matters affecting the political and financial life of the realm. No taxes could be raised without the consent of those who paid them, a practice that remained in place until the centralizing policies of Isabella and Ferdinand in the late fifteenth century.

Alfonso VIII's grandson, Ferdinand III (1217–1252 in Castile, 1230–1252 in Leon), was the great beneficiary of his grandfather's triumphs and policies. Under Ferdinand III, a cousin and contemporary of St. Louis and like him also canonized as a saint, the kingdom was organized in distinct territorial units. A royal official, a *merino*, represented the Crown in judicial, fiscal, and administrative matters. By the 1240s, the language of royal administration shifted from Latin to Castilian; the kingdom was thus the first in Europe to embrace the vernacular as the language of everyday business and government. In the 1230s and 1240s, most of the South was conquered by Ferdinand III's armies, with Seville and Cordoba as the signal prizes of his efforts. We now know that Ferdinand III was also at the vanguard of important legal reforms. By granting the vernacular Romance version of the Visigothic law known as the Fuero Juzgo, as a charter to individual towns in the newly conquered lands, the king sought to institute a unified system of law throughout the realm. When he died in 1252, he left a united and powerful country. Chroniclers and literary works from the period were already beginning to emphasize the unique attributes of Castile and to forge a sense of national identity.

His son, Alfonso X, the Wise (1252–1284), followed in the steps of his father, now ruling over the united realms of Castile and Leon. His court became the center for lively cultural exchanges. Jews, Muslims, and Christians worked side by side in Alfonso's *scriptorium*, producing scientific, literary, magical, and scientific works. Besides being the patron of this cultural revival, Alfonso X was himself a main contributor in the fields of lyrical poetry, scientific/ magical works, and the law. His ambitious legal program, the *Siete Partidas*, an extensive compilation of Roman-based law, sought to unify the entire country under the rational rule of law. In this he failed. Noble and urban resistance against legal encroachment on their ancient rights; the ambitions of his own son, Sancho; a downturn in the economy; and other social upheavals led to civil strife and to the overthrow of the king's ambitious program. From 1284 onward, with a few notable exceptions, Castile was plagued by royal minorities, usurpation of power, wanton and selfish violence by the nobility, and disorder. This long series of crises lasted with small respites along the way, until Isabella and Ferdinand restored order to Castile.

The Crown of Aragon

One of the most remarkable and interesting political entities in the medieval West was the Crown of Aragon. Out of the collapse of Navarrese power in the 1030s, Sancho III's children and relatives carved out kingdoms throughout northern Spain. In the northeast corner of Iberia, two significant political units emerged. The kingdom of Aragon was an inland kingdom, scarcely populated, mostly dependant on a rural economy, with only a handful of important towns—Zaragoza, the capital; Calatayud; and others. Perched between the Pyrenees and the Mediterranean, Catalonia or the County of Barcelona was a prosperous area, tracing its political history back to Charlemagne. Dominated by the great city of Barcelona and its commercial interests, Catalonia shared with its Occitanian neighbors language and culture. When Ramiro II's (1134–1137) daughter, Petronila, married the ruler of the County of Barcelona, Ramiro Berenguer IV (1131–1162), a new entity came into being, the Crown of Aragon (*La corona de Aragon*).

Ramiro Berenguer and his heirs ruled over Aragon as kings of Aragon, following the customs, laws, and traditions of the Aragonese realm. They came to the Cortes (the parliament) of Aragon to ask for subsidies and taxes and dealt with the powerful and unruly Aragonese nobility the best way they could. In Catalonia, they ruled as counts of Barcelona, and also had to come hat in hand to ask for the cooperation and financial and military support of the proud merchants and urban nobility of Barcelona. In Aragon, the king spoke a form of Castilian with Aragonese intonation and words. In Catalonia, the language of the people was Catalan. All official documents were written in Latin.

When Jaume I (1213–1276), a great, learned, and enterprising king, conquered the city of Valencia and its rich hinterland, these new possessions were not annexed to one of the existing kingdoms but became an independent entity within the Crown of Aragon. Valencia also had its own Cortes or parliament, its own laws, and its own traditions. The king of the Crown of Aragon had to deal with each individual kingdom and its diverse and often conflicting needs one at the time. Thus, strong royal authority never truly developed in Aragon until the coming of the Bourbons to Spain in the eighteenth century.

After the conquest of Valencia, the Crown of Aragon turned its energies toward the Mediterranean. In the late thirteenth century, Aragonese and Catalan armies landed in Sicily, and the island, together with the kingdom of Naples, became either part of the sprawling Aragonese-Catalan Empire or was ruled by members of the Crown of Aragon's royal family. The Catalans played a distinct role in the Byzantine Empire as well. But all was not well. In Catalonia, the thirteenth century witnessed a harsh reintroduction of serfdom at a time when serfdom was waning throughout the West. Barcelona, the great Mediterranean commercial depot, began its slow decline, affecting the Catalan hinterland. Its volatile politics and fierce sense of its own liberties served as a deterrent to the consolidation of political authority within the eastern Iberian kingdoms.

Far to the West was Portugal. Surviving Castilian encroachments, Portugal carved out its own unique space in the Iberian peninsula. After the great conquests of the early thirteenth century and the demise of Islam from western Andalusia, Portugal embraced its maritime vocation. The Portuguese began their seafaring adventures from the great port of Lisbon on the Atlantic Ocean. Such sophisticated endeavors required a great deal of political and financial organization, and the Portuguese, as their Castilian neighbors had done, developed bureaucratic structures, taxation systems, and a sense of their own identity vis-à-vis their powerful and expanding neighbors based solidly on their own separate language and sense of the land as distinct from the rest of Spain.

The Development of France:
From Hugh Capet to Philip the Fair

The Capetians, 987–1226. When Hugh Capet (c. 938–996) came to the throne of France in 987, he was the first of a male line that was to continue uninterrupted for almost 350 years. Like the Byzantine emperors, but with better luck, the Capetians had procured the election and coronation of the king's eldest son during his father's lifetime. When the father died, the son would already be king. This principle of co-adoption became an important component of Capetian success and was in use into the thirteenth century.

For a hundred years before the accession of Hugh Capet, his ancestors had been rivals of the Carolingians for the throne. As king of France, Hugh was recognized by all the feudal lords as their suzerain, but they were actually more powerful than he. Although Hugh had the right to collect the aid (military service), the counsel, and the feudal dues that his vassals in theory owed him, he was seldom able to exercise these rights fully. But, he was also lord of his own domain, the Ile-de-France, a piece of land including Paris and the area immediately adjacent and extending south to Orleans on the Loire River. It was far smaller than the domain of any of the great feudal lords, yet it was compact, central, easy to govern, and advantageously located. Hugh and his immediate successors concentrated on consolidating the administration of their center of power.

The Capetians also enjoyed the sanctity of kingship that came with coronation and unction (anointing) with holy oil, although this was a later development, mythologized for the purpose of royal propaganda. In the eyes of the people, this ecclesiastical ceremony brought the king very close to God. In this way the king was raised above all other feudal lords, however powerful. Furthermore, the church was his partner. In the great sees near Paris, the king could nominate successors to vacant bishoprics and archbishoprics, and he could collect the income of bishoprics during vacancies. As in Germany, these royal powers aroused the opposition of the papacy, but the French kings abandoned lay investiture without a prolonged struggle. The king retained his right of intervention in episcopal elections, and the bishops still took oaths of fealty to the king and accepted their regalia at his hands. This unbroken partnership with the church greatly strengthened the early Capetian kings.

The history of the Capetians during their first two centuries of rule in France is, on the surface, far less eventful than the contemporary history of several of their great vassals, such as the dukes of Normandy, who were conquering England and whose vassals were establishing a great state in Sicily, or the dukes of Burgundy, whose relatives married the daughters of Alfonso VI of Castile. One of them became the first king of Portugal in the early twelfth century. The Capetian kings stayed at home, made good their authority within their own domain, and, piece by piece, added a little neighboring territory to it. Within the royal domain, the Capetians increased their control over the *curia regis* (king's court), which consisted of an enlargement of the royal household. The great offices at first tended to become hereditary, thus concentrating power in the hands of a few families. Under Louis VI (1108–1137) one man held the key household offices of chancellor and *seneschal* (steward) as well as five important posts in the church. Louis VI, however, ousted this man and his relatives from their posts and made appointments of his own choosing. These new men were lesser nobles, lower churchmen, and members of the bourgeoisie that were now emerging in the towns. Since they owed their careers to the Crown alone, they were loyal and trustworthy royal servants. Most important among them was Suger (1081–1151), the abbot of St. Denis, a man of humble origin and learned attainments who efficiently served both Louis VI and Louis VII (1137–1180) for decades.

The most important single factor in the development of Capetian France, however, was the relationship of the kings with their most powerful vassals, the dukes of Normandy. By the mid-eleventh century, these dukes had made great strides in making the administration of their own duchy more efficient by compelling their vassals to render military service, forbidding them to coin their own money, and curbing their rights of justice. The viscounts, agents of the ducal regime, exercised local control. After Duke William conquered England in 1066 and became its king, he and his successors were still vassals of the Capetians for Normandy. But they became so much more powerful than their overlords that they did not hesitate to conduct regular warfare against them. Norman power grew even greater during the early twelfth century, when Matilda, a royal princes, and soon to be Queen of England after her father's death (Henry I, d. 1135), married another great vassal of the French king, Geoffrey IV, count of Anjou. In the person of their son, King Henry II of England (1154–1189), England was united with the French fiefs of Normandy, Anjou, Maine, and Touraine in what is sometimes called the Angevin, or English-French, Empire.

But this was not all. King Louis VII of France had married Eleanor, the heiress of Aquitaine, a great duchy in the southwest of France. When he had the marriage annulled (1152) for lack of a male heir, Eleanor lost no time in marrying Henry II and adding Aquitaine to his already substantial French holdings, and giving four sons to Henry as well. So when Henry became king of England in 1154, he was also lord of more than half of France. He added Brittany and still other French territories.

Philip II, or Philip Augustus (1180–1223), first supported Henry II's rebellious sons against him. Then, after Henry's death, Philip plotted with Henry's younger son, John, against John's older brother, Richard the Lionhearted. Philip married a Danish princess with the idea of using the Danish fleet against England and making himself heir to the Danish claims to the English throne. He later divorced her, but the mighty pope Innocent III was able to force him to take her back in 1198. Even Innocent, however, could not force Philip to accept papal mediation in his English quarrel. When John succeeded Richard in 1199, Philip Augustus supported a rival claimant to the English throne—John's nephew, the young Arthur of Brittany.

Through legal use of his position as feudal suzerain, Philip managed to ruin John. In 1200 John married a young woman who was betrothed to someone else. Her father, a vassal of the king of France, complained to Philip, his suzerain and John's. Philip declared John's fiefs forfeit and planned to conquer them with Arthur's supporters. John murdered Arthur and lost his supporters on the Continent, and in 1204 he had to surrender Normandy, Brittany, Anjou, Maine, and Touraine to Philip Augustus. Only Aquitaine was now left to the English, who had been expelled from France north of the Loire. In 1214, at the battle of Bouvines in Flanders, Philip Augustus, in alliance with Frederick II, now supported by the pope, defeated an army of Germans and English under Emperor Otto IV, John's ally. Unable to win back their French possessions, the English finally confirmed this territorial settlement by treaty in 1259.

The Winning of the South.   The Capetians next moved to take over the rich Mediterranean South. The areas of Toulouse and Provence were not directly part of the kingdom of France, although the counts of Toulouse were, in theory, vassals of the kings of France. This southern region, known as Occitania, comprised a cultural and linguistic homogeneous area, extending from the actual French borders with northwestern Italy to the borders with Catalonia in the South. It was a turbulent region, with fiercely independent lordships, a relaxed attitude toward orthodoxy, large and thriving cities, and a flourishing civilization. It was the world of the *langue d'oc,* linguistically different from northern France and the heartland of the French kingdom. A large number of the inhabitants of the Languedoc or Occitania belonged to the heretical church of the Cathars, with its center in the town of Albi. Hence they were called *Albigensians,* but the Cathars were also popular in other important Occitanian towns—Toulouse, Montpellier, and others—and in the countryside.

The Cathars believed that the history of the universe was one long struggle between the forces of light (good) and the forces of darkness (evil). The evil forces (Satan) created man and the earth, but Adam had some measure of goodness. Jesus was not born of a woman, nor was he crucified, because he was wholly good, wholly light. The Jehovah of the Old Testament was the god of evil. Cathars or Albigensians often had the support of nobles, and particularly women, who adopted their views to combat the church politically. Innocent III called for a Crusade against the Albigensians in 1208.

Philip Augustus did not at first participate in the expeditions of his nobles, who rushed south to plunder in the name of the Catholic church. Northern French nobles were soon staking out their claims to the lands of southern nobles who embraced the heresy. By the year of Philip's death (1223), after the war had gone on intermittently for fourteen years, the territorial issue had become confounded with the religious one. So Philip sponsored an expedition led by his son, Louis VIII (1223–1226). Assisted by a special clerical court called the Inquisition, Louis VIII and his son Louis IX (1226–1270) carried on the campaign. The South was almost entirely taken over by the Crown, and it was arranged that the lands of the count of Toulouse, the greatest lord in the region, would come by marriage to the brother of the king of France when the last count died.

We must make a small digression here. The birth of the Inquisition in the early thirteenth century was symptomatic of the widespread mental changes discussed in an earlier chapter. The Inquisition marked a shift in the policy of trying to convince heretics of their errors by peaceful means. Instead, prison, public humiliation, and burning at the stake became the weapons to ferret out heterodoxy. Together with the influential Fourth Lateran Council (1215)—which required identifying signs on the clothing of Jews, condemned the doctrine of courtly love, and strengthened restrictions on lepers and those now declared to be either polluted or unacceptable to Christian society— western Europe as a whole took a turn to a more aggressive identification and punishment of difference. At the same time that regional identities were emerging in the West, discourses of difference and harsh persecution defined those who were not to be included in nascent regional and national projects.

Royal Administration.   Administrative advances kept pace with territorial gains. Philip Augustus systematically collected detailed information on precisely what was owed to him from the different royal fiefs. He increased the number of his own vassals and exacted stringent guarantees—such as a promise that if a vassal did not perform his duties within a month, he would surrender his person as a prisoner until the situation was resolved. Philip and his officials were alert to increase royal power by purchasing new estates, by interfering as much as possible in the inheritance of fiefs upon the death of their holders, and by providing husbands of their own choosing for the great heiresses. A lady would sometimes outlast three or four husbands, inheriting from each; thus she became a more desirable prize each time and offered the king a chance to marry her off with profit to himself.

The local officials of the Crown, the *prévôts* (provosts), had regularly been rewarded by grants of land. The Crown lost income and power as well as popularity when a local provost imposed taxes on his own behalf. Early in his reign Philip Augustus appointed a new sort of official—not resident in the countryside, but tied to the court—who would travel about, enforcing the king's will in royal lands, rendering royal justice, and collecting moneys due to the king. This official was a civil servant appointed by the king, who paid him a salary and could remove him at will. In the North, he was called a *bailli* (bailiff) and his territory a *baillage* (bailiwick). In the South, he was called a *sénéchal* and his district a *sénéchaussée*. Both of these administrative innovations had been borrowed from practices already in place in recently conquered Normandy.

A bailli or sénéchal ruled far from Paris and could become just as independent and unjust as the old provosts had been, without the king's awareness. Louis IX had to limit the power of these officials. He made it easy for complaints against them to be brought to his personal attention, and he appointed a new kind of official to take care of the caretakers. These were the *enquéteurs* (investigators)—royal officials who had supervisory authority over the baillis and sénéchals and traveled about the country inspecting their work. This complex of new civil servants introduced in the late twelfth and thirteenth centuries meant that the king could interfere with almost all local and private transactions.

The king's household slowly differentiated itself into departments, most of which had little to do with government. The *curia regis* consisted not only of retainers but also of clerics and others who served as advisers on day-to-day problems. When a major policy question affecting the realm was up for decision or when a major legal case needed to be tried, the king was entitled to summon his vassals (both lay and clerical) for counsel, and those he summoned were obliged to come. When the curia regis sat in judgment on a case, it came to be known as the *Parlements*, a high judicial tribunal. Naturally, as the laws grew more complex, trained lawyers had to handle more and more of the judicial business. At first they explained the law to the vassals sitting in judgment, and then, as time passed, they formed a court of justice and arrived at decisions themselves in the name of the king. By the fourteenth century this court of justice was called the *Parlement de Paris.* The first kingdomwide representative assemblies in France did not meet until the early fourteenth century, although provincial and local assemblies with bourgeois representation had been in operation for almost a century before that. When the curia regis sat in a special session on financial matters, auditing the reports of income and expenditure, it acted as a kind of government accounting department. By the fourteenth century, this was called the chamber of accounts. Naturally enough, it engaged professional full-time employees, clerks, auditors, and the like.

Cash flowed to the Crown from the lands of the royal domain, from customs due and special tolls, from fees for government services, and from money paid by vassals in order to avoid rendering such services as entertaining the king and his court. However, the king could not levy regular direct taxes on his subjects. A special levy was imposed on those who stayed home from the Crusade that set out in 1147. In 1188 Philip Augustus collected one tenth of the movable property and one tenth of a year's income from all who failed to join in a Crusade. These extraordinary imposts, however, aroused a storm of protest.

St. Louis, 1226–1270.   Further advances in royal power came with Louis IX. Deeply pious, Louis carried his high standards over into his role as king. He wore simple clothes, gave alms to beggars, washed the feet of lepers, built hospitals, and created in Paris the Sainte-Chapelle (Holy Chapel) to hold a reliquary containing Christ's Crown of Thorns. The church made Louis a saint in 1297 for personally leading two Crusades against the Muslims. St. Louis did not let his own devotion to the church stop him from defending royal prerogatives against every attempt to infringe upon them. For example, when the popes tried to assess the churches of France for money and men for papal military campaigns, the king declared that church property in France was "for the requirements of himself and his realm" and was not to be despoiled by Rome (1247). Yet when he himself became deeply interested in the crusading movement, he needed papal support to enable him to tax the French clergy. The clergy then complained to the pope about the king's demands for funds.

With the townspeople, too, there were difficulties during Louis's reign. These difficulties arose in large measure out of internal conflicts between the small patrician groups of rich merchants and the lower groups of tradespeople and artisans. When the Crown intervened, it was out of concern not so much for the poor and humble as for the maintenance of order and the continued flow of funds to the royal coffers. In 1262 Louis issued a decree requiring that the towns present their accounts annually. This decree was a new sort of enactment, an *ordonnance,* or royal command issued for all of France without the previous assent of all the vassals. Royal power and prestige had now so progressed that Louis did not feel the need to obtain all his vassals' consent each time he wished to govern their behavior; ordonnances signed by some vassals governed all. Examples of Louis's ordonnances were his prohibition of private warfare and his law providing that royal money was valid everywhere in France. Royal justice had now become widely desired. The royal court of justice alone came to be recognized as competent to try cases of treason and of breaking the king's peace. The extension of royal justice to the towns was secured by bringing into the Parlement's deliberations representatives of the urban centers—the *bourgeois.* So fair and reasonable was the king's justice felt to be that his subjects often applied to him personally for it. He made himself available to them by sitting under an oak tree in the forest of Vincennes near Paris and listening to the case of anyone, high or low, who wished to appeal to the king. Louis was a remarkable man. In his devotion to the crusading enterprise, he was wholeheartedly embracing the highest ideals of the period. But he never seemed to realize that the Holy Lands could not be won by more Crusades. Moreover, it cost France a great deal to have the king delayed abroad for years and to have him languish in captivity from which he was redeemed only at great expense. Yet for all his human failings, St. Louis typifies the medieval ideal that the divine law of God's revelation was mirrored in human law. As God ordered the universe, so human law established the proper relationships of individuals to one another in society.

Philip the Fair, 1285–1314. After the death of St. Louis, the French monarchy experienced a trend toward greater consolidation of administrative functions. Following from the policies of Philip Augustus and St. Louis, Philip IV (1285–1314), "the Fair," strongly pushed for greater royal power over his subjects. The towns, the nobles, and the church suffered further invasions of their rights by his agents. The *gens du roi,* "the king's men," often university-trained lower nobility, bourgeois, and clergymen, sought to expand the authority of the Crown throughout the realm. Members of the Parlement of Paris now traveled to the remotest regions of France, bringing royal justice to all parts of the king's own domain and more and more taking over the machinery of justice in the great lordships.

In the same period, the most intimate advisers of the king in the curia regis became differentiated as the "narrow" or "secret" council, while the larger group of advisers, consisting of the remaining lords and high clerics, was called the "full council." In 1302, apparently for the first time, representatives of the towns attended a meeting of this larger council. There began the long transition to a new kind of assembly, the Estates General. An *estate* in the sense used in early fourteenth-century France stood for one of the social orders in the tripartite division of society. Traditionally, the clergy is considered the first estate, the nobility the second, and the townspeople the third. When all three estates are present, an assembly is therefore an Estates General, although such a designation was not used until much later.

War with England and Flanders kept Philip pressed for cash during much of his reign. He summoned the estates to explain his need for money and to obtain their approval for his proceeding to raise it. Since medieval lords felt that no action was proper unless it was customary, whenever the king wanted to do anything new he had to try to make it seem like something old. Philip tried all the known ways of getting money. One of the most effective was to demand military service of a man and then permit him to buy himself out of it. Forced loans, debasement of coinage, additional customs dues, and royal levies on commercial transactions also added to the royal income. Although it was need for money for purely local problems that lay behind the most famous episode of Philip's reign—his fierce quarrel with the papacy— its importance and the significance of its outcome had a major impact on the medieval world.

In his papal opponent, Boniface VIII (1294–1303), Philip was tangling with a fit successor to Gregory VII and Innocent III. A Roman aristocrat and already an old man when elected pope, Boniface suffered from a malady that kept him in great pain and probably partly accounted for his undoubted bad temper and fierce language. Philip claimed the right to tax the clergy for the defense of France in his wars against England; the English monarch was taxing the clergy in his French possessions. Boniface issued a papal bull (from the papal seal, or *bulla,* on it), *Clericos laicos* (1296), declaring that kings lacked the right to tax clerics; Philip slapped an embargo on exports from France of precious metals, jewelry, and currency, which severely threatened the elaborate financial system of the papacy. The pope retreated, saying in 1297 that in an emergency the king of France could tax the clergy without papal consent and that the king would decide when an emergency had arisen. The right to tax the clergy and the laity for the defense of the realm was thus established with papal acquiescence.

But a new quarrel arose in 1301. When Boniface named one of Philip IV's enemies, Bernard Saisset, as bishop of Pamiers, Philip used the excuse that Bernard had spoken ill of the king and the queen to bring him up on charges in front of the Parlement of Paris (a royal court of appeal). A series of angry exchanges between the pope and the French king followed. Philip IV called a meeting of the Estates General to Paris in 1302. By applying a great deal of pressure on the clergymen and secular representatives and by appealing to their sense of loyalty to the king and to France, Philip the Fair was able to elicit their support in his struggle with the pope. Essentially, he turned the conflict into one between the French "nation" and the pope.

Boniface pushed his claims still further in the famous *Unam sanctam* bull, which declared that it was necessary for salvation for every person throughout the world to be subject to the pope. This was the single strongest statement made concerning the authority of the church over the state. When he also threatened to excommunicate the king, Philip issued a series of extreme charges against Boniface and sent one of his most trusted men, William of Nogaret, and a small armed force to capture the pope, then in residence at Anagni. As was discussed earlier, Nogaret and his French troops joined a group of Boniface's Italian enemies. They captured the pope, stole his treasure, and thoroughly humiliated the elderly Boniface until the people of Anagni rose up in arms and expelled the invaders. Nonetheless, Boniface, who was over eighty, died not long after this humiliation. The most remarkable thing about the whole affair is that few voices in Christian Europe, with the exception of Dante (who placed Boniface in hell anyway), rose to defend Boniface or to decry the attack on the Vicar of Christ. Most chroniclers and commentators noted the event as one more example of the political nature of the conflict between Rome and secular rulers.

In 1305 Philip obtained the election of a French pope, Clement V (1305–1314), who went to Avignon, on the border between France and the Holy Roman Empire, and made this city his permanent residence. Thus began the "Babylonian captivity" of the papacy at Avignon (1309–1377). Clement issued bulls reversing Boniface's claims, lifted the sentence of excommunication from Boniface's attackers, and praised Philip the Fair for his piety. For three quarters of a century the papacy in Avignon was seen as a tool of the French monarchy, although this was not always true. Just before Philip died in 1314, the towns joined with the lords in protest against the king's having raised money for a war in Flanders and then made peace instead of fighting. Louis X (1314–1316) calmed the unrest by revoking the aid, returning some of the money, and making scapegoats of the more unpopular bureaucrats. He also issued a series of charters to several of the great vassals that confirmed their liberties. But taxation was still thought of as inseparably connected with military service, and military service was an unquestioned feudal right of the king. So the king was still free to declare a military emergency, to summon his vassals to fight, and then to commute the service for money. For this reason the charters of Louis X did not effectively halt the advance of royal power. In 1328, the last of the Capetians died without a male heir, and a new dynasty, that of the Valois, came to the throne of France.

The Development of England

England became a major player in Continental affairs as the result of the Norman Conquest of 1066. That year William, duke of Normandy (c. 1027–1087), defeated the Anglo-Saxon forces at Hastings on the south coast of England. The Anglo-Saxon monarchy had, since the death of Canute in 1035, fallen prey to factions. Upon the death of Edward the Confessor (1042–1066), who had been a pious but somewhat ineffectual monarch, his brother-in-law, Harold Godwinson, succeeded to the throne with the endorsement of the Witan. Harold defeated an invasion from his brother Tostig and his ally, Harald (III)

Hardraka, king of Norway (1046–1066), at the battle of Stamford Bridge in 1066. But William of Normandy, claiming that Harold Godwinson had promised to support his bid for England in 1064, crossed the Channel and defeated Harold's forces at Hastings.

The Norman Conquest, 1066. Before the conquest of England, William had successfully asserted his rights over the vigorous and tough Norman nobility. He allowed no castle to be built without his license and insisted that, once built, each castle be put at his disposal on demand. The Norman feudal cavalry was formidable and early perfected the technique of charging with the lance held couched, so that all the force of horse and rider was concentrated in the point of the weapon at the moment of impact. Infantry and bowmen supported the charge. As a result of trade with Scandinavia and England, Normandy was prosperous even beyond the norms of the eleventh-century economic revival. It enjoyed a flourishing agriculture, growing towns, a flowering of monastic learning and church building under ducal patronage, and an effective fiscal administration. Moreover, because William put down private warfare and efficiently dispensed justice, there was peace and order.

While facing England across the Channel, Normandy had always maintained contact with the Scandinavian lands of Norman origin. After the Danish invasions of England all three regions were closely involved in commercial relations and were often in strife. It was Norman nobles, favorites of Edward the Confessor, who built the first castles in England shortly before the conquest. Edward gave important posts in the English church to Norman clerics, and as early as 1051 Edward had recognized William as his rightful heir.

William's invasion had the blessing of the papacy, which recognized his claim to the throne of England. William landed successfully and established two fortified beachheads on the Sussex coast. All was over in one hard day's fighting as Norman horsemen and bowmen slaughtered Harold's close-packed warriors, who were fighting on foot with battle-axes. William was crowned on Christmas Day 1066 by the archbishop of York. William seems to have taken special pains to restore order. *The Anglo-Saxon Chronicle*, a collection of contemporary vernacular histories, says of him: "Amongst other things the good security that he made in this country is not forgotten—so that any man could travel over his kingdom without injury, with his bosom full of gold; and no one dared strike another, however much wrong he had done him."*

In 1072 the Conqueror won the submission of the king of Scotland, who became his vassal. Each state was marked by the building of new castles to hold the region and enforce order; the former ruling class of England was replaced by Norman and French nobles. All of England belonged to William

---

The Anglo-Saxon Chronicle, ed. Dorothy Whitelock, D. C. Douglas, and S. I. Tucker. London: Oxford University Press, 1961, 164.

This scene from the Bayeux tapesty (c. eleventh century) shows the encounter between a Norman army on horseback and a Saxon light infantry. The battle of Hastings led to the Norman conquest of England. (Giraudon/Art Resource)

by right of conquest. He kept about one sixth as royal domain, gave about half as fiefs to his great Norman barons, and returned to the church the quarter that it had held before. The barons owed military service only to William, and they swore primary allegiance to him in the Salisbury Oath of 1086, giving him authority that no French king enjoyed at that time. The bishops and abbots also owed him feudal services. He forbade private war and allowed only royal coinage. He kept the Anglo-Saxon system of courts and bound local officials closely to the Crown by giving them wide local authority at the expense of bishop and earl. The Conqueror thus maintained old English custom and law, while superimposing on it Norman feudal structure with its mounted knights and castles. The sheriffs (the king's agents in the shire) provided continuity. The Norman curia regis met regularly three times a year, but could be summoned at any time to give counsel and try the cases of the great vassals. Its members also could be asked to perform special tasks in the shires—local administrative units that had been established in the early eleventh century and were divided into smaller units known as hundreds—for adjusting taxation, maintaining the peace, and settling local pleas.

In 1086 William ordered a careful survey of all landed property in England. The record of that survey is the *Domesday Book,* which included a full statement of ownership, past and present, for every piece of land, and a listing of all resources, so that the royal administration might learn whether and where more revenue could be obtained. Tenants, plows, forest land, fish ponds—all were listed in *Domesday Book.* Those who collected the information from the old Anglo-Saxon subdivisions arranged it under the new Norman divisions. The *Domesday Book,* then, was a formal written record attesting to the introduction of feudal landholding and law into England.

With the assistance of an able Italian, Lanfranc (d. 1089), whom he made archbishop of Canterbury, William established Continental practices in the English church. Norman churchmen gradually replaced the English bishops. To commemorate the victory at Hastings, William founded Battle Abbey on the site of the battlefield; other monastic foundations followed, notably in the North, an area that had been particularly devastated by the Norman invasion and William's policies. Norman abbots brought Latin books and learning from the Continent, and for a time vernacular writing in English ceased. William refused the pope's demand that feudal homage be paid to him as overlord of England; he agreed only to pay the accustomed dues to the church of Rome. The English church recognized no new pope without the king's approval and accepted no papal commands without his assent.

Henry I and Henry II, 1100–1189. William's immediate successors extended his system. They made their administrators depend on the king alone by paying them fixed salaries. Household and curia regis grew in size, and special functions began to develop. Within the curia regis the king's immediate advisers became, as was the case in France, a "small council," and the full body met less often. The royal chancery (secretariat) also grew. Henry I (1100–1135) allowed his vassals to make "scutage" payments to buy themselves out of military service. He also collected still heavier payments from royal towns or boroughs. To handle the increased income, the first specialized treasury department came into existence, the exchequer.

Because Henry's only legitimate son drowned, the succession was disputed between Henry's daughter, Matilda, wife of Geoffrey IV of Anjou, and Henry's nephew, Stephen of Blois. A civil war (1135–1151) between their partisans produced virtual anarchy in England. Yet when Henry II (1154–1189), son of Matilda and Geoffrey, succeeded to the throne, he found the foundations of a powerful monarchy. Stormy and energetic, Henry II had more than eleven hundred unlicensed castles destroyed. From the contemporary *Dialogue Concerning the Exchequer,* written by his treasurer, we learn how the money rolled in: from scutage plus special fees for the privilege of paying it, from fines, from tallage paid by the boroughs, and from a new tax collected from the knights who did not go on Crusades.

Even more important than this strengthening of financial institutions was Henry's contribution to the law of England. Law was what had always existed, and it was the job of the lawyers and government officials to discover what this was and to proclaim it. Henry II therefore did not fill statute books with new enactments; instead he asserted that he was ruling in accordance with the law of Edward the Confessor. By developing old instruments in new combinations, he created the new common law—law common to all of England because it was administered by the royal courts. The chief royal instruments were writs, juries, and traveling justices. If, for example, someone seized a subject's property, by the middle of Henry II's reign the victim could buy a royal writ: an order from the king directing a royal official to give the plaintiff a hearing. The official would assemble a group of twelve neighbors who knew the facts in the case, called a jury. They then told the truth as they knew it about whether dispossession had taken place, answering yes or no, and thus giving a verdict. These early juries were not trial juries in the modern sense, but men who were presumed to be in the best position to know the facts already.

By similar machinery of writ and jury, inheritances unjustly detained could be recovered, and a person unjustly held as a serf could be freed. No matter who won, the royal exchequer profited, since the loser had to pay a fine. Building on the practice begun by Henry I, Henry II also regularly sent justices out to the shires. On their travels they were instructed to receive reports from the local officials and to try all cases pending in the shire court. Moreover, the sheriffs had to bring before the justices from each hundred and township a group of sworn men to report under oath all crimes that had occurred since the last visit of the justices and to indicate whom they considered to be the probable criminal in each case. This was another use of the jury, the jury of *presentment*, since it "presented" the names of suspect criminals. Again the treasury profited, as the justices imposed heavy fines.

Henry II, however, failed to limit the competing system of canon law. He had appointed his friend and chancellor Thomas à Becket (1118–1170) archbishop of Canterbury. But once he had become archbishop, Becket proved determined not to yield any of the church's rights, but rather to add to them whenever he could. A great quarrel between the two broke out over the question of clerics convicted of crime. In publishing a collection of largely earlier customs relating to the church (*Constitutions of Clarendon*, 1164), Henry included a provision that clerics charged with crimes should be indicted in the royal court before being tried by the bishop's court, and then, if convicted, returned to the royal authorities for punishment. Becket refused to agree to this part of the document and appealed to the pope for support.

Although the issue was compromised after a dispute that lasted six years, Henry in a fit of temper asked whether no one would rid him of Becket. Four of his knights responded by murdering Becket in his own cathedral at Canterbury. Henry swore to the pope that he was innocent of complicity in the murder, but, although the extent of his complicity in Becket's murder is controversial, he had to undergo a humiliating penance and, more important, had to yield on the issue. The church in England won the sole right to punish its clergy. Moreover, Henry had to accept the right of litigants in church courts to appeal to Rome directly, without royal intervention of any sort. This meant that the papacy had the ultimate say in an important area of English life. It was a severe defeat for Henry's program of extending royal justice. Yet the other clauses in the *Constitutions of Clarendon* were not challenged, and the king continued to prevent the pope from directly taxing the English clergy.

Richard I and John, 1189–1216. Henry II's son, Richard the Lionhearted (1189–1199), spent less than six months of his ten-year reign in England, but thanks to Henry II the bureaucracy functioned without the presence of the king. Indeed, it functioned all too well for the liking of the population, since Richard needed more money than had ever been needed before to pay for his Crusade, for his ransom from captivity, and for his wars against Philip Augustus of France. Heavy taxes were levied on income and on personal property; certain possessions, including silver plate, were simply confiscated; many charters were sold to cities. Thus it was that Richard's brother John (1199–1216) succeeded to a throne whose resources had been squandered. John had the misfortune to face three adversaries who proved too strong for him: Philip Augustus, who expelled the English from France north of the Loire; the pope, Innocent III; and the outraged English barons.

In 1206 the election to the archbishopric of Canterbury was disputed between two candidates, one of whom was favored by John. The pope refused to accept either, and in 1207 procured the election of a third, Stephen Langton (c. 1155–1228), who was a learned English scholar at Paris. John exiled the monks of Canterbury and confiscated the property of the see. Innocent responded by putting England under an interdict and by excommunicating John. He threatened to depose John and corresponded with Philip Augustus, who prepared to invade England. Fearing with good reason that such an invasion would strain the loyalty of his own vassals, John gave in (1213). Not only did he accept Langton as archbishop of Canterbury and promise to restore church property and to reinstate banished priests, but he also recognized England and Ireland as fiefs of the papacy and did homage to the pope for them. Thereafter Innocent sided with John in his quarrel with a large faction of the English barons.

Magna Carta, 1215. A quarrel with perhaps a third of the English barons arose from John's ruthlessness in raising money for the campaign in France and from his practice of punishing vassals without trial. The barons hostile to John renounced their homage to him and drew up a list of demands, most of which they forced him to accept on 15 June 1215, at a meadow called Runnymede on the banks of the Thames. The document that he agreed to send out under the royal seal to all the shires in England had sixty-three chapters, in the legal form of a feudal grant or conveyance, and it is known as *Magna Carta*, the Great Charter. *Magna Carta* was a feudal document, a list of specific commissions drawn up in the interest of a group of barons at odds with their feudal lord, the king. The king promised reform and made certain concessions to the peasantry, the tradespeople, and the church. This medieval document is often called the foundation stone of present liberties in Britain and North America largely because some of its provisions were given new and

---

The Written Record

MAGNA CARTA

The following are a few excerpts from *Magna Carta:*

20. A freeman shall be amerced [fined] for a small offence only according to the degree of the offence; and for a grave offence he shall be amerced according to the gravity of the offence, saving his contenement [property necessary for sustenance of his family and himself]. And a merchant shall be amerced in the same way, saving his merchandise; and a villein in the same way, saving his wainage [harvested crops needed for seed]—should they fall into our mercy. . . .

28. No constable or other bailiff of ours shall take grain or other chattels of any one without immediate payment therefor in money, unless by the will of the seller he may secure postponement of that payment.

29. No constable shall distrain [require] any knight to pay money for castle-guard when he is willing to perform that service himself, or through another good man if for reasonable cause he is unable to perform it himself. . . .

30. No sheriff or bailiff of ours, nor any other person, shall take the horses or carts of any freeman for carrying service, except by the will of that freeman.

From *Sources of English Constitutional Theory*, ed. Carl Stephenson and Frederick George Maitland (New York: Harper and Row, 1937, 1964).

---

expanded meanings in later centuries. In 1215, however, *Magna Carta* was essentially a baronial document, reiterating feudal rights. It emphasized two general principles, common to other medieval realms as well: that the king was subject to the law and that he might, if necessary, be forced to observe it.

As soon as John had accepted the charter, he tried to break his promises. The pope declared the charter null and void, and Langton and the barons opposed to John became supporters of a French monarch for England. Philip Augustus's son actually occupied London briefly; but John died in 1216 and was succeeded by his nine-year-old son, Henry III (1216–1272), to whose side the barons rallied. The barons expelled the French from England, and it was not until 1258 that the king found himself again in an open clash with a faction of his own barons.

Henry reissued *Magna Carta*, formally ratifying it. Nonetheless, the barons felt that he did not fully adhere to it. The clash came to a head in 1258, a year of bad harvest, when Henry asked for one third of the revenues of England as an extra grant for the pope. The barons came armed to the session of the great council and secured the appointment of a committee of twenty-four of their number, who then issued a document known as the Provisions of

Oxford. This document created a council of fifteen without whose advice the king could do nothing. The committee put its own men in the high offices of state, and it replaced the full great council with a baronial body of twelve. But the barons could not agree among themselves, and Henry III resumed his personal rule. Open civil war broke out in 1263 between the king and the baronial party headed by Simon de Montfort (c. 1208–1265). When in the next year Louis IX was called in to arbitrate, he ruled in favor of the king and against the barons. Simon, however, would not accept the decision. He captured the king and set up a regime of his own, based on the restoration of the Provisions of Oxford. This regime lasted fifteen months. In 1265 Simon called an assembly of his supporters, but the heir to the throne, Prince Edward, defeated and killed Simon and restored his father, Henry III, to the throne. For the last seven years of Henry's reign (1265–1272), as well as for the next thirty-five years of his own rule (1272–1307), Edward I was the true ruler of England.

The Origins of Parliament, 1258–1265.   It is to these years under Henry III that historians turn for the earliest signs of the development of parliament. The word "parliament" comes from French and simply means a "talk" or "parley"—a conference of any kind. The word was applied in France to that part of the curia regis that acted as a court of justice. In England during the thirteenth century, the word often referred to the assemblies summoned by the king, especially those that were to hear petitions for legal redress. In short, a parliament in England in the thirteenth century was much like the parlement in France—a session of the king's large council acting as a court of justice.

The Norman kings made attendance at sessions of the great council compulsory; it was the king's privilege, not his duty, to receive counsel, and it was the vassal's duty, not his privilege, to offer it. But by requiring the barons to help govern England, the kings strengthened the assembly of vassals, the great council. The feeling gradually grew that the king must consult the council. Yet the kings generally consulted only the small council of their permanent advisers; the great council met only occasionally and when summoned by the king. The barons who sat on the great council thus developed a sense of being excluded from the work of government in which they felt entitled to participate. It was baronial discontent that led to the troubles under Henry III. When the barons took over the government in 1258, they determined that the great council should meet three times a year, and they called it a parliament. When Henry III regained power, he continued to summon the feudal magnates to the great council, to parliament.

The increasing prosperity of England in the thirteenth century had enriched many members of the landed gentry who were not necessarily the king's direct vassals. The inhabitants of the towns had also increased in number and importance with the growth of trade. As in Leon-Castile in the late twelfth and early thirteenth centuries, representatives of these newly important classes in country and town now began to attend parliament at the king's summons. They were the knights of the shire, two from each shire, and the burgesses of the towns. As was the case elsewhere, the chief reason for the king's summons to the shire and town representatives was his need for money. By the thirteenth century the sources of royal income were not enough to pay the king's ever-mounting bills. Thus he was obliged, according to feudal custom, to ask for "gracious aids" from his vassals.

These aids were in the form of percentages of personal property, and the vassals had to assent to their collection. So large and so numerous were the aids that the king's immediate vassals naturally collected what they could from their vassals to help make up the sums. Since these subvassals would contribute such a goodly part of the aid, they, too, came to feel that they should consent to the levies. The first occasion for which there is clear evidence of the king summoning subvassals for this purpose was the meeting of the great council in 1254. The towns also came to feel that they should be consulted on taxes, since in practice they could often negotiate with the royal authorities for a reduction in the levy imposed on them. Burgesses of some towns were included for the first time in Simon de Montfort's "parliament" of 1265. Knights of the shire also attended this meeting because Simon apparently wanted to muster the widest possible support for his program. But only known supporters of Simon were invited to attend the parliament.

Edward I, 1272–1307.   By the late thirteenth century Edward I enacted a great series of systematizing statutes. Edward's statutes were framed by the experts of the small council, who elaborated and expanded the machinery of government. Each of the statutes was really a large bundle of different enactments. Taken together, they show us an England in which the suzerain-vassal relationship was becoming a mere landlord-tenant relationship and in which the old duties of fighting were becoming less important than financial obligations. The second Statute of Westminster (1285), for example, was designed to assure the great landowner that an estate granted to a tenant could not be disposed of except by direct inheritance: This is what we could call entail. Similarly, the Statute of Mortmain (1279) prevented transfer of land to the church without the consent of the suzerain. The church placed a "dead hand" (*mortmain*) on land and could hold on forever to any land it received; lay landlords, therefore, found it highly unprofitable to see portions of their holdings transferred to clerical hands. Besides these statutes, which protected the interest of the landlord, Edward I, in a statute of 1290, commanded the barons to show by what authority (*quo warranto*) they held any privilege, such as the right to have their own court of justice.

Under Edward the business of royal justice increased steadily, and specialized courts began to appear. The Court of Common Pleas, which handled cases that arose between subjects, had begun to take shape earlier, but now it crystallized into a recognizable, separate body. The new Court of King's Bench handled criminal and Crown cases, and a special Court of Exchequer dealt with disputes about royal finance. Edward I also regularized and improved existing financial and military practices. He made permanent the king's share in export duties on wool and leather, the burden of which fell mostly on foreigners, and in customs dues on foreign merchandise, which soon became the most important single source of royal income—eloquent testimony to the flourishing commerce of the period. At the request of parliament, Edward did away with an important source of loans, expelling the Jews from England in 1290. Edward I's parliament of 1295 is traditionally called the Model Parliament because it included all classes of the kingdom—not only barons, higher clergy, knights of the shire, and burgesses, but also representatives of the lower clergy. In the royal summons of 1295 appeared a celebrated clause: "What touches all should be approved by all." This formula, which appears in other parts of medieval Europe in this period, became the foundations for Bartolus de Sassaferrato's first preliminary discussion of the idea of sovereignty.

Edward required all freemen to equip themselves for military service. The less wealthy served as foot soldiers, but those with a certain minimum amount of property were compelled to become knights and serve on horseback, in part for financial reasons: Once they had achieved knight's status, the king could collect feudal dues from them. Edward's vigorous extension of royal power aroused the same sort of opposition that had plagued John and undone Henry III. In 1297 both the clergy (under the influence of Pope Boniface VIII) and the barons refused to grant the aid that Edward wanted; they were able to make him confirm *Magna Carta* and promise not to make any nonfeudal levy without first obtaining consent.

Four different models of organizing territory and people can be seen in the preceding discussion. In Castile, a martial kingship derived its authority from the long struggle against Islam. Because of the universal need to obtain the consent of the ruled for any important fiscal or military action, the Leonese and Castilian kings encouraged the development of representative assemblies. On the other hand, these kings deployed symbols of authority quite distinct from those present in England and France. The Crown of Aragon developed into a federated monarchy, with very strong representative assemblies in each of the political entities composing the entire realm. Thus, the rulers of the Crown of Aragon had no choice but to accept strong limitations to their power.

In France, sacral kingship with coronation, anointment, and thaumaturgical claims as the centerpiece of their authority yielded a long process of consolidating the realm and creating a "religion of monarchy." Representative assemblies also played a role, but the French kings preferred, on the whole, to deal with the different regions of France on a piecemeal basis. England—a small, compact, and well organized country—allowed the monarchs to exert their power with the consent of the nobility, the clergy, and the urban representatives. Parliament emerged as a symbol of royal authority, developing only much later into a restraint on the power of kings. Different political developments yielded different outcomes. And yet, these were not the only solutions to the question of how to organize people into viable political entities. In other parts of Europe and on the periphery of the West, other political structures flourished. It is to them that we turn in the next chapter.

SUMMARY

From 1031 onward, the demise of the caliphate of Cordoba allowed for the emergence of large and fairly aggressive Christian kingdoms in Iberia. The kingdom of Castile, occupying the central part of the Iberian peninsula, claimed hegemony over the rest of Christian Spain and led the long struggle to recover Muslim-held lands. The kings of Castile could command powers not yet possible to other monarchs in the West. In a society organized for warfare, greater liberties were conferred to peasants and towns, and representative assemblies came together to finance and approve the royal raids on Muslim lands.

To the east of Castile, the Crown of Aragon emerged as a federated monarchy. Each of its constituent parts—Aragon, Catalonia, and Valencia—fought for the preservation of ancestral rights and liberties. The monarchs of the Crown of Aragon always found their authority to be limited and spent most of their energies dealing with their rebellious kingdoms.

Between 987 and 1314 the French monarchy grew in power and prestige until it dominated the machinery of government. France became the first large, unified state in the medieval West. The Capetian kings made good their authority over their own territory and piece by piece added to it. By 1214 at the battle of Bouvines they had overcome the Norman-Angevin threat; in the south under Louis IX (St. Louis) they drove the Albigensian heresy underground and took over Mediterranean lands. They increased their control over the curia regis, the king's court, and under Philip IV, the Fair, they consolidated the royal hold on power against the towns, the nobles, and the church.

After the Norman Conquest of England in 1066, English kings developed existing Anglo-Saxon institutions into a strong and unified kingdom. Henry I and Henry II extended William the Conqueror's system of administration. The development of common law brought power to the monarch and security to the subjects. However, the united opposition of the English barons limited the royal power. By the early fourteenth century a recognizable parliament began to emerge.

EIGHT

Political Communities: Center and Periphery

In the previous chapter we examined the rise of feudal monarchies (France and England, with the addition of the Iberian realms). We also described briefly those structures that were necessary for the emergence of the nation-state in the medieval West. As was mentioned, the traditional historiography has often described the political history of medieval Europe as taking place in two distinct areas. England and France (sometimes with part of Italy and Germany) have been seen as part of the core areas of western Europe. Political developments in France and England constituted a paradigm against which other national histories have been compared. Although the idea of establishing contrasts between center and peripheries in European political life is essentially incorrect, one must reiterate that a great deal of the manner in which Europe's political history has been written and taught emphasizes the differences between specific institutional and political models, that is, those of France and England and the experiences of other polities. In reality, the differences were not as pointed as has been assumed. Moreover, as was noted earlier, there is no reason to judge one type of political organization or nation-building strategy as superior to another. What we know is that, away from the so-called core areas of western Europe, or within the central regions of western Europe itself, other political communities endured, were transformed, or passed out of existence. The dynamics of their growth, survival, or demise were sometimes significantly different from the territorial, ethnic, and linguistically based monarchies we examined in the previous chapter. In many other respects, they were not.

Byzantium and the rising Ottoman Empire were multilinguistic, multireligious, and multiethnic empires. The Italian cities were small land-based political units, carving independent spaces in the midst of larger entities (the empire, the church). They embraced intense civic lives and symbols quite distinct from the ideological and symbolic programs of sacral, or even nonsacral, kingship espoused by the monarchies to the west. In Scandinavia, Poland, Russia, Hungary, and elsewhere, the road to the nation was different, in many respects, from that of the western monarchies. At the very heart of all these developments one finds elements in common—dependence on rising bureaucracies, the development of armies, deployment of a symbolic language of power and authority—but the manner in which this took place was different. Only in hindsight could one argue for the superiority of one system over another. In the period after 1000, it was all open-ended and unpredictable.

Byzantium, 1081–1453

The most enduring presence in the medieval East was that of Byzantium. Its institutional structure was more than a millennium old when the first signs of broader political organization beyond the fragmented and private arrangements of feudal Europe began to take place. Byzantium had a bureaucracy, an army, and a sophisticated court life in place from the sixth century onward. It had inherited many of its political structures from Rome and transformed them through the centuries. It was a model to be imitated, and imitated it was. In many respects the parallel and intertwined histories of Byzantium and its eventual conqueror and heir, the Ottoman Empire, need to be told to their dramatic denouement in 1453.

From the time of the First Crusade in the late eleventh century, the fate of the Byzantine Empire increasingly depended upon western Europe. The flood of crusaders first made the Byzantines uneasy and ultimately destroyed them. From 1204 to 1261, while the Byzantine government was in exile from its own capital, its chief aim was to drive out the hated Latins. But even after the Byzantine leaders had recaptured Constantinople in 1261, they still could not shake off the West.

The western attitude toward Byzantium is revealed in the crisp words of the great fourteenth-century Italian poet Petrarch:

> I do not know whether it is worse to have lost Jerusalem or to possess Byzantium. In the former Christ is not recognized; in the latter he is neglected while being worshiped. The Turks are enemies but the schismatic Greeks are worse than enemies. The Turks openly attack our Empire [the Empire of the West]; the Greeks say that the Roman Church is their mother, to whom they are devoted sons; but they do not receive the commands of the Roman pontiff. The Turks hate us because they fear us less. The Greeks both hate and fear us deep in their bellies.*

The Greek attitude is revealed by a fifteenth-century Greek churchman who said that he would rather see the turban of the Turk in Constantinople than the red hat of a cardinal. Those who shared this opinion got their wish in 1453. One of the great ironies of history is that the fate of eastern Christendom was settled, to some extent, by western Christendom's weakening of Byzantium first and by their neglect of it later. The Muslim rule that the Latin West

---

*From H. A. Gibbons, *Foundation of the Ottoman Empire* (New York: Century, 1916), p. 133.

had sought to roll back was, paradoxically, vastly extended by the actions of western Christians. It is clear to see the role the Turk played in both these points of views, that of Petrarch and of the Byzantine cleric. Byzantium stood between these two enemies in a vulnerable and exposed position. That it survived for so long and that it mounted a successful revival it is a testimony to the strength of its ancient institutions and resolve. All these transformations, however, need to be put in some larger context. The political landscape of the Middle East and of eastern Europe was also determined by the shattering impact of the Mongol invasions in the thirteenth century. Later on we will have the opportunity to examine the world of Ghengis Khan, but for now let us return to Byzantium.

Byzantine Decline, 1081–1204

The drama of Byzantium's last centuries was played out to the accompaniment of internal decay. Alexius I Comnenus had captured the throne in 1081. Thereafter the imperial accumulation of land seems to have gone unchecked. With the weakening of the central government and the emergence of the local magnates, a form of feudalism became the characteristic way of life, as free peasants increasingly were forced by economic decline to sell their lands to the great landowners and sink into serfdom. Severe depopulation of the countryside followed, while in the cities imperial police officials or local garrison commanders acted as virtually independent rulers. Economic ruin and social misery mounted steadily in the twelfth century. The tax collectors demanded food and lodging, presents and bribes. They would seize cattle on the pretext that they were needed for work on state projects, and then sell them back to the owners and keep the money for themselves. Irregular taxes for defense gave further chances to oppress the population. With the decline of the navy, piracy became a major problem. The coasts of Greece and the Aegean islands became nests of raiders, preying not only on merchant shipping but also upon the population on shore.

In 1171 Emperor Manuel I Comnenus made a desperate effort to rid the capital of Venetian merchants by suddenly arresting all he could lay his hands on in one day. But the economic hold of Venice was too strong, and the emperor was soon forced to restore its privileges. In 1182 a passionate wave of anti-Latin feeling led to a massacre of thousands of westerners living in Constantinople. In 1185 the Normans of Sicily avenged the Latins by sacking Thessalonica. The last of the Comnenian dynasty, Andronicus I (1182–1185), was tortured to death by the frantic citizens of Constantinople as the Norman forces approached the city walls. The weak dynasty of the Angeloi succeeded, and in 1204 Constantinople fell to the West.

The Latin Empire, 1204–1261

After the sack of Constantinople, the Latins elected Baldwin of Flanders as the first Latin emperor (1204–1205), and the title continued in his family during the fifty-seven years of Latin occupation. The Venetians chose the first

Latin patriarch and kept a monopoly on that rich office. The territories of the empire were divided on paper, since most of them had not yet been conquered. The Venetians secured the long sea route from Venice by claiming the best coastal towns and strategic islands. A hybrid state was created in which the emperor's council consisted half of his own barons and half of Venetian merchants. Although in theory the Latin emperors were the successors of Constantine and Justinian, in practice they never commanded the loyalty of the Greek population and could not make important decisions without the counsel of their barons.

In Asia Minor Greek refugees from Constantinople set up a state in Nicaea and constantly threatened to recapture Constantinople. Outnumbered, incompetent as diplomats, and miserably poor after the treasures of Byzantium had been wasted, the westerners could not maintain their empire. When the popes became deeply involved in their quarrel with the western emperor Frederick II, the Latin Empire was doomed. In 1261 the Greeks of Nicaea seized Constantinople and reestablished the Byzantine Empire. Meanwhile, however, the Latins had fanned out from Constantinople. Greece was divided into a series of feudal principalities. The Peloponnesus became the principality of Achaia, with twelve feudal baronies and many minor lordships. Thessalonica became the capital of a new kingdom, which, however, fell to the Greeks in 1224. In the Aegean a Venetian adventurer established the duchy of Naxos, and other barons, mostly Italian, founded their own tiny lordships among the islands. The Venetians held Crete. These feudal states lasted for varying periods, but most of them were wiped out during the Turkish conquest in the fifteenth century.

Despite its decline, Byzantium in the eleventh and twelfth centuries retained much vitality. Economic activity appears to have increased as government controls were relaxed. Literature, law, and scholarship flourished. Vernacular literature was popularized; heresy grew, and alien cultures were viewed with less suspicion. A class of professional intellectuals emerged, as did a new aristocracy. Such social changes did not enable Byzantium to retain its earlier sense of pride, however. Unlike the West, where some provincial towns became important centers of learning or trade, Byzantine towns did not develop beyond an artisanal level. International trade was left to foreigners.

Byzantium after 1261

When the Greeks of Nicaea under Michael VIII Palaeologus (1259–1282) recaptured Constantinople, they found it depopulated and badly damaged and the old territory of the empire mostly in Latin hands. It was impossible for Michael to reconquer all of Greece or the islands, to push the frontier in Asia Minor east of the Seljuk capital of Konia, or to deal effectively with the Serbians in the Balkans. However, he staved off the threat posed to his empire by Charles of Anjou, younger brother of St. Louis. Just as a new and powerful force seemed headed for Byzantium in 1282, a revolt known as the Sicilian Vespers—when Sicilians rose up in arms, with the support of the Aragonese,

against the French troops occupying the island—forestalled invasion and
Charles of Anjou's plans had to be abandoned.

So incompetent and frivolous were most of the successors of Michael VIII
that they contributed materially to the decline of their own beleaguered
empire. Wars among rival claimants for the throne tore the empire apart
internally. Social unrest reappeared as Thessalonica was torn by civil strife.
The value of the currency was allowed to decline. New controversy (that of
the Hesychast movement; see later) divided the clergy, already tormented by
the choice between uniting with Rome or, it appeared, perishing.

From about 1330 a new movement was reviving monasticism throughout
the whole of eastern Europe, a revival associated with *Hesychasm* (from the
Greek *hesychia*, "quietude"). In the tenth century, monks of the Orthodox eastern church had founded at Mount Athos in northern Greece a remarkable
monastery from which females, human or animal, were banned. Responsible
directly to the patriarch of Constantinople, these monks preserved their independence, governing themselves and devoting their energies to self-
sufficiency and to scholarship. From Mount Athos many monks founded
other movements. One of these monks, St. Gregory of Sinai, set up a monastery
in southeastern Bulgaria that emphasized the Hesychast goal: a mystical state
of recollection and inner silence that would be achieved after man's victory
over his passions. Only contemplative prayer could lead to God, although
bodily exercises meant to aid spiritual concentration were also important.

In the early fourteenth century monastic churches within the walls of Constantinople were restored under the patronage of wealthy men. Byzantine
churchmen took a renewed interest in scholarship, in the maintenance of
libraries, and in the Greek heritage, preserving for future generations the
knowledge of the past. Byzantine society recognized both the life of the
world and the life of the spirit. Some monks emphasized Greek literature and
philosophy, known as the "outer" wisdom, which prepared one for the truth;
others, often illiterate, emphasized the "inner" knowledge that came from
the "divine light" that illuminated the soul. Humans were sanctified through
this divine light, through a direct experience that involved the body and the
soul. Obviously such teachings posed grave problems for the traditional
views of the Orthodox church, and many commentators ridiculed the Hesychast movement. Nonetheless, the mystical movement initiated a renaissance
of learning and spirituality in fourteenth-century Byzantium.

Byzantium and the Ottoman Turks, 1354–1453

By the fourteenth century the Ottoman Turks had begun to press against the
borders of Byzantine Asia Minor. Economic and political unrest led the dis-
contented population of this region to prefer the Ottomans to the harsh and
ineffectual Byzantine officials. Farmers willingly paid tribute to the Turks,
and as time went on many of them converted to Islam to avoid payment.
Having absorbed the Byzantine territories in Asia Minor, the Turks built a
fleet and began raiding in the Sea of Marmora and the Aegean. In 1354 one of
the rivals for the Byzantine throne allowed them to establish themselves in

Europe. Soon they had occupied much of Thrace. In 1363 they moved their capital to Adrianople, well beyond the European side of the Straits. Constantinople was now surrounded by Turkish territory and could be reached from the West only by sea. To survive at all, the later emperors had to make humiliating arrangements with the Turkish rulers.

Although the Byzantine Empire lasted to 1453, its survival was no longer in its own hands. The Turks chose to attack much of the Balkan region first, conquering the Bulgars and Serbs in the 1370s and 1380s. A French and German "crusade" against the Turks was wiped out at Nicopolis on the Danube in 1396. But further Turkish conquests were delayed for half a century when a new wave of Mongols under Timur the Lame (celebrated in literature as Tamerlane, c. 1336–1405) emerged from central Asia in 1402 and defeated the Ottoman armies at Ankara. Like most Mongol military efforts, this proved temporary, and the Ottoman armies and state recovered. In the 1420s and 1430s the Turks moved into Greece. The West, now thoroughly alarmed at the spread of Turkish power in Europe, tried to bolster the Byzantine defenses by proposing a union of the eastern and western churches in 1439 and by dispatching another "crusade," this time to Bulgaria in 1444. Both efforts proved futile.

With the accession of Muhammad II (also called Mehmed the Conqueror) to the Ottoman throne in 1451 (he ruled until 1481), the doom of Constantinople was sealed. New Turkish castles on the Bosporus prevented ships from delivering supplies to the city. In 1453 strong forces of troops and artillery were drawn up in siege array, and the Turks even dragged a fleet of small boats uphill on runners and slid them down the other side into the Golden Horn itself. The last emperor, Constantine XI (1448–1453), died bravely defending the walls against the Turkish attack. On 29 May 1453, with the walls breached and the emperor dead, the Turks took the city. Muhammad II gave thanks to Allah in Hagia Sophia; thenceforth, it was to be a mosque. Shortly thereafter, he installed a new Greek patriarch and proclaimed himself protector of the Christian church. On the whole, during the centuries that followed the Orthodox church accepted the sultans as the secular successors to the Byzantine emperors.

The Ottoman System

The Ottomans showed tolerance to their infidel subjects, permitting Christians and Jews to serve the state and allowing the patriarch of Constantinople and the Grand Rabbi to act as leaders of their own religious communities, or *millets*. The religious leader not only represented his people in their dealings with the Ottoman state but also had civil authority over them in matters that affected them alone. Non-Muslims paid a head tax and lived in comparative peace. From 1280 to 1566 ten able sultans ruled the Ottomans. In theory, the sultan possessed the entire wealth of his dominions, and his object was to exploit it to the full. To do so he maintained an elaborate system of administrators whose lives and property belonged absolutely to him. To belong to the ruling class, a man had to be loyal to the sultan, a Muslim, and a true Ottoman—that is, he had to master the "Ottoman way" of speaking and behaving. Anyone who lacked one or more of these attributes was not a member of the ruling class but a subject (*raya*). Any raya could become an Ottoman by acquiring the necessary attributes. Beyond collecting, spending, and increasing the imperial revenues and defending and adding to the imperial possessions, the Ottomans had no duties. Thus, unlike the West, membership in the ruling elite depended on a series of factors that had to do more with culture and religion than with ethnicity or place of birth.

The Ottoman ruling class included four subdivisions: the men of the emperor, the men of the sword, the men of the pen, and the sages. The first comprised an inner service, embracing the sultan himself and his wives, sons, servants, private purse, and palace attendants, including the entire harem. In addition, there was an outer service, including the grand viziers and the other highest officers of the state, those who directed all the other branches of the service. A grand vizier presided over the council of state, and if the sultan trusted him might exercise great influence; but the sultan, too, could depose or kill him.

In the early days of the Ottoman Empire, the Turkish princely families from Anatolia virtually monopolized both the inner and the outer services of this imperial class. But by the fourteenth century the sultans had learned to balance their influence by recruiting new talent from among their Christian subjects. Some entered the system as prisoners of war; some the sultan bought or received as presents. But most he obtained through the regular levying of a tribute of male children between the ages of ten and twenty that took place every four years. The recruits had to accept Islam, and so these recruits, all originally Christian, competed with the older Turkish aristocratic families for the honor of staffing the imperial class.

The men of the sword included all those connected with the Ottoman armies. Besides the usual irregular troops and garrison forces, these were the cavalrymen who predominated in early Ottoman history. They received fiefs of land in exchange for service and could administer these fiefs as they wished, collecting taxes from their tenants and keeping order and justice among them. With the introduction of gunpowder and the development of artil'ery and rifles, the Ottomans founded a special new corps to use these weapons, the janissaries. Most of the janissaries came from the recruits who were not selected for training for the imperial class. The janissaries lived in special barracks in the capital and enjoyed special privileges. They were both a source of strength and a constant potential danger to the state.

The men of the pen performed the other duties of government, striving to see that all land was tilled and that all trade was carried on as profitably as possible, so that the sultan might obtain his share in taxes. Once the money came in, these officials spent it on the necessary expenses of state, including salaries for troops and other employees. To keep an official honest and zealous, the Ottoman system often rewarded him by giving him in place of a salary a portion of the sultan's property as a kind of fief to exploit for himself. In the country every farm and village, in town every business and trade, and in government every job thus became a kind of fief.

The sages (*ulema*) included all those connected with religion: the judges who applied Muslim law in the courts, the teachers in the schools, and the scholars of the Qur'an and the holy law (*shari'a*), the *muftis*. The muftis answered questions that arose from lawsuits. They applied the sacred law of Islam and usually gave short replies without explanation. The grand mufti in Istanbul whom the sultan himself consulted was known as *Sheikh-ul-Islam*, the ancient or elder of Islam, and outranked everyone except the grand vizier. Since he could speak the final word on the sacred law, he exercised a kind of check on the absolute power of the sultan himself. He alone could proclaim the beginning of war or denounce a sultan for transgressing the sacred law.

In the early modern period, the Ottoman Empire represented one of the most powerful and successful political entities in Europe. Its development followed along very different paths than those associated with political ruler-ship in the core western areas, but it led to the same centralization of power as elsewhere.

Russia, Poland-Lithuania, and the Politics of Eastern Europe

Poland emerged as a political community around 1000, mostly through the work of Boleslav I (992–1025). Pressured from the West by the unrelenting German eastern expansion and from the South and East by new emerging powers (Bulgars, Moravians, and others), the Poles, as the Hungarians had done, embraced Catholicism and cast their fate with the West. Boleslav I's rule was notable for his organization of an army capable of withstanding German pressures in the West and adding territories in the Baltic and the region around Krakow, a city that would become the spiritual center of the Polish people. Boleslav's career is typical, in many respects, of the meteoric rise of capable chieftains who, by their personal abilities, were capable of establishing their authority over substantial holdings. Only shortly before his death did he become king, formalizing the emergence of Poland as a king-dom. In many respects, the patterns are somewhat similar to developments in the West: military might, the beginnings of a rudimentary administrative apparatus (a bureaucracy), a new religion that served significant political purposes, a new sacral center at Krakow.

Polish rulers, however, followed tradition by dividing their kingdom and possessions among their heirs. This led to endless strife and allowed for the Polish nobility (the great men) to acquire powers that often placed them beyond royal control. The earlier Polish rulers, Casimir I (1038–1058) and Boleslav II (1058–1079) among them, fought to establish a hereditary princi-ple and to put an end to political strife. Civil disorder, however, was height-ened in the 1240s with the Mongol invasion (see later), which added to the political instability but also created a vacuum for further German penetration into western Poland. The weakness of central authority led to the election by the nobility of foreigners as kings, which serves as a pointed reminder of the interconnectedness of western and eastern Europe in the Middle Ages and beyond. Louis of Anjou (1370–1382), a member of the French royal family, and Henry of Valois in the late sixteenth century are just some examples of the foreign elected kings throughout the late fourteenth and fifteenth centuries. This development also accentuated the emergence of Poland into a kingdom—eventually a republic with an elected king—in which centralization did not prosper and different institutions and ways of organizing territory and people emerged. The Polish nobility acquired unprecedented powers and was able to check any concentration of authority in royal hands. The feudal anarchy of the fourteenth and fifteenth centuries was not very different from the strife that overcame France, England, or the Iberian kingdoms in the same period, but the outcome by the late fifteenth century was very different indeed. At the end, geographical location, topography (Poland lacked easily defendable borders), and who one's neighbors were (Poland was placed between two growing and expansionist powers) had a great deal to do with a realm's eventual fate.

The other important development in late medieval Polish history was its symbiotic relation with the Great Duchy of Lithuania. After the late fourteenth century, Polish and Lithuanian history were deeply intertwined. These developments are beyond the chronological boundaries of this book, but one should note in passing the conversion of Lithuanians to Roman Catholicism in the late fourteenth century, the dynastic and familial ties between royal and noble families in both countries, and the spectacular growth of the Polish-Lithuanian realm in the fifteenth century. For a brief period of time, the Polish-Lithuanian kingdom (duchy) expanded into regions of what today is Hungary and Moldavia, from the Baltic to the Black Sea and eastward to the very gates of Moscow. It was a territorially expansive realm; the future, however, did not lie there but with Russia.

From Kievan Rus to Moscowy

In a previous chapter we saw the early development of Kievan Rus, emerging as an Orthodox Christian kingdom from the interaction between Viking migrations and settlements along river networks and Byzantine cultural and religious influence. From the late twelfth century onward, the collapse of Kievan Rus led to the formation of a series of virtually independent petty principalities. These entities—Vladimir, Novgorod, and others—were too weak and disunited to resist the constant pressure from the Mongols, the Poles, and the Lithuanians. By 1240 the Mongols captured Kiev and established a khanate (of the Golden Horde) that would control most of what is today the Ukraine and parts of southern Russia for over two centuries and collect heavy tribute from Russian principalities. In the North, successive Germanic and Scandinavian attacks threatened the survival of the principalities of Vladimir and Novgorod (the latter an important trading town on the Baltic with long-standing links to the Hanseatic League, a mercantile league of German cities carrying trade from eastern markets on the Baltic to western Europe). From this period, Alexander Nevski, ruler of Vladimir and Nov-

This fifteenth-century icon representing St. George slaying a dragon reveals the artistic sensibilities of Russian artists and the Byzantine influence on their work. (*Scala/Art Resource, NY*)

gorod (1236–1263), won important battles against the Swedes and the Teutonic Knights. Nevski became part of legend and, eventually, a national icon in the uncertain beginnings of the Russian nation and state.

By the early fourteenth century, the grand duke of Lithuania, with his capital at Vilna, ruled nominally over most of western Russia. The Lithuanians, still mostly pagan, gradually took over the language and manners of their Russian vassals. But, as was noted earlier, in 1386 the grand duke married the heiress to the Polish throne and became king of Poland. As a result, the Polish Roman Catholic church and the Polish nobility came to the fore in Lithuania. Any hopes of a peaceful integration of Lithuania and the emerging Russian principalities fractured along the religious divide between Catholics and Orthodox Christians.

As in the West, the economic basis of society in western Russia was manorial, and restrictions were placed on the freedoms of the peasant farmer quite early. Paradoxically, as serfdom waned in the West (around 1300, with the exception of Catalonia), it began to rise in the East, lasting until the nineteenth century. In the north the commonwealth of Novgorod came to rule over the vast, empty, infertile regions that were explored by armed merchants and pioneers in search of furs and other products. The town council, or *veche*, became very strong. Internally, Novgorod had a rigid class system. The representatives of the richer merchants came to control the veche, and a few powerful families concentrated the city's wealth in their hands and vied for political power. The gap between rich and poor grew wide. A man who could not pay his debts would be made a slave, and slaves frequently revolted and became brigands. Because the surrounding countryside had little good soil, the city depended upon the region to the southeast, around Moscow, for its grain. In 1478 the ruler of Moscow conquered Novgorod and deported the upper classes to central Russia. Russia as a political entity now became a player in the affairs of eastern Europe.

Russia's, or to be more precise, Muscovy's churchmen were entirely familiar with Rome's claim to world empire and with Constantinople's centuries-long position as "new Rome." With the fall of Constantinople to the Turks, they elaborated a theory that Moscow was the successor to the two former world capitals. Russian churchmen spread the story that Rurik, the first political organizer of Russia, was descended from the brother of Augustus. They claimed that the Russian czars had inherited certain insignia and regalia not only from the Byzantines but even from the Babylonians. All the czars down to the last, Nicholas II (1894–1917), were crowned with a cap and clothed with a jacket that were of Byzantine manufacture. Thus the church supplied the state with justification for its acts. Royal authority and the role of Moscow (and Russia) in political affairs were thus legitimized through a combination of political and religious claims of great antiquity. In the late thirteenth century, however, all of that was still in the future, and that future was still uncertain since the Mongols remained the undisputable power in the region.

The Tatars or Mongols, 1223–1400

By the early thirteenth century Genghis Khan had consolidated under his command the Mongolian nomads of central Asia—Huns, Avars, and Polovtsy—who had erupted repeatedly into Europe. Having conquered northern China and Asia from Manchuria to the Caspian Sea, Genghis Khan's generals, Subedai and Sebe, led the Tatars across the Caucasus Mountains and into the steppes of southern Russia, defeating the Russians and dissident Polovtsky together near the Sea of Azov in 1223. Although Genghis Khan died in Asia in 1227, Batu Khan (d. 1255) brought the Tatars back again in the 1230s, sacked Moscow in 1237 and Kiev in 1240, and moved into western Russia, Poland, Hungary, and Bohemia.

Tatar success seems to have come largely because of their excellent military organization: unified command, general staff, clever intelligence service, and

A later (fourteenth-century) image of Ghengis Khan and his sons, rulers of the vast Mongol Empire. (Art Resource, NY)

deceptive battle tactics. Although Batu defeated the Poles and the Germans in 1241, political affairs in Asia—the election of a new Khan—drew him eastward, and the Tatars never again appeared so far to the west. Batu retreated across Europe, and at Sarai Berke, near the great bend of the Volga and close to present-day Volgograd, he founded the capital of a new kingdom—the Golden Horde—which accepted the overlordship of the far-off central government of the Mongols in Peking. Other Mongol leaders ended the Abbasid caliphate in 1258, but their advance westward came to a halt when they were defeated by the Mamluks in Ain Yalut (Palestine) in 1260. The enmity between Mongols and Muslims led the leaders of western Europe to hope that they could convert the Mongol rulers to Christianity and ally with them against the Muslims. Several embassies, including the well-known travels of Marco Polo and other merchants and missionaries, were sent to Mongolia and China during the thirteenth and fourteenth centuries with this end in view. Nothing came of it except a great increase in geographical knowledge derived from the accounts of European ambassadors and travelers.

The most lasting effect of the Tatar invasions was in Russia. Here the Tatars' main purpose was the efficient collection of tribute. Although they ravaged Russia while they were conquering it, after the conquest they shifted to a policy of extracting as much income as possible. They took a survey of available resources and assessed tribute at the limit of what the traffic would bear. They did not disturb economic life as long as their authority was recognized. They did draft Russian recruits for their armies, but they made the local Russian princes responsible for the delivery of manpower and money, and they stayed out of Russian territory except to take censuses, survey property, and punish rebels. Each tributary Russian prince traveled to Sarai on his election to do homage. Toward the end of the fourteenth century the Russians grew bolder. The first Russian victories over the Tatars, scored by Dimitri

Donskoi, a prince of Moscow, in 1378 and 1380, were fiercely avenged. Yet they showed that the Tatars could be defeated. The Golden Horde did not disintegrate until the early fifteenth century, and even then the Tatars did not disappear from Russian life. Three separate khanates, or Tatar political entities, were formed: one at Kazan on the middle Volga, one at Astrakhan at the mouth of the Volga on the Caspian, and one in Crimea.

The World of Islam

The Mongol or Tatar invasions and their disruptive impact were not restricted to Russia. They shook all of the eastern frontier of Europe, and their taking of Baghdad became a watershed in the history of Islam. Islamic historians see these events as marking a sea change in the later developments of Islamic societies in the Middle East and as the end of the Golden Age of the Baghdad caliphate. But the Mongol invasions also disrupted international lines of trade and communications in other ways. A recent historian has, in fact, traced the beginnings of European hegemony to the disruptions of the trade carried along the Silk Road and to the slow decline of Muslim power in the Fertile Crescent and the Middle East. There is a great deal of truth in this assessment. A similar pattern of rearrangement of Muslim trade in the western Mediterranean, above all in Spain, has been described by Olivia Constable. Trade, formerly in the hands of Muslim and Jewish merchants, linking eastern ports with western markets in Iberia and North Africa was replaced or overtaken by Iberia's trade with northern Europe after the Christian conquest of Andalusia in 1230s and 1240s. Thus the Iberian peninsula, which had been one of the main entry points for Muslim trade from sub-Sahara Africa and from the eastern Mediterranean, now turned its back on these mercantile connections and embraced European markets.

Nonetheless, although Baghdad was taken by the Mongols, Muslim power receded in Iberia, and aggressive Italian and Catalan merchants began to compete with Muslim merchants in the eastern Mediterranean, the world of Islam prospered in Africa, south of the Sahara, in the Far East, and in Europe. While Christians made gains in the West, the Ottomans began their inexorable march into Europe. By the fifteenth century, they had become, as was shown earlier, a major European power, and Islam advanced into the Balkans and to the very gates of Vienna. It is only in hindsight that one can argue for the eventual hegemony of the West after the early seventeenth century. At the end of the Middle Ages, the matter was still very much unsettled.

Scandinavia

From the Northmen's expansion in the ninth century onward, the Scandinavian realms played a significant role in Europe's economy and political life. Scandinavian princesses married kings in France, Castile, and elsewhere, linking the northern European royal houses with their counterparts in the rest of western Europe. Grain from Scandinavia made its way to markets in the south, as did fish (there was a great demand for salted herring throughout Europe), wood, furs, and other products. After 1000, the economy of Scandinavian realms was deeply linked to markets in the core areas of western Europe and, through them, to the rest of the known world. Three kingdoms emerged in the period between 1000 and 1300—Denmark, Sweden, and Norway.

Several important factors determined the political structure of the northern realms. The first was conversion to Christianity. Early attempts at conversion, while not fully successful, occurred in Denmark during the rule of Knut the Great (1014–1035), and even earlier in Sweden, while Norway initially converted under Olaf I (995–1000), but mostly under Olaf II (1016–1028). Conversion to Christianity, mostly the conversion of the ruling elites and the slow imposition of the new religion over the general population, meant also the coming of new political and cultural influences from England, Germany, and elsewhere. Feudal structures, which never developed fully as they did in other parts of the West, came late and seem to have been associated with the introduction of cavalry (in Denmark not until the first half of the twelfth century). Regardless of some feudalizing trends, the kings of Denmark, Sweden, and Norway gained considerable power in relation to their subjects.

The expansionist policies of the three kingdoms may have heightened the power of kings as leaders of Crusades to the east or as promoters of the conquest of new territories. Denmark had close ties with England (under Knut) and, under Waldemar I (1157–1182), Knut II (1182–1202), and Waldemar II (1202–1241), eastward into Pomerania, Livonia, and the eastern Baltic Sea region. As was the case elsewhere in the West, by the late thirteenth century the kings of Denmark granted political representation to the clergy, nobility, and urban representatives. Eric V's charter of 1282 recognized the existence of a national assembly or parliament and placed the king under the law of the realm. In Sweden, the development of the monarchy was slower and often impeded by an elective monarchy in which power and election were shared by Swedes and Goths throughout a great part of the twelfth century. Under the rule of Earl Birger Magnusson (the power behind the throne) in the mid-thirteenth century, Sweden's king (Magnusson's son) sought to reform the realm, end serfdom, and obtain the support of the emerging urban centers. This led to the establishment of a hereditary monarchy by the late thirteenth century, but within an increasingly feudalized society and growing political interference from the high nobility.

Although troubled by disputed successions, the kings of Norway established a fairly successful rule over nobles and clergy. Under Sverre (1184–1202) and Haakon IV (1223–1262), the Crown expanded its authority. The success of Norway's kings was also related to its expansionist policies (not all of them successful) in Iceland and Scotland, to Norway's inclusion within the Hanseatic trade league, and to the rise of urban populations. As was the case elsewhere in Europe, religion, incipient bureaucratic structures, language, territorial expansion, and a strong kingship (or absence of it) were some of the factors leading to more stable polities and a growing sense of communal identity.

Germany, Italy, and the Low Countries

The diversity of political structures throughout Europe is most vivid in the particular ways chosen by Germany and Italy. Both failed to develop into early modern nation-states, but that did not mean failure. In many respects, their ways of organizing territory and people were as effective (and different from each other) as those of England, France, or Castile. If in the sixteenth and seventeenth centuries what today we call Germany and Italy did not play as central a political role as other western nations did, it had more to do with economic (opening of Atlantic trade), and religious (the devastating religious wars that wrecked Germany) reasons than with political and administrative structures.

Germany and the Empire to 1254

Just before the year 1000, Germany was emerging from the last throes of Carolingian rule. Power was fragmented, and the great lords (dukes and counts) ruled their lands as private property. In Chapter 5 we outlined the emergence of German imperial authority, which, beginning with the Saxon ruler Henry I (919–936), sought to establish a more effective rule over the dispersed territories that comprised Germany and over its independently minded nobility. The history of Germany in the eleventh and early twelfth centuries was deeply bounded with that of the papacy and, as was seen earlier, with the conflict over lay investiture. We should, for the sake of clarity, briefly sketch out some of the salient events in these centuries (with emphasis on the political and institutional changes that took place during the papal-imperial disputes) before focusing on German affairs in the years after the Concordat of Worms in 1122.

Otto the Great's grandson, the brilliant young Otto III (983–1002), used a seal with the words "Renewal of the Roman Empire." In Rome itself he strove to restore a Roman imperial palace, Roman titles, and Roman glory. He also put German officials on church lands to keep these lands out of the hands of the Italian nobility and appointed German bishops to Italian sees in an effort to build up the sort of government he had at home. Since Otto III paid careful attention to relations between Germany and the Slavs, German contemporaries seem to have felt that his intervention in Italy was proper and legitimate. He was not trying to dominate the entire West but rather to establish himself as emperor in the new sense and to consolidate the rule of the Saxon dynasty.

German culture and trade benefited from the Italian connection. By the early eleventh century, the right of each new German king to be king of Italy and emperor was taken for granted. Italy benefited as the long period of anarchy finally came to an end. The emperors raised the level of the papacy from the degradation it had reached in the tenth century. But as the emperors sponsored reform within the church, they set in motion forces that would make the papacy a world power. When the Saxon dynasty died out in 1024, Conrad II (1024–1039) was elected king. The new dynasty, which came from Franconia, produced activist administrators, notably Henry III (1039–1056). Conrad began training members of the lower orders of society to serve as administrators. The church had long used such men to run its great estates, and now the kings used them to run the lands of the Crown. They often received lands as a reward, and their lands became hereditary. Thus these *ministeriales* depended directly on the Crown, had a status that could not be described as feudal, and remained as a social group peculiar to Germany. Although free landholders had no feudal ties, they had no royal ties either. So when the attack came on the increasing claims for power by the emperor in eleventh-century Germany, it came from these free landowners. They had strengthened their position by becoming the guardians or "advocates" of monasteries. In 973 there were 108 abbeys in Germany, probably all attached to the Crown; in 1075 there were more than 700, and almost all the new ones were attached to great nobles and landholders. Founding a new monastery in Germany was not solely a sign of the founder's piety, for monks colonized new lands, and the resulting revenues went to the founder of the house. To keep these valuable monasteries out of royal hands, the German nobles often made them the legal property of the pope. Thus in Germany a "noble" church based largely on monastic foundations grew up side by side with what may be termed the "royal" church and its bishops.

Opposition to the royal church, to the power of the low-born ministeriales, and to the trend toward greater monarchical power led the German nobility to revolt. In 1073 the nobles rose in Saxony against Emperor Henry IV (1056–1106), although in 1075 Henry crushed the uprising. But only a few weeks later there began the open struggle with the papacy that gave the nobles new occasion to rebel. This was the investiture controversy (already described in Chapter 5), which lasted half a century. Over the next century and a half, power in Germany shifted steadily from the emperor to the princes of the particular states. It is not surprising therefore that some of the most energetic German rulers attempted to build power bases elsewhere. Frederick I (Barbarossa, 1152–1190) styled himself Holy Roman emperor and sought his fortune outside Germany. Frederick I began by consolidating his own holdings in Germany. He also settled his differences with the German nobility by granting them almost total autonomy and attempted to impose imperial control over Italy. He led six expeditions to Italy, notable for the defeat of imperial troops by an Italian urban militia at Legnano in 1176. After Legnano, the Italian communities still recognized imperial suzerainty, but they became, in fact, independent. Thwarted in Italy, Barbarossa took the cross and drowned in a river while leading the Third Crusade in 1190.

His grandson and namesake, the great Hohenstaufen ruler Frederick II (1211–1250), preferred to rule his Italian possessions, Sicily and southern Italy, inherited from his Norman mother Constance, the daughter of Roger II of Sicily, than to deal with independent German princes. Frederick II was one of the most extraordinary figures in medieval history. A learned man, his court was the center for intellectual exchanges among Muslims, Jews, heretics, and Christians. He wrote a book on falconry that remains one of the most thorough and intelligent treatments of the subject. He ruled Sicily and southern Italy with an iron hand, intruding on the movement of his subjects (requiring passports, forbidding them to study abroad, etc.) in ways that were unprecedented in medieval statecraft. His long struggle with the church and the popes, the latter committed to the extinction of the Hohenstaufen family, is a premature glimpse at the secularizing trends of European realms much later. Sicily and southern Italy under the Roman law–inspired Constitution of Amalfi (1231) was as centralized as a medieval kingdom could have been in the early twelfth century, and Frederick ruled authoritatively, decisively, and well. When he died unexpectedly in 1250, however, his program came apart and Sicily after a long struggle fell to French hands and, in 1282, to the king of the Crown of Aragon, Peter III, the husband of Constance, the last Hohenstaufen heir. In the end, despite all adversity, Sicily was ruled by one of Frederick's descendants.

The Princes and the Empire, 1254–1493

After Frederick II's death, there was no emperor at all for almost two decades. This was the Great Interregnum (1254–1273), following the death of the last Hohenstaufen king, Conrad IV. During this time the princes grew even stronger at the expense of the monarchy, and the old links between Germany and Italy were dramatically reduced. The imperial title survived. It went to Rudolf of Habsburg (1273–1291), whose estates lay mostly in Switzerland. Rudolf wanted to establish a hereditary monarchy for his family and to make his monarchy as rich and as powerful as possible. He added Austria to the family holdings, and his descendants ruled at Vienna until 1918. Rudolf made concessions to the French in the West to get their support for the new Habsburg monarchy. After 1270, consequently, the French moved into imperial territories that had once belonged to the old Carolingian middle kingdom. The German princes, however, opposed the Habsburg policy of appeasing the French.

Thus, during the century following the Interregnum, two parties developed in Germany. The Habsburg party, eastern-based and pro-French, favored a strong hereditary monarchy. The opposition party, western-based and anti-French, was against a strong hereditary monarchy. Toward the middle of the fourteenth century, the princes as a class secured a great victory, which was embodied in the Golden Bull of 1356, issued by Emperor Charles IV. It affirmed that imperial majesty derived from God, that the German electoral princes chose the emperor, and that the choice of the majority of the electors needed no confirmation by the pope. The electors were to number seven: three ecclesiastical princes—the archbishops of Mainz, Trier, and Cologne—and four secular princes—the count Palatine of the Rhine, the duke of Saxony, the margrave of Brandenburg, and the king of Bohemia. The rights of the four secular electors were to pass to their eldest sons, and their territories could never be divided. Each of the seven electors was to be all but sovereign in his own territory.

Throughout the fourteenth century the German princes faced the threat of new political fragmentation, especially from their administrative officials, the ministeriales. To levy taxes the princes had to obtain the consent of the nobles and knights, along with that of the other two orders—the clergy and the towns. These three orders regularly won privileges from the princes in exchange for money. This period also saw the rise of the Hansa (a league of merchants) in North German commercial towns and the increasing prominence of sovereign "free cities," such as Hamburg and Frankfurt, all over Germany.

After about 1400 the princes who were not electors gradually adopted for their own principalities the rules of primogeniture (inheritance by the first-born) and indivisibility that the Golden Bull had prescribed for the electoral principalities. The princes were assisted in their assertion of authority by the spread of Roman law, which helped them make good their claims to absolute control of public rights and offices. Gradually, in dozens of petty states, orderly finance, indivisible princely domains, and taxation granted by the estates became typical. With numerous sovereign princes firmly established and with free cities enjoying virtual independence, the imperial title had become almost meaningless politically, although it retained its symbolic importance into the early modern period. It had lost control not only over the western lands taken by France but also over other frontier areas, notably Switzerland.

Italy: Despots and Condottieri, 1268–1513

In Italy the medieval struggle between popes and emperors had promoted the growth of independent communes and towns, particularly in northern Italy. In the twelfth and thirteenth centuries many of these communes were oligarchic republics. The ruling oligarchies, however, were torn by the strife between Guelfs and Ghibellines. These two factions dated back to the conflict between the popes and the emperors in the late eleventh and early twelfth centuries. The Guelfs were usually associated with the pro-papal party; the Ghibellines favored the emperor. By the thirteenth century, however, these ancient affiliations had lost a great deal of their meaning. The Guelfs often represented guild masters, craftsmen, and businessmen, while the Ghibellines attracted to their ranks nobles (who in Italy often lived in cities) and well-to-do bankers and financiers.

This redrawing of the political map sometimes led to something close to class warfare between the wealthy, on the one hand, and the small shop-keepers and wage earners, on the other. Dissension grew so bitter that arbitrary one-man government seemed the only remedy. Sometimes a despot seized power; sometimes he was invited in from outside by the contending factions; often he was a *condottiere,* a mercenary commander the states had hired under contract to fight their wars. One of the first great condottieri was an Englishman, Sir John Hawkwood, who as a soldier of fortune sold himself to various communes. In the fifteenth century the most celebrated condottieri were drawn from noble dynasties like the Gonzaga of Mantua or were ambitious plebeians such as Francesco Sforza, who became duke of Milan (1450–1466).

Italy developed politically along models quite different from those of other European realms and regions. Only the Low Countries, specifically the region of Flanders, may have experienced similar developments. In Jacob Burkhardt's incomparable *The Civilization of the Renaissance in Italy* (1860), he argued that the state developed in Italy "as a work of art." Even though one can question the validity of the word "state" at such an early period, what Burkhardt meant was irrefutable, that is, that in some communes in Italy political power was wielded as the work of men, without recourse to ecclesiastical mediation or without any arguments as to the human (violence, statecraft, secular) sources of power. Many rulers in Milan, Florence, Ferrara, and other Italian communities legitimized their power by force and by their patronage of the arts. Many of them were new men, and they built their authority either by tyrannical force, as the Visconti did in Milan; by political cunning and manipulation, as the Medici did in Florence; or by legitimizing the authority of a small oligarchical elite by depriving most of the population from franchise, as was accomplished by the leading families of Venice in the late thirteenth century. But there were other roads to political organization. Guilds played a significant role in political affairs and in some cases exercised political control of the city. The Italian experience thus differed dramatically within Italy itself from one town to another and from that of their European neighbors. The result, however, was no different: the ability to wield power ever more effectively through the creation of more complex administrative structures and the deployment of stirring symbols of city pride and independence.

Although there were myriad Italian communities, all of them competing for a place in the sun, several cities (with their respective territories) or kingdoms dominated Italian politics by the thirteenth century: Naples in the south, the states of the church in the center, and the duchy of Milan and the republics of Florence and Venice in the north.

The Kingdom of Naples and the Papal Monarchy

The kingdom of Naples, which during certain periods included Sicily, had long been subject to foreign domination. As was noted earlier, in 1266 Charles of Anjou conquered the territory. The kingdom of Sicily revolted (1282) and passed to the control of Aragon, and eventually to the Spain of Ferdinand and Isabella. Naples remained under Angevin rule until 1435, when it was taken by Alfonso the Magnanimous of Aragon. On his death it became independent once more under his illegitimate son Ferrante (Ferdinand I, 1458–1494). Naples was a monarchy. Unlike most of the rest of Italy, feudal structures flourished there and a powerful rural nobility played a significant role in the affairs of the kingdom. Economically, Naples became an important outpost for merchants from other Italian cities, mostly Genoa, who profited from the Neapolitan transhumance (the movement of flocks from winter to spring pasture) and the exportation of raw material: wool, tallow, hides, and so on.

The lands of the church experienced a material decline in the fourteenth and early fifteenth centuries. While the papacy was at Avignon, Rome passed to the control of rival princely families; outlying papal territories fell to local lords or despots. The angry Romans, determined to bring the papacy back to their city permanently, intimidated the French-dominated College of Cardinals into electing an Italian as Urban VI. The new pope alarmed the cardinals with his plans for drastic reform, and thirteen of them proceeded to declare his election invalid and chose a rival to rule the church from Avignon, "Clement VII" (1378–1394). (The quotation marks indicate that he does not rank as a legitimate pope and distinguish him from the sixteenth-century Pope Clement VII.) These events inaugurated the Great Schism (1378–1417), during which there were two popes, each with his own College of Cardinals—one at Rome, the other at Avignon.

Against the scandal of the Great Schism the church rallied in the Conciliar Movement, which began when both Colleges of Cardinals agreed to summon a general council of five hundred prelates and representatives from Catholic Europe. The Council of Pisa (1409–1410) deposed both papal claimants and elected an Italian, "John XXIII" (1410–1414). Since neither of the rival popes accepted the council's actions, there was now a triple split. A second general council, called jointly by Pope "John XXIII" and the Holy Roman Emperor Segismund and meeting at Constance (1414–1417), finally ended the Great Schism and elected Martin V (1417–1431), a Roman aristocrat, who restored the formal unity of western Christendom. On other issues, however, the Conciliar Movement was less successful. The Council of Constance tried the Bohemian reformer Jan Hus (c. 1369–1415) for doctrinal heresy and had him burned at the stake in violation of a guarantee of his safety. The movement Hus had started continued until the Hussites, after a ferocious crusade against them, were again granted communion at the Council of Basel in 1436. Neither this council nor its successors, which met sporadically until 1449, managed to purge the church of corruption and worldliness. And their efforts to transform the papacy from an absolute monarchy into a constitutional one, by making general councils a permanent feature of ecclesiastical government, were thwarted. Nevertheless, important limitations were placed on the pope's authority. A notable example was the Pragmatic Sanction of Bourges, which in 1438 gave the Gallican church a large measure of autonomy. In Italy, however, the papal monarchy functioned as another political entity, often at war with its main rivals in the peninsula and often struggling for territorial gains.

The Duchy of Milan, 1277–1535

Milan lay in the midst of the fertile plain of Lombardy and was the terminus of trade routes from northern Europe and also a textile and metalworking center. It had played a major political role since the twelfth century, when it headed the Lombard League that defeated Frederick Barbarossa at Legnano. Milan was then a republic, run by the nobility in conjunction with a parlamento, or great council, in which all citizens of modest means could participate. This precarious balance between aristocracy and democracy was upset by outbreaks of Guelf and Ghibelline factionalism. In 1277 authority was seized by the noble Visconti family, who in 1395 finally secured recognition from the emperor as dukes of Milan. The Visconti, above all Gian Galeazzo Visconti, ruled Milan in a tyrannical fashion and imposed their will on their subjects, often by extreme measures. When the direct Visconti line died out in 1447, Francesco Sforza usurped the ducal office in 1450. The most famous of the Sforza dukes was a younger son of Francesco, Ludovico il Moro (1451–1508). Ludovico made the court of Milan possibly the most brilliant in Europe by assembling a retinue of outstanding artists and intellectuals, headed by Leonardo da Vinci (1452–1519). His craftiness could not protect him against the armies of France and Spain, which invaded Italy in the 1490s, the former power coming into Italy at Ludovico's invitation.

Florence

The Republic of Florence, like that of Milan, was a fragile combination of aristocratic and democratic elements. It was badly shaken by Guelf-Ghibelline rivalries and by the emergence of an ambitious wealthy faction of bankers and merchants. In the twelfth century the commune had acquired a dominant position. Florence exemplified the growth of social mobility, new wealth, extensive trade, and complex credit operations. Increasingly, society was based on the need to work cooperatively, as best shown by the widespread use of credit in both public and private finance. There grew a productive tension between the cult of poverty (and insecurity) that was deeply rooted in monastic and philosophical Christian thought and the desire for wealth (and security) that lay at the base of the growth of the Italian cities. The factionalism, therefore, was not simply political, for it expressed very major concerns in a changing society and economy.

In the late 1200s Guelf masters of the crafts (the *Artes*) prevailed over the Ghibelline aristocrats and revised the constitution of the republic so that a virtual monopoly of key government offices rested with the seven major guilds. These guilds were controlled by the great masters of the wool and silk trade, bankers, and exporters. They denied any effective political voice to the artisans and shopkeepers of the fourteen lesser guilds, as well as to Ghibellines, many nobles, and common laborers. But feuds within Guelf ranks soon caused a new exodus of political exiles in the late thirteenth and early fourteenth centuries, including the poet Dante, who was exiled from the city in 1302. Throughout the fourteenth century and into the fifteenth, political factionalism and social and economic tensions tormented Florence, although they did not prevent a remarkable cultural growth. The politically unprivileged sought to make the republic more democratic. In the long run, attempts at reform faltered because of the oligarchy's resilience and also because the reformers themselves were torn by the hostility between the lesser guilds and the ciompi or poor day laborers. The English king Edward III's repudiation of his debts to the Florentine bankers, followed in the 1340s by disastrous bank failures, weakened the major guilds enough to permit the fourteen lesser guilds to gain supremacy. Unrest persisted, however, reaching a climax with the revolution of the ciompi in 1378. Wool carders, weavers, and dyers gained the right to form their own guilds and to have a minor voice in politics. But continued turbulence permitted the wealthy to gain the upper hand over both the ciompi and the lesser guilds. The prestige of the reestablished oligarchy rose when it defended the city against the threat of annexation by the aggressive Visconti of Milan. Finally, in the early 1400s, a new rash of bankruptcies and a series of military reverses weakened the hold of the oligarchy. In 1434 some of its leaders were forced into exile, and power passed to Cosimo de Medici.

For the next sixty years (1434–1494) Florence was run by the Medici, who were perhaps the wealthiest family in all Italy. Their application of the graduated income tax bore heavily on the rich, particularly on their political enemies, while the resources of the Medici bank were employed to weaken their opponents and assist their friends. They operated quietly behind the façade of republican institutions. Cosimo, for example, seldom held any public office and kept himself in the background. The grandson of Cosimo was Lorenzo, ruler of Florence from 1469 to 1492 and known as the Magnificent. Although possessing the wide-ranging interests admired by his contemporaries, Lorenzo was not without flaws. His neglect of military matters and his financial carelessness, which contributed to the failure of the Medici bank, left Florence poorly prepared for the wars that were to engulf Italy in the late 1400s.

Venice

The third great northern Italian state, Venice, enjoyed a political stability that contrasted with the turbulence of Milan and Florence. By the fifteenth century the Republic of Saint Mark, as it was called, was in fact an empire that controlled the lower Po valley on the Italian mainland, the Dalmatian coast of the Adriatic, the Ionian islands, and part of mainland Greece. The Po territories had been annexed to secure the defenses and food supply of the island capital, and the others were the legacy of its aggressive role in the Crusades.

The Venetian constitution assumed its definitive form in the early fourteenth century. Earlier, the chief executive had been the *doge*, or "duke," first appointed by the Byzantine emperor, then elected; the legislature had been a general assembly of all the citizens. However, the Venetian merchants feared that a powerful doge might establish a hereditary monarchy, and they found the assembly unwieldy and unbusinesslike. Accordingly, they relegated the doge to a ceremonial role and transformed the old assembly into the Great Council, whose membership of 240 men was limited to the families listed in a special *Golden Book*. The Great Council, in turn, elected the doge and the members of the smaller councils, which really ran the government. Foremost among these was the Council of Ten, charged with maintaining the security of the republic.

The Venetian system gave a permanent monopoly of political power to the old merchant families listed in the *Golden Book*. Yet the oligarchs of Venice, while denying the majority a voice in politics and sternly repressing all opposition, instituted many projects that served the general welfare, from neighborhood fountains to a great naval arsenal. They treated the subject cities of the empire with fairness and generosity and developed a corps of diplomats to serve the far-reaching concerns of a great commercial power. Venice was unique among Italian states for its political calm and order.

The Low Countries

The Low Countries, or, more accurately, Flanders, remained under the suzerainty of a lord, the count of Flanders. Not unlike most of the Italian polities, Flanders, Hainault, and Brabant were intensely urban, and the towns had developed as important textile manufacturing and mercantile centers from the eleventh century onward. Cities like Bruges, Ghent, Lille, Arras, Cambrai, and others gained independence from feudal rule. Also not unlike its Italian counterparts, the proud Flemish bourgeoisie could meet the challenge of foreign invaders, as the French found to their discomfort at the battle of the Golden Spurs in 1302 at Courtrai. There urban militias, manned by merchants and craftsmen, inflicted heavy casualties and a humiliating defeat to a large French army composed mostly of knights.

Of great importance to the English economy and political life (England sought Flemish alliances as a way to neutralize the French and Flanders was the natural market for English wool) and to France, which claimed feudal suzerainty over the land, the count of Flanders and the fairly autonomous city councils of the Flemish cities (ruled by well-entrenched oligarchies) lived an uncertain political independence in the shadows of their far more powerful neighbors. The point, however, is that regardless of the final outcome, Flemish towns developed political institutions that allowed for a great deal of prosperity and dazzling cultural achievements. The world portrayed by Huizinga (a great twentieth-century Dutch historian) in his remarkable *The Autumn of the Middle Ages* is a signal example of the manner in which diverse political forms yielded positive results. The French, Castilian, or English model proved to be successful in the long run, but for men and women in late medieval Europe other alternatives—the loose political associations of the Crown of Aragon or Germany, the city-centered politics of Italy and Flanders, the pluralistic society of the Ottoman Empire—may have been at the end far more congenial than the slow and intrusive centralization of power in the hands of kings.

SUMMARY

The Byzantine Empire had been in decline even before crusaders looted its palaces and churches in 1204. Official corruption had contributed to economic and social decay. Under the Latin emperors, the Byzantine Empire was divided into feudal states, but in 1261, the Greeks of Nicaea ousted the Latin emperors from Constantinople. Rival claims to the throne, social unrest, and religious controversy led to further decay in the empire. Thus weakened, the Byzantine Empire could not withstand the advance of the Ottoman Turks in the fourteenth century. In 1453, even the supposedly impregnable city of Constantinople fell to the invaders and was renamed Istanbul.

Ottoman rulers were generally tolerant of other religions, including Christianity. They organized their state based on a strong ruling class that included men of the emperor, men of the sword, men of the pen, and the sages. The Turks expanded their empire into Africa, Persia, and Europe. Ottoman armies besieged Vienna twice, but each time they were turned back. In the thirteenth century Genghis Khan and his successors invaded Russia. Tatars collected tribute from the Russians for two hundred years, although they allowed Russian princes to rule themselves. In the fourteenth and fifteenth centuries the princes of Moscow challenged Tatar rule and eventually, with the support of the church, established an absolute autocratic state. Poland and Lithuania emerged in this period as realms or political entities. In Poland, the power of the nobility thwarted any royal attempts at centralization, but the establishment of a ritual center at Krakow, the conversion to Catholic Christianity, and long struggles against enemies on all frontiers helped shape a Polish sense of identity.

The kingdoms of Denmark, Sweden, and Norway came into being in northern Europe around 1000 and entered the European political scene. In Germany, the Saxon emperors first sponsored church reform, but later clashed with the papacy over the investiture of bishops and the emperors' attempts to dominate Italy. The church emerged victorious from this struggle, but with diminished prestige and power. The emperors failed to develop a strong government in either Germany or Italy; thus both areas were divided into petty, frequently quarrelsome local states. The principle of an elective monarchy triumphed in the fourteenth century and was confirmed in the Golden Bull of 1356. Sovereign princes and free cities ruled their own territories. After 1483, Holy Roman emperors, although elected, were always members of the house of Habsburg.

In Italy, individual city-states rather than any central authority prevented the development of national awareness. Of the three most powerful states of northern Italy—Milan, Florence, and Venice—only Venice enjoyed political stability under a mercantile and aristocratic oligarchy. Venice introduced the idea of establishing diplomatic embassies throughout Europe. In the Low Countries, independent or quasi-independent cities also emerged along the lines of the Italian experience. These urban centers developed important cultural and administrative institutions that lasted into the early modern period.

NINE

The Late Medieval Crisis and the Transition to the Early Modern Period

In the previous two chapters we witnessed the very early stages of nation-state formation and the slow process by which national identities began to be forged. This final chapter examines the crisis (or crises) of late medieval society and its impact on the development of late medieval values and the state. How did medieval men and women and their governments deal with famine, war, plague, and rebellion? What were the responses with which they met more than a century of continuous crises? The most important of these responses may have been the consolidation of royal authority in France, England, and the Christian kingdoms of Spain. This represented what Max Weber once described as "the legalized monopoly of violence." These new assertions of power took place within a period of turbulent social, economic, and cultural changes. But the rise of the nation-state was by no means the sole response to the crisis, nor was the rise of fairly centralized feudal monarchies unavoidable.

The Crisis of Late Medieval Society

It is important to note that as western European cultural production and intellectual achievements were reaching their highest point from the mid-thirteenth century until the late fifteenth, late medieval society was facing a series of disasters that contemporaries often deemed insurmountable and that scholars have come to lump together under the general heading of "the crisis of late medieval society." The work of Dante in the early fourteenth century coincided with a ferocious famine that devastated most of northwestern Europe. Petrarch wrote as the plague swept throughout Europe, killing his beloved Laura in Avignon. Chaucer's enchanting stories were told against the backdrop of the Hundred Years' War raging in France and other parts of the West. But the crisis, or series of crises, that almost brought medieval society to its knees cannot be defined solely by a series of easily recognizable catastrophes such as plague, famine, rebellions, or war. Many of the causes were structural and had been in the making even during the long run of prosperity that marked the eleventh, twelfth, and the early half of the thirteenth centuries. Yet, the extraordinary thing about the late medieval crisis was not merely its widespread impact and virulence; it was that medieval society endured and that it responded by creating, out of the ruins of successive disasters, a new and dynamic civilization.

The Structural Crises

The late medieval crisis, its causes and ramifications, is one of the most debated issues in medieval historiography. For more than five decades historians have argued about the reasons for the crisis and about its overall effect on medieval men and women and on the fledgling institutions developed in the twelfth and early thirteenth centuries. Rather than one single explanation, it may be useful to see the crisis as an overlapping series of social and economic transformations. The late medieval crisis did not have the same trigger mechanisms across the wide geographical expanse of the medieval West. Local conditions affected the nature and extent of the crises. Nonetheless, their impact was equally nefarious throughout the medieval West.

The Malthusian Explanation: Weather, Soil, and the Social Transformation of the Village Community

By the mid-thirteenth century, and most certainly by the end of the century, the climate took a turn for the worse. Colder summers and abundant rain during the growing and harvest seasons reduced food production and made land cultivation more difficult. This mini–ice age, which can be traced historically through the study of advancing glaciers and the width of tree rings, elicited numerous references in the chronicles and histories of the period. Many of those recording the events of their day noted the deteriorating weather patterns: the incessant rain, the increasing cold. But hostile weather turned out to be just one of the problems.

Historians of the late Middle Ages have argued that the rise of population—which resulted from the expansion of the arable and increased production of food in the eleventh and twelfth centuries—led to growing pressures on the land. Marginal lands, that is, lands that were not very productive and that demanded considerable amount of additional work to make them yield fruit, were now cultivated with diminished returns. The late medieval crisis has been ascribed, by many historians, to a kind of Malthusian cycle (after Thomas Malthus, author of an influential treatise on population published in 1799): a population growing too fast and outstripping its ability to produce food. To be sure, areas in France and England had a denser population in the late thirteenth century than they do today, but demographic pressures cannot fully explain the full extent of the crisis.

In certain areas of medieval Europe—in the kingdom of Castile, for one—the onset of the crisis in the mid-thirteenth century stemmed from both low population density in certain areas and demographic dislocation (people migrating to the newly conquered lands in the South and abandoning traditional cereal cultivation in the North). These demographic shifts were accompanied by a sharp decline in food production, inflation of food prices, and, at times, even food scarcity. Thus, in Castile and other places in the West, insufficient population rather than demographic pressures were the precipitating factor. Other explanations are necessary for a better understanding of how the crisis came about.

From the mid-thirteenth century, village communities in the medieval West underwent important social and economic changes. The intrusion of urban capital into the countryside and the rise of well-to-do farmers brought important disruptions to the workings of the rural economy. The accumulation of property into the hands of the few sent peasants off the land and into the cities in search of work or turned them into agricultural day laborers, thus creating a veritable landless peasant population. This process of growing class distinctions in what had been a fairly egalitarian rural world continued into the early modern period. In the late thirteenth century, it was exacerbated by deteriorating weather conditions and sharp price increases. Rapid inflation constituted a transformation from the slow rise in prices and wages that had kept a steady pace over the course of almost three centuries. This slow pace benefited the peasants who paid fixed dues and meant bad news for the great lords (monasteries, nobles) who received most of their income from land rents that had been established long ago by the customs of the locality. A sharp decline in what may be called feudal rents (the money that peasants paid as rent to their lords) brought about increased violence, as lords scrambled madly to keep their social standing and conspicuous expenses unchanged.

The role of violence in the making of the late medieval crisis cannot be ignored. When in need, lords would often resort to the most extreme actions to extort income from their helpless tenants (although peasants at times resisted quite successfully). Around the mid-fourteenth century, those in power attempted to enserf the free peasants anew or to revive the harsh conditions under which they had toiled before the spread of peasant freedom in the twelfth century. In places such as Castile the efforts failed. In England, it led to an unsuccessful peasant uprising. In Catalonia, it further added restrictions to an extensive servile peasantry.

In this regard, we must not neglect the role that the new and far more centralized monarchies in some regions of the West played in accelerating the onset of the crisis in the late thirteenth century. The growing expense of government, above all the frightful expense of maintaining garrisons and armed contingents, prompted rulers to seek new sources of income or to squeeze harder on old ones. The case of Philip IV, the Fair (1285–1314), king of France, is emblematic of the new fiscal claims of the nascent state. These economic needs led to extraordinary fiscal demands and royal intrusiveness. In successive ventures, Philip extorted money from the Jews by threatening to expel them (and then collected money from the Christian population to carry out the actual expulsion). He raided the funds of his own Lombard bankers and then exiled them from France. The Templars (who acted as bankers to the Crown and were supposed to own untold wealth) were dealt with in violent fashion. Accusing them of heresy, sodomy, and necromancy, Philip forced the dissolution of the Templar Order and publicly executed its leaders. He pushed his subjects so hard that they finally rose up in protest by the end of his reign. The reality is that frequent warfare in the late thirteenth century between England and France, between England and Scottish rebels, between Castile and Muslims in the Granada area, and between city-states in Italy placed added burdens on the financial stability of medieval society.

The Challenge of Crisis: Famine, War, Plague, and Rebellion

Structural crises were highlighted by four distinct catastrophes that severely tested the endurance of medieval men and women and threatened the collapse of medieval institutions. In rapid succession Europe was confronted in the fourteenth and fifteenth centuries with major disasters. Some, such as famine and the plague, were brought on by natural phenomena and could not, in theory, have been prevented. Others, such as wars and rebellions, resulted from shifts in medieval structures and the oppressive nature of medieval lordship. We tend to think of these disasters as one episode in the long history of the Middle Ages, but, in reality, they were recurring events. Famines struck most of Europe in the period between 1315 and 1321, but local and regional bouts of famine were a part of European life until the agricultural revolution of the late seventeenth and early eighteenth centuries. The plague (the Black Death) struck Europe between 1347 and 1353 (although its most virulent impact took place between 1348 and 1351) with catastrophic consequences and recurred every generation, although not with the same extensive mortality, until the seventeenth century. War became endemic in European history; revolutions disturbed the social order into the modern period. What was the nature of these particular disasters, and what was their long-term impact on medieval men and women?

Famine

The changes in weather patterns together with other structural factors (a rising population, the cultivation of marginal lands, growing social antagonisms within the village community) came to a head in 1315. That year, throughout most of northern Europe (the Mediterranean lands were spared), crops failed. From the Ural Mountains, in what today is Russia, to Ireland, incessant rain in late spring and through the summer led to failed crops. Hay could not be cured and rotted on the fields. Because of diminished sunshine, salt was hard to get (because there was no evaporation of seawater), causing an immediate sharp rise in its price. In England, the price of wheat rose from 20 shillings per quarter in early spring to 40 shillings by June. In Louvain (Flanders), wheat prices rose by 320 percent. In some locations the scarcity of food (mainly grain) affected even the powerful. The chronicles tell us that Edward II, king of England, stopped at St. Albans on 10 August 1315 and could find no bread to purchase.

Widespread famine brought about a wave of crimes against property, as men and women sought to survive at all costs. Some found sustenance in tree bark, grass, or other far less appealing products. Some chroniclers even report instances of cannibalism, although such mentions should always be read with caution. Some localities lost between one quarter and one half of their population; the rate of infanticide—mostly female infanticide, which had always been high in medieval Europe—rose dramatically.

The famines of 1315–1321 must be placed in the context of endemic hunger affecting the lower peasantry and urban poor in western society. What was different this time was the magnitude and the geographical range of the famine. Unlike regional food scarcity, where help could be found next door, most of northern European society was equally beset by the crisis. Religious processions, prayers, and civil attempts to deal with the famine proved futile and underscored the inability of religion and royal power to solve such wide-spread problems. Far more troubling, the famines of these years affected animals as well. Illnesses such as anthrax, animal murrain, and other diseases plagued farm animals, while dysentery and other sicknesses affected humans. The decline in the number and strength of work animals complicated matters, lowering the ability to produce food. In the end, the famine weakened the general population and rendered it vulnerable to more dangerous diseases and other disasters. Far worse was to come.

War

Medieval men and women lived in an extremely violent world. Private warfare, lordly excesses, mutilations of defeated enemies, rape, the selling into slavery of conquered people, and other such deeds were part of the fabric of everyday life. It was a cruel and hostile world. Organized warfare—with the exception of large-scale military efforts such as the Crusades—seldom meant the mobilization of substantial forces or the presence of standing armies. The cost of mounting campaigns limited the carnage and the range of battle in the medieval West. This explains in part why medieval people were unprepared for the social and psychological consequences or the butchery of the Hundred Years' War. England and France had long engaged in periodic conflict, much of which was dictated by their uneasy relationship. On the one hand, most English nobles were French in culture and lifestyle in the thirteenth and fourteenth centuries. Many of them still owned feudal holdings in France and spoke a language that was closer to French than to the English that was

A depiction of the battle of Crecy between the English and the French fails to note the role of foot soldiers and archers fighting for England in the final outcome of the battle. Instead it emphasizes the role of knights in warfare. (HIP/Scala/Art Resource, NY)

spoken by the common people in England. On the other hand, the kings of England—who recognized no superior as ruler of England—held important territories in France (Normandy until 1216), Gascony, and other lands as vassals of the king of France. It was an impossible situation, and it became untenable in a world in which national identities were in the making.

Since a substantial part of the history of the Hundred Years' War is integral to the emerging national histories of England and France, the details and highlights of the conflict are discussed in the context of the final emergence of the nation-state in the next volume of this series. Nonetheless, several salient points should be made now, for the war contributed to the shaping of the late medieval crisis.

The Scope of the War. The Hundred Years' War was not just a conflict between England and France. Its maelstrom drew into its swirling abyss most western European countries at one time or another. The kingdom of Castile became a battlefield in the 1360s, when Bertrand du Guesclin, constable of France, marched his rowdy companies of mercenaries into Spain to support the illegitimate claims of Henry of Trastámara against his own half-brother, Peter I (1350–1365). The latter was supported by the English, and so it was that the fabled Black Prince, Edward, prince of Wales, saw action in the Iberian peninsula. The Castilian fleet played a decisive role in sea battles in the English Channel on both sides of the conflict. Portugal was also an actor in the war. Flanders, long coveted by the French, was pivotal in the long struggle. The Flemish town militias inflicted a frightful defeat to a large French army at Courtrai at the beginning of the fourteenth century. Although nominally under French lordship, the powerful Flemish urban centers (and those from Brabant and Hainault) were de facto independent. On the other side of the conflict, England's economic well-being depended on securing access to Flemish markets for its wool exports. Scotland also played a role, as did the German princes on the Rhineland and the Italian communes. The Hundred Years' War was a European-wide conflict, and its ripples were felt far across the Continent.

Suzerainty and Sovereignty. The war began with the feudal claims of Edward III (1327–1377) to the throne of France. It was first and foremost a dynastic conflict to determine rights of inheritance and line of descent. The war sought to resolve complicated issues of suzerainty—that is, could Edward III of England legally challenge his rightful lord, Philip VI of France (1328–1350)? And could he do so, having paid homage, including liege homage, to the French king twice before? But if the war began as a feudal conflict, it turned into a struggle between nations, with questions of sovereignty at stake. By the mid-fifteenth century, the war, and other factors triggered by the long struggle, had led to the emergence of "national" identities. The rise of Joan of Arc (Jeanne d'Arc, b. between 1408 and 1412, d. 1431) would have been unimaginable without the growing sense of national identity among the French, who were no longer willing to tolerate the English presence on their soil. Although the phenomenon of national identity did not come to fruition fully until the nineteenth century, this development from below was codified, in the mid-fourteenth century, by complex theories of sovereignty—that stipulated, for example, that the ruler should recognize no superior within the borders of his realm. These ideas were then turned into administrative practices.

Technologies: Big Battles and Little Battles. The war can be summarized as a series of great battles in which a superior French army fighting within the codes established by feudal tradition and a culture of chivalry—heavy armored noble cavalry charges and individual combat—was repeatedly defeated by smaller English contingents fighting in unconventional style (emphasizing strategic positioning, deploying longbow archers, and withholding its heavy cavalry from the initial charge). The English claimed that they were forced to fight in such fashion because of numerical inferiority, but at Crecy (1346), Poitiers (1356), and Agincourt (1415) a much smaller English army smashed their rivals by their choice of tactics and superior military technology. The social implications of the new realities of war—a humble Welsh bowman could shoot ten arrows per minute, and these longbow (made of yew trees and as high as six feet) arrows could pierce French armor—brought an end, once and for all, to the nobility's supremacy in the battlefield. As many well-appointed and groomed French lords found out in these great battles, war was no longer heroic or fun. Even though nobles retained a great deal of their social, economic, and political status, and their military roles remained significant until the modern age, by the late fifteenth century the infantry had come to dominate the European battlefields. The medieval chivalrous ideal was relegated to the pageantry of the tournament and the choreographed warfare of the joust. In short, armor could no longer provide protection from the craft of socially inferior opponents, who could kill from a distance with a well-placed arrow. And longbows were only one of the nasty new weapons deployed during the Hundred Years' War. Powerful crossbows, mostly the monopoly of Italian mercenaries, created havoc. Firearms and artillery came into use in the fifteenth century and, although not yet very efficient, transformed warfare's social landscape.

If the French were peculiarly unsuccessful in large pitched battles, they were, however, quite adept at waging the equivalent of modern guerilla warfare in those instances in which their sense overcame their pride. Small raids, continuous attacks, disrupting the English lines of supplies, denying the invaders the ability to rely on local resources, hiring efficient foreign mercenaries—all these proved winning tactics. There was nothing chivalrous about these methods, but, when confronted with the reality of almost two thirds of their country occupied by the English, these tactics brought the French ultimate victory. One must remember that England was a very small kingdom when compared to France (the most populous country in western medieval Europe) and that mounting campaigns across the English Channel for over a hundred years placed an extraordinary burden on English resources. As long as the war meant raiding the enemy's lands, stealing the goods of those defeated, and taking wealthy French lords prisoner for substantial ransom—as occurred when the king of France, John the Good, was captured at Poitiers—the war effort was sustainable. But when it meant conquering and ruling the country—as was the case after Henry V's victory at Agincourt—that was another matter altogether.

Honor. Because the war became such a grim business and social hierarchies were turned topsy-turvy, the nobility and courts sought refuge in elaborate codes of honor, fancy festive displays, and tournaments. These intricate activities became an answer to the nobility's eroding role as warriors. The writings of Froissart, the best chronicler of the war, and other chroniclers of the period are filled with minute and dazzling descriptions of the great nobles' heroic deeds. A revival of courtly ideals led to actions such as those of Bertrand du

*By the late Middle Ages jousting and elaborate courtly spectacles provided the ruling classes
with a convenient and fairly controlled alternative to the mayhem of the Hundred Years'
War. Note the elaborate armor (as compared to the coat of mail of an earlier age; see Chapter
Five) and finery.* (HIP/Scala/Art Resource, NY)

Guesclin, the constable of France, who charged into battle with one eye closed
for the honor of his lady. He was not to open his eye until he had smitten some
of his enemies. The fabled Black Prince wore black as a sign of his faithfulness
to his lady. Elaborate jousts, a controlled form of warfare open only to those of
noble blood, became a welcome and elaborate substitute for the randomness
of the new type of warfare. Kings in Castile, England, and France and the
rulers of the Low Countries created new orders of chivalry—the Order of the
Golden Fleece, the Order of Santiago, the Order of the Garter, the Order of
the Star. These intimate, and exclusive, groupings of the high nobility reiterated the difference between those on top and those on the bottom.

But all these displays could not obscure the reality of combat or the cruelty
and excesses of the combatants. Peasants were often caught between warring
armies, their lands ravaged by marauding companies. Their lives were taken;
their wives and children, raped. At Agincourt, Henry V, the hero of several of

Shakespeare's plays, ordered countless French prisoners to be slaughtered. Such deeds were part of the everyday violence of late medieval society.

The Black Death

The greatest trauma for medieval society was the Black Death, which was most virulent between 1348 and 1350. It has been estimated that the plague killed one third to one half of an already weakened European population. This ghastly epidemic apparently marked the first appearance in Europe of bubonic plague, introduced by caravans coming from China to the Crimea and then by ship to Sicily. Propagated by flea bites, prevalent wherever there were rats, and also carried in the air by sneezing and coughing, the plague wiped out entire communities. Death from bubonic plague was particularly horrific, with very painful boils beginning in the groin, armpit, or on the neck, followed by bleeding under the skin and the spitting of blood, uncontrolled excrement, heavy sweating, and blackened urine. It was often swift in killing its victims.

Recurring in the 1360s and 1370s, the plague altered the socioeconomic pyramid and initiated a steady decline in population that lasted until the late fifteenth century. A major social consequence of the plague was a severe shortage of labor. Laws were enacted in England, Castile, and elsewhere to limit wages and, in some cases, to bind peasants to the land once again in 1351. The peasants and workers who had survived the epidemic, however, benefited from the existing conditions and the availability of better lands.

The Black Death also had far-reaching psychological effects. Attitudes toward death became more morbid, and fascination with the rituals of death and dying grew, until by the fifteenth century the horror of physical death and of bodily decay had become an obsession. The Black Death erupted again in 1388–1390, and with this visit the cult of death developed even greater strength. Dance, decoration, art, and public ceremony used death as a centerpiece. Cemeteries were surrounded by charnel houses that displayed the bones of the deceased. In enclosed places, the infection of one person meant the likely death of all, and entire monasteries were wiped out. Not knowing the cause of such sweeping disasters, people looked to demons, superstition, and the wrath of God for explanation. The Black Death also strained the moral fabric of Europe. Some chose to embrace lives of debauchery and excess; others joined endless processions. Nothing worked. Governments proved, once again, to be quite incompetent to deal with the crisis. Appeals to God brought no relief. Parents abandoned their children and fled for their lives. Children abandoned their parents, husbands their wives. Selflessness usually ended in death. Selfishness, fleeing the illness, was often rewarded with life.

Medieval medicine helped very little. When the plague began its sweep across Europe, medical theory rested on the notion of humors. The human body was believed to have four humors—blood, phlegm, yellow bile, and

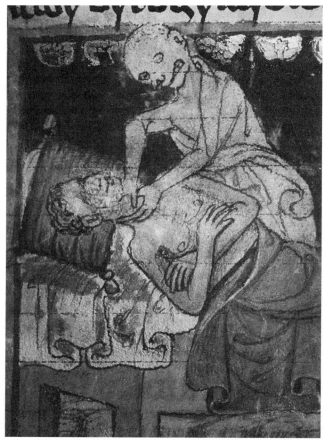

A manuscript illumination from fourteenth-century Europe shows a morbid image of the Black Death strangling an infected victim.   (Werner Forman/Art Resource, NY)

black bile. Each was related to specific organs, phlegm coming from the brain, blood from the heart, and so forth. Good health meant that the humors were in balance; if one were sick, the physician must restore that balance, for example, by changing the diet or by bloodletting. When the plague swept over Europe, the physicians did not know what to do. None of the hundreds of medical treatises written on the plague correctly adduced its cause—indeed, medical science would not understand plague until the early twentieth century. Almost no one saw any connection between the plague and the piles of dead rodents to be found prior to an outbreak. As to causes, most commentators favored either the astral or the environmental theory. The astral theory held that a conjunction of three higher planets—Mars, Jupiter, and Saturn—

in the sign of Aquarius corrupted the air, bringing poisonous material to the heart and lungs. The environmental theory held that a series of earthquakes between 1345 and 1347 had released poisonous fumes from the center of the earth. Others ascribed the plague to southerly winds and warmer weather.

The crisis of the plague and consequent search for remedies led to the professional evolution of medicine. As the older medical leaders perished in the plague, other physicians took their place. Surgeons displaced traditional physicians; in 1390 the medical faculty at the University of Paris invited surgeons to join the faculty as equals. The lay public also began to demand that medical writing be in vernacular tongues so that the patient might attempt to understand his or her own problems. The role of hospitals changed. Before the plague anyone who was placed in a hospital was treated as though dead, and the institutionalized person's property was sold. After the Black Death, hospitals sought to cure the sick. Patients who had only broken bones were placed in separate wards, where they might hope to be protected from those with infectious diseases.

From the middle of the fourteenth century to the end of the fifteenth, no one could know, from day to day, whether he or she would live or die. Recurrent cycles of plague taught a lesson about human helplessness in the face of nature, influencing religious belief, social organization, and the movement toward experimental science. Those who survived the plague may have been better off—there were fewer people, wages rose as labor was scarce, and many restrictive remnants of feudal ties fell into disuse—but, as a poem at the time put it, for most people the world was truly "turned upside down."

The fourteenth century was particularly frightening, for even the climate turned against the rural population. In the midst of one of the earth's great climatic swings from an earlier time when wheat was grown in Sweden and there were vineyards in Newfoundland, Europe passed through a long succession of wet years when crops rotted, and panic, famine, and death were common in the countryside. Hygiene was generally lacking, even at court; disease was the normal state of things, even when there was no plague, for antisepsis was unknown, and simple injuries easily led to death. Even the presumed innocence of childhood was no joy, for while the children of the well-to-do certainly had toys, most were seen simply as small adults and expected to behave as adults long before they were into their teens.

No action in history is without its reaction, and few disasters do not also lead to beneficial change, as in the rise of medical knowledge after the Black Death. One group benefited: middle-class women, particularly in England, who experienced what some scholars have called a "golden age" between about 1370 and 1470. The more secure position of women in society arose in part from depopulation, so that women were more valued for their work, knowledge, and property, and in part from other changes in society. Prior to this time women were legally viewed as "one flesh" with their husbands, but widows were able to break free from this categorization. A widow was able to make a will and testament; in London especially she could continue her husband's business and occupy the family house (whereas elsewhere and earlier a widow had to vacate her dead husband's home in forty days), and she was able to join in the social and economic life of guilds, companies, and fraternities, although she was denied the political activities of such groups. Some women—the widows of tanners, for example—had to struggle to keep a position in their craft and were seldom admitted to the guilds, but by and large the "custom of London" allowed growing participation.

Throughout western Europe a widow was entitled to dower: a share in a husband's real estate at his death. She also shared in the husband's goods and chattels by the custom of *legitim,* which meant that she kept half (or a third if there were surviving children) of the husband's movable goods. Dower in land reverted to the husband's heirs at the widow's death, but the dower in chattel was hers to sell or use as she wished, and this made it possible for widows to enter business for themselves. Upperclass women also acquired property, and some, such as Elizabeth de Burgh, Lady of Clare (1295–1360), in England or Leonor de Albuquerque in fifteenth-century Castile, maintained and ran large estates, engaged in significant public benefactions, and were the center of social gatherings.

This improved status for women declined when the population began to rebound from the Black Death. The poetry and romances of the fourteenth and fifteenth centuries are particularly virulent in their misogyny. The witch craze, which targeted mostly women, was already underway by the late fifteenth century. Thus, some gains made by women and peasants as a result of population decline and social instability were soon denied by the increasing hierarchical and patriarchal nature of late medieval society.

Other Responses to the Black Death.   Historians have long debated the extent of the Black Death's impact on European society. Some have seen the spread of the bubonic plague as an important watershed, shaping the subsequent course of European life and culture for centuries. Others point to the short duration of the plague—it did not last for more than six months in any specific locality—and to the resilience of medieval institutions and people to rebound within a short period of time. As we have seen, various sectors of medieval society gained from the onslaught of the plague. The truth about the long-term impact of the Black Death may lie somewhere between these two conflicting interpretations.

One of the most disturbing responses to the plague was to blame those on the margins of society for the calamity. Lepers, Jews, and Muslims (in Iberia) were accused of poisoning wells. Attacks against these groups were widespread, but they were most frequent in Germany and Spain. In some cases, the attacks preceded the coming of the plague. In others, they followed the appearance of the sickness. Flagellants, traveling in groups of thirty-three and whipping themselves into a bloody mess, roamed the countryside and urban centers, driving themselves and onlookers into a frenzy, spreading the Black Death as they went from one town to another.

We know some specific facts about the plague. Proportionally, the poor died in greater percentages than the rich (50 percent versus 25 percent). Contrary to popular perception and later representations, Jews, who lived in crowded quarters, also died in greater numbers. As noted earlier, the selfish—those who fled the coming of the plague—were often rewarded with survival. The selfless—those who remained behind and tried to care for the ill—almost always died. That reality shook the very fabric of medieval society and weakened the church's long-held grip on European beliefs and loyalty. In addition, new cultural transformations—notably, the Italian Renaissance, its beginnings dating roughly to the years of the plague—and deep structural changes, such as the changes in the village community, poverty of soil, and climate mentioned earlier, pushed medieval men and women inexorably toward a new direction. But the plague was not all that medieval men and women had to withstand.

Rebellions

The Middle Ages often experienced outbursts of violence. Villagers rose up in arms against predatory lords. Millenarian expectations swept western Europe in the wake of the year 1000 and under the impact of the First Crusade. None of these uprisings or convulsions, however, came close to the broad rebellions of peasants and urban poor that challenged the normative society of orders in the fourteenth and fifteenth centuries. The rebellion of the Karls (Flanders) and the Pastoreaux (France) in the 1320s, the Jacquerie in the region of Paris (1356–1358), and the uprising of non-guild workers (the ciompi) in Florence in 1378 were followed by the great English peasant revolt—spreading throughout most of southeast England in 1381. The next century featured the wars of the *remenças* (those who had to pay a fee—a *remença*—to buy their freedom) in late fifteenth-century Catalonia—the only successful peasant uprising in medieval western European history. Continuing into the early modern period, the unrest of the medieval poor exploded in the German peasant uprisings in 1524–1525 and in a series of peasant rebellions that swept most of Europe into the seventeenth century.

What made these risings new was an awareness by those below (and even by those on top of) the wide social and economic gap separating the rich from the poor. The "common people" or "lean folk," as the chroniclers refer to them, could no longer tolerate or accept the notion that such inequalities were God-ordained and a natural concomitant of a society of orders. As John Ball, a priest and one of the ideologues of the English peasant uprising, argued in a famous speech on 13 June 1381, shortly after being released from prison: "When Adam delved and Eve spun/Where was then the gentleman?" Ball's call to the equality of all men—who were after all the children of the same parents, Adam and Eve—was often replicated, in word and deed, by rebels throughout Europe. Like the popular violence that erupted in the face of the oppressive medieval practices, rebels' grievances were rooted in the social and economic dislocations that the late medieval crisis produced. The Jacquerie came about, to a large extent, because of the French nobility's inability to protect the peasantry from the ravages of mercenary companies roaming the countryside after the French defeat at Poitiers. The English peasant uprising of 1381 followed the Crown's efforts to raise additional taxes to finance the war in France. Other factors also played an important role. Feeding on patristic sources and age-old peasant fantasies about the land of Cockaigne (an imaginary utopian world where work was unnecessary and the most delectable foods flew into one's mouth), the peasants' calls for an egalitarian world and the coming of Christian justice on earth fanned the desire for redress for the glaring injustices of the medieval social order.

The peasants and urban poor often articulated their distress in the most violent fashion. Froissart, who was no friend of the French peasants taking up arms in 1356, describes with gory details (embellishing the earlier chronicle of Jean le Bel) the peasants' cruelty and excesses. He describes vividly the rape of noble women, the roasting alive of their husbands and fathers, and the forced feeding of the executed's flesh to the surviving relatives. But what Froissart conveniently omits from his narrative is that after a few successes, the rebels throughout Europe—with the already noted exception of the Catalonian serfs—were slaughtered by noble armies with equal or surpassing ferocity.

Research over the last twenty years, above all on the English and Catalan risings, shows that the peasants taking part in insurrections were not the very poor or destitute rebelling against unbearable conditions. Rather, the evidence points to the contrary; that is, that the leadership of the Jacquerie, of the English peasant uprising, and even of the Catalan *remenças* came from fairly well-to-do peasant stock and even from the lower nobility, and that some of them had gained military experience in the Hundred Years' War. Above all, the rebels reacted to increased social and economic pressure brought on by the late medieval crisis.

To the average citizen, then, these late Middle Ages must have seemed a time of incredible calamity and hardship. The Black Death ravaged the streets and the countryside. The Hundred Years' War brought political and social collapse to much of western Europe, sweeping aside old ways. Soldiers experienced an unprecedented death rate, as gunpowder and heavy artillery came into widespread use for the first time. The great schisms within the church forced Christians to take sides in a complex dispute that involved competing popes. The Turks were on the march, threatening the gates of Europe, as the powerful armies of the West fought one another. And yet, although the time may have seemed one of exceptional decline and instability, it also presaged rebirth.

The Answers of Late Medieval Society

While these problems may have been pervasive and nearly catastrophic, medieval society did not collapse as classical civilization had done under the onslaught of similar challenges in late antiquity. Instead, medieval people came up with novel ways of organizing society and articulated their personal and cultural concerns in new and creative forms.

Culture

New universities rose throughout Europe in the fourteenth and fifteenth centuries, especially in Germany. Thomas Aquinas's folding of Aristotelian thought into Christian theology (a new form of scholasticism) became the dominant scholarly discourse in European medieval universities. Scholasticism, however, had worthy rivals. Radical interpretations of Aristotelian philosophy—mostly based upon Averröes's commentaries—opened different ways of interpreting Aristotle's legacy. The innovative philosophical approach of such figures as William of Ockham (1300–1349/1350), Siger de Brabant (d. 1285), and John Duns Scotus (d. 1308) pointed a way to the future, laying down the philosophical foundations of the long process by which western Europe would become secular.

In Italy, a world unto its own, cultural developments pioneered by Francesco Petrarch (1304–1374), Giovanni Boccaccio (1313–1375), Leonardo Bruni (1370–1444), and others emphasized the study of Latin literature, above all Virgil and Cicero, in direct opposition to scholastic concerns. They also argued that their cultural project, the study of the humanities, represented a revival or "renaissance" of the classical past. Ethics—the study of how to live a morally commendable life—became more relevant for these scholars than the philosophical and metaphysical disputations that dominated the universities. Italian scholars, often writing outside the context of the university, stressed the study of the humanities, thus begetting the word humanism. The Renaissance in Italy is beyond the scope of this volume, but all in all, the Italian Renaissance achievements in literature, art, architecture, and thought may be viewed as one of the cultural responses to the late medieval crisis.

In other parts of western Europe new literary forms written mostly in the vernacular—the works of Juan Ruiz, the archpriest of Hita in Castile; Geoffrey Chaucer in England; François Villon in France; and others—brought a breath of fresh air and boldly addressed new themes in western culture. All of these authors wrote in the midst of the chaos caused by war, plague, and rebellion. Similarly, art and architecture—the final flourishing of the Gothic and the high point of medieval illumination and painting—produced bold and new depictions of men, women, and their world.

Religion

The late medieval crisis led to new forms of spirituality. We have already seen how the Black Death generated an extraordinary high level of morbidity, but late medieval religion emphasized far more than the remembrance of or reflection on one's own mortality, *memento mori*. Private devotions, private chapels, funeral art, and pious readings among the bourgeoisie and the upper classes stood in sharp contrast to the popularity of romances and books of chivalry in this period. The great success of Thomas à Kempis's *The Imitation of Christ* attests to the individual preoccupation with personal salvation, the desire to imitate Christ in daily life, and, far more important, the strength of lay religion at the end of the Middle Ages. In many respects, two different and radically opposing forces were at work: (1) a greater interest in personal religion and (2) a secularizing trend powered by institutional and cultural transformations.

The church underwent its own particular crisis. After the removal of the papacy to Avignon in 1305, the church reached unprecedented heights in terms of temporal power and financial well-being; but what it gained in riches, it lost in spiritual prestige. In 1378 the church suffered through the Great Schism, as different parts of Christendom competed for the supremacy of their own particular popes. The crisis also brought about a decisive response from the church hierarchy. Bishops throughout the Christian West came together in the Conciliar Movement to restore order and unity to the church. At a series of councils (Pisa, 1409–1410; Constance, 1414–1417; Basel, 1431–1449), a gathering of high church dignitaries, inspired by the writings of Jean Gerson and Pierre d'Ailly, argued for the superiority of a general council of the church over the theocratic pretensions of the popes. Although such theories were soon discarded by a reinvigorated papacy, one of the main consequences of the Conciliar Movement was the return of the popes to Rome and the beginnings of the Renaissance papacy, a period of dazzling artistic achievements.

The New Monarchies

Perhaps the most decisive response to the challenges of the late medieval crisis was the eventual genesis of the nation-state. Out of the crucible of war, rebellion, plague, famine, and the renewed defiance of a feudal nobility very much aware of the threat that a centralized state and a strong monarch posed to its well-being, a few places in western Europe (Portugal, Castile, France, and England) met the crisis by consolidating royal power and centralizing administrative reforms. This process was not easy; nor did it develop evenly. Other regions, such as Germany and Italy, which did not become nations until the nineteenth century, followed different paths. In 1400, or even 1500, it was not yet clear whether the nation-state was the best option for political organization. Only in hindsight can we see the advantages in this type of political system, but we also see its disadvantages: the intrusive nature of the state, its coercive methods, its use and misuse of religion for political purposes, and, eventually, the threat of absolutism. Perhaps the most promising development was the Italian formula of independent city-states and small principalities, where, as was already discussed in the previous chapter, the state came into being as—to use Jacob Burkhardt's felicitous phrase—"a work of art," crafted by men unencumbered by links to the sacred.

As early as the mid-fourteenth century, the growth of the state coincided with newly conceptualized theories of sovereignty. The works of Bartolus of Sassoferrato (d. 1352), Marsiglio of Padua (1275–1342), and others postulated new ideas about power: who holds it, where it comes from, how it is to be

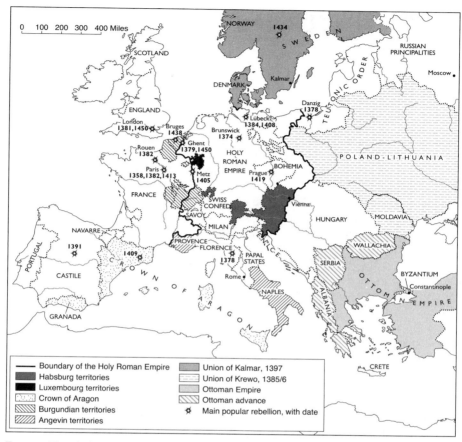

Europe, Circa 1400

wielded. Together with new practical and more onerous forms of taxation, the emergence of standing armies (created mostly because of the exigencies of war), and new forms of representing royal power through festive displays, royal entries, and performative rituals, the enunciation of political theories about the purpose and nature of the state yielded, by the late fifteenth century, new monarchies with powers that would have been unthinkable in an earlier period. How was this done?

The Final Genesis of the Nation-State

The Social Context

During the fourteenth and fifteenth centuries forms and attitudes that had prevailed in western politics became less flexible and less creative. The Holy Roman Emperor Henry VII in the early 1300s sought to straighten out the affairs of Italy in the old Ghibelline tradition, even though he had few of the resources that had been at the command of Frederick Barbarossa. The nobles of France and England, exploiting the confusion of the Hundred Years' War, built private armies and great castles and attempted to transfer power back from the monarch to themselves. Their movement has been called bastard feudalism, for service in these neo-feudal armies hinged upon money, not the traditional values of personal loyalty, mutual respect, and guarantees.

Such manifestations have been interpreted as symptoms of decline, but they may also be viewed as experiments in adjusting old institutions to new demands. The nobles who practiced bastard feudalism were also putting soldiers in the field when neither French nor English monarchies could sustain a military effort. The importance of the monetary factor was also characteristic of the passage from medieval to modern. By the close of the fifteenth century it was evident that the future lay not with the nobility but with the so-called new monarchs who were committed to power politics. Although politics and power had always gone hand in hand, the "new" monarchs did not hide their pursuit of power behind the trappings of the church, and they were served by better instruments of government and more fully equipped and better-trained soldiers, diplomats, and bureaucrats. Outstanding representatives of the new professionalism were Louis XI of France, Henry VII of England, and Ferdinand and Isabella of Spain. The princes of the various German states and the despots of the Italian city-states exemplified the new businesslike political behavior.

Meanwhile, the economy and society of western Europe underwent even more strain and upheaval. In the countryside the traditional patterns of manorialism, serfdom, and payment in kind coexisted with a free peasantry producing goods for a cash market and paying rents and taxes in cash. The economy and society showed some of the same symptoms of upheaval affecting political life. Former serfs, who thought they were free peasants by law, often found that a lord could still oblige them to use his oven or flour mill or wine press and charge a stiff fee for the privilege. But they also discovered that they could no longer turn to a lord for protection in troubled times. The uncertainty and insecurity of a world no longer wholly medieval nor yet wholly modern provoked, as we have seen, numerous outbreaks of rural violence. The crisis also convulsed urban life. Civil war broke out in the prosperous wool-manufacturing town of Flanders, and chronic strife developed between the wealthy and poorer classes in Florence. Although life for the peasant man or woman was confined, harsh, and, on the whole, short, rural life showed a bewildering variety. Broad generalization is therefore difficult beyond noting a slow increase in the value of labor in western Europe and a slow descent into serfdom in eastern Europe. Towns often served as political and economic buffers between nobles and peasants, and where there was no growth in towns or rise in urban class consciousness, the gap between rich and poor widened significantly.

Men of the upper classes and middling sorts continued to be warriors and priests. Upper-class medieval women were placed on a pedestal, to be admired for their attainments in conversation, embroidery, or household management (although the revival of courtly literature in the fourteenth and fifteenth centuries introduced, as was already noted, a nasty misogynist bent); lower-class women were sent with their husbands into the fields. The arranged marriages of royalty and nobility typically took place in childhood; the arranged marriages of the peasantry came at a later age, and many peasant women did not marry because of a shortage of eligible landholding males. Daughters were, therefore, frequently put out to service, creating a class of permanent domestic workers. Most marriages were arranged and not for love. Families were large, and children were esteemed for their labor value or to make economic and political alliances through marriage. Therefore, the children of the nobility often married by the time they were thirteen, and the daughters of the working class by the age of sixteen or later. Peasants often married even later. Men were older at marriage, and the age of both men and women at marriage rose in the fifteenth century. These economic considerations do not mean that there was no love in marriage—the letters between John and Margaret Paston, married circa 1439, clearly demonstrate that there was—or that children were not treated affectionately, especially as the church encouraged paternal care. Divorce did not exist (although annulment, especially for the powerful, did). Unions ended only with the death of a partner; this meant that husbands and wives often felt it best to attempt to get along. Still, there were many private contracts of marriage, made in secret and without the blessings of the clergy, and these often led to disputes about property and the marriage agreement, which eventually had to be adjudicated by an ecclesiastical court. It is within this changing context that the nation-state came into being.

Into the Modern Period

Rebirths and Encounters

By 1500 many things had changed in western Europe, and the slow transition to the early modern period was already well underway. No one year or event can be singled out as marking the end of the Middle Ages. In many ways, some medieval structures and cultural themes remain part of western society today. Nonetheless, by the early sixteenth century deep social, economic, cultural, and political transformations signaled a dramatic shift in European life. Some dates resonate in the popular imagination and in historical writings as watersheds in European history. The year 1453, which witnessed the conquest of Constantinople, brought to an end more than a thousand years of Byzantine civilization. In many respects, 1453 marked the final end of the Roman Empire. Although it had survived in a radically different form than originally envisioned by its founder Constantine in the early fourth century, Byzantium stood, symbolically and materially, for the enduring presence of Rome in the East. A Middle Ages that could perhaps be said to have begun with Constantine's conversion ended, in part, with the taking of his city more than a thousand years afterward.

The 1460s saw the beginnings of printing in the West (the Chinese had been printing books already for centuries before). Over the next decades, the rise in the number of books available at an accessible price to a growing reading public increased exponentially. The combination of a larger reading public and access to printed books changed the European cultural landscape. The year 1492 witnessed Columbus's epoch-making voyage across the Atlantic and the European encounter with an unknown New World. Together with the bold Portuguese voyages of exploration along the coast of Africa, culminating in the epic voyage by Vasco da Gama to India, the new awareness of a wider world opened a new era for the West. Discoveries, encounters, and conquests extended Europe's commercial networks far beyond its ancient historical borders. It also opened new cultural horizons.

Europe and the World

At the beginning of our long journey over the millennium we call the Middle Ages, this book emphasized European society's openness to the wider world. Economic exchanges and cultural transmissions linked western Europe to Africa and Asia. In truth, these contacts diminished over the long and troubled centuries that followed the collapse of the Roman Empire in the West, but the ties to the outside world never disappeared fully. Despite the receding boundaries of the European heartland, Muslim and Jewish traders and scholars, adventurous European travelers, and missionaries kept open conduits to the known world outside. Although obscured by the feverish imagings of people outside Christian Europe as "monstrous races" and by fantastic descriptions of foreign locales and people in some medieval travel accounts—John of Mandeville's travel account was among the most influential in constructing these fantastic tales—the late Middle Ages was veritably a period of reopening to the outside world and of establishing permanent ties, although often these ties were those of colonization and oppression, with the entire world. These different processes marked the end of the medieval world and the beginnings of European hegemony over most parts of the globe. It was, in many respects, the beginnings of globalization.

Europe reached out to the world beyond its borders in many different ways, but two in particular are emblematic of the expansive changes that ushered in the modern period: cultural transformations and the encounter with, and expansion into, other worlds.

Cultural Transformations: The Renaissance

As was noted in the previous chapter, the great cultural rebirth known as the Renaissance in Italy is not discussed in detail in this volume. However, we will discuss some specific aspects of Renaissance's scholarly inquiries that went beyond the recovery of Roman classical culture or of its well-known artistic achievements.

Looking Back in Time.   One of the most important developments of fifteenth-century Renaissance culture was a new and, in many ways, revolutionary awareness of time. Rather than just a rebirth or recovery of the Roman past, a good number of Renaissance thinkers, most notably among them Marsiglio Ficino and Pico della Mirandola (writing in the second half of the fifteenth century), sought to go back beyond Rome into "deep time." They believed that the further one could go back in historical time, the closer one would get to the pristine sources of truth and to the original sources of knowledge. In many respects, therefore, this preoccupation with very ancient time meant a veritable discovery and exploration of cultures (Egyptian, Chaldean, and other ancient cultures) that had been long erased from, or exoticized by, western memory. It was a new opening to a different kind of outside world—one that was alive only in ancient and esoteric texts and in faint remembrances.

This consciousness of time led to the writing and thinking of new types of history. The works of Guicciardini, Machiavelli, and other Italian historians signaled a sharp break with medieval historiographical traditions. This new concern with history, the older the better, also led to a search for the historical origins of one's city or country, to the writing of elaborate historical accounts (often fictitious) of one's collective past, and to an almost obsessive interest in genealogy and genealogical trees. How did this happen?

The most immediate past to which the Renaissance humanist had direct access was, of course, that of Rome, and from the mid-fourteenth century onward many scholars inspected and studied the antiquities around them. They collected and copied epigraphic material, reading the past in the stones. By the mid-fifteenth century, a series of developments uncovered for the Renaissance intellectual elite a different kind of past, a far more remote and, until then, fairly inaccessible kind of past. These new ideas about time were rooted in the Renaissance's rejection of medieval philosophy and culture and in its fierce attachment to the classical tradition. The latter held implicitly to the belief in a golden past and in the slow decline of mankind from an age of gold, to one of silver, to one of iron. Thus, some aspects of Renaissance thought, unlike that of the Middle Ages, were intrinsically conservative, seeking to recover rather than to create new ideas. But far more important, this search for the deep past and esoteric knowledge represented, in many respects, a new form of knowing, of spirituality, and it turned upside down the latent sense of progress found in the Judeo-Christian tradition.

The Mysteries.   The Renaissance also witnessed the revival of what one may describe as pagan mysteries, a series of esoteric and mysterious forms of knowledge given great validity by their ancient provenance. These included alchemy, magic, hermeticism, and astrology. Alchemical, astrological, and magical treatises had long entered the West through the Arabs. These works, many of which claimed to reveal very ancient knowledge, had already been translated into Latin in the twelfth century. Others came in the mid-fifteenth century (as was the case with Hermeticism) and attracted the keen interest of a few scholars inclined to these types of esoteric knowledge. Although familiarity with these works was restricted to a small elite, many of these ideas— magical and astrological—did spread into popular culture, although they often did so in a distorted fashion.

Far more important, the Ottoman conquest of Constantinople in 1453 led to a massive migration of Greek scholars to the West. They brought with them numerous ancient texts. Many of these texts were not known in the West or were not available in western libraries and were known only secondhand. Florence, already the most important cultural center in Renaissance Italy, became the repository of many of these texts and the site for the translations and interpretations of ancient lore. The key figure in the adaptation of some of these diverse and esoteric types of knowledge was Marsiglio Ficino, a fifteenth-century scholar working in Florence under the patronage of the Medici. The most significant texts for the opening of new perspectives in European culture were such fundamental western works as Plato's *Republic* and his *Symposium,* but they also included the mysterious *Corpus Hermeticum* and the *Aesclepius,* the foundations of Hermeticism. In the fifteenth century scholars considered these latter works as far more important than the Platonic dialogues. Pico della Mirandola, in his paradigmatic *Oration on the Dignity of Man,* cited Hermetic, Chaldean, astrological, kabbalistic, and Christian sources. At the end, the popularity of Hermeticism waned, and the reception of other philosophical traditions in the fifteenth century came to play a significant role. Together with Plato, the works of the Greek Skeptics—Sextus Empiricus, Pyrrhus, and others—also entered the European intellectual world. In many respects the great scientific revolution of the sixteenth and seventeenth centuries traces its origins to the revival of these works. These texts were newly discovered worlds as well.

The Encounter with Other Worlds

The European expansion and encounter with unknown worlds developed over the long course of centuries. Nonetheless, from the late fourteenth century the pace accelerated as the Portuguese and Castilians sailed into the Atlantic and along the coast of Africa. The Castilian and Portuguese conquests of the Canary Islands and the Azores respectively and the Portuguese settlement of trade centers on the western coast of Africa opened the way to the Americas and to India. But these enterprises were concomitant with cultural and practical developments that revolutionized the European worldview and seafaring. A greater and better knowledge of geography and astronomy resulted from the recovery of classical texts. Pierre d'Ailly's *Imago Mundi,* written in 1410, reproduced a great deal of the classical knowledge about the world. Most seafarers in the fifteenth century knew the book; Christopher Columbus, for example, read *Imago Mundi* and was influenced by it. New practical knowledge of cartography and of the use of the compass and the astrolabe made sailing into the open waters of the Atlantic a matter of skill and technical know-how rather than an unpredictable adventure. New types of ships, the Portuguese-designed *caravela redonda* most of all, combined square rigging with lateen sails and allowed for open sea-going vessels, unlike the oar-powered galleys of the Mediterranean, capable of sailing into the Atlantic. In the late fifteenth century, the Portuguese adoption of broadside artillery in their ships led to their superiority over native fleets in the Indian Ocean.

The Portuguese were at the vanguard of European expansion, and their precocity gave them an extraordinary advantage. Sailing along the west coast of Africa, the Portuguese established trading stations on African shores and profited immensely from the beginnings of the slave trade. But Africa was only the gateway to even more profitable enterprises. After rounding the Cape of Good Hope in the southernmost tip of Africa, the way to the fabulous riches of India lay open to them. Vasco da Gama's signal sea voyage to India and his return to Europe in 1499 was, from the perspective of contemporaries, an extraordinary event besides which even Columbus's recent claims to have discovered a westward route to India paled in comparison.

As preposterous as Columbus's claims were in the context of what was known about the world in 1492, his heady mix of superb sailing skills, an almost apocalyptic religious fervor, and measureless ambition carried him to convince the Catholic Monarchs, Ferdinand and Isabella, to sponsor his enterprise, leading to his momentous voyage across the Ocean Sea. At the end, his mistaken search for the Indies by sailing westward had immense consequences for Europe and the world and signaled emphatically the transition to the early modern world.

The Caribbean, the Valley of Mexico, Its Natives, and the Shock of the New

After landfall on 12 October 1492, Europeans attempted to make sense of the strange new lands and people they had found in the Caribbean and, later on, in the Americas. The first narrative of the encounter between the Old World and the New (rewritten by Bartolomé de las Casas after the lost manuscript of Columbus's account) sought to create a positive image of Columbus and of New World natives. The account of the first voyage presented a vision of the Caribbean Islands (those first visited by Columbus in 1492) as paradisaical and of its inhabitants as people living a state of nature: the pre-Lapsarian "natural man." Columbus returned to the Old World after his first voyage and skillfully made his voyage appear far more profitable than it was in reality. The printed announcement heralding Columbus's voyage to the Indies circulated widely through Europe, a good example of the power of printing to create a new vision of the world. The second expedition to the New World in 1493 was a large enterprise with many ships and men, and it involved a determined commitment to settle the islands of the Caribbean with Castilians. From exploration, the Europeans had turned to the colonization of the New World.

The most reliable account of the second voyage, that of Dr. Alvarez Chanca, carefully describes the flora and fauna of the Antilles in amazed tones, but his representations of the natives are often ambivalent and include descriptions of some of the inhabitants as "beastly." This became even more accusatory in Chanca's description of the Caribs. He describes them as cannibals. Chanca's account also provides an account of the difficulties faced by the Spaniards in adapting to the food and climate of the Caribbean. One also finds the first references to the wave of diseases spreading among the native population, to the sexual abuses perpetrated by the Spaniards, and to the slow awareness among the colonizers and the authorities back in the metropolis that the islands had neither gold nor spices. Instead of immediate wealth, an ecological and human catastrophe swiftly followed the coming of the Europeans into the Caribbean.

As the inhabitants of the Caribbean began to die of disease and overwork, the colonizers began to demand new working forces. Slowly, African slaves began to be ferried across the Atlantic to the New World to replace the dying natives. The conjunction of large plantations, the growth of export commodities (sugar), and African slavery led to the emergence of new forms of bondage unknown in the Middle Ages. The embryonic beginnings of capitalism also played a significant role in the genesis of Atlantic slavery. The islands in the Caribbean, however, also proved to be useful stations between Europe and America's mainland. By the sixteenth century, two annual fleets linked Spain to its colonies. Moreover, the Caribbean Islands served as launching points for the exploration and conquest of the mainland. Indeed, Mexico and Central America were first encountered and then conquered not from the European metropolis but from the Caribbean Islands. The supplies and manpower for the next bold move in European expansion came from the Caribbean.

In the 1510s the Spaniards began to explore the coast of Mexico and Central America, establishing contacts with cultures that were far more sophisticated than those of the Caribbean Islands. By the late 1510s the Spaniards began to move inland from the coast. Led by Hernán Cortés, who disregarded his orders to remain on the coast and wait for reinforcements, the Spaniards, few in number and with even fewer resources, mounted an expedition into the very heart of the powerful Aztec Empire. By 1521, after a harsh and bloody struggle and with the substantial help of native allies, Cortés conquered the great Aztec capital. Perhaps the true end of the Middle Ages lies not in Europe but in the smoldering ruins of Tenochtitlán. There, among the remains of the largest city in the Western Hemisphere, Spain lay claim to the first world empire, an idea unimaginable to the medieval mind.

By the early 1500s the realization that this was a New World and not the Indies spread throughout Europe's learned circles. This new knowledge, an experiential one, had a profound impact on European culture and life. In the early stages of colonization the Europeans had seen the New World through the lens of classical writings and medieval travel accounts (Pliny, John of Mandeville, and others), but by the 1520s these ancient paradigms became no longer tenable and were discarded. New ideas about the world and the people who lived in it had to be created. A new age was at hand.

Chronology

212	The Edict of Caracalla grants Roman citizenship to all those living within the borders of the empire
235	Death of Emperor Alexander Severus
c. 235–285	The crisis of the third century
284–305	Rule of Diocletian
285	Edict of the Tetrarchy
312	28 October, battle at the Milvian Bridge
c. 312–325	Constantine converts to Christianity
313	Edict of Milan
312–337	Constantine's rule in the West
324–337	Constantine's rule over the whole empire
325	Council of Nicaea
332	Edict of the Colonate
c. 340–397	Ambrose
c. 340–420	Jerome (translation of the Bible into Latin)
354–430	Augustine of Hippo (*The Confessions, The City of God,* and other works)
378	Battle of Adrianople (victory of the Visigoths over a Roman army)
392	Christianity becomes the official religion of the empire
406	Vandals invade Spain and North Africa
410	Visgoths sack Rome
476	The last Roman emperor in the western part of the empire is deposed
c. 480–524	Boethius (*On the Consolation of Philosophy*)
c. 480–c. 547	St. Benedict of Nursia
c. 490–575	Cassiodorus (Vivarium and the *scriptoria*)
c. 500	Anglo-Saxon tribes enter England
527–565	Reign of Justinian
529–532	Publication of the *Corpus Iuris Civilis iuris civilis*
533	Conquest of North Africa by Justinian
536	Justinian's conquest of part of the Italian peninsula

c. 540–604	Gregory the Great
551	Visigothic kingdom in Toledo
568	Lombards conquer northern Italy
c. 570–636	St. Isidore of Seville
572–586	Leovigild, king of the Visigoths
587	Recared's conversion from Arian to Catholic Christianity
589	Third Council of Toledo; Catholicism declared the religion of the kingdom
622	Hijra of Muhammad from Mecca to Medina; beginning of the Islamic era
630	Muhammad conquers Mecca
632	Death of Muhammad; Abu Bakr becomes the first caliph
633–437	Arabs conquer Syria and Iraq
639–642	Conquest of Egypt
649	*Liber judiciorum,* composition of Roman-influenced legal code
656–661	Murder of Ali; beginnings of first Muslim civil war; Umayyad caliphate dynasty begins
696	Abd al Malik introduces Arab coinage as part of the reorganization of imperial administration
710	Muslims from North Africa land in Spain
711	Defeat of Visigoths; beginning of the conquest of Spain by Muslims
717	Charles Martel, mayor of the palace in Merovingian France
721–725	Battle of Covadonga (721); King Pelayo in Cangas (Asturias)
739	Alfonso I, king of Asturias
750	Fall of the Umayyads, accession of the Abbasid caliphate
751	Arabs capture Chinese paper makers in Central Asia
751	Pepin III, the Short, becomes king of the Franks
755	Abd al-Rahman I, independent emir
756	Cordoba declares its independence
762–763	Foundation of Baghdad
768	Charles (Charlemagne) succeeds his father Pepin III as king of the Franks
791	Alfonso II, king of Asturias in Oviedo
800	Ptolemy's *Geography* translated into Arabic
800	Charlemagne crowned emperor
801	Louis the Pious captures Barcelona

803	Harun al-Rashid, ruler in Baghdad
814	Death of Charlemagne; his son Louis the Pious becomes emperor
825	Beginning of the Muslim conquest of Sicily
830s?	First mention of the tomb of St. James at Compostela
850	Ordoño I, king of Asturias; beginning of repopulation; rise of the county of Castile
866	Alfonso III the Great, king of Asturias
910	Foundation of the monastery of Cluny
919–936	Henry the Fowler, emperor in Germany (Holy Roman Empire)
929	Descendants of Abd al-Rahman proclaimed caliphs in Cordoba
936–973	Otto the Great, emperor in Germany
946	The county of Castile independent
955	Battle of Lechfeld (defeat of Magyars)
978–1002	Rule of al-Mansur in Cordoba
987–996	Hugh Capet elected king of France
983–1002	Otto III, emperor in Germany
1031	End of Cordoba caliphate
1035	Kingdoms of *taifas* established
1037	Death of Avicenna
1039–1056	Henry III, emperor in Germany
c. 1040	First example of Castilian literature, *las jarchas*
1042–1066	Edward the Confessor, king of England
c. 1043	Ruy Díaz de Vivar, el Cid, is born
1046	Council of Sutri
1049–1054	Pope Leo IX
c. 1053	Birth of Guibert of Nogent
1054	Schism between the eastern and western Christian churches (Orthodox and Catholic)
1056–1106	Henry IV, emperor of Germany
c. 1058	The *Usatges* (a law code) of Barcelona are written down
1059	Papal election decree
1066	William the Conqueror, king of England, duke of Normandy
1066	Battle of Hastings
1072	Death of Peter Damiani
1072	Alfonso VI, king of Castile-Leon

1073–1085	Gregory VII elected pope
1075–1122	Investiture controversy
1077	Canossa
1080	Council of Burgos; end of Mozarabic liturgy; imposition of Roman (Cluniac) rites
c. 1080	*Song of Roland* in substantially its present form
1085	Conquest of Toledo
1086	Invasion of Almoravids
1086	William IX, lord of Aquitaine and Poitou (a troubadour and father of Eleanor of Aquitaine)
1086	*Domesday Book*
1088–1099	Pope Urban II
1090	Ivo appointed bishop of Chartres
1093	Anselm appointed archbishop of Canterbury
1094	El Cid conquers Valencia
1095	First Crusade preached at Clermont
1095–1099	First Crusade
1098	Foundation of Citeaux; Anselm, *Cur Deus Homo*
1099	Jerusalem captured by First Crusade
1099	Death of el Cid
1099–1118	Pope Paschal II
1100–1135	Henry I, king of England (curia regis, sheriffs, exchequer)
1102	Almoravids take Valencia
1104	Guibert appointed abbot of Nogent
1106–1125	Henry V, emperor of Germany
1108–1137	Louis VI, king of France (construction of St. Denis)
1108	Guibert, *Gesta Dei per Francos*
1109	Death of Anselm of Canterbury
1114	Abelard teaching in Paris
1115	Bernard appointed abbot of Clairvaux
1116	Guibert completes his autobiography
1117	Death of Anselm of Laon
1122	Concordat of Worms
1123	Abelard, *Sic et Non*; death of Guibert of Nogent
1128/1140	Abelard, *Paraclete Hymnbook*

1129/1141	Bernard, *de Diligendo Deo*
1133	Abelard, *Commentary on Romans* and *Historia Calamitatum*
1134	New west front begun at Chartres
1135	Abelard, *Ethics*
1135/1153	Bernard at work on his sermons on Song of Songs
1135/1160	Hugh "Primas" of Orleans writing
1135	Alfonso VII, emperor of all the Spains
1136	Invasion of Almohads
1137	Louis VII of France marries Eleanor of Aquitaine
1140	Abelard condemned by Council of Sens, at insistence of St. Bernard
c. 1140s	Beginning of the spread of Catharism throughout most of southern France
1142	Death of Abelard
1144	Consecration of east end of St. Denis, built by Suger
c. 1145	Early work of Bernard of Ventadour
1145	Otto of Freising, *The Two Cities*
1150	Peter Lombard, *Book of Sentences;* Bernard of Clairvaux, *De consideratione*
1152	Henry of Anjou marries Eleanor of Aquitaine
1154–1189	Henry II (Plantagenet), king of England
c. 1155	Bernard of Ventadour in England at Henry II's court
1158–1214	Alfonso VIII, king of Castile
1159	John of Salisbury, *Metalogicon* and *Policraticus*
1162–1196	Alfonso II, king of Aragon
1164	Archpoet, "Confession"
1170	Murder of Thomas à Becket
c. 1170	Chrétien de Troyes, *Erec and Enide*
c. 1180	Death of John of Salisbury
c. 1180	Chrétien de Troyes, *Knight of the Lion* and *Knight of the Cart*
c. 1180s	Spread of the Waldensian heresy
1180–1223	Rule of Philip Augustus, king of France
c. 1185	Chrétien de Troyes, *The Story of the Grail*
1187	Fall of Jerusalem to Saladin
1188	First meeting of the Cortes of Leon-Castile
1189	Death of Henry II of England

c. 1195	Birth of Gonzalo de Berceo, author of *Miracles of Our Lady* and other works
1198–1216	Pope Innocent III
1204	Sack of Constantinople by the Fourth Crusade
c. 1206	Composition of the *Poem of the Cid*
1209	The Franciscan order is founded
1212	Battle of Las Navas de Tolosa
1215	Fourth Lateran Council
1215	*Magna Carta*
1215	Foundation of the University of Salamanca
1216	Foundation of the Dominican Order
1226–1270	Louis IX, king of France
1230	Final Union of Castile and Leon
1236	Conquest of Cordoba
1237–1240s	Mongols' conquest of Slavic realms
1238	Conquest of Valencia
1238	Nasrid rule established in Granada
1248	Conquest of Seville
1264	Mudejar rebellions in Andalusia
1265–1321	Dante Aligheri
1282	Conquest of Sicily by Peter III of Aragon (Sicilian Vespers)
1285–1314	Philip IV, the Fair, king of France; first meeting of the Estates General in Paris 1302
1304–1374	Petrarch
1315–1321	The Great Famine (most acute in 1315 and 1317)
1337–1453	Hundred Years' War
1346	Battle of Crecy; defeat of the French armies at the hands of a numerically inferior English army
1347–1353	The Black Death (most virulent between 1348 and 1351)
1350–1365	Civil war in Castile
1356	Battle of Poitiers; capture of the French king, John the Good
1358	The "Jacquerie" rebellion
1369	Henry II of Trastámara, king of Castile
1378	The revolt of the ciompi in Florence
1381	The English peasant uprisings

1391	Attacks on Jews in Spain; large number of conversions
1405	Battle of Agincourt
1412	Compromise of Caspe—the regent of Castile, Fernando de Antequera, becomes king of the Crown of Aragon
1415	Ceuta is taken by the Portuguese
1420s–1430s	Portuguese colonization of Madeira and Azores islands
1429–1430	Joan of Arc leads the French armies
1442–1443	Alfonso V of Aragon gains control of Naples
1449	Anti-*Converso* riots in Toledo
1453	Ottoman Turks conquer Constantinople
1462–1472	Civil and *remença* wars in Catalonia
1469	The marriage of Ferdinand and Isabella
1473	Massacre of *Conversos;* printing arrives in Spain
1478	Setting up of the Inquisition
1479	Dynastic union of Castile and Aragon
1488	Bartolomeu Dias reaches the cape of Good Hope
1492	Conquest of Granada; expulsion of the Jews; encounter with the New World
1497–1498	Vasco da Gama reaches the great spice-trading areas in India
1502	*Moriscos* forced to choose between baptism and expulsion

Suggested Readings

CHAPTER 1:   The End of the Ancient World

Primary Sources

Augustine of Hippo. *Confessions.* Trans. H. Chadwick. Oxford: Oxford University Press, 1998.

Lane, Eugene, et al. *Paganism and Christianity, 100–425 CE: A Sourcebook.* Minneapolis: Fortress Press, 1992.

Louth, Andrew. *Early Christian Writings: The Apostolic Fathers.* New York, Penguin, 1987.

Williams, Margaret. *The Jews Among the Greeks and Romans: A Diasporan Sourcebook.* London: Duckworth, 1998.

Secondary Sources

Barnes, Timothy. *Constantine and Eusebius.* Cambridge, MA: Harvard University Press, 1981.

Bowersock, G. W. *Julian the Apostate.* Cambridge, MA: Harvard University Press, 1978.

Bowersock, G. W., et al. *Late Antiquity: A Guide to the Postclassical World.* Cambridge, MA: Belknap Press, 1999.

Brown, Peter. *Augustine of Hippo: A Biography.* Rev. Ed. London: Faber and Faber, 2000.

———. *The Rise of Western Christendom. Triumph and Diversity, AD 200–1000.* Oxford: Blackwell, 1996.

———. *The Cult of the Saints. Its Rise and Function in Latin Christianity.* Chicago: Chicago University Press, 1981.

———. *Religion and Society in the Age of Saint Augustine.* London: Faber and Faber, 1972.

———. *The World of Late Antiquity, AD 150–750.* New York: Harcourt Brace Jovanovich, 1971.

Cameron, Averil. *The Later Roman Empire, AD 284–430.* London: Fontana, 1993.

Corcoran, Simon. *The Empire of the Tetrarchs: Imperial Pronouncements and Government, AD 284–324.* Rev. Ed. Oxford: Oxford University Press, 2000.

Curran, John R. *Pagan City and Christian Capital: Rome in the Fourth Century.* Oxford: Oxford University Press, 2000.

Dunn, Marilyn. *The Emergence of Monasticism: From the Desert Fathers to the Early Middle Ages.* Oxford: Blackwell, 2000.

Elsner, Jas. *Imperial Rome and Christian Triumph: The Art of the Roman Empire AD 100–450.* Oxford: Oxford University Press, 1998.

Herrin, Judith. *The Formation of Christendom.* Princeton, NJ: Princeton University Press, 1987.

Jones, A. H. M. *The Later Roman Empire, AD 284–602: A Social, Economic, and Administrative Survey.* Oxford: Blackwell, 1986.

MacMullen, Ramsay. *Christianity and Paganism in the Fourth to Eighth Centuries.* New Haven, CT: Yale University Press, 1997.

McLynn, Neil. *Ambrose of Milan: Church and Court in a Christian Capital.* Berkeley: University of California Press, 1994.

Raven, Susan. *Rome in Africa.* 3rd Ed. London: Routledge, 1992.

Rousselle, Aline. *Porneia: On Desire and the Body in Antiquity.* Oxford: Blackwell, 1988.

Salzman, Michele Renee. *On Roman Time: The Codex-Calendar of 354 and the Rhythms of Urban Life in Late Antiquity.* Berkeley: University of California Press, 1990.

Whittaker, C. R. *Frontiers of the Roman Empire: A Social and Economic Study.* Baltimore: Johns Hopkins University Press, 1994.

Williams, Stephen. *Diocletian and the Roman Recovery.* New York: Routledge, 1997.

Wills, Garry. *Saint Augustine.* New York: Viking, 1999.

Wolfram, Herwig. *The Roman Empire and Its Germanic Peoples.* Berkeley: University of California Press, 1997.

CHAPTER 2:   Byzantium and Islam, 500–1000

Primary Sources

Geanakoplos, Deno John, ed. *Byzantium: Church, Society, and Civilization Seen Through Contemporary Eyes.* Chicago: University of Chicago Press, 1986.

Head, Constance. *Imperial Byzantine Portraits: A Verbal and Graphic Gallery.* New Rochelle, NY: Caratzas, 1982.

Lewis, Bernard, ed. *Islam: From the Prophet Muhammad to the Capture of Constantinople.* 2 vols. New York: Harper & Row, 1987.

Procopius. *The Secret History.* Trans. R. Atwater. Ann Arbor: University of Michigan Press, 1964.

Secondary Sources

Ahmed, Leila. *Women and Gender in Islam: Historical Roots of a Modern Debate.* New Haven, CT: Yale University Press, 1992.

Browning, Robert. *Justinian and Theodora.* London: Thames & Hudson, 1987.

Cameron, Averil. *Procopius and the Sixth Century.* London: Routledge, 1996.

Crone, Patricia. *Meccan Trade and the Rise of Islam.* Princeton, NJ: Princeton University Press, 1987.

Haldon, J. F. *Byzantium in the Seventh Century: The Transformation of a Culture.* Cambridge: Cambridge University Press, 1990.

Herrin, Judith, *Women in Purple. Rulers of Medieval Byzantium.* London: Weidenfeld & Nicolson, 2001.

Hodges, Richard, et al. *Mohammed and Charlemagne: The Origins of Europe.* London: Duckworth, 1983.

Hodgson, Marshall G. S. *The Venture of Islam: Conscience and History in a World Civilization.* Volume 1: *The Classical Age of Islam.* Chicago: University of Chicago Press, 1974.

Hourani, Albert. *A History of the Arab Peoples.* New York: Warner, 1992.

Jenkins, Romilly. *Byzantium: The Imperial Centuries, AD 610–1071.* London: Weidenfeld and Nicolson, 1966.

Kennedy, Hugh. *The Prophet and the Age of the Caliphates: The Islamic Near East from the Sixth to the Eleventh Century.* New York: Longman, 1989.

Lewis, Bernard. *Islam in History: Ideas, People, and Events in the Middle East.* Chicago: Open Court, 1993.

Mango, Cyril. *Byzantium: The Empire of New Rome.* New York: Scribner, 1980.

Mottahedeh, Roy. *Loyalty and Leadership in an Early Islamic Society.* Princeton, NJ: Princeton University Press, 1980.

Norwich, John Julius. *Byzantium: The Early Centuries.* London: Viking, 1989.

Ostrogorski, George. *History of the Byzantine State.* Trans. Joan Hussey. Oxford: Blackwell, 1968.

Pirenne, Henri. *Mohammed and Charlemagne.* 1935. Trans. Bernard Miall. London: Unwin, 1974.

Spellberg, Denise. *Politics, Gender, and the Islamic Past.* New York: Columbia University Press, 1994.

Turteltaub, H. N. *Justinian.* New York: Forge Books, 1998.

Weitzmann, Kurt. *The Icon: Holy Images, Sixth to Fourteenth Century.* New York: George Braziller, 1978.

Whittow, Mark. *The Making of Byzantium, 600–1025.* Berkeley: University of California Press, 1996.

Wilson, N. G. *Scholars of Byzantium.* Rev. Ed. London: Duckworth, 1996.

CHAPTER 3: Medieval Society in the West

Primary Sources

Beowulf. Trans. Seamus Heaney. New York: Norton, 2002.

Dutton, Paul Edward. *Carolingian Civilization: A Reader.* Peterborough, Ontario: Broadview Press, 1993.

Einhard and Notker the Stammerer. Two Lives of Charlemagne. Trans. Lewis Thorpe. New York: Penguin, 1969.

Gregory of Tours. *History of the Franks.* Trans. Lewis Thorpe. New York: Penguin, 1974.

Whitelock, Dorothy, ed. *English Historical Documents.* Volume 1: AD 500–1042. 2nd Ed. London: Eyre & Spottiswoode, 1979.

Secondary Sources

Beckwith, John. *Early Medieval Art: Carolingian, Ottonian, Romanesque.* Rev. Ed. London: Thames & Hudson, 1988.

Carver, Marvin. *Sutton Hoo: Burial Grounds of Kings?* London: British Museum Press, 1998.

Collins, Roger. *Medieval Spain: Unity in Diversity, 400–1000.* New York: St. Martin's Press, 1983.

Duby, Georges. *The Early Growth of the European Economy: Warriors and Peasants from the Seventh to the Twelfth Century.* Trans. H. B. Clarke. Ithaca, NY: Cornell University Press, 1974.

Fichtenau, Heinrich. *Living in the Tenth Century: Studies in Mentalities and Social Orders.* Toronto: University of Toronto Press, 1957.

Frantzen, Allen. *King Alfred.* Boston: Twayne, 1986.

Geary, Patrick. *The Myth of Nations. The Medieval Origins of Europe.* Princeton, NJ: Princeton University Press, 2002.

———. *Before France and Germany: The Creation and Transformation of the Merovingian World.* Oxford: Oxford University Press, 1988.

Lawrence, C. H. *Medieval Monasticism: Forms of Religious Life in Western Europe in the Middle Ages.* 3rd Ed. New York: Longman, 2001.

McKitterick, Rosamund. *The Frankish Kingdoms Under the Carolingians, 751–987.* New York: Longman, 1983.

————. *Carolingian Culture: Emulation and Innovation.* Cambridge: Cambridge University Press, 1994.

Raftis, J. A., ed. *Pathways to Medieval Peasants.* Toronto: University of Toronto Press, 1981.

Reuter, Timothy. *Germany in the Early Middle Ages, c. 800–1056.* New York: Longman, 1991.

Reynolds, Susan. *Fiefs and Vassals: The Medieval Evidence Reinterpreted.* Oxford: Oxford University Press, 1996.

Riché, Pierre. *Daily Life in the World of Charlemagne.* Trans. Jo Ann McNamara. Philadelphia: University of Pennsylvania Press, 1988.

Stenton, Frank. *Anglo-Saxon England.* 3rd Ed. Oxford: Clarendon Press, 1971.

Straw, Carole. *Gregory the Great: Perfection in Imperfection.* Berkeley: University of California Press, 1988.

Sweeney, Del. *Agriculture in the Middle Ages: Technology, Practice, and Representation.* Philadelphia: University of Pennsylvania Press, 1995.

Wemple, Suzanne Fonay. *Women in Frankish Society: Marriage and the Cloister, 500 to 800.* Philadelphia: University of Pennsylvania Press, 1981.

Wickham, Chris. *Early Medieval Italy: Central Power and Local Society, 400–1100.* London: Macmillan, 1981.

Wilson, David. *The Vikings and Their Origins: Scandinavia in the First Millennium.* Rev. Ed. London: Thames & Hudson, 1989.

CHAPTERS 4 and 5:   Medieval Society *and* Those Who Pray

Primary Sources

Abelard, Peter, and Heloise. *Letters of Abelard and Heloise.* Trans. Betty Radice. New York: Penguin, 1974.

Benton, John F., ed. *Self and Society in Medieval France: The Memoirs of Abbot Guibert of Nogent (1064?–c. 1125).* Rev. Ed. Toronto: University of Toronto Press, 1984.

Peters, Edward, ed. *The First Crusade: The Chronicle of Fulcher of Chartres and Other Source Materials.* Philadelphia: University of Pennsylvania Press, 1971.

The Song of Roland. Trans. Glyn Burgess. New York: Penguin, 1990.

Tierney, Brian, ed. *The Crisis of Church and State, 1050–1300.* Toronto: University of Toronto Press, 1964.

Secondary Sources

Barber, Richard. *The Knight and Chivalry.* Rochester, NY: Boydell Press, 1995.

Benson, Robert L., et al. *Renaissance and Renewal in the Twelfth Century.* Toronto: University of Toronto Press, 1982.

Bisson, Thomas N., ed. *Cultures of Power: Lordship, Status, and Process in Twelfth-Century Europe.* Philadelphia: University of Pennsylvania Press, 1995.

Bloch, Marc. *Feudal Society.* Trans. L. A. Manyon. New York: Routledge, 1961.

Bouchard, Constance B. *Holy Entrepreneurs: Cistercians, Knights, and Economic Exchange in Twelfth-Century Burgundy.* Ithaca, NY: Cornell University Press, 1991.

Brundage, James. *Medieval Canon Law.* New York: Longman, 1995.

Clanchy, Michael. *Abelard: A Medieval Life.* Oxford: Blackwell, 1997.

Constable, Giles. *The Reformation of the Twelfth Century.* Cambridge: Cambridge University Press, 1996.

Erdmann, Carl. *The Origin of the Idea of Crusade.* Trans. N. Baldwin and G. Goffart. Princeton, NJ: Princeton University Press, 1977.

Ferruolo, Stephen C. *The Origins of the University: The Schools of Paris and their Critics, 1100–1215.* Stanford, CA: Stanford University Press, 1985.

Haskins, Charles Homer. *The Renaissance of the Twelfth Century.* 1927. Cambridge, MA: Harvard University Press, 1971.

Head, Thomas, et al. *The Peace of God: Social Violence and Religious Response in France Around the Year 1000.* Ithaca, NY: Cornell University Press, 1992.

Herlihy, David. *Medieval Households.* Cambridge, MA: Harvard University Press, 1985.

Lynch, Joseph. *The Medieval Church: A Brief History.* New York: Longman, 1992.

Poly, Jean-Pierre, et al. *The Feudal Transformation: 900–1200.* New York: Holmes & Meier, 1991.

Riley-Smith, Jonathan. *The Crusades: A Short History.* London: Athlone, 1987.

Robinson, I. S. *The Papacy, 1073–1198: Continuity and Innovation.* Cambridge: Cambridge University Press, 1990.

Southern, Richard W. *The Making of the Middle Ages.* 1955. New Haven: Yale University Press, 1970.

Tellenbach, Gerd. *The Church in Western Europe from the Tenth to the Twelfth Century.* Cambridge: Cambridge University Press, 1993.

Venarde, Bruce. *Women's Monasticism and Medieval Society: Nunneries in France and England, 890–1215.* Ithaca, NY: Cornell University Press, 1997.

CHAPTER 6:   Culture and Learning in Late Medieval Europe

Primary Sources

Andreas Capellanus. *The Art of Courtly Love.* Trans. John Jay Parry. New York: Columbia University Press, 1960.

Chrétien de Troyes. *Yvain: The Knight of the Lion.* Trans. Burton Raffel. New Haven, CT: Yale University Press, 1987.

Dante Alighieri. *The Divine Comedy.* Trans. Charles Singleton. 6 vols. Princeton, NJ: Princeton University Press, 1977.

Goldin, Frederick. *Lyrics of the Troubadours and Trouvères: Original Texts with Translations.* Garden City, NY: Anchor Books, 1973.

St. Francis. *The Little Flowers of St. Francis.* Trans. Raphael Brown. New York: Doubleday, 1991.

Secondary Sources

Baldwin, John. *The Scholastic Culture of the Middle Ages, 1000–1300.* Lexington: Heath, 1971.

Bouchard, Constance B. *"Strong of Body, Brave, and Noble": Chivalry and Society in Medieval France.* Ithaca, NY: Cornell University Press, 1988.

Bynum, Caroline Walker. *Jesus as Mother: Studies in the Spirituality of the High Middle Ages.* Berkeley: University of California Press, 1982.

Camille, Michael. *Gothic Art: Glorious Visions.* New York: Abrams, 1996.

Crouch, David. *William Marshal: Knighthood, War, and Chivalry, 1147–1219.* 2nd Ed. New York: Longman, 2002.

Duby, Georges. *The Knight, the Lady, and the Priest: The Making of Modern Marriage in Medieval France.* Trans. Barbara Bray. Chicago: University of Chicago Press, 1993.

Epstein, Steven. *Wage Labor and Guilds in Medieval Europe.* Chapel Hill: University of North Carolina Press, 1991.

Gies, Frances and Joseph. *Cathedral, Forge, and Waterwheel: Technology and Innovation in the Middle Ages*. New York: HarperCollins, 1994.

Hanawalt, Barbara, et al., eds. *City and Spectacle in Medieval Europe*. Minneapolis: University of Minnesota Press, 1994.

Lambert, Malcolm. *Medieval Heresy: Popular Movements from the Gregorian Reform to the Reformation*. 3rd Ed. Oxford: Blackwell, 2002.

LeRoy Ladurie, Emmanuel. *Montaillou: The Promised Land of Error*. Trans. Barbara Bray. New York: Vintage, 1979.

Lilley, Keith D. *Urban Life in the Middle Ages, 1000 to 1450*. New York: Palgrave, 2002.

Little, Lester K. *Religious Poverty and the Profit Economy in Medieval Europe*. Ithaca, NY: Cornell University Press, 1978.

Lopez, Robert S. *The Commercial Revolution of the Middle Ages*. Cambridge: Cambridge University Press, 1971.

Mollat, Michel. *The Poor in the Middle Ages: An Essay in Social History*. Trans. Arthur Goldhammer. New Haven, CT: Yale University Press, 1986.

Moore, R. I. *The Formation of a Persecuting Society: Power and Deviance in Western Europe, 950–1250*. Oxford: Blackwell, 1987.

Panofsky, Erwin. *Gothic Architecture and Scholasticism*. New York: Meridian, 1951.

Parkes, James W. *The Jew in the Medieval Community*. London: Sepher-Hermon, 1976.

Paterson, Linda. *The World of the Troubadours: Medieval Occitan Society, c. 1100–1300*. Cambridge: Cambridge University Press, 1995.

Wieruszowski, Helene. *The Medieval University*. Princeton, NJ: Van Nostrand, 1966.

CHAPTER 7:   Politics and Society

Primary Sources

Bisson, Thomas, ed. *The Fiscal Accounts of Catalonia Under the Early Count-Kings (1151–1213)*. Berkeley: University of California Press, 1984.

Fitz Stephen, William. *Norman London*. Trans. F. D. Logan. New York: Italica Press, 1990.

Stenton, Frank. *The Bayeux Tapestry*. 2nd Ed. London: Phaidon, 1965.

(Abbot) Suger. *The Deeds of Louis the Fat*. Trans. R. Cusimano and J. Moorhead. Washington, DC: Catholic University of America Press, 1992.

Wood, Charles T. *Philip the Fair and Boniface VIII: State vs. Papacy*. 2nd Ed. New York: Holt, Rinehart and Winston, 1971.

Secondary Sources

Baldwin, John W. *The Government of Philip Augustus: Foundations of French Royal Power in the Middle Ages*. Berkeley: University of California Press, 1986.

Beaune, Colette. *The Birth of an Ideology: Myths and Symbols of Nations in Late Medieval France*. Berkeley: University of California Press, 1991.

Bisson, Thomas N. *The Medieval Crown of Aragon: A Short History*. Oxford: Clarendon Press, 1986.

Clanchy, Michael. *From Memory to Written Record: England 1066–1307*. 2nd Ed. Oxford: Blackwell, 1993.

———. *England and Its Rulers, 1066–1272*. New York: B&N Imports, 1983.

Douglas, David C. *William the Conqueror: The Norman Impact upon England*. London: Eyre & Spottiswoode, 1964.

Dunbabin, Jean. *France in the Making, 843–1180.* 2nd Ed. Oxford: Oxford University Press, 2000.

Fletcher, Richard. *Moorish Spain.* London: Weidenfeld & Nicolson, 1992.

Green, Judith A. *The Government of England Under Henry I.* Cambridge: Cambridge University Press, 1986.

Hallam, Elizabeth M. *Capetian France, 987–1328.* 2nd Ed. New York: Longman, 2001.

Hudson, John. *The Formation of English Common Law: Law and Society in England from the Norman Conquest to Magna Carta.* New York: Longman, 1996.

Richard, Jean. *Saint Louis: Crusader King of France.* Trans. Jean Birrell. Cambridge: Cambridge University Press, 1992.

Richardson, H. G., et al. *The English Parliament in the Middle Ages.* Rio Grande, OH: Hambledon, 1981.

Holt, J. C. *Magna Carta.* 2nd Ed. Cambridge: Cambridge University Press, 1982.

Jordan, William C. *The French Monarchy and the Jews: From Philip Augustus to the Late Capetians.* Philadelphia: University of Pennsylvania Press, 1989.

Kantorowicz, Ernst. *The King's Two Bodies: A Study in Medieval Political Theology.* Princeton, NJ: Princeton University Press, 1957.

O'Callaghan, Joseph F. *Alfonso X, the Cortes, and Government in Medieval Spain.* Brookfield, VT: Ashgate, 1998.

Strayer, Joseph R. *The Reign of Philip the Fair.* Princeton, NJ: Princeton University Press, 1980.

———. *On the Medieval Origins of the Modern State.* Princeton, NJ: Princeton University Press, 1970.

Warren, William L. *Henry II.* Berkeley: University of California Press, 1973.

CHAPTER 8:   Political Communities

Primary Sources

Dmytryshyn, Basil. *Medieval Russia: A Source Book.* 3rd Ed. Fort Worth, TX: Harcourt Brace Jovanovich College, 1991.

Otto of Freising. *The Deeds of Frederick Barbarossa.* Trans. C. C. Mierow. 1953. Toronto: University of Toronto Press, 1994.

Powell, J. M., ed. *The Liber Augustalis, or the Constitutions of Melfi Promulgated by Emperor Frederick II for the Kingdom of Sicily in 1231.* Syracuse, NY: Syracuse University Press, 1971.

Secondary Sources

Abulafia, David. *Frederick II: A Medieval Emperor.* London: Allen Lane, 1988.

Arnold, Benjamin. *Medieval Germany, 500–1300: A Political Interpretation.* Toronto: University of Toronto Press, 1997.

Barraclough, Geoffrey. *The Origins of Modern Germany.* New York: Norton, 1963.

———. *Eastern and Western Europe in the Middle Ages.* New York: Harcourt Brace Jovanovich, 1970.

Bartlett, Robert. *The Making of Europe: Conquest, Colonization, and Cultural Change, 950–1350.* Princeton, NJ: Princeton University Press, 1993.

Brentano, Robert. *Rome Before Avignon: A Social History of Thirteenth-Century Rome.* New York: Basic Books, 1974.

Davies, Norman. *God's Playground: A History of Poland.* Volume 1: *The Origins to 1795.* New York: Columbia University Press, 1982.

Durham, Thomas. *Serbia: The Rise and Fall of a Medieval Empire.* New York: Sessions, 1989.

Fine, John V. A., Jr. *The Early Medieval Balkans: A Critical Survey from the Sixth to the Late Twelfth Century.* Ann Arbor: University of Michigan Press, 1983.

Fuhrmann, Horst. *Germany in the High Middle Ages, c. 1050–1200.* Trans. T. Reuter. Cambridge: Cambridge University Press, 1986.

Hyde, John K. *Society and Politics in Medieval Italy: The Evolution of the Civil Life, 1000–1350.* London: Macmillan, 1973.

Jordan, Karl. *Henry the Lion: A Biography.* Trans. P. S. Falla. Oxford: Clarendon Press, 1986.

Kantorowicz, Ernst. *Frederick the Second, 1194–1250.* Trans. E. O. Lorimer. 1931. Princeton, NJ: Princeton University Press, 1997.

Manteuffel, Tadeusz. *The Formation of the Polish State: The Period of Ducal Rule, 963–1164.* Trans. A. Gorski. Detroit: Wayne State University Press, 1982.

Martin, Janet. *Medieval Russia, 980–1584.* Cambridge: Cambridge University Press, 1995.

Martines, Lauro. *Power and Imagination: City-States in Renaissance Italy.* New York: Knopf, 1979.

Partner, Peter. *The Lands of St. Peter: The Papal State in the Middle Ages and the Early Renaissance.* Berkeley: University of California Press, 1972.

Saunders, John Joseph. *The History of the Mongol Conquests.* Rev. Ed. Philadelphia: University of Pennsylvania Press, 2001.

Sawyer, Birgit. *Medieval Scandinavia: From Conversion to Reformation, c. 800–1500.* Minneapolis: University of Minnesota Press, 1993.

Sawyer, P. H. *Kings and Vikings: Scandinavia and Europe, 700–1100.* London: Methuen, 1982.

Sedlar, Jean W. *East Central Europe in the Middle Ages, 1000–1500.* Seattle: University of Washington Press, 1994.

Vernadsky, George. *Kievan Russia.* New Haven, CT: Yale University Press, 1973.

CHAPTER 9: The Late Medieval Crisis and the Transition to the Early Modern Period

Primary Sources

Brucker, Gene, ed. *The Society of Renaissance Florence: A Documentary Study.* New York: Harper & Row, 1971.

Christine de Pisan. *The Book of the City of Ladies.* Trans. Earl Jeffrey Richards. London: Persea Books, 1982.

Cortés, Hernan. *Letters from Mexico.* Ed. A. Pagden and J. Elliot. 2nd ED. New Haven, CT: Yale University Press, 2001.

Froissart, Jean. *Chronicles.* Trans. Geoffrey Brereton. New York: Penguin, 1968.

Fuson, Robert H., ed. *The Log of Columbus.* Camden, ME: International Marine Publishing, 1987.

Giovanni Boccaccio. *The Decameron.* Trans. G. H. McWilliam. New York: Penguin, 1995.

Horrox, Rosemary, ed. *The Black Death.* New York: St. Martin's Press, 1994.

Machiavelli, Niccolò. *The Prince.* Trans. George Bull. New York: Penguin, 1999.

Pernoud, Régine, ed. *Joan of Arc: By Herself and Her Witnesses.* New York: Stein & Day, 1966.

Secondary Sources

Allmand, Christopher. *The Hundred Years' War: England and France at War, c. 1300–1450.* Cambridge: Cambridge University Press, 1988.

Aston, Margaret. *The Fifteenth Century: The Prospect of Europe.* New York: Norton, 1968.

Baron, Hans. *The Crisis of the Early Italian Renaissance.* Princeton, NJ: Princeton University Press, 1966.

Baxandall, Michael. *Painting and Experience in Fifteenth-Century Italy.* Oxford: Oxford University Press, 1972.

Bennett, H. S. *Chaucer and the Fifteenth Century.* Oxford: Oxford University Press, 1961.

Bois, Guy. *The Crisis of Feudalism: Economy and Society in Eastern Normandy, c. 1300–1550.* Cambridge: Cambridge University Press, 1984.

Brucker, Gene. *Florence: The Golden Age, 1138–1737.* Berkeley: University of California Press, 1998.

Burke, Peter. *Culture and Society in Renaissance Italy.* Princeton, NJ: Princeton University Press, 1999.

Crosby, A. W. *The Columbian Exchange: Biological and Cultural Consequences of 1492.* Westport, CT: Greenwood Press, 1972.

Dollinger, P. *The German Hansa.* Stanford: Stanford University Press, 1970.

Eisenstein, Elizabeth. *The Printing Press as an Agent of Change.* 2 vols. Cambridge: Cambridge University Press, 1979.

Fernandez-Armesto, Felipe. *Before Columbus: Exploration and Colonization from the Mediterranean to the Atlantic, 1229–1492.* London: Macmillan, 1987.

———. *Columbus.* Oxford: Oxford University Press, 1991.

Geremek, Bronislaw. *The Margins of Society in Late Medieval Paris.* Cambridge: Cambridge University Press, 1987.

Gillingham, John. *The Wars of the Roses: Peace and Conflict in Fifteenth-Century England.* London: Weidenfeld & Nicolson, 1981.

Hanawalt, Barbara. *The Ties That Bound: Peasant Families in Medieval England.* Oxford: Oxford University Press, 1986.

Harvey, L. P. *Islamic Spain, 1250–1500.* Chicago: University of Chicago Press, 1990.

Herlihy, David. *The Black Death and the Transformation of the West.* Cambridge, MA: Harvard University Press, 1997.

Herlihy, David, and Christiane Klapisch-Zuber. *Tuscans and Their Families: A Study of the Florentine Catasto of 1427.* New Haven, CT: Yale University Press, 1985.

Hilton, R. H. *Bond Men Made Free: Medieval Peasant Movements and the English Rising of 1381.* London: Routledge, 1988.

Huizinga, Johann. *The Autumn of the Middle Ages.* Ed. and Trans. R. J. Payton and U. Mammitzsch. Chicago: University of Chicago Press, 1996.

Huppert, George. *After the Black Death: A Social History of Early Modern Europe.* 2nd Ed. Bloomington: Indiana University Press, 1998.

Jardine, Lisa. *Worldly Goods: A New History of the Renaissance.* New York: Norton, 1996.

Kaeuper, Richard W. *War, Justice, and Public Order: England and France in the Later Middle Ages.* Oxford: Oxford University Press, 1988.

Knecht, R. J. *French Renaissance Monarchy.* New York: Longman, 1984.

Leff, Gordon. *Heresy in the Later Middle Ages: The Relation of Heterodoxy to Dissent, c. 1250–1450.* 2 vols. Manchester: Manchester University Press, 1967.

Martines, Lauro, ed. *Violence and Disorder in Italian Cities, 1200–1500.* Berkeley: University of California Press, 1972.

Mattingly, Garrett. *Renaissance Diplomacy.* New York: Penguin, 1971.

McAlister, Lyle. *Spain and Portugal in the New World, 1492–1700.* Minneapolis: University of Minnesota Press, 1984.

Miskimim, H. A. *The Economy of Early Renaissance Europe, 1300–1460.* Cambridge: Cambridge University Press, 1975.

Mollat, Michel, et al. *The Popular Revolutions of the Late Middle Ages.* London: Allen & Unwin, 1973.

Nicholas, David. *The Growth of the Medieval City: From Late Antiquity to the Early Fourteenth Century.* New York: Longman, 1997.

Nirenberg, David. *Communities of Violence: The Persecution of Minorities in the Middle Ages.* Princeton, NJ: Princeton University Press, 1998.

Ozment, Stephen. *The Age of Reform, 1250–1550.* New Haven, CT: Yale University Press, 1980.

Parry, J. H. *The Age of Reconnaissance.* New York: New American Library, 1963.

Rady, Martyn. *The Emperor Charles V.* New York: Longman, 1988.

Rice, Eugene E., Jr. *The Foundations of Early Modern Europe, 1460–1559.* New York: Norton, 1970.

Skinner, Quentin. *Machiavelli.* Oxford: Oxford University Press, 1981.

Subrahmanyam, Sanjay. *The Career and Legend of Vasco da Gama.* Cambridge: Cambridge University Press, 1997.

Vaughan, Richard. *Valois Burgundy.* Hampden, CT: Shoestring Press, 1975.

Waugh, Scott, et al., eds. *Christendom and Its Discontents: Exclusion, Persecution, and Rebellion, 1000–1500.* Cambridge: Cambridge University Press, 1995.

Index

DATE DUE